Integrating Computer Technology into the Classroom

Integrating Computer Technology into the Classroom

THIRD EDITION

Gary R. Morrison
Wayne State University

Deborah L. Lowther
University of Memphis

Upper Saddle River, New Jersey
Columbus, Ohio

Library of Congress Cataloging-in-Publication Data
Morrison, Gary R., Ed.D.
Integrating computer technology into the classroom / Gary R. Morrison, Deborah L. Lowther.—3rd ed.
p. cm.
Includes bibliographical references and index.
ISBN 0-13-142116-6
1. Computer-assisted instruction. 2. Computer managed instruction. 3. Computers—Study and teaching. 4. Instructional systems—Design. I. Lowther, Deborah L. II. Title.

LB1028.5.M6373 2004
371.33'4—dc22

2004009264

Vice President and Executive Publisher: Jeffery W. Johnston
Executive Editor: Debra A. Stollenwerk
Development Editor: Kimberly J. Lundy
Assistant Editor: Amy Nelson
Editorial Assistant: Mary Morrill
Production Editor: Kris Roach
Production Coordination: Carlisle Publishers Services
Design Coordinator: Diane C. Lorenzo
Cover Designer: Jeff Vanik
Cover Image: Getty One
Photo Coordinator: Lori Whitley
Production Manager: Pamela D. Bennett
Director of Marketing: Ann Castel Davis
Marketing Manager: Darcy Betts Prybella
Marketing Coordinator: Tyra Poole
This book was set in Sabon by Carlisle Communications, Ltd. It was printed and bound by R. R. Donnelley & Sons Company. The cover was printed by Coral Graphics Services.

Photo Credits: John Paul Endress/Silver Burdett Ginn, p. 2; Gary R. Morrison, pp. 8, 15, 27, 33, 65, 80, 103, 140, 152, 175, 185, 208, 213, 242, 248, 269, 291, 332, 341, 364; Kathy Kirtland/Merrill, p. 22; Anthony Magnacca/Merrill, pp. 38, 88, 126, 164, 226, 282, 302; Silver Burdett Ginn, p. 47; Anne Vega/Merrill, pp. 52, 274; David Mager/Pearson Learning, p. 62; Modern Curriculum Press/Pearson Learning, p. 114; Mike Peters/Silver Burdett Ginn, p. 196; Scott Cunningham/Merrill, pp. 254, 259, 310, 357; Tom Watson/Merrill, p. 319; Shirley Zeiberg/PH College, p. 326; Frank LaBua/PH College, p. 350.

Pearson Education Ltd.
Pearson Education Singapore Pte. Ltd.
Pearson Education Canada, Ltd.
Pearson Education—Japan
Pearson Education Australia Pty. Limited
Pearson Education North Asia Ltd.
Pearson Educatión de Mexico, S. A. de C. V.
Pearson Education Malaysia Pte. Ltd.

PEARSON
Merrill
Prentice Hall

10 9 8 7 6 5 4 3 2 1
ISBN: 0-13-142116-6

Preface

Our goal is to teach students how to use computers as a tool to solve problems while learning core subject area content. We provide a rationale and model for integrating computer technology into the curriculum by using it as a tool rather than as an instructional delivery device. This book presents an approach to creating an integrated inquiry lesson; however, we do not propose that it is the only way to teach. Our approach is structured to include the standards or benchmarks of the school district or state. We believe that computers can make a difference in student learning when teachers change the way they have students use computer technology in the classroom.

By using computers as a tool for problem solving, we are providing an instructional environment that allows learners to construct meaning based on their individual experiences. This approach is quite different from the traditional approach of using computers for drill-and-practice and tutorials to help learners memorize information for a test. Our approach incorporates a variety of cognitive and constructive practices to create a student-centered learning environment that is highly active and motivational—resulting in increased student achievement.

Our goal is not to have teachers integrate computers into every lesson, but rather to teach them how to determine if computers should be used and how to use them. In addition, please note that the primary focus in this book is not on developing basic computer literacy skills (although skill levels will increase as new functions are introduced and used). The focus is to develop new methods for using computers in the classrooms.

THE AUDIENCE FOR THIS BOOK

We have written this textbook for both the preservice and the inservice teacher. For the preservice teacher, this book could be used in an introductory instructional technology course. It can also be used as a text in a methods course that is focused on problem-based learning. For the inservice teacher, this book makes an excellent text for a graduate level technology course, or for an advanced methods course with a focus on problem-based learning.

Additionally, this text is well suited for a course that focuses on integration of computer technology into the classroom. An instructor can use this text with a variety of teaching methods to illustrate how to integrate computers as a learning tool.

ORGANIZATION OF THIS TEXT

In this third edition, we have made additions and revisions that provide a description and discussion of developing NTeQ lesson plans, implementing a lesson plan, assessing learning in an open-ended learning environment, and integrating educational software in a meaningful way. The 10-step NTeQ model remains the same in this edition, but we have refined the concepts and increased our emphasis on the role of *teacher as designer.* In this section, we describe what is new to this edition, and provide a brief summary of the chapter contents.

New to This Edition

Getting Ready

- ***What Do I Know?*** is a series of focus questions at the beginning of each chapter to stimulate interest and focus learning.
- A ***Classroom Snapshot*** is presented before the chapter content to illustrate the key concepts of the chapter in an authentic context.
- ***NTeQ Portfolio Activities*** are provided at the end of each chapter. These tasks include reflection on the chapter content and various hands-on activities to reinforce learning. Students who complete each of these activities can develop either a paper or electronic-based portfolio for teaching.
- ***ISTE NETS for Students*** are integrated into the text. We provide examples of how teachers can address the NETS standards with the content of the chapter.
- ***Check It Out*** activities are Web-based and directly related to examples given in the text. Some allow you to actually work with and manipulate referenced data and information while others provide URLs to sites with relevant information.

The following is a brief summary of the chapters. In the third edition, we have resequenced some of the chapters to provide what we believe is a logical approach to teaching technology integration.

Chapter 1 introduces the NTeQ model and provides a basis for using computer technology as a tool for solving problems.

Chapter 2 presents a rationale for rethinking the use of computers in the classroom and establishes the foundational research base of the NTeQ model.

Chapter 3, the first Teacher as Designer chapter, describes a set of tools to help teachers plan effective lessons: e.g., topic and task analysis, writing objectives, learner analysis, and assessment.

Chapter 4, the second Teacher as Designer chapter, focuses on how to use the 10-step NTeQ model to develop technology integration lessons.

Chapters 5, 6, and 7 describe how to integrate student use of word processing, spreadsheets, and databases into inquiry-based lesson plans.

Chapter 8 focuses on how students can use different computer tools to publish or present the results of the problem-solving activities.

Chapter 9 presents ideas for how to integrate a wide variety of Internet resources into the classroom.

Chapter 10 describes how to assess and meaningfully integrate both traditional and inquiry-based educational software into an NTeQ lesson plan.

Chapter 11 presents easy-to-follow guidelines for implementing a lesson in which students use computers in a problem-solving context.

Chapters 12 and 13 describe how to facilitate and manage students using computers in a classroom.

Chapter 14 presents guidelines and approaches for assessing student learning with the use of traditional and alternative methods such as task lists and rubrics.

Special Features to Help the Learner Process the Content

Additional features in the third edition of *Integrating Computer Technology into the Classroom* include the following:

- ***Key Topics*** at the beginning of each chapter provide a quick outline of the chapter contents.
- ***An introduction*** at the beginning of each chapter orients the student to information and ideas presented in the chapter.
- ***Power Tips*** throughout the book provide ideas for using specific software or computer features and often include a listing of valuable resources.
- ***Tool chapters*** (i.e., Chapters 5 to 7) include instructions on how to write lesson plans in which students use specific functions of basic software applications to enhance learning.
- ***Classroom Snapshots*** highlight successful computer integration lessons that have been implemented by K–12 teachers.
- ***The Teacher's Diary*** provides practical tips, suggestions, and encouragement from K–12 teachers who are integrating computers into their classrooms.
- ***At the Classroom's Doorstep*** includes *Questions Teachers Ask* about the chapter and answers to those questions.
- ***Screen shots and graphics*** are used throughout each chapter to illustrate lesson ideas.
- ***URLs*** for accessing Internet resources support chapter content; however, these sites often change locations or suddenly drop from cyberspace. We have tried to identify locations that are resistant to "cyber rust."
- ***Companion Website*** and ***www.NTeQ.com*** **website** provide links to resources and a variety of lesson plans that span key content areas and K–12 grade levels. The NTeQ website has more than 1,500 lesson plans contributed by individuals like yourself.

Special Features to Help Learners Integrate Technology

We have developed a mix of new and old features that will help preservice and inservice teachers integrate computer technology into their classroom. These features include the following:

- ***NTeQ Lesson Plans*** are provided at the end of selected chapters to illustrate how to use the NTeQ model at different grade levels and in different disciplines.
- ***Lesson Ideas*** at the end of selected chapters provide possible topics for developing integrated lessons.

- ***Classroom Snapshots*** at the beginning of each chapter illustrates both good and bad examples of technology integration. These examples can provide ideas and models for effectively integrating technology.
- ***The NTeQ Portfolio*** provides challenging activities for the students. In some chapters, students are challenged to reflect and develop their own perspective on teaching with technology. Other chapters provide a framework for the students to develop an integrated lesson plan for their own classrooms for immediate or future use.
- ***Check It Out*** activities provide access to resources on the Internet to help students develop innovative lesson plans.

SUPPLEMENTS TO THE TEXT

All supplements are provided free of charge to instructors who adopt this text. To request any of the following supplements, please contact your Prentice Hall representative or visit our website at *www.prenhall.com*. (If you do not know how to contact a local sales representative, please call faculty services at 1–800–526–0485 for assistance.)

Instructor's Manual

Our instructor's manual provides you with a variety of chapter-by-chapter resources and ready-to-use classroom activities. This instructor's manual is divided into two sections. The first section provides a sample outline for a 13-week course using *Integrating Computer Technology into the Classroom*. The second section of the manual provides teaching strategies for each of the chapters. Each chapter includes the following:

Introduction

Key chapter topics

Getting Ready

This section provides suggestions on how to prepare and plan for the instruction on each chapter.

Lesson Tips

In this section, we provide a number of activities for your students that range from sample lesson plans to activities to help them develop an integrated lesson plan.

Handouts

When appropriate, we have provided handouts for the various activities that you can duplicate or modify.

Computerized Test Bank

A customizable test bank on disk is available for both Macintosh and Windows users to assist in the preparation of classroom assessments.

Companion Website (*http://www.prenhall.com/morrison*)

The Companion Website provides activities to engage the learner and provide additional examples of how to integrate technology into the classroom. These activities include:

- ***Reflection activities*** that provide guidance to help the learner reflect upon the content in the chapter.
- ***Integration activities*** that provide a framework for discussing and incorporating a variety of activities related to technology integration.
- ***Web destinations*** link students to websites that provide information relevant to the topics in the chapter and answer or discuss questions regarding the information.
- ***Check It Out activities*** from the text allow students to perform the tasks presented.
- ***NTeQ portfolio activities*** give students a starting point to be creative and develop their own teaching portfolio.
- ***Resources*** links to the NTeQ website.
- ***Message Board*** is a Web resource where you can post questions that other students can answer and discuss.
- ***Chat*** is a live chat area for members of a single class or a combination of students from several universities to discuss a topic of interest.

www.nteq.com

The NTeQ website includes a variety of resources for preservice and inservice teachers. One of the most popular features of the website is the lesson planner. Students and teachers can create a lesson plan online that is available to others. Site visitors can also search for lesson plans by grade level, subject area, and topic area. There are also a number of other resources provided by teachers.

ACKNOWLEDGMENTS

Most of the ideas for the lesson plans in this book were conceived or suggested by our colleagues and classroom teachers, whom we want to thank for sharing. For ideas presented in the first edition we would like to offer a special thanks to the Project SMART teachers, and to Dr. Richard Petersen, who gave us ideas and helped us develop some of the materials.

Several people deserve a special thank you. First, we want to thank Dr. Katherine Abraham, the Project SMART director, who was always willing to provide us with ideas related to the math curriculum and help with our spreadsheet and database problems. For the third edition, we would like to acknowledge ideas from the Anytime Anywhere Learning teachers in the Walled Lake Consolidated Schools and from many of our colleagues, including Steve M. Ross and Gary J. Anglin.

Second, we want to thank Fran Clark, who not only helped us refine but also tested the NTeQ model in her third-grade classroom. She documented her experiences in many of *The Teacher's Diary* sections that appear in each chapter. We also want to thank Thomas J. Buggey for his contributions to "Meeting the Needs of Students with Disabilities" in Chapter 12. As we developed this book, several of our graduate assistants provided feedback and used the manuscript in their courses.

Third, we want to thank the reviewers who gave us helpful and constructive comments and suggestions: Joan Hanor, California State University, San Marcus; Toni Stokes Jones, Eastern Michigan University; Judith E. Rodgers, St. Cloud State University; and Ellen W. Wiley, Valdosta State University.

We want to thank our editors, Debbie Stollenwerk and Kim Lundy, who supported our ideas from the beginning and provided us with numerous suggestions during chapter development. We would also like to thank our many colleagues, administrators, and classroom teachers who have shared stories of success, ideas for lessons, and suggestions for improving the book.

Gary R. Morrison

Deborah L. Lowther

DEAR TEACHER

Microcomputers were introduced into the K–12 classroom almost 25 years ago. We have gone from the Altair, Commodore, and Apple I to the PC and Macintosh, which individually have more memory and drive storage than an entire lab of the earliest computers. Even though we have observed large leaps in technology and in the number of computers in the classroom, we have seen little change in the way teachers teach or the way students use computers. Teachers, parents, principals, superintendents, and school boards are beginning to question their investments in computer technology: "What do we have to show for all of these computers?" Most students today are educated in the same way students were educated a generation or two ago. Students are no more likely to sit in front of a computer for all of their instruction than they were to sit with one of Skinner's programmed learning machines. Why has the computer not revolutionized education as some scholars predicted?

A recent survey of computer applications used by K–12 students indicates that 78% of the students spend time playing games in school (Digest of Educational Statistics, 2000). Few, if any, elementary or middle school students reported using spreadsheets or databases, and only 6% of the high school students reported using spreadsheets or databases. In contrast, we find that employers require their employees to use productivity tools such as word processing, spreadsheets, databases, e-mail, and personal information managers. Individuals in the workplace are using computers as a tool, whereas educators generally tend to think of computers as an instructional delivery device—something to replace the teacher, much like Skinner's teaching machine. This observation is interesting because most individuals believe that computers are placed in the schools to prepare students for the workforce—where, as mentioned earlier, computers are used as a tool.

We have transitioned from the early fears that computers would replace teachers to a view of how teachers and students can use computers to learn in new ways. Technology changes almost daily, and it is difficult to keep abreast of all the changes. However, the teaching environment is changing, too. Before the Internet was introduced to the classroom, a class was defined by a textbook and four walls. Today, there are no boundaries, because the World Wide Web provides a massive database of information that students can access faster than most teachers can redirect a question. For example, five years ago a student might ask a question and the teacher would suggest the student research the question in the library and report the findings, fully knowing the student may forget the question by the end of class. Recently, we observed a student in a laptop class with wireless Internet access asking a question about the gestation period for a particular mammal. *Before* the teacher could suggest she look it up, three hands were waving. These three students had searched with Google and found the answer.

Ten years ago, the teacher was the expert in the classroom. Today, experts from around the world are readily available to your students. The role of the successful teacher changes from that of expert to one who is *wise*. Wise teachers realize they are not experts, but know where to find resources for themselves and their students. Resources include not only the scholarly expertise available on the Web, but also the technological expertise of the students themselves. Our goal is to create wise teachers who can facilitate learning by effectively utilizing and managing resources and the classroom.

The type of computer you have does not matter. All your students need is access to integrated software such as AppleWorks, Microsoft Works, Microsoft Office, or individual applications for spreadsheets, databases, word processing, drawing, presentations, and Internet browsing. Teachers who have collected the older Macintoshes and PCs discarded by other teachers, parents, or businesses were able to provide a large number of computers in their classrooms. How many of us really need a computer with a 2.2-gigahertz processor when we can barely type 27 words a minute! This book is written for the pre-service and practicing teacher who has very basic computer skills such as using a mouse; opening, creating, and saving documents; and using menus. Software is not as important as learning how to use the tool in a productive manner to learn core content and skills. The type and capability of the software you use in your classroom will likely change, and some programs will be replaced by more powerful software in the near future.

Recently, we were visiting a sixth-grade classroom with a colleague, and the teacher was implementing an integrated lesson she had developed with the NTeQ (iNtegrating Technology for inQuiry) model introduced in this text. The students in each of her five science classes were testing various paper products. One student suddenly stopped his work and asked the teacher why they couldn't create an index to determine which products were the best across all five of her classes. We stared at one another in amazement, thinking that it would be great to hear a graduate student make such a leap in knowledge when analyzing research data!

As you integrate technology into your classroom, we hope you will share your ideas with others on the NTeQ Website and Companion Website. Let's work together to start a revolution in the way students learn in each classroom.

Gary R. Morrison and Deborah L. Lowther

REFERENCES

Digest of Educational Statistics. (2000). Retrieved August 29, 2003, from *http://nces.ed.gov/pubs2001/digest/dt426.asp*.

Educator Learning Center: An Invaluable Online Resource

Merrill Education and the Association for Supervision and Curriculum Development (ASCD) invite you to take advantage of a new online resource, one that provides access to the top research and proven strategies associated with ASCD and Merrill—the Educator Learning Center. At *www.EducatorLearningCenter.com* you will find resources that will enhance your students' understanding of course topics and of current educational issues, in addition to being invaluable for further research.

How the Educator Learning Center Will Help Your Students Become Better Teachers

With the combined resources of Merrill Education and ASCD, you and your students will find a wealth of tools and materials to better prepare them for the classroom.

Research

- More than 600 articles from the ASCD journal *Educational Leadership* discuss everyday issues faced by practicing teachers.
- A direct link on the site to Research Navigator™ gives students access to many of the leading education journals, as well as extensive content detailing the research process.
- Excerpts from Merrill Education texts give your students insights on important topics of instructional methods, diverse populations, assessment, classroom management, technology, and refining classroom practice.

Classroom Practice

- Hundreds of lesson plans and teaching strategies are categorized by content area and age range.
- Case studies and classroom video footage provide virtual field experience for student reflection.
- Computer simulations and other electronic tools keep your students abreast of today's classrooms and current technologies.

Look Into the Value of Educator Learning Center Yourself

A four-month subscription to Educator Learning Center is $25 but is FREE when used in conjunction with this text. To obtain free passcodes for your students, simply contact your local Merrill/Prentice Hall sales representative, and your representative will give you a special ISBN to give your bookstore when ordering your textbooks. To preview the value of this website to you and your students, please go to *www.EducatorLearningCenter.com* and click on "Demo."

About the Authors

Gary R. Morrison received his doctorate in Instructional Systems Technology from Indiana University. Since then, he has worked as instructional designer at the University of Mid-America, Solar Turbines International, General Electric Company's Corporate Consulting Group, and Tenneco Oil Company. As a professor at the University of Memphis, he taught courses in instructional design and served as a faculty associate in the Center of Academic Excellence. Presently, he is a professor in the Instructional Technology Program at Wayne State University, where he teaches courses in instructional design and distance learning. His credits include print projects, multimedia projects, and more than 30 hours of instructional video programs, including a five-part series that was aired nationally on PBS-affiliated stations.

Dr. Morrison has written more than 100 papers on topics related to instructional design and computer-based instruction and has contributed to several books and instructional software packages. He is co-author of *Designing Effective Instruction* with Steven M. Ross and Jerold E. Kemp. He is the associate editor of the research section of *Educational Technology Research and Development* and past president of AECT's Research and Theory Division, and Design and Development Division.

Deborah L. Lowther received her Ph.D. in Educational Technology from Arizona State University. Before completing her doctoral work, she was a seventh-grade science teacher. She is currently an associate professor in the Department of Instruction and Curriculum Leadership at the University of Memphis. Her area of concentration is Instructional Design and Technology. She teaches courses primarily focused toward preparing preservice and inservice teachers to integrate computer technology into their curriculum. She also teaches courses that lead to state certification in instructional computing applications. Her research is centered on factors influencing the integration of technology into various learning environments. Over the past 8 years, Dr. Lowther has been very involved with technology integration from the international to the local level. Her involvement includes conference presentations; co-guest editing *Technology in the K–12 Schools,* a special edition of a national journal; working with multiple grants focused toward technology integration; providing professional development to K–12 schools across the nation. She is currently the Principal Investigator of Professional Development for the Appalachian Technology in Education Consortium.

Brief Contents

Contents

Note: *Every effort has been made to provide accurate and current Internet information in this book. However, the Internet and information posted on it are constantly changing, so it is inevitable that some of the Internet addresses listed in this textbook will change.*

KEY TOPICS

Conceptions of Technology
- The Use of Computers in Schools
- The Use of Computers in Business
- Computers as Tools to Make Us Smarter

The NTeQ Model
- The Ten-Step Approach
- NTeQ Philosophy
- NTeQ and the Standards

Chapter 1

Rethinking Computers and Instruction

The United States has a history of introducing technology into the schools to solve educational problems (Figure 1-1). Shortly after the launch of Sputnik in 1957, Congress passed the National Defense Education Act to improve science and math achievement in public schools. One aspect of this plan was to place an overhead projector in most if not all of the K–12 classrooms. In the 1960s we saw the introduction of both programmed instruction and educational television in the classroom. In the early 1980s microcomputers were introduced into the classroom. During the 1990s, we saw federal and state initiatives enacted to place more computer technology in the P–12 classrooms in hope that technology would again solve our educational problems. At the start of the 21st century, we saw schools adding wireless connections and laptops to the classroom. Although Bork (1987) predicted that microcomputers would revolutionize our schools, we have yet to see any large-scale gains attributed to the infusion of this latest technology into the classroom. One reason the revolution has yet to start may be due to our conceptions of how we should use technology versus how we are using it.

GETTING STARTED

What Do I Know?

1. Each of my students will have a laptop next year; what do I do?
2. Do I need to teach differently if I have computers in my classroom?
3. I was told I must take my class to the computer lab this year; what do I do?
4. Will computers really teach my students?
5. Isn't having students use computers a lot of work?

Classroom Snapshot

We were waiting for Ms. Londhe's social studies class to start. The ninth-grade students were entering the classroom and taking a laptop computer from the cart. Our first hint that this class would be quite different from any other was the way the students were seated. Some were clustered in spots on the furniture and floor around the perimeter of the room. Others were moving desks together to accommodate groups of four or five students. We were expecting the students to start their laptop and begin taking notes as soon as Ms. Londhe started her lecture. Her "lecture" was the shortest we have ever observed—it rivaled the start of the Indianapolis 500-mile race. She simply said, "Class, let's get started." Immediately, the students started to work, and we did not hear Ms. Londhe address the class until about 5 minutes before the end.

The students were engaged in a project to determine how the economy of one state depends on that of another. They were researching industries in each state, mapping the major roads and rails from manufacturing centers, finding information on employment and income, and determining what each state manufactured, as well as the source of natural resources needed for the products. Their goal was to illustrate how the economy of the state they had selected influenced the economy of other states and was affected by the economy of other states. Some groups of students were working together on one computer while other teams appeared to have divided the work amongst individual team members. URLs, tables, and charts were all e-mailed to other members of the team when a piece of information that could solve the problem was found.

Next, we visited Mr. Diglio's biology class, where the students were studying the human skeleton. The students were sitting two at a computer and working through a program to help them memorize the name of each of the bones. The software had two modes. In the tutorial mode, a student could move the cursor over a bone, so the name appeared and the student could hear the correct pronunciation. There seemed to be little dialog between the students other than an occasional disagreement on the spelling of a bone or which bone to do next. Mr. Diglio's room was very orderly and quiet compared to Ms. Londhe's class.

CONCEPTIONS OF TECHNOLOGY

If you were to survey teachers on what type of software they use, what do you think they would say they use most often? Your results would probably reflect the results of other surveys (Archer, 1998; Becker, 1991) indicating computers were used most often for drill-and-practice, tutorials, and educational games. Let's examine these three types of software.

The Use of Computers in Schools

Drill-and-practice software was quite common and readily available in the 1970s and 1980s and often mimicked flash cards. The computer would display a stimulus, such as a math problem or foreign vocabulary word, and the student would select or enter an answer. After evaluating the response, the program would provide some type of response ranging from a simple line of text indicating the correctness of the an-

FIGURE 1-1 Incoming Technology

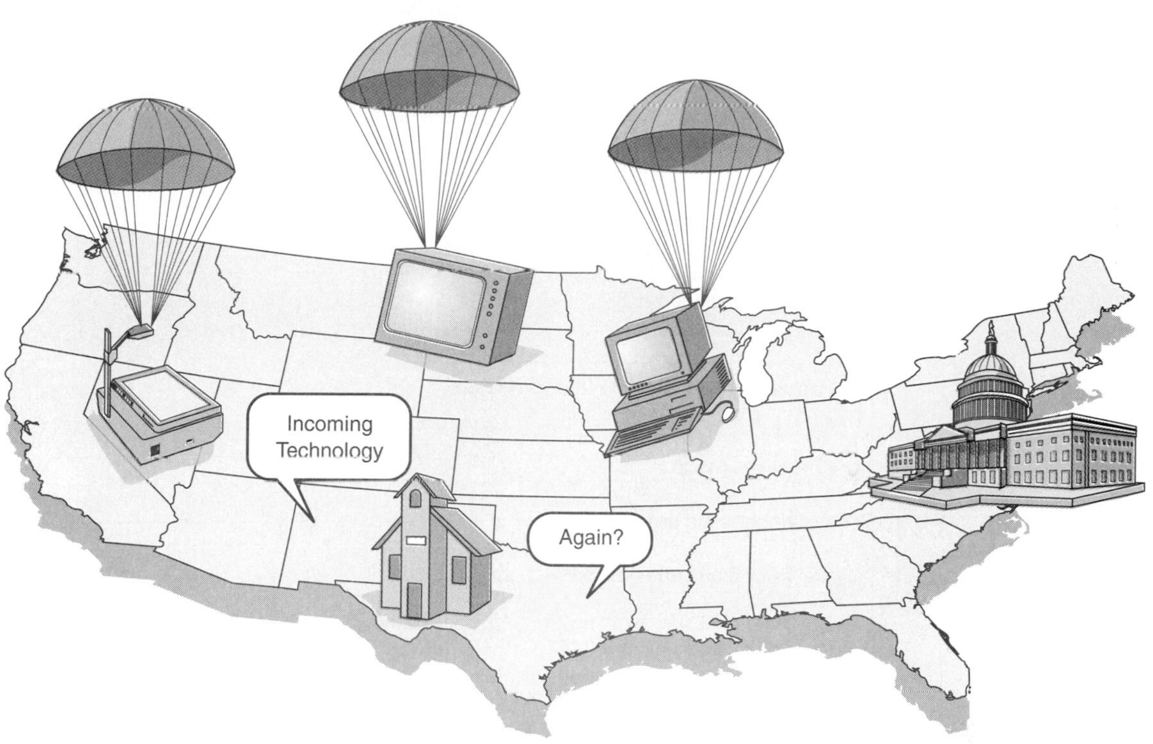

swer to eye-catching graphics and sounds. Sometimes the displays for an incorrect answer were more intriguing than for a correct answer, which led students to purposefully select incorrect answers. Drill-and-practice software is not used to teach new information; rather, it reinforces existing knowledge, such as multiplication facts. Although drill-and-practice software is an efficient way to achieve rote-learning objectives, current educational trends question the value of the rote learning this type of software promotes.

Tutorials are another form of popular instructional software. This approach, however, attempts to teach the learner new information. Strategies used with tutorial software can range from a simple implementation of programmed instruction to a highly sophisticated application that allows for branching and adaptation to individual differences (Figure 1-2) (Ross & Morrison, 1988). Tutorials are still useful for introduction of new content and remediation; however, they typically do not provide a sophisticated context for exploration and experimentation.

Educational games are often based on a drill-and-practice approach and usually provide an interesting theme such as solving a math problem to save Earth from an alien attack. Games are often a variation of drill-and-practice software, sometimes adding a time variable. Students must complete a task within a set amount of time to prevent a catastrophic event (such as an alien destroying the computer screen). The reward structures of the game may involve more graphic and sound displays than a

FIGURE 1-2 Examples of Branching and Adapting Instruction

Lesson 3

Converting Fractions
to Decimals

You may select from 2 to 10 practice examples.
Recommended Level: 7 Examples
Enter your selection (2-10):

You answered 12. It appears that you have subtracted 3 from 15.

The problem is 15/3.

The / symbol is the division symbol.

Divide 15 by 3 and enter the answer. ________

Branching Example

Jamie had entered a contract with Mr. Keegan to finish her work on time. She has earned 6 hours of free time from Mr. Keegan to paint. She divides her free time into sessions of 3/4 hours. How many sessions will Jamie have to paint?

Adaptive example from "A computer-based strategy for personalizing verbal problems in teaching mathematics," S. M. Ross and P. Anand, 1987, *Educational Communication* and *Technology Journal* 35, 151–162.

typical drill-and-practice application. Like drill-and-practice software, educational games often promote rote learning.

Educators have typically viewed technology as a means to *deliver* instruction to students. Lumsdaine (1964) characterized this view as Technology Type I, which stresses the importance of teaching aids. This view assumes the technology of the *machine* is intimately associated with the technology of *teaching* (Davies, 1973). The overhead projectors placed in the classroom after the launch of Sputnik were seen as amplifying the teacher's message by projecting it on a screen. Similarly, educational television during the 1960s was seen as amplifying and extending the message of the master teacher.

In contrast to the overhead projector and television, we would classify computer-based instruction as Technology Type II, which emphasizes *software* designed through the application of scientific principles. Lumsdaine (1964) provided programmed instruction as an example of this type of technology because it applied learning principles (e.g., shaping and reinforcement) to the design of the materials. Technology Type II *replaced* the teacher as opposed to amplifying the teacher's message.

Both types of technology emphasized the *delivery* of instruction using technology. This view of technology is best expressed by Thomas Edison, who championed the motion picture by stating that anything a teacher could teach could be taught by film (Heinich, Molenda, Russell, & Smaldino, 1996).

The Use of Computers in Business

We have seen that schools use computers to deliver instruction through games, drill-and-practice, and tutorial software. If we were to conduct a survey of the students' parents who use computers at work, we would most likely find that parents use computers differently. Computers are used as a *tool* to solve problems in the workplace. This use of computers was verified in the U.S. Departments of Labor and Education's report entitled "What Work Requires of Schools: A SCANS Report for America 2000," which includes the following as one of the five competencies needed by today's workforce (SCANS, 1991, pp. xvii–xviii):

- Works with a variety of technologies
- Selects technology—chooses procedures, tools, or equipment, including computers and related technologies
- Applies technology to task—understands intent and proper procedures for setup and operation of equipment
- Maintains and troubleshoots equipment—prevents, identifies, or solves problems with equipment, including computers and other technologies

The types of applications most frequently used by employees include "bookkeeping/invoicing (66 percent), word processing (57 percent), communications (47 percent), analysis/spreadsheets (41 percent), and calendar/schedule (38 percent)" (Digest of Educational Statistics, 2001). Earnest W. Deavenport, Jr., chairman and CEO of Eastman Chemical Company has stated that an individual taking an entry-level position with his company must have good computer skills and understand how to use computers to get the job (Archer, 1998). The use and conceptualization of computers as tools in the workplace stands in stark contrast to an educator's view of computers as instructional delivery mechanisms. We can probably conclude that Mr. Deavenport has little use for an individual's skill in blasting aliens or driving a simulated racecar around a closed track. Rather, he and others, as revealed by the SCANS report, are looking for students who have skill in using productivity applications to solve problems. Many of these competencies are also reflected in the National Educational Technology Standards for Students or NETS (International Society for Technology in Education, 2000), which is available at *http://cnets.iste.org/getdocs.html*.

The American Association of University Women (AAUW) (2000) suggest that just teaching students about databases, spreadsheets, and other tools is not enough. Rather, our focus must be on developing problem-solving skills. That is, developing

Students discussing the best way to collect data.

the intellectual skills to use the data and information we generate with technology. Thus just teaching students how to use these productivity tools is not adequate. They must learn to use the tools to solve problems and generate new ideas and knowledge.

Although we can find isolated examples of successful computer utilization in education, we have not seen the revolution in learning as predicted by Bork (1987). If we consider the effect of computers on our work culture, then we see a revolution that has affected everything from tracking an overnight Federal Express package via a telephone keypad as a computer interface to the design of new computers by other computers, to creating corporate financial models to predict revenue, to doing delicate surgery with robotics controlled by a computer. Could we start a revolution in education, as predicted by Bork, if we changed our conception of computers from a delivery mechanism to a tool?

Computers as Tools to Make Us Smarter

Norman (1993) believes that human cognition is aided by artifacts. Physical artifacts that we use for cognition include pencils and paper, calculators, and computers. Reading, mathematics, language, mnemonics, and procedures (e.g., the formula for calculating the area of a rectangle) are examples of mental artifacts. We invent new artifacts to help us improve our thinking process. For example, you might draw a map to give someone directions to your favorite restaurant. The map is an artifact you created to represent the streets and turns to take to the desired location. You might create a mnemonic or mental artifact to help you remember the names of the Great Lakes. Our brains have limited processing capabilities; therefore we seek ways to increase our thinking ability. One tool humans have invented to help us increase our thinking ability is the computer.

Computers are a physical artifact that we can use to help us become smarter (Norman, 1993). Professionals, researchers, cashiers, teachers, mechanics, and pilots all use computers daily to make themselves smarter and more efficient. But can computers make students smarter? Yes, but they can also have a negative effect if not used correctly. How can computers make students smarter? We will illustrate several strategies you can use as a teacher. Let's start by describing two ideas. First, students can use a computer to create a graph of data they have collected. This representation of the data can help the students *reflect* and *identify* patterns and trends, to generate new ideas. Second, students can use computers to store data, much like using a filing cabinet. They can then use a database to recall important data or sort the data into a particular order to discover a new relationship. The point is to use computer technology to encourage reflection and synthesis of ideas. Computers can make our students smarter when students begin to *process* the *data* they have generated with the computer. It is through this cognitive processing that students create new knowledge and solutions that are the result of understanding relationships.

THE NTEQ MODEL

As a teacher, how can you integrate computer technology into your classroom to achieve these goals of teaching the students how to use a computer as a tool and encouraging higher-level thinking and processing activities? This book presents a method for creating lesson plans that achieve these goals. In this section, we will introduce you to the iNtegrating Technology for inQuiry NTeQ model, explain the philosophy of the model, and describe its relationship to standards and school reform.

The Ten-Step Approach

The NTeQ model (Figure 1-3) involves 10 steps for *creating* a lesson plan that integrates computer technology into the classroom. The steps may seem out of order at first glance; however, the sequencing will become clear as you practice each step. We will provide more detail on each step in subsequent chapters.

Specify Objectives

Each integrated lesson plan begins with a statement of the objectives. These objectives are based on standards, benchmarks, and curriculum materials. Clearly stated objectives will guide your preparation of the lesson plan.

Match Computer Functions

Next, you need to identify any relationships between your objectives and the functions a computer can perform. For example, if the verb in your objective is "analyze," then you have a match with a function in either a spreadsheet or database. If the objective is draw or design, you have a match with a function in a drawing or graphics program. There will not be a match with every objective; similarly, computers are not used in every lesson.

FIGURE 1-3 NTeQ Lesson Plan Model

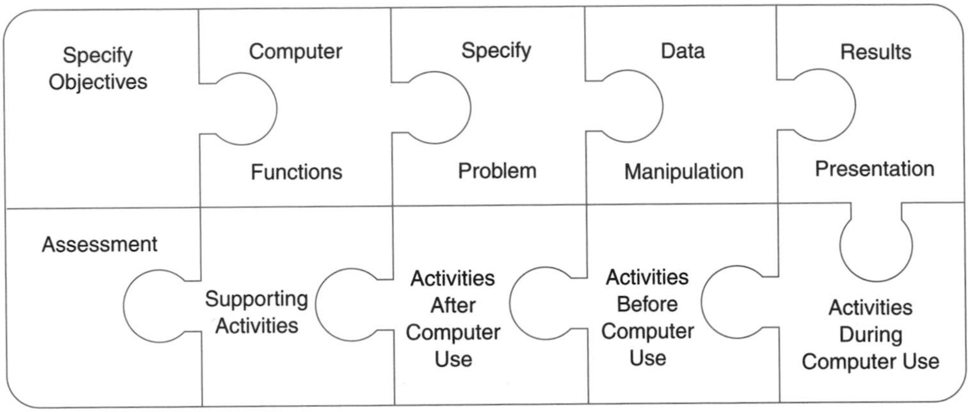

Specify the Problem

The NTeQ lesson uses an inquiry or problem-based approach. Students are given or identify a problem to solve and then learn the needed content as they work to solve the problem. Problems can come from your existing lesson plans or students can work with you to identify a relevant problem. A good problem is one that students can relate to and understand.

Data Manipulation

During the problem-solving process, the students will gather data through observations or experimentation, or from an Internet search. Once they have collected the data, what do you expect them to do with it? That is, how will they manipulate it? Will they, for example, calculate the mean, create a graph or create a drawing, etc. This step requires careful planning to ensure the objectives are addressed. It is not unusual to find lessons in which students collect data in one class (social studies) and manipulate it in another (e.g., math).

Results Presentation

As the students solve the problem, they gain an understanding of relationships and create new knowledge. In the results presentation step, you will need to plan how the students will present their knowledge. Presentations can take the form, for example, of written and oral reports, newspapers and magazines, posters, Web pages, or books.

Activities During Computer Use

Classrooms with only four or five computers require more planning of the activities than classrooms in which each student has unlimited access to a laptop computer.

Thoughtful planning, however, allows not only more efficient use of class time but also fewer problems and less frustration. You need to determine what activities the students will complete at the computer. For example, are they searching the Internet for information, writing a report, entering data, or creating a graph or drawing? You need to have clear expectations of how the students will use the technology.

Activities Before Computer Use

Now that you have a clear idea of what the students will do with the computer, you can plan the activities they need to complete to make the computer time efficient and effective. For example, if they are searching for information, you can have the students generate a list of search terms before starting the search. If they are creating a graph, they need to organize their data; if they are writing a report, they need to prepare an outline of the report.

Activities After Computer Use

It is a fairly simple process to conduct an Internet search and find hundreds if not thousands of pages of data, to create a graph, or report the results of an observation. The key, however, is to engage the students in reflective, higher-level thinking about the data they have collected and manipulated. For younger students, it might simply involve the largest and smallest items in a bar graph or pie chart. For more advanced students, it might involve explaining or hypothesizing why there are differences in the bar graph. To encourage this higher-level thinking, you will need to develop questions and a plan for encouraging the students to reflect and analyze.

Supporting Activities

There are objectives that do not require the active use of a computer but are essential to the lesson. Activities that support these objectives are labeled as supporting activities. In classrooms with only a few computers, students will need to engage in other meaningful activities when they are not using a computer. These supporting activities can include silent reading, group discussion, teacher-led discussions, and use of manipulatives, as a few examples. When managing a classroom with limited computer access, the supporting activities might include those that support objectives in other units of instruction as well as other disciplines.

Assessment

Given the variety of products and levels of learning, a traditional paper-and-pencil test may not be adequate or appropriate to assess the students' learning. You may need to develop alternative forms of assessment for integrated lessons.

The planning for each of these steps will be covered in detail in the remaining chapters of the book. We will provide examples for each step, as well as complete lesson plans.

NTeQ Philosophy

The five basic components of the NTeQ philosophy are the teacher, the student, the computer, the lesson, and the multidimensional environment. The NTeQ model, when successfully implemented, will have the following results:

1. The teacher is technologically competent and assumes the roles of designer, manager, and facilitator (Lowther, Bassoppo-Moyo, & Morrison, 1998).
2. The student actively engages in the learning process, assumes the role of researcher, and becomes technologically competent.
3. The computer is used as a tool, as it is in the workplace, to enhance learning through the use of real-world data to solve problems.
4. The lesson is student-centered, problem-based, and authentic, and technology is an integral component.
5. The environment incorporates multiple resource-rich activities.

NTeQ and the Teacher

As computers become increasingly available to students, teachers obviously need to know how to use the computers. As a result, teachers may attend workshops and seminars to learn the basics of how a computer works. It is assumed that if teachers learn how to use word processing, a browser, and a spreadsheet or become computer literate, they will be able to integrate technology into their lessons. Yet many teachers who have attended basic literacy sessions often let the computers sit idly at the back of the classroom or have students use them for simple drill-and-practice or educational games (Durham, Morrison, & Ross, 1995).

We propose that teachers need to go beyond computer literacy to become technologically competent. The three steps for this process to occur are as follows:

1. Teachers need to experience using the computer as a tool to learn new information.
2. Teachers need to understand the relationship between basic computer functions and student learning.
3. Teachers need to use their knowledge of student learning and technology to design, manage, and facilitate a student-centered, multidimensional learning environment.

Teachers need to experience using the computer as a tool to learn new information. Most of us have spent the majority of our academic life in a traditional classroom. In this setting, the teacher typically lectured while the students listened and sometimes took notes. Classroom activities included answering questions at the back of the book or on a worksheet, copying diagrams from books, drawing pictures, writing stories, doing science activities, and taking quizzes. So, when we ask teachers to assume the new role of a facilitator and to create lessons that integrate the use of technology as a tool, they have little if any prior experience or models to draw upon. Therefore it is imperative for teachers to experience learning activities similar to those that they are expected to use with their students. This simulation of a student activity not only will let the teachers experience the benefits of using technology to enhance learning but also will let them encounter some of the frustrations that tend to arise when computers are used.

Teachers need to understand the relationship between basic computer functions and student learning. Teachers typically learn how to use basic computer applications such as creating a test with word processing, a spreadsheet grade book, or a database with student information. However, they do not learn how to analyze the actual computer functions to determine how these functions can help students learn.

An analysis of a database will reveal that it can sort, match, find, and group sets of information. The next logical step is to determine how students can use these capabilities to achieve one or more lesson objectives. For example, in a traditional lesson studying endangered species, students might learn which animals are endangered, where they live, what they eat, and why they are endangered by reading the textbook, completing worksheets, and writing a report on an animal of their choice. If teachers realize that students can place the endangered species information into a database, the students can then discover some of the common elements or patterns that exist. Students could manipulate the data in numerous ways, such as by sorting where the animals live or what they eat or why they are endangered. As students work with the data, patterns begin to emerge, giving rise to new questions and new ways to look at the data. For example, are carnivores or omnivores more likely to become extinct? Which continent has the most endangered species? Which group of animals is the most threatened? Students can also identify other information to add to the database. By having the students use a database to examine the information rather than fill in blanks on a worksheet or answer questions from the back of a book, they not only learn the information, but they manipulate the data (e.g., sort or match records) to solve problems and discover new information.

Teachers need to use their knowledge of student learning and technology to design, facilitate, and manage a student-centered, multidimensional learning environment. Once teachers understand the basic computer functions, they can combine this understanding with what they know about how students learn, to create an environment that integrates technology to enhance learning. Generating the *design* is the first step (see Chapter 3). When the teacher assumes the role of a designer, each aspect of the lesson must be considered and carefully arranged to support and foster meaningful student learning.

The next step in creating the learning environment involves the teacher assuming the role of a *facilitator* (see Chapter 12). In a traditional classroom, the teacher provides the students with what they are to learn, typically with a lecture or students reading a chapter of the textbook. The facilitator process is different because a facilitator does not tell the students the information they need to learn but rather provides a resource-rich environment through which the students are guided into learning. In this environment, the students work collaboratively to learn or solve a problem. The teacher as facilitator keeps a close watch on the progress of each group and asks directed questions to stimulate student thinking and decision making. Facilitation also involves teachers modeling various processes for the students. This modeling can include both physical processes, such as how to create fields in a database, and cognitive processes, such as describing each step the teacher might take to solve a problem. Facilitation also ensures students receive the necessary scaffolding or remediation to proceed with the lesson (Vygotsky, 1978).

The last step to create the environment is *classroom management* (see Chapter 13). This aspect not only involves planning but also the actual management of a classroom that now has several computers. The NTeQ lesson plan depicts what the students do before they go to the computer, at the computer, and after finishing with the computer. However, the lesson plan does not designate how or when they will rotate to and from the computers. One way to plan for managing a technology-based lesson is for the teacher to actually use the software to create a product similar to what the students will produce during the lesson. This activity not only gives the teacher the expertise to handle student problems as they arise but also ensures that the lesson can be completed. The management plan also should include procedures for addressing two technology-related issues: lack of student computer skills and technical problems. The use of job aids (simple instruction sheets posted in the computer area) can help, and teachers can employ the assistance of the students who are "computer experts." With the NTeQ model, teachers themselves gain technological competence. They create a learning environment in which students use technology to enhance their learning in a way similar to what they will use in the workforce.

NTeQ and the Student

When examining the role of students in relation to the NTeQ model, we find the students are impacted in the following three important ways:

1. The student is actively engaged in the learning process.
2. The student assumes the role of a researcher.
3. The student becomes technologically competent.

The student is actively engaged in the learning process. Students involved in a lesson based on the NTeQ model spend very little time, if any at all, sitting quietly at their desks while they take notes on the teacher's lecture. They also very rarely, if ever, answer the chapter questions in their history or science books. Instead, the students are involved in a learning environment that has small groups of students collaboratively solving problems using real-life resources. This approach is seen in the scenario of Ms. Londhe's class presented in the Classroom Snapshot. In this learning environment, the students were actively and collaboratively engaged in collecting and analyzing actual data that affect each state's economy. This type of active engagement and discussion with peers reinforces what is being learned by giving students the opportunity to apply their knowledge.

The student assumes the role of a researcher. The inquiry approach taken with the NTeQ model places students in the role of researchers. The students are not merely given the information they must learn, rather they are given situations they must investigate. During the investigation, or problem-solving process, the students work collaboratively to solve the problem, which leads to learning the appropriate concepts and principles. For the students to solve the situation or problem, they must use the techniques of a researcher, or the scientific method: identify the problem, formulate a hypothesis, collect and analyze data, and draw conclusions. Chapter 11, Implementation: From Plan to Action introduces the NTeQ Problem-Solving Process to help guide students through the steps needed to successfully conduct an inquiry.

The student becomes technologically competent. When students are given the opportunity to learn in an environment that is based on the NTeQ model, they will begin to become technologically competent. Technological competence means the student has achieved the following:

- Is a capable user of the basic computer applications often found in the workplace, such as word processing, database, spreadsheet, draw, Internet browser, e-mail, and presentation
- Understands the capabilities of each type of computer application and when and where it is appropriate to use each one

This technological competence will enable students to gain more from their K–12 and postsecondary education and benefit them throughout their future careers.

NTeQ and the Computer

The role of the computer in the NTeQ model is different because it is seen from two vantage points. First, the computer is not the point of emphasis, yet it is a critical component. In other words, there is no emphasis on learning the history of comput-

With an open environment, students collaboratively decide how to solve problems.

ers or the electronic functions of a computer. Most people in the business world know very little about how computers operate, yet, for example, they use computers all day long to solve complex financial problems for major corporations.

Second, we view the computer as a learning tool, similar to a calculator. When calculators were introduced into the classroom, students were not expected to learn the history of calculators or how the electronic circuitry enabled the calculator to function. Instead, students were shown the basics of how a calculator could assist them in solving math problems. The computer should be viewed in the same manner. It is a tool that can help students look at information in new and different ways.

The computer is used as an extension of what the students are able to do for themselves because computer functions closely align with students' abilities. The computer, however, is more efficient in performing these functions (see Appendix A for a list of computer functions aligned to learning tasks). Students then can place a greater emphasis on discovering new ideas rather than on sorting and classifying data. For example, students in Ms. Londhe's class could have compared states without a computer, but it would have taken a tremendous amount of time for the students to experiment with the different economic factors. With the use of a spreadsheet, the students can quickly and accurately experiment with the information to reach the best solution. Both the spreadsheet and the state information sheets are artifacts we use to make us smarter (Norman, 1993). The computer, however, is more efficient and allows the students more time to attend to higher-order thinking tasks. The students studying the endangered species could have placed their information on note cards rather than in a database. When looking at various sets of data (e.g., all the reptiles who eat plants and live in Europe), though, it would take much more time for students to gather this information from note cards. With the database, it could be done within a few minutes. Students are then free to focus on the "why, what, and where" questions that can help them discover relevant principles. If we use the computer as a tool for solving problems, it can enhance interest and motivation, provide access to information outside the classroom, and allow students to manipulate data in a variety of ways (Blumenfeld et al., 1991).

Because the NTeQ model closely aligns what the students are learning to the functions of a computer, the computer becomes an integral part of the lesson. The students must use a computer to answer the questions in an efficient and effective manner. After students have used computers in this manner, *they* begin to ask the teacher if they can use the computer. They start to realize that the information they are learning becomes more meaningful when they can categorize the information and place it into a database. Students may express an interest in composing their reports with a word processor because they can import bar graphs to support their results or clip art to add meaning to what they have written. In other words, each student begins to recognize that the computer is an integral part of his or her learning process.

NTeQ and the Lesson

The NTeQ lesson is composed of 10 major components (see Figure 1-3). The components fit together to create lessons that are student-centered, problem-based, authentic, and dependent on the integration of technology.

The lessons are designed to keep the students actively involved in the learning process. With the students playing a greater role in the classroom, the teacher assumes the role of facilitator and guide. The lessons are also formulated around problems that are embedded in a context that is meaningful and authentic for the students. This context is created by incorporating the use of real resources that the students gather themselves. For example, clothing or pizza prices, the cost of a movie, water quality, local voting behaviors, mileage to a favorite place, or endangered species. This data gathering and manipulation makes the information something that is real and more meaningful than the information lifted from their textbook. Students can relate to the material because they are involved in the collection process, that is, deciding what to collect, finding the information, and determining what part of the information is relevant. Plus, they have a reason for collecting and analyzing the information—they need to solve the problem. Thus the lessons are student centered, problem based, and authentic. But, as the name iNtegrating Technology for inQuiry implies, the NTeQ model focuses on the integration of technology, so the lessons are also dependent on the integration of technology.

The NTeQ model is not intended for use with *every* lesson taught. It takes a careful analysis of what the students are going to learn to determine if technology can be integrated. The technologically competent teacher determines whether there is a correlation between what the students are learning and the functions of a computer. If it is determined that the students will benefit from using the computer to gather, manage, manipulate, retrieve, or present the information, then the model can be applied.

NTeQ and the Standards

Today's teachers must address two types of standards in their planning and teaching. First, they must address the national, state, and local district's standards, or benchmarks. These standards focus primarily on content such as writing a coherent paragraph or explaining the reasons for migrations to the western states. Second, teachers must address the National Educational Technology Standards (NETS) for Students. These standards address the students' use of computer technology. The following paragraphs describe how these standards are addressed by the NTeQ model.

Content Standards

National content standards are prepared by professional organizations such as the National Council of Teachers of Mathematics (*www.nctm.org*), National Council for the Social Studies (*www.ncss.org*), National Science Teachers Association (*www.nsta.org*), and National Council of Teachers of English (*www.ncte.org*). State and local school districts may also develop or modify these national standards for use in local schools (see *www.education-world.com/standards/* for a listing of state standards). These standards prescribe the skills and knowledge students must master in each subject area at each grade level. Teachers then use these standards to plan the individual class curriculum.

How do teachers use these standards with the NTeQ model? The standards are simply guidelines as they are presented. Each teacher must translate the standards into an instructional objective that provides a meaningful context for the desired learning. Once you have translated your standards into an objective, you can use the NTeQ model to first determine if there is a match with a computer function; then you can begin to develop an integrated lesson. Similarly, you can purposely translate a standard into an objective that has a match with a computer function. An integrated lesson developed with the NTeQ model can address a variety of objectives.

NETS for Students

In contrast to the content standards, the NETS standards (*http://cnets.iste.org/*) focus on technology skills and knowledge. The technology standards are organized into six broad categories: basic operations and concepts; social, ethical, and human issues; technology productivity tools; technology communication tools; technology research tools; and technology problem-solving and decision-making tools. Integrated lessons developed with the NTeQ model can address the standards in each of these six broad categories.

SUMMARY

The NTeQ model is an inquiry-based approach used to create a student-centered learning environment. Teachers can use the 10-step NTeQ model to create integrated lesson plans that incorporate the use of computers as a tool for solving problems. Students use computers to create artifacts that are used to solve problems and develop understanding. This approach requires teachers to design or adapt lessons, assume the role of facilitator, and plan the management of the classroom. Students take on the active role of a researcher rather than that of a passive listener. The result is a student-centered classroom in which students are actively engaged in learning.

AT THE CLASSROOM'S DOORSTEP

Questions Teachers Ask

Must I use a problem-based learning approach in my classroom to use computers as a tool?

No, you do not need to use a problem-based learning approach. We have found that integrating computers as a tool works best in an open-ended environment. The most common approach to creating this type of learning environment is some form of problem-based learning, inquiry, or guided design. The approach presented in this text is flexible and will allow teachers to adapt it to their own teaching style.

Can I still use tutorials and drill-and-practice software?

Yes, there is a place for computer-based instruction (CBI) if it is used appropriately. CBI is most useful when it supports the scaffolding the students need to solve a problem. Thus you need to carefully select applications that support your objectives for the unit. Chapter 10, Educational Software, provides more detail on effectively using educational software.

Won't I have to spend a great deal of time to develop these units of instruction?

It does take some time and effort to develop an integrated computer lesson. Many times you can adapt a unit you are currently using, or you might work with a group of teachers in the same grade level or closely grouped grades. The payback in developing one of these units comes from using it more than one time. It will take less effort to implement the unit each time you use it. Starting with the second use, you should be able to focus on minor modifications to strengthen the lesson.

Won't every student need a computer to use it as a tool?

Ideally, every student would have a computer, just like every student has a pen and notepad. The NTeQ model works well when each student has a computer (see Ross, Lowther, Morrison, & Plants, 2000, in Chapter 2). However, the NTeQ model was designed to work in classrooms that have four to six computers, with students working in groups. This book focuses on this type of classroom and includes a variety of strategies and management plans for the implementation.

TECHNOLOGY INTEGRATION ACTIVITIES

To access the activities that connect the content of the text with the Companion Website and other technology, please go to the Activities module in Chapter 1 of the Companion Website at *http://www.prenhall.com/morrison.*

NTEQ PORTFOLIO ACTIVITIES

The following activities are designed to help you build your NTeQ Portfolio for teaching.

Reflections

There are many approaches to teaching and to using computers in the classroom. Have you given any thought as to how you will use computers in your classroom? For your NTeQ portfolio entry for Chapter 1, write a description of your view of how you will use computers in your classroom. Next, enter your definition of technology integration. That is, what does technology integration mean to you?

REFERENCES

American Association of University Women. (2000). *Executive summary: Tech-savvy—Educating girls in the new computer age (2000)* [On-line]. Available: http://www.aauw.org/research/techexecsumm.cfm.

Archer, J. (October 1, 1998). The link to higher scores. *Technology Counts '98. Education Week*, *18*(5), 10–20.

Becker, H. J. (1991). How computers are used in United States schools: Basic data from the 1989 I.E.A. computers in education survey. *Journal of Educational Computing Research, 7*, 385–406.

Blumenfeld, P. C., Soloway, E., Marx, R., Krajcik, J. S., Guzdial, M., & Palincsar, A. (1991). Motivating project-based learning: Sustaining the doing, supporting the learning. *Educational Psychologist, 26*(3 & 4), 369–398.

Bork, A. (1987). *Learning with personal computers*. New York: Harper & Row.

Davies, I. K. (1973). *Competency-based learning: Technology, management, and design*. New York: McGraw-Hill.

Digest of educational statistics (2001). [On-line]. Available: http://nces.ed.gov/pubs2002/digest2001/ch7.asp.

Durham, P., Morrison, G. R., & Ross, S. M. (1995). Technology training of 21st century classroom teachers. *Tennessee Educational Leadership, 22*, 41–45.

Heinich, R., Molenda, M., Russell, J. D., & Smaldino, S. E. (1996). *Instructional media and technologies for learning*. Upper Saddle River, NJ: Merrill.

International Society for Technology in Education. (2000). *National educational technology standards*. Eugene, OR: International Society for Technology in Education.

Lowther, D. L., Bassoppo-Moyo, T., & Morrison, G. R. (1998). Moving from computer literate to technological competent: The next educational reform. *Computers and Human Behavior, 14*, 93–109.

Lumsdaine, A. A. (1964). Educational technology, programmed instruction, and instructional science. In E. R. Hilgard (Ed.). *Theories of learning and instruction: The sixty-third yearbook of the National Society for the Study of Education* (pp. 371–401). Chicago: National Society for the Study of Education.

Norman, D. A. (1993). *Things that make us smart: Defending human attributes in the age of the machine*. Cambridge, MA: Perseus Books.

Ross, S. M., Lowther, D. L., Morrison, G. R., & Plants, R. (2000). *Anytime anywhere learning: Final evaluation of the laptop program*. Memphis, TN: University of Memphis. [On-line]. Available: http://www.nteq.com/report.htm.

Ross, S. M., & Morrison, G. R. (1988). Adapting instruction to learner performance and background variables. In D. Jonassen (Ed.), *Instructional designs for microcomputer courseware* (pp. 227–245). Hillsdale, NJ: Lawrence Erlbaum Associates.

Savery, J. R., & Duffy, T. M. (1995). Problem-based learning: An instructional model and its constructivist framework. *Educational Technology, 45*, 31–38.

SCANS (June, 1991). *What work requires of schools: A SCANS Report for America 2000* (pp. xvii–xviii.). U.S. Department of Labor and Education. Available: http://wdr.doleta.gov/opr/fulltext/document.cfm?docn–6140.

Vygotsky, L. (1978). *Mind in society*. Cambridge, MA: Harvard University Press.

KEY TOPICS

Chapter 2

NTeQ: A Research-Based Model

The No Child Left Behind Act of 2002 (*www.ed.gov*) stresses the importance of adopting instructional strategies that have been proven effective with rigorous research. This research must verify that the instructional practice is effective and improves student learning. In this chapter, we provide an introduction to research on practices that are foundational aspects of the NTeQ model, as well as two studies that support the educational effectiveness of implementing the NTeQ model.

GETTING STARTED

What Do I Know?

1. Today, teachers are expected to use "research-based" models; does the NTeQ Model meet this criterion?
2. How will the NTeQ model fit in with the comprehensive school reform model adopted by my school?
3. What evidence do you have that the NTeQ model increases learning?

Classroom Snapshot

Mr. Marshall was getting ready to start his 19th year of teaching seventh- and eighth-grade science and social studies. Although he was well liked by the students and perceived as making his classroom a fun place, Mr. Marshall felt like he was no longer connecting with his students. They seem to have a lot of energy and even more questions. Home computers and Internet access were enjoyed by almost everyone in the school. Over the past few years, he had noticed how nice the student reports were with lots of graphics and easy-to-read text with few if any spelling or grammar errors. But his students did not seem excited about learning any more. Was he getting too old to teach this young group? Maybe it was time to switch to the community college.

The community for Sugar Creek Middle School is quite conservative. Four years ago, when the new school was started, the parents indicated they wanted a tried and traditional approach of basics for the curriculum. Achievement scores for the school, however, were not as high as one would expect. Trying something new would not be well received by the parents, but might be worth the risk if Mr. Marshall could once again connect with his students. He was interested in creating a student-centered learning environment rather than his traditional teacher-centered classroom. The research suggested a student-centered environment could enhance student learning, but Mr. Marshall realized he would need data to support this change. During the year, he decided to have his students create a portfolio of their projects and papers. The portfolios would show smaller changes from grading period to grading period and, hopefully, significant changes between the first and last assignments of the year. He also had access to the state's achievement test scores for writing, math, and social studies. If all works well, he would have the evidence needed to show his new method was effective.

The results from Mr. Marshall's new approach were very good. The portfolio provided a means of comparing the students' writing at the beginning of the year to that at the end of the year. At the open house, parents commented on visible improvement in their children's writing. Similarly, the math, writing, and social studies scores on the state achievement test showed significant increases for Mr. Marshall's class over scores of other students in the district. As a result, other teachers and the principal are interested in changing the way they teach next year.

EDUCATIONAL REFORM AND TECHNOLOGY

Since the beginning of the 20th century, schools in the United States have operated on a factory model. Their aim was to create obedient and competent workers for the many factories and industries that were a part of the industrial revolution. Thus, like factory workers, students sat individually in rows, completing their individual tasks, memorizing their work, and learning not to question, but rather to obey authority. As the century continued, industry changed. Specialized workers with communication skills, who could work as part of a team, think independently, and question the status quo were needed.

Schools, however, have remained essentially unchanged since the early 1900s. Soon after the publication of *A Nation at Risk* (National Commission on Excellence in Education, 1983), educators, politicians, parents, and citizens began to look critically at the educational process, which resulted in the current educational reform movement. These various reforms have taken many paths, but a consistent theme was to break from the traditional factory models of education. One criticism of both the past and current reform movements is the lack of a relationship between educational reform and educational technology (Means, 1994). Educational reform and technology have developed innovative approaches to teaching. Those restructuring the schools, however, often have failed to consider the use of technology when designing new programs. Similarly, the instructional technologists often have failed to consider the redesign of the school when implementing technology. For example, how can laptop computers be charged during class or how can laptops be stabilized on desks with slanted tops?

One reason for the lack of technology integration into the restructured schools may be attributed to both the way technology is used and the types of technology available. As previously mentioned, technology has typically been used to *deliver* instruction in the classroom. The most common type of software used in the classroom is drill-and-practice, which is based on a behavioral approach to teaching and emphasizes rote memorization (Archer, 1998; Becker, 1991). Both the approach to using technology and the software used often are inconsistent with the current reform approaches and current views of instruction. Today's educational reform is based on a student-centered approach in an open-ended environment and is not usually supported by the more traditional uses of computer technology. Technology and a student-centered approach to education do not, however, need to be at odds with one another. If we change our view of computers from merely a means to deliver instruction to one of a tool to solve problems, then the reform movement can influence the use of technology and technology can influence the reform of education.

Two Views of Teaching

The emphasis on increasing student achievement and school reform has resulted in an increased use of standardized achievement tests to assess student progress. These tests range from state-developed tests (e.g., MEAP and TCAPS) to traditional tests such as the Iowa Tests of Basic Skills. Teachers must focus on how they can improve their students' achievement as measured on a specific test. There seems to be a clear dichotomy of approaches teachers take in addressing the benchmarks and standards assessed by these tests (Newmann, Bryk, & Nagaoka, 2001). One approach is teacher centered, with a focus on memorization of facts, formulas, dates, names, and so on. The student is then expected to recall the exact information for the test. The second approach is one that focuses on authentic intellectual work in a student-centered environment. This approach requires students to formulate problems, collect information and data, organize and manipulate the information and data, and then formulate an answer. The debate between these two approaches has been fueled by the increased demand for accountability required by the No Child Left Behind Act, which often translates into increased use of standardized tests.

A study by Newmann et al. (2001) suggests that the authentic learning approach in a student-centered environment produced substantially more achievement gains than the teacher-centered memorization approach. Let's examine the results of this study. Newmann and his associates studied 400 classrooms in 19 different elementary schools. They analyzed over 2,000 classroom assignments and standardized scores for almost 5,000 students. When they analyzed the results of classrooms using high-quality assignments (i.e., those involving authentic intellectual activities), they found that the learning gains were 20% greater than the national average. Students who were in classrooms that focused primarily on a memorization approach gained 25% *less* in reading and 22% *less* in mathematics than the national average. Additional analyses were conducted to determine whether there was a relationship between achievement and classroom composition such as prior achievement, race, gender, and socioeconomic status. Their analysis found only a weak, insignificant relationship between the teacher's assignments and students' prior achievement. Newmann and his colleagues also found that high-quality assignments in mathematics tended to help the low-achieving students even more than their high-achieving classmates. The low-achieving students showed a 29% gain in achievement over similar students in classes that focused on a more direct instructional approach. Overall, the results indicate that both high- and low-achieving students in a classroom that stresses high-quality intellectual assignments benefit with resulting increases in achievement.

These studies suggest that combining the use of computer technology as a tool with an emphasis on problem solving and reflection will result in increased student achievement. Creating lessons that incorporate these ideas will help you create a student-centered learning environment.

Student-Centered Instruction

Let's start our discussion by examining three basic premises of a student-centered learning environment. First, student-centered learning emphasizes understanding one's world rather than mimicking (i.e., rote memorization of) the content. Understanding is a result of the learner reshaping and transforming information (Gardner, 1991). Understanding one's world requires the student to actively process and manipulate information. Second, students will strive to reduce discrepancies between what they know and what they observe. Savery and Duffy (1995) refer to this phenomenon as *puzzlement*. This cognitive dissonance (Festinger, 1957) between what the student knows and what is observed is a motivating factor for seeking resolution of the difference by developing a new understanding (Brooks & Brooks, 1993). Third, one's knowledge is refined through negotiations with others and evaluation of individual understanding (Savery & Duffy, 1995). Students use other students to test their understanding and examine the understanding of others. This collection of understanding provides a means for an individual to evaluate and understand propositions, which when grouped together are called *knowledge*. Collaborative groups allow a student to learn the views of others in order to challenge and test the viability of his or her own views. The teacher's responsibility is to understand what and how students think.

In the following sections, we will examine the three components of a student-centered learning environment that form the basis of our approach to integrating computers into the curriculum. These three components are open-ended learning environments, learning context, and collaborative learning.

A small group of students using the computer as a tool.

Open-Ended Learning Environments

One characteristic of a student-centered teaching approach is the use of open-ended learning environments. These environments often require students to solve a problem, which exposes them to new information. As a result, students gain new understanding by reshaping and transforming their knowledge. Let's examine inquiry learning and problem-based learning as ways of creating an open-ended learning environment.

The new social studies movement of the 1960s used a discovery approach (Bruner, 1960, 1966) to teach students conceptual knowledge about the social sciences (Hertzberg, 1981). Using the inquiry approach, teachers created inquiry units that required students to seek information in order to discover concepts and principles. As part of this process, students discovered new concepts (e.g., classifications) and relationships (e.g., principles) between the concepts (Bruner, 1960). Although the instruction in an inquiry unit was carefully structured (Woolever & Scott, 1988), the units were student centered and they encouraged students to ask questions and find the answers. Recent research (Edelson, Gordin, & Pea, 1999; Greeno, Collins, & Resnick, 1996) suggests support for inquiry-based activities that use projects and authentic contexts to enhance learning.

More recently, the differences between inquiry learning, discovery learning, and problem-based learning have become blurred. All three focus on providing a realistic context for the learner. Learners then solve a problem that leads to understanding of the content. Problem-based learning (PBL) strategies have recently caught the attention of P–12 educators (Barrows & Kelson, 1996; Savery & Duffy, 1995) as a strategy consistent with a student-centered approach. PBL models the problem-solving approach experts use to solve real-world problems (Barrows & Kelson, 1996).

Barrows (1985) describes this approach as follows: Students are provided with the problem first, before they begin studying the material. Students must then think about what they know individually and collectively and what they need to learn to solve the problem. By determining what they need to know, the students develop knowledge structures based on problem-solving approaches rather than traditional subject matter approaches as presented in textbooks.

Like the inquiry approach, PBL is based on the use of the scientific method for gathering information, generating hypotheses, manipulating the data, testing hypotheses, and identifying a solution. Problems are designed to entice the learner into acquiring the knowledge and skills of a domain of knowledge (Barrows & Kelson, 1996). Students are motivated to learn new information they can use to solve problems. This approach fosters self-directed learning based on intrinsic rewards, such as finding a solution, rather than an extrinsic reward, such as a score on a test.

Inquiry lessons provide a unique environment for the learner. Students have an opportunity to learn the practices of a discipline such as science by engaging in the practice of science (Edleson et al., 1999). Bruner (1960) suggests that the activities a cancer researcher engages in while in her lab or a novelist engages in at his desk are the same as those of anyone who is seeking to achieve understanding. For students there are two ways to learn physics, biology, math, grammar, or art. First, they can read a textbook and engage in discussions about conclusions in the field of inquiry. According to Bruner, physics, biology, math, grammar, and art when taught in a traditional manner look very little like the actual practice of the disciplines in the real world by scientists, writers, and artists. The second approach is to have the student engage in inquiry in the field just as the scientist, writer, or artist. This approach provides the learner with a chance to behave like the scientist and develop an understanding of the field.

Features of Open-Ended Learning Environments

The open-ended learning environments described focus on the learner by allowing the learner to make decisions about what information is needed and what approach should be taken to solve a problem. These environments stand in contrast to traditional instruction, in which content is selected and transmitted through lectures and assigned readings in textbooks. Each of these open-ended methods can also vary in the amount of structure and direction the teacher can provide (Albanese & Mitchell, 1993; Land & Hannafin, 1997). Direction from the teacher can range from providing specific tutoring or resources to coaching individual students on how to identify needed information.

Open-ended learning environments also require the teacher to adopt new approaches. The primary mode of teaching switches from one of lecturing to one of facilitating student investigation. Teachers work as facilitators and tutors to help students understand the material and to provide the necessary scaffolding. The emphasis is on the student developing an understanding of the material through direct contact with information, data collection, and data manipulation. Students then generate and test hypotheses and determine the best solution.

Selecting content for an open-ended learning unit is a process of negotiation involving input from students and knowledge of the curriculum frameworks. Teachers must consider standards imposed by the schools and recommended by their professional societies (e.g., National Council of Teachers of Mathematics) when designing the units. Similarly, students should have input based on their interests. The final objectives for the unit evolve from discussions between the teacher and students on how to address the needs expressed by society and the interests of the students.

Inquiry learning and PBL both use a problem-solving approach to acquire knowledge. These approaches place more responsibility on the learner for solving the problem and acquiring the knowledge the *individual* needs to solve the problem. As a result, students using one of these approaches are more likely to have a better understanding of the problem and solution than students in a direct teaching environment.

Learning Context

Traditional textbooks and instruction separate learning from the context. The effectiveness and appropriateness of this practice has been (Bruner, 1960) and is now questioned by researchers (Brown, Collins, & Duguid, 1989). For example, a common time–distance math problem might appear as "It is 932 miles between Philadelphia and St. Louis. A car leaves Philadelphia at 8:00 A.M. headed west and is traveling at 65 miles per hour. A second car leaves St. Louis at 8:00 A.M. and is headed east traveling at 57 miles per hour. What time will they meet?" A logical answer is never, because the car from Philadelphia is headed to Chicago and the car from St. Louis is headed to Nashville! The "author" of this fictional problem (and others like it) intended both cars to take the same route and for the student to calculate when they would meet. Consider, however, a student who lives in Memphis or Houston and the probability that he has either traveled the route from St. Louis to Philadelphia or whether he has visited the two cities. For most students, the names of the two cities are just names, or they may be names associated with a big McDonald's-type arch or the Liberty Bell. The instruction was abstract and failed to provide a meaningful context for the learner.

Collaborative Learning

Teachers and students today are required now more than ever to collaborate in their work. Reform movements push teachers toward site-based management, team planning, peer coaching, and community partnerships; thus we can no longer accept the notion of the teacher as an isolated decision maker. Our evolving society requires citizens to have specialized skills. Employees must be able to work as part of a team, support a larger vision, and communicate and work effectively with others. Therefore teachers are not only modeling collaboration in their own work, but they are also required to use instructional processes that facilitate collaboration and the development of social skills among their students.

The Social Nature of Learning

The social impact on learning has been discussed for centuries by scholars such as Aristotle, Dewey (1916), and Vygotsky (1978). Although constructivists emphasize the self-construction of meaning, it would be a misconception to believe that whatever an individual thinks is in fact "the truth." Rather than subscribing to this form of relativism, constructivists support the notion of the self-construction of meaning within a

TABLE 2-1 Cooperative Versus Traditional Groups

Cooperative Groups	Traditional Learning Groups
Heterogeneous	Homogeneous
Social skills emphasized Task and group maintenance emphasized	Social skills assumed Only task emphasized
Teacher observes and facilitates Shared leadership and responsibility	Teacher ignores group functioning One leader and self-responsibility
Interdependent	No interdependence

Adapted from Johnson & Johnson, 1984.

social context. As people attempt to find meaning in an experience or encounter, they reflect on their beliefs, values, and concepts, which all arise from a common and shared understanding within their culture. The collaborative environment can create advantages for the learner; however, students also often benefit from the opportunity to "articulate, reflect, and scaffold" (Herrington & Oliver, 2000) with a partner.

Cooperative Versus Traditional Group Work

How can teachers effectively capitalize on the social nature of learning? Many educators are now taught to integrate small-group learning into their pedagogy. However, as more teachers move toward the use of group learning such as dyads, triads, and cooperative learning, it is important to distinguish among features of teaching that promote cooperation and the development of social skills and features of traditional group work (Table 2–1).

The development of group social skills is necessary when integrating technology as a tool. A collaborative group is doomed to failure when given a task without appropriate teacher support to develop the necessary social and technical skills needed to complete the assignment. We often have seen some group members passively sit while others work at the computer. Had the teacher required these groups to divide responsibilities and accept responsibility for one another, this type of problem might have been overcome. The use of technology in group work also provides the opportunity for students to educate one another. For example, if a student is unfamiliar with Web browsers, the teacher might decide to assign that student the responsibility for locating Websites on a given topic with the support of a knowledgeable student sitting by his or her side as they work. The learners are empowered as they acquire new skills, and the student serving as coach becomes empowered through the opportunity to educate others.

STARTING THE REVOLUTION

You say you want a revolution
Well, you know
We all want to change the world.

"Revolution" by Lennon and McCartney

Four Steps for Starting a Revolution

It has been over 15 years since Bork (1987) made his prediction that computers would revolutionize the way students learn. We have yet to see computers have any major impact. Perhaps the revolution will begin now that we have a better understanding of how to use computers in the classroom for the following reasons:

1. After experimenting with computers in the classroom for some 20 years, we now know what does and does not work.
2. We are approaching the critical mass of computers in the classroom; that is, they are readily available to nearly every classroom.
3. Teachers, administrators, politicians, and parents are ready for a new approach to using computers.
4. Current teaching practices emphasize using realistic contexts for learning.

First, after experimenting with computers in the classroom for approximately 20 years, we now know what works and what does not work. Using computers as a delivery device *has not* produced the results we expected. We predict that if we integrate computers into the curriculum as a tool for solving real-world problems, we will start a revolution that can affect how students learn. This shift in thinking about computers as a tool instead of a delivery mechanism is consistent with the use of computers outside of the classroom. Our focus will shift from the skill of just using a computer (e.g., keyboarding) to one of knowing not only how and when to use a computer, but how to use the computer to solve a problem. More importantly, the tool-using approach is consistent with the current constructivist approach in education. During the past 20 years, the primary mechanism driving the computer-delivery approach has been a behavioral perspective, which has often taken a passive approach to learning. Using computers as tools can help teachers create a student-centered learning environment. Students create an understanding of the world that will lead to the development of knowledge.

Second, we are approaching the critical mass of computers in the classroom. Today we see more computers in classrooms, not just in computer labs. For example, 84% of 7,000 fourth-grade students reported that they had computers in the classroom and 79% had computer labs at their schools (Jerald & Orlofsky, 1999). To use a computer lab, teachers have to schedule the lab in advance and move the class between rooms (Pruett, Morrison, Dietrich, & Smith, 1993). These labs are not always available and might require scheduling several weeks in advance. This lack of easy access makes it difficult to plan a lesson integrating computers. In addition, the focus is on computer literacy and computer-based instruction (Lowther, Bassoppo-Moyo, & Morrison, 1998). As a result, computer labs encourage the use of computers as delivery mechanisms. Placing computers in the classroom, where they are readily available throughout the school day, allows students to use them as a tool. Consider the effect of a school that allowed students to use a pencil and paper *only* in the school cafeteria. In addition, only one class could use the cafeteria at a time. Teachers probably would have a difficult time trying to use paper and pencils in their lesson plans. A typical trip to the "cafeteria writing lab" might result in nothing more than drawing some pictures or copying some letters or words. When students are allowed to use pencil and paper in the classroom at any time, they can use them as tools. Similarly, when computers are readily available in the classroom, teachers can take a different approach to integrating them into a lesson.

Third, teachers, administrators, politicians, and parents are ready for a new approach to using computers. Schools, states, and the federal government have invested a great deal of money in hardware and software without seeing revolutionary changes in student learning. Changing our approach from one of a delivery mechanism to one of computers as tools allows for better integration of computers into the curriculum and the development of real-life skills and knowledge. There is currently little economic need for a student who has progressed to the sixth level of destroying alien ships. There is, however, a need for a student who knows when and how to use a computer to solve problems.

Fourth, current teaching practices emphasize using realistic contexts for learning. Using computers as tools provides both support and a means of extending this practice. Students can apply solutions used in the real world to analyze and manipulate real-world problems. Today's microcomputers and Internet access allow teachers and students to extend problems and search for answers beyond the classroom, community, state, and nation.

The focus of this book is to illustrate how to combine an open-ended learning environment with using computers as a tool to create a new approach to integrating computers in the classroom.

The Revolution

During the 1999 to 2000 school year, more than 400 fifth- and sixth-grade students and their teachers implemented the NTeQ model in the Walled Lake Consolidated Schools (*www.walledlake.k12.mi.us/*). The students were part of an Anytime Anywhere Learning project (*http://www.microsoft.com/education/aal/default.asp*) in which each student's parents leased or purchased a laptop computer for the student. The teachers developed integrated lesson plans using the NTeQ model.

An evaluation of the project (Ross, Lowther, Morrison, & Plants, 2000) identified differences between the classrooms using the NTeQ model and those using a more traditional approach to instruction. Table 2–2 provides a list of significant differences between the classrooms using the NTeQ model and the traditional classrooms.

TABLE 2-2 Evaluation Results

Classrooms using the NTeQ model for instruction were more likely to demonstrate:
Independent inquiry by the students
Use of the computer as a tool
Cooperative learning
Project-based learning
Higher levels of feedback from the teacher
Teacher serving as facilitator
Computer used as a research tool to locate information
Improved writing ability

When NTeQ is implemented, students are engaged in a variety of activities.

When teachers were asked what improvements they observed in the students' project, they reported improved research skills, use of problem skills, and ability to synthesize information. A survey of parents and students suggested they were pleased with the project and felt their (or their children's) research skills were improved (Ross, et al., 2000). "Laptop students are much more fluent than other students with using the technology of the 21st century for learning, research, and production. For them, computers are fully integrated with and a natural part of their educational experiences both at school and at home" (p. 13). A second study completed in 2002 (Lowther, Ross, and Morrison, 2003) found substantial and significant gains in writing and problem solving for students in the laptop program. These two studies provide support for the use of an integrated approach to teaching and learning when using computer technology.

THE TEACHER'S DIARY

I think back on the past 8 months of teaching a class of students equipped with laptops and can't imagine doing it any other way. Teaching a classroom of students using laptops as a tool for learning has had a positive impact on every aspect of my career. Although it was a bit scary to be one of the first to teach in this way, I am glad I overcame my fears and gave it a try.

I attribute my success with the program to taking part in a staff development course that provided inspiration and encouragement, as well as an inner drive to

Continued

make the program work for my students. I learned how exciting learning can be by doing a few simple, instructor-guided activities (my role was that of a student). In addition, I practiced the teacher role, working collaboratively with other teachers to plan and develop units that could be used in my own classroom. In this process, I "bought into" the philosophy of teaching and learning using the NTeQ model.

It hasn't been easy; the planning is time-consuming, and troubleshooting problems often requires more time than might seem possible. However, I feel that it is worth it. I've come to expect the unexpected. Some of my best teaching moments this year have come from unplanned lessons—when students take an open-ended question and delve into it in their own way. The research tools are now at the students' fingertips, which makes it possible to reach as high as they desire.

Computers have allowed me to change my whole teaching style. There are more options of teaching any concept now that I am no longer limited to the use of the student textbook. Now the possibilities are endless. Students have access to an electronic encyclopedia that has video and audio clips, as well as all the opportunities that the Internet provides. Students learn to become responsible for their own learning instead of looking for me to be the one directing and making all the decisions.

Pam Shoemaker
Sixth-Grade Teacher

SUMMARY

Computers have been a part of the classroom for the past 25 years, yet we have not seen significant gains in achievement as a result of their use. An examination of past and current practices suggest that computers are used primarily as an instructional delivery device. That is, we expect students to learn *from* the computer and to use it as a substitute for the teacher. These practices, however, differ significantly from how computers are used in the world beyond the classroom. Recent studies also suggest that students who engage in higher-level learning activities perform significantly better on standardized achievement tests. One question we might ask, then, is how can we combine the higher-level instructional activities with computer usage? The NTeQ model combines a student-centered approach with computer technology used as a tool for problem solving. This approach provides a flexible means for addressing both content and technology standards for students at any grade level.

AT THE CLASSROOM'S DOORSTEP

Questions Teachers Ask

Am I limited to instructional methods that have scientific research support?

Yes and no. If your school or district is seeking Federal support to improve your schools, you must use methods that have been proven to be effective in enhancing student learning. This approach makes sense from the standpoint of an effective teacher. Why use an unproven method that has the potential to inhibit student learning? We do not see this approach as limiting your choice to only proven methods, because we see opportunities to test new ideas and gather data to support their effectiveness, much as Mr. Marshall did in the Classroom Snapshot in this chapter.

Where will I find supporting research for the methods I want to use?

As educators and researchers, we have created a very rich database of research studies that is readily available in university libraries, with the more recent studies being available online. The journals in your discipline and general research journals (e.g., *Review of Educational Research*) provide a rich resource. Electronic databases such as ERIC allow you to create custom searches to find most any article or report published in the past 35 years.

Will I be able to understand the research?

Journals are written for different audiences and purposes. Rigorous research journals such as the *Journal of Educational Psychology* and *Educational Technology Research and Development* provide in-depth reports of research. Although you might not be able to follow the statistical analysis presented in the article, you might be able to find support and ideas for methods you want to use. Other journals such as the *Journal of Research in Science and Teaching, Theory and Research in Social Education*, or *Journal for Research in Mathematics Education* might provide studies that are more easily understood by teachers in the discipline. There are a host of other scholarly journals that provide research reports geared to your teaching grade level and discipline. Often these journals provide review or synthesis of the research studies that is more easily understood than the original research studies.

TECHNOLOGY INTEGRATION ACTIVITIES

To access the activities that connect the content of the text with the Companion Website and other technology, please go to the Activities module in Chapter 2 of the Companion Website at *http://www.prenhall.com/morrison*.

NTEQ PORTFOLIO ACTIVITIES: A RESEARCH-BASED MODEL

The following activities are designed to help you build your NTeQ portfolio for teaching.

Reflections

There are two parts to this chapter's NTeQ portfolio. First, review the No Child Left Behind Act (*http://www.nclb.gov/index.html* or *http://www.ed.gov*). What are the implications for you as teacher? Reflect on the act and record your thoughts in your portfolio.

Second, the NTeQ model incorporates inquiry and problem-based learning and collaborative groups into a student-centered learning environment. Find at least one research study that supports each of these ideas, and write a brief summary of the study for your NTeQ portfolio for this chapter.

You can find studies by searching ERIC (*http://ericir.syr.edu/Eric/*) or using one of the electronic or text databases in your library, such as PsycINFO.

REFERENCES

Albanese, M. A., & Mitchell, S. (1993). Problem-based learning: A review of the literature on its outcomes and implementation issues. *Academic Medicine, 68*, 52–81.

Archer, J. (October 1,1998). The link to higher scores. *Technology Counts '98. Education Week, 18* (5), 10–20.

Barrows, H. S. (1985). *How to design a problem-based curriculum for the preclinical years.* New York: Springer.

Barrows, H. S., & Kelson, A. M. (1996). *Problem-based learning: A total approach to education.* (Unpublished monograph.) Springfield, IL: Southern Illinois School of Medicine.

Becker, H. J. (1991). How computers are used in United States schools: Basic data from the 1989 I.E.A. computers in education survey. *Journal of Educational Computing Research, 7*, 385–406.

Bork, A. (1987). *Learning with personal computers.* New York: Harper & Row.

Brooks, J. G., & Brooks, M. G. (1993). *In search of understanding: The case for constructivist classrooms.* Alexandria, VA: Association for Supervision and Curriculum Development.

Brown, J. S., Collins, A., & Duguid, P. (1989). Situated cognition and the culture of learning. *Educational Researcher, 18*, 32–42.

Bruner, J. S. (1960). *The process of education.* Cambridge, MA: Harvard University Press.

Bruner, J. S. (1966). *Toward a theory of instruction.* Cambridge, MA: Harvard University Press.

Dewey, J. (1916). *Democracy and education.* New York: Macmillan.

Edelson, D. C., Gordin, D. N., & Pea, R. D. (1999). Addressing the challenges of inquiry-based learning through technology and curriculum design. *Journal of the Learning Sciences, 8*, 391–450.

Festinger, L. (1957). *A theory of cognitive dissonance.* Stanford, CA: Stanford University Press.

Gardner, H. (1991). *The unschooled mind: How children think and how schools should teach.* New York: Basic Books.

Greeno, J., Collins, A., & Resnick, L. B. (1996). Cognition and learning. In R. Calfee, and D. Berliner (Eds.), *Handbook of educational psychology.* New York: Macmillan.

Herrington, J., & Oliver, R. (2000). An instructional design framework for authentic learning environments. *Educational Technology Research and Development, 48*, 23–48.

Hertzberg, H. (1981). *Social studies reform, 1880–1980* (A Project SPAN Report). Boulder, CO: Social Science Education Consortium.

Jerald, C. D., & Orlofsky, G. F. (1999). Raising the bar on school technology. *Technology Counts '99. Education Week, 19*(4), 58–69.

Land, S. M., & Hannafin, M. J. (1997). Patterns of understanding with open-ended learning environments: A qualitative study. *Educational Technology Research & Development, 45*, 47–73.

Lowther, D. L., Bassoppo-Moyo, T., & Morrison, G. R. (1998). Moving from computer literate to technological competent: The next educational reform. *Computers and Human Behavior, 14*, 93–109.

Lowther, D. L., Ross, S. M., & Morrison, G. R. (2003). The laptop classroom: The effect on instruction and achievement. *Educational Technology, Research, and Development, 51*, 23–44.

Means, B. (1994). Introduction: Using technology to advance educational goals. In B. Means (Ed.), *Technology and educational reform*, (pp. 1–21). San Francisco: Jossey-Bass.

National Commission on Excellence in Education. (1983). *A nation at risk: The imperative for educational reform.* Washington, DC: Decision Resources Corporation.

Newmann, F. M., Bryk, A. S., & Nagaoka, J. K. (2001). *Authentic intellectual work and standardized tests: Conflict or coexistence?* Consortium on Chicago School Research. [On-line]. Available: http://www.consortium-chicago.org/publications/pdfs/p0a02.pdf.

Pruett, P. L., Morrison, G. R., Dietrich, A. P., & Smith, L. J. (1993). Integration of the microcomputer into the mathematics classroom. *Computers and Human Behavior, 9*, 17–26.

Ross, S. M., Lowther, D. L., Morrison, G. R., & Plants, R. (2000). Anytime anywhere learning: Final evaluation of the laptop program. Memphis, TN: University of Memphis. [On-line]. Available: http://www.nteq.com/report.htm.

Savery, J. R., & Duffy, T. M. (1995). Problem-based learning: An instructional model and its constructivist framework. *Educational Technology, 45*, 31–38.

Vygotsky, L. (1978). *Mind in society*. Cambridge, MA: Harvard University Press.

Woolever, R., & Scott, K. P. (1988). *Active learning in social studies: Promoting cognitive and social growth.* Glenview, IL: Scott, Foresman and Company.

KEY TOPICS

Why Planning?
Learner Analysis
- Student Learning Variables
- Determining Student Learning Preferences
- Changing the Learning Environment

Writing Instructional Objectives
- Where Do Objectives Come From?

Analyzing Topics and Tasks
- Topic Analysis
- Procedural Analysis

Instructional Strategies
- Presentation
- Generative Strategies

Chapter 3

Teacher as Designer I: Teacher's Toolbox

A wide variety of curriculum guides and materials are available for classroom use. Some guides are very thorough and include lecture notes, handouts, PowerPoint presentations, overhead transparencies, tests, and worksheets. A teacher or substitute teacher can pick up a package and teach a class in a matter of a few minutes. Planning to achieve successful learning, however, can take a good deal of time. In this chapter, we will introduce you to the basic skills you will need for developing an integrated technology lesson plan. In Chapter 4 we will introduce you to the steps of the NTeQ model, which are similar to a recipe or instructions on the back of a TV dinner. This model will guide you through the lesson planning process.

GETTING STARTED

What Do I Know?

1. How do I plan an integrated lesson that will work with my students?
2. Do I need objectives to help with my planning and lesson development?
3. How can I encourage my students to engage in the processing of information?

Classroom Snapshot

Ms. Nunez is really excited because she just found the "Easy Integration" Website, which has tons of lesson plans that all integrate the use of technology. She plans to begin with a science lesson on vertebrates and searches the on-line database of science lessons. She quickly finds one that looks easy to follow because it only has three sections: Lesson Topic, Materials, and Activities, which included the use of technology. Ms. Nunez download lesson and the worksheets and makes copies. The worksheets have two technology activities included: the first is a list of Websites with information and activities related to vertebrates; the second is a word processing activity that has students write a paper on what they learned about vertebrates from the Websites. She never knew technology integration could be so easy!

On the day of the lesson, the students went to the computer lab and Ms. Nunez gave a brief introduction that told the students they would visit some interesting sites with vertebrate information and photos, then write a paper about what they learned. She noted that it was very important to take careful notes as they visit the sites, because they would use these to write their papers. The students were able to find the Internet sites quite easily and found lots of great animal photos on each one. However, there was so much information about vertebrates that the students had no idea of where to begin or which sites to visit. In addition, many of the sites were difficult to use because the information was written for adults or much older students, making the information hard to understand. The students tried their best to take some notes and write a paper about vertebrates, but the final papers were on numerous aspects of the topic and had very little information that was worthwhile.

Ms. Nunez was disappointed and quite surprised that the Internet could have a poorly written lesson plan posted on a Website. In reflection, she realized that she had not done enough planning to ensure that the lesson actually met the needs of her students, had learning objectives, focused on the most important topics, and engaged students in meaningful activities. Next time, she will plan carefully and add the missing parts for any lesson that is not complete.

WHY PLANNING?

The amount of time devoted to lesson planning can vary depending on available resources and objectives. For example, it will not take as long to adapt an existing lesson plan to an integrated computer unit as it does to design such a plan from scratch. One approach to preparing a lesson plan is to follow a process that will guide you through each step of developing the lesson plan. You might think of this process as an approach similar to cooking. Those of us (i.e., the authors) who are naive cooks need very specific directions, such as those found on the back of a frozen meal, to create a culinary delight. We tend to follow every step of the instructions to the "T" and have even been known to ask how many holes do we punch in the plastic covering of a microwave meal! Experienced chefs probably started their early career in much the same manner. However, as they gained experience they began to modify the recipe and directions in an attempt to create a slightly different dish (we experimented once with not punching holes in the plastic covering of the microwave dish). These chefs, though, always follow basic rules, such as never packing flour into a measure cup.

An approach to developing lesson plans is similar to a style of cooking. At first, you follow each step of the process. Then as you gain experience and know what works and does not work, you can begin to modify your approach and try different steps. It is like moving to a new town and finding one way to drive to work that you follow for a while. Then, as the landmarks become familiar, you begin to experiment as you try to find a better way. This chapter will present the basic skills needed to develop a lesson plan. These skills include learner analysis, writing objectives, analyzing the content, and developing the instructional strategies.

LEARNER ANALYSIS

Walking into a classroom of 6, 20, 30, or even 400 students for the first time can be an unsettling experience. For example, we typically teach classes with 15 to 30 adult students. In a recent class, there were a few elementary and secondary teachers, an Internal Revenue Service auditor, a manager for a manufacturing company, an owner and manager of a food services company, a librarian, a marine reserve officer, and a parole officer. At first, this class seems very diverse compared to a typical third-grade class. If we examine the two classes, we would find that both instructors would want to know similar information about the two classes. The students in the two classes would vary in different ways on many of the same characteristics. This information about the students is used to create an appropriate learning environment for the students.

One problem with attempting to address the various learning styles in a classroom is the need for *multiple* forms of instruction for each different learning style. Unfortunately, most textbooks and other classroom materials are available only in a generic, one-approach-fits-all learning style. Although this approach might be easy, it places an extra burden on the teacher to come up with a variety of approaches, which is more time consuming and not always practical. A more viable approach is one of adapting the learning environment to various learning *preferences*. Let's examine the variables you can change in a learning environment and how to determine a student's learning preferences, then consider ways of adapting the learning environment based on learner preferences.

Student Learning Variables

Dunn and Dunn (1978) identified four major groupings of variables related to student preferences for learning. As a teacher, you often can change these variables to enhance the learning environment as opposed to creating a variety of instructional materials. We will examine each of these groupings—environmental, emotional, sociological, and physical—as they apply to the classroom.

Environmental

The classroom environment includes sound, light, temperature, and design elements. Have you ever compared the way you work at home with the way you worked in a classroom as a grade school student? If your classroom was like most of ours, it was quiet. At home, however, we often have some music or the television as background noise while we work. One environmental variable you can manipulate is the availability of sound (e.g., music and class discussions) for students. Remember, though, the range of preferences is from complete quiet to some noise. The second environmental variable is the amount of light provided in the work areas. Some students might prefer to work in a softer light provided by an incandescent bulb while others might prefer the brighter light of a high-intensity bulb, window, or florescent lights. Temperature is the third environmental variable and is probably the one you will have the least control over—it will either be too hot or too cold! The fourth environmental variable is the design of the classroom. Preferences for design range from a very informal layout (e.g., a rug and bean bags) to a very formal layout with desks and chairs in perfect rows and students exhibiting good posture.

Emotional

The emotional variable refers to persistence, motivation, and structure—elements you can manipulate through instructional assignments. *Persistence* refers to an individual's ability to stay focused on a task until completion. Persistence varies from student to student and even among subject areas for a given student. Those with low persistence in a given subject may give up in frustration and not complete the task. Responsibility is the ability to work without teacher or adult supervision on a given task until it is completed. *Structure* refers to the number of options you can give a student. For example, some students are capable of electing and working on several assignments, while other students cannot make a decision when given different options.

Sociological

The sociological group of elements describes how students like to work with others. For example, some students only want to work by themselves and resent working on a team or with another student. Others want to work with the teacher or an adult, while other students prefer to work with their peers.

Physical

The physical grouping includes a variety of ways students perceive information and the modes they prefer for learning. Dunn and Dunn (1978) describe *perceptual strengths* as the way students like to learn. Although students might have a preference such as reading instead of listening to a lecture, there is little evidence to suggest that students learn *only* in the preferred mode (Jonassen & Grabowski, 1993). A second variable in this category is intake, which refers to eating or drinking while studying or working. Some of us prefer to drink coffee or a soft drink and nibble on crackers while working. Time of day for studying or working is the third variable in this category. As a college student, you probably expressed your learning preference by attempting to select classes that met at your best learning times. That is, if you were a night person, then you probably tried to avoid classes before noon. The last variable in this grouping is mobility, which refers to a student's preference to move about or sit in one location while studying. For example, some of us prefer to walk around the block or around the room while trying to find a solution to a problem.

Many of the elements in these four groupings are under your control as the teacher. You can make changes and create different zones or areas in your classroom to meet the needs of the students. Before you can make these changes, however, you must determine your students' preferences.

Determining Student Learning Preferences

Park (1996) suggests that there is a lack of empirical evidence supporting the use of learning styles for enhancing instruction. There is, however, considerable research on the Dunn and Dunn inventory (Dunn, 1990, 1995; Dunn & Dunn, 1978). This research suggests that changing the environment to match *learners' preferences* results in enhanced motivation and learning. This inventory provides ways of changing the learning environment, a more viable solution for a classroom teacher than designing alternative forms of instruction, to adapt to various learning styles. The following is a brief discussion of the Dunn and Dunn inventory.

Dunn and Dunn's Learning Style Inventory

One of the more thoroughly researched inventories was developed by Dunn and Dunn (1978). The Learning Styles Inventory (LSI) is designed for use in grades 3 to 12 and takes approximately 30 minutes to complete. Sample items include "I concentrate best when I feel cool," "It's hard for me to sit in one place for a long time," and "I can ignore most sound when I study." An analysis of the student's response produces a profile of how the student prefers to learn. Dunn and Dunn also suggest creating an observation instrument (Figure 3-1) a teacher can use and then verify by administering the inventory.

Web-Based Inventories

A search of the World Wide Web produced several learning profile inventories that students can take on-line (Check It Out 3-1). Although these inventories have several questions and constructs similar to Dunn and Dunn's LSI, no statistical information regarding the development and validity of the inventory was provided.

Decisions concerning the structuring of your classroom environment should be based on data from a variety of sources. Once you decide to offer background music, different lighting, or food, you should monitor the effect of this change on student behavior and learning and make appropriate adjustments as needed.

Changing the Learning Environment

Once you have determined student preferences for learning, the next step is to create a learning environment that supports the activities in the NTeQ lesson. Two basic classroom designs are presented in Chapter 13, Managing the Classroom, for rooms with four to six computers. The following paragraphs suggest some additional designs to support learning in an open-ended environment while implementing an integrated technology lesson.

FIGURE 3-1 Learning Style Preferences Observation

Learning Style Preferences

Student ______________________________

Environmental Preferences

Sound		Yes	No
	Easily distracted by noise		
	Background music appears to bother		
Light			
	Avoids bright light		
	Prefers subdued light		
Temperature			
	Shows preference for cool temperatures		
	Shows preference for warm temperatures		
Design			
	Prefers a neat work area		
	Works well in a messy area		

Emotional

Motivation		Yes	No
	Follows directions		
	Eager to learn		
Persistence			
	Works on task until complete		
	Gives up when frustrated		
	Easily distracted		
Responsibility			
	Works without supervision		
	Distractible		
Structure			
	Can choose between options		
	Unable to focus on one choice		

Adapted from Dunn & Dunn, 1978.

FIGURE 3-1 Continued

Sociological

Group Work		Yes	No
	Enjoys working in a group		
	Prefers to work individually		
	Prefers to work with peers		
	Prefers to work with adults		

Physical

Perceptual Strengths		Yes	No
	Prefers to read for information		
	Prefers to listen to others provide information		
	Prefers to learn from pictures		
	Prefers to learn tactually		
	Prefers to learn from experience		
	Prefers to learn from a combination of senses		

CHECK IT OUT 3-1

How to Determine Your Learning Style

There are a number of learning style inventories on the Internet, although the sites come and go. You can use the following sets of search terms to identify different inventories that are on the Web. We used *www.google.com* for our search.

Link to these resources and activities in the Check It Out module for this chapter of the Companion Website.

Environmental Changes

The various activities in an open-ended lesson can generate a higher level of noise and activity than a typical classroom. If you have students who are easily distracted by noise, you can create a quiet area in the room that uses a screen(s) to block some of the sound. Another option is to provide headphones and appropriate music for those who want to isolate themselves from the classroom sounds. Screens and window coverings also can be used to create areas with subdued or incandescent lighting for students who do not prefer bright lighting. Computer screens are usually most legible when away from bright lights. For example, you may need to block out bright lights that are directly overhead and arrange them so students do not face a window when working at the computers. Temperature is one environmental variable that is difficult to control. Careful planning to place areas either close to or away from heating and air-conditioning units may produce some variations in temperature. Students can bring sweaters or sweatshirts for use when it is cold. You can also designate formal and informal areas in the room to accommodate different styles (Figure 3-2). Informal areas might include a carpet, pillows, or other comfortable chairs.

Emotional. You can create different learning environments by how you assign and manage the various NTeQ lesson activities. For unmotivated students and those with a short attention span, you can create smaller tasks that will maintain their interest. For example, you may need to break the data analysis process into several small steps to keep some students on task. You also can offer various levels of guidance to those students who have not developed a high level of responsibility for completing their work. The emotional variables will draw heavily on your skills as a facilitator (see Chapter 12).

Sociological. To address the various sociological learning preferences of your students, you may want to arrange your classroom environment to support a variety of

FIGURE 3-2 Redesigning the Environment

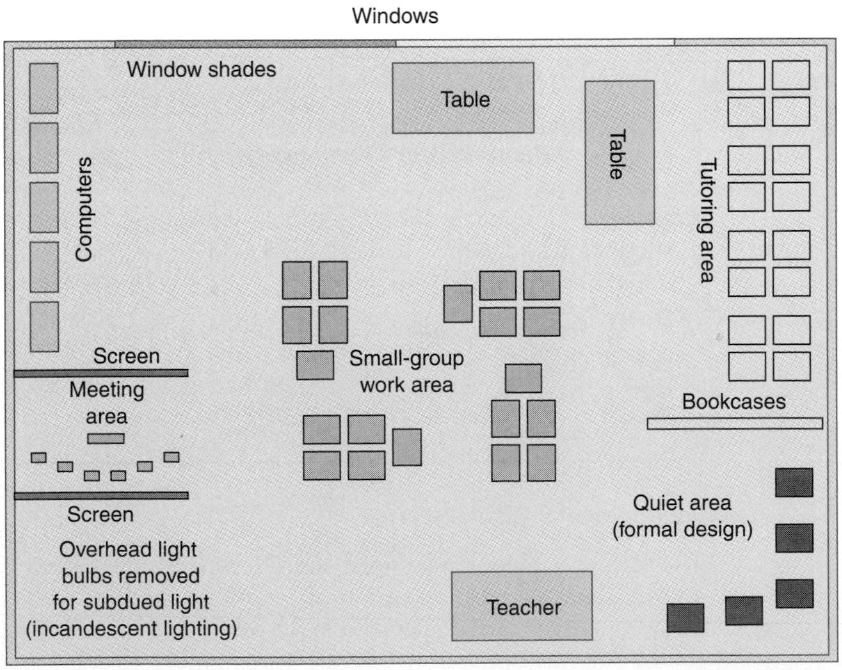

learning activities. For example, Figure 3-2 shows areas for small-group work, individual work, group tutoring, and a meeting area where students can work with an adult such as a parent or expert from the community. As you rearrange your classroom, consider the noise and activity level of each area and try to separate the noisier areas from the quiet areas. You can involve the students in the redesign and let them both help plan and help with the rearrangement. A week or so after you implement the design, you may need to consider additional changes to enhance the environment.

Physical. You may have already addressed the room environment for students' preference for intake and mobility as you designed it for the other variables. Intake and mobility may require some management rules to prevent accidents (e.g., no food or drink at the computers) and to keep "mobile" students from disrupting students working in other areas. The time variable presents more of a problem for most classrooms. Using the NTeQ model, however, you have some freedom to structure work periods by allowing students to work on different projects and different aspects of a project to meet their time preference.

Redesigning your classroom environment can enhance student activities when working on an NTeQ lesson. Using learning centers grouped by type of activity to allow for various learning preferences also can enhance motivation and achievement. For example, you can create work areas for computer preparation work, which might include both small-group work areas and individual research areas. You can create small-group, individual, and tutoring areas for use after completing work at the computer and in supporting activities.

The NTeQ model is more easily implemented with a flexible classroom arrangement.

WRITING INSTRUCTIONAL OBJECTIVES

An effective lesson plan always starts with the instructional objectives. Well-written objectives serve two purposes. First, objectives function as a guide in developing a lesson plan. They help us stay focused on the important points and select instructional strategies that will help the learners achieve the objectives. Second, objectives help in planning how we will assess our students' achievement. If we know what we expect our students to do at the end of the unit, then we can devise a strategy to assess our expectations or objectives. Further information about assessment is presented in Chapter 14.

Where Do Objectives Come From?

Our best answer is "it all depends." Objectives are not a new concept to education; they have had their ups and downs through time. Sometime when you are in the library, glance at an educational journal such as the *Phi Delta Kappan* or a teacher-oriented type of journal from the early 1970s. You can probably find classified advertisements for lists of thousands of objectives in your chosen discipline. Today, you are more likely to find objectives in the form of national standards for a discipline such as science (*http://www.nsta.org/*), math (*www.nctm.org*), social studies (*http://www.ncss.org/*), or language arts (*http://www.ncte.org/*). Or, you may have specific state or district standards or benchmarks.

These standards provide guidelines for the instruction in your classroom. The standards, however, are not meant to be blindly implemented. Rather, you need to adapt these standards to the context of your students and classroom. This adaptation will make each standard more meaningful and realistic to your students. There are also times when you may decide to go beyond the standard. The result is an objective you have created based on a standard or benchmark.

The objectives for your unit of instruction may consist of your own objectives, objectives from the textbook or curriculum, objectives from the standards, or a combination. Your next task is to refine these initial statements of intent into tactical statements. Two popular methods for writing instructional objectives are the behavioral (e.g., Mager type) and cognitive approaches. Objectives specify what the learner *can do* when he or she finishes the instruction. The following sections describe the application of each type of objective and how to write each. The same process applies whether you are creating new objectives or adapting existing objectives for your instruction.

Behavioral Objectives

Mager (1984) popularized the use of behavioral objectives in instruction. These objectives are useful when you can identify *specific behaviors* you want the student to demonstrate. For example, calculating an average, identifying a sonnet, or arranging a list alphabetically are specific behaviors. With each of these behaviors, you can devise a simple test item such as "Determine the average of the following numbers . . . " to determine if the student has mastered the content. A Mager type objective has three parts—the action verb and related content, the criteria, and the conditions. For example, "*Given* a right triangle, the student will *correctly calculate* the length of the hypotenuse." Let's examine how to construct a behavioral objective using each of these three parts.

TABLE 3-1 Action Verbs for a Behavior Objective

Direct Observation	Results Observation
Choose	Analyze
Dramatize	Compose
Diagram	Support
Pronounce	Order
Operate	Review
Sketch	Compare
Identify	Judge
Demonstrate	Apply

The first part of a behavioral objective is an *action verb*. Action verbs describe a behavior you can observe (e.g., "Draw a triangle.") or the result of the behavior that you can observe (e.g., "Calculate the average."). A verb such as *understands* is not an action verb, because we cannot observe how someone understands. The only observable related behavior or result from asking a student if he or she understands is usually a nod of the head *suggesting* that the student does understand, even when the student has no idea of what you just asked. Table 3-1 provides examples of behaviors we can directly observe and those for which we can observe the results of the behavior.

An action verb in an objective is meaningless by itself. For example, "The student will divide with 100% accuracy" is not very descriptive. Each action verb must include a content description. The content part describes the subject matter the student will act on or use. Dividing a line in half, a cup of sugar into thirds, or word into syllables all require different behaviors and dramatically change one's perspective of the objective. One purpose of a behavioral objective is to reduce ambiguity. The action verb *and* the related content are both necessary to communicate our intent. Consider, for example, how different teachers might view the objective in the second sentence of this paragraph. Someone teaching nutrition might think of dividing a large recipe into smaller portions while a technical instructor might consider a series of problems that require a student to develop a model that divides the load of the roof onto several walls. The content information is needed to narrowly define our objective and to communicate our intent.

Examples of action verbs and the content reference are as follows:

- Identify the parts of speech in a sentence.
- Demonstrate how to operate a camcorder.
- Compare two viewpoints on campaign spending.

The second component of the behavioral objective is the *criteria*, or performance standard. This standard describes *how well* the learner must perform. Sometimes the criteria are left out of the objective, implying 100% accuracy; however, we strongly believe that you should always state the criteria. These standards can specify how much (e.g., 8 out of 10 or 100% correct), how accurate (e.g., within a quarter of an inch), or how fast (e.g., in 5 minutes or less).

The following examples include the action verb, content reference, and criteria:

- Identify the parts of speech in a sentence *with 100% accuracy.*
- Demonstrate how to operate a camcorder *by producing a 3-minute tape with no jerky movement and that is in focus.*
- Compare two viewpoints on campaign spending *by summarizing three critical issues related to the topic.*

The third component describes the *conditions* of the performance. For example, if you want students to calculate the average population of a five-county region, can they use a calculator or spreadsheet on the test? Other conditions can specify resources the student can or cannot use, such as a book or chart. Conditions also can describe the testing situation, such as "given a paragraph . . ."

The following objectives illustrate all three parts of the behavioral objective:

- Given 10 sentences, the student will identify the parts of speech in a sentence with 100% accuracy.
- Given a tripod, videotape, and camcorder, the student will demonstrate how to operate the camcorder by producing a 3-minute tape with no jerky movement and that is in focus.
- Using resources on the Internet, the student will compare two viewpoints on campaign spending by summarizing three critical issues related to the topic.

Cognitive Objectives

An alternative approach to behavioral objectives is cognitive objectives (Gronlund, 1985, 1995). Cognitive objectives are used to describe student learning and are not easily specified in a single sentence. Objectives that cover such topics as interpreting a graph, searching the Internet for information, working effectively in a group, or writing an essay or report are not easily reduced to a few words or explained in a single behavioral objective. Cognitive objectives provide a means to specify a number of behaviors that can describe the achievement of the objective.

Cognitive objectives consist of two parts. The first part is a general instructional objective that is stated in broad terms (Morrison, Ross, & Kemp, 2004). Examples include the following:

- Selects information using Yahoo
- Interprets a chart of classroom cookie sales
- Explains the meaning of a story

The second part of the cognitive objective includes one or more statements describing specific performances that indicate mastery of the objective. The following examples illustrate specific behaviors that indicate mastery of the general statements.

- Selects information using Yahoo
  - Finds a specific article related to the problem
  - Compiles a list of Websites related to the problem
  - Identifies productive search terms

- Interprets a chart of classroom cookie sales
  - Identifies the student with the most sales
  - Compares this year's sales with the sales during the previous 3 years
  - Identifies the students who sold more than the class average
- Explains the meaning of a story
  - Summarizes the plot
  - Identifies the characters
  - Explains the meanings of the characters' actions

Cognitive objectives are useful for describing higher-level learning tasks that allow for more than one approach to mastery. Behaviors such as apply, interpret, solve, or evaluate suggest that there is *more* than one solution to a problem. In the example involving the interpretation of the graph, there are various questions a student could answer to demonstrate the ability to interpret a graph. In contrast, a behavioral objective might simply focus on a specific behavior. "Given a graph, the student will correctly identify the bar that shows the maximum sales." Although the objective indicates that the student will need to learn to interpret a graph, it is a very specific interpretation. In contrast, a cognitive objective allows for greater flexibility without the specifics, which places a greater emphasis on teacher interpretation and implementation of the instruction.

As you write your objectives, remember to focus on what the *student* will do (e.g., demonstrate a skill or knowledge) as a result of the instruction rather than what the *teacher* will do. For example, many teachers and instructors mistakenly use objectives to write descriptions of what will happen during the instruction by using such phrasing as "to teach the learner how to calculate an average." This type of statement is an activity (Morrison, et al., 2004). A simple test for an objective is to ask if the objective specifies what the learner will demonstrate *after* the instruction. Both cognitive and behavioral objectives focus on the outcomes or product of the learning process. This product is what the learner can demonstrate, not the instructional activities themselves.

ANALYZING TOPICS AND TASKS

Once you have defined what the learners must demonstrate through either behavioral or cognitive objectives, you need to determine what content the students must master. We will consider two types of content. The first is a list of topics, and the second is a list of steps to complete a task.

Topic Analysis

As a student, you sat through many lectures while taking detailed notes. Your notes might have resembled an outline format indicating different levels of information. Now, reverse the situation. You are a teacher preparing your lecture; what would you do? One approach is to create an outline of the ideas you want to present. This outline is a topic analysis.

A topic analysis is a listing of the key points and supporting information our learners need to understand in order to achieve an objective. If you are adapting a unit of

An NTeQ lesson plan requires thoughtful planning by the teacher.

instruction from your existing curriculum materials, your topic analysis will include information from the student materials and additional information needed to achieve the objectives. The topic analysis will help you identify the facts, concepts, and principles (Morrison, et al., 2004) in the content.

Consider a topic analysis for a psychology class on learning. It might include the following content:

- **I.** Learning
  - **A.** A relatively permanent change in behavior
  - **B.** Applies to humans and animals
  - **C.** Types of learning
    - **1.** Classical conditioning
    - **2.** Operant conditioning
- **II.** Classical conditioning
  - **A.** Pavlov
    - **1.** Russian physiologist
    - **2.** Studied digestion in dogs
  - **B.** Conditional response
    - **1.** Pairing a stimulus such as a bell with food
    - **2.** Stimulus and response must occur close together in time and space
- **III.** Operant conditioning
  - **A.** First studied by Thorndike, who rewarded chicks with food
  - **B.** Skinner extended Thorndike's work and named it operant conditioning

C. Principles of operant conditioning
   1. Shaping—Rewards for successive approximations of the desired behavior
   2. Chaining—Performing a series of behaviors
   3. Schedules of reinforcement
      a. Continuous schedule of reinforcement
      b. Partial schedule of reinforcement
      c. Fixed-ratio schedule of reinforcement
      d. Variable-ratio schedule

You can now use this topic analysis to plan your instruction. For example, you might have your students search for information on noted psychologists such as Pavlov and Skinner and then prepare a presentation or report. You might also have your students participate in an on-line psychology experiment that demonstrates various reinforcement schedules. The topic analysis provides a framework for the information the students must learn to achieve the objectives. Your task is to design the various strategies students can use to learn the content. Some of your strategies will involve the use of a computer and others will not. For example, you could teach the various forms of reinforcement schedules without a computer, or you could have the students perform different experiments and graph their results using a spreadsheet. If we refer back to the Classroom Snapshot, we see that Ms. Nunez would have had greater success with her vertebrate lesson if she had conducted a topic analysis to identify the specific information she wanted her students to learn.

Procedural Analysis

A second type of analysis, procedural analysis, is used to determine the steps needed to perform a task. These tasks can range from how to calculate the area of a room, to the steps a student needs to complete to perform an experiment, to how to create hyperlinks in PowerPoint. It is often helpful to have another person assist you with this process, because it is easy to overlook some of the more subtle steps. The process is one of listing the steps in sequential order of completion. For example, what are the steps for setting up a document for typing a research report?

1. Create a new document in a word processor.
2. Set all the margins to 1 inch.
3. Create a header with a short title page number.
4. Center the title of the paper on the first page.
5. Change the size and weight of the title to 14 points and bold.
6. Add the author's name about 3 inches below the title and center it.
7. Add the content subject area centered below the author's name.
8. Add the date, centered below the subject area.
9. Change the font size of the author's name, subject area, and date to 12 points.
10. Insert a page break after the subject area.

Once you have completed the initial draft of the procedural analysis, you should test it. First, go through each step and complete the process. By following each step and doing what you have stated, you can identify any missing steps. Second, ask someone else to complete the task by *carefully* following the steps you have listed. You can then identify problems the person encounters as you observe the person completing the task.

Procedural analysis is a useful tool for preparing job aids for your students and instructions for various tasks they must perform. Like the topic analysis, the procedural analysis identifies the steps the students need to learn to master skill-related objectives.

INSTRUCTIONAL STRATEGIES

Instructional strategies are the methods or tactics you will use to help your students master the content needed to achieve the unit's objectives. There are a variety of strategies ranging from lecturing and reading to discovery learning through conducting experiments or solving problems. An instructional strategy has two components (Morrison et al., 2004). The first is the presentation; that is, how you will present the information to the learner. The second is the generative strategy, or the method you will use to help the learner develop an understanding of the information. The following sections examine each of these components.

Presentation

How do you present the information the students need in a manner that they can understand? You can help the learner grasp the meaning of the new material by making it as concrete as possible. You can make material concrete through the use of words or with pictures.

Using Words to Make the Instruction Concrete

All of us have read a book, a magazine article, or journal piece and then stopped and realized that we did not understand anything we had just read. How could the author have made the material more comprehensible? To make material understandable to a reader, first, use words that are meaningful to the reader. That is, use words that provide a *referent* for the learner. For example, younger readers might have more success if the author used a familiar term such as "car" rather than "vehicle" when writing about automobiles, because the term "car" helps evoke an image of the family's car. Using familiar words can aid the students' understanding. Second, we can use consistent terms throughout a lesson. If you were explaining the theme of a story and then in the next sentence you used the term "thesis," you might easily confuse your students. You should not interpret these suggestions as a rule for not introducing new terms; rather, they are guidelines for helping the student develop an understanding of the materials.

Using Pictures to Make Instruction Concrete

A picture provides the student with a concrete referent for a word. For example, if we were talking about Morel mushrooms, you might have an image of a toadstool. I could provide an explanation of how it looks somewhat like a sponge, but then you

FIGURE 3-3 Morel Mushroom

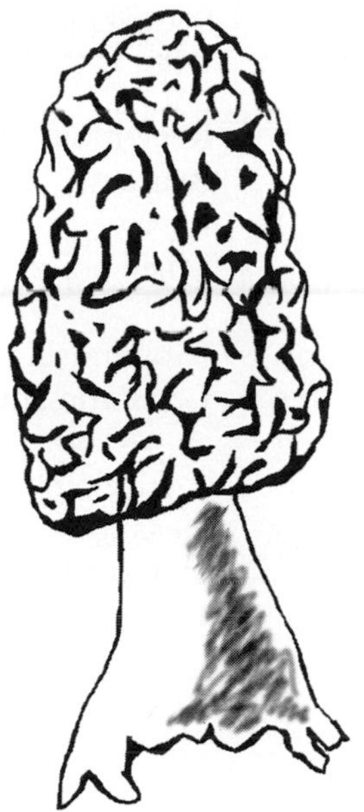

might conjure an image of a rectangular plant that resembles a toadstool, with a top shaped like a sponge you use in the kitchen. By providing a picture (Figure 3-3), the student is given a concrete image to associate with the label "Morel." This image provides a referent for the word, making it concrete. During the initial instruction, you should try to find pictures, posters, actual objects, or videotapes that can provide the students with the images to associate with words.

Generative Strategies

The last step in the strategy design is to develop the generative strategy. Generative strategies are tactics you can use to help the learner understand new information. These strategies help learners construct meaningful understandings of the new information and link this new information with what they already know.

The strategies used to create the Think Sheets come from Wittrock's (1974a, 1974b) *generative learning model*. Wittrock views the student as an *active* processor of information who works to construct relationships and meaning from the environment. Wittrock (1991) identifies two types of student-generated relationships. First, the student creates relationships among the various ideas from the instruction. Second, the student then actively relates these new ideas to what is already known. When the learner creates these relationships, new understandings of the information are created. There are four classes of generative strategies we can use in a Think Sheet (described below) to help the student develop these relationships between the new ideas and between the new ideas and what is already known (Jonassen, 1988). These four classes are seen in Table 3-2 and are explained in the following paragraphs.

TABLE 3-2 Generative Strategies

Type of Generative Strategy	Suggested Activities
Recall Helpful for learning facts, and lists for verbatim recall	Repetition Rehearsal (e.g., mental practice) Review Mnemonics
Integration Useful for transforming information into a more easily remembered form	Paraphrasing Generating questions or examples
Organizational Helps learner identify how new ideas relate to existing ideas.	Analyzing key ideas (identify ideas then interrelate them) Outlining Categorizing
Elaboration Requires learner to add their ideas to the new information	Generation of mental images Physical diagrams Sentence elaboration

Adapted from Morrison, G. R., Ross, S. M., & Kemp, J. E (2004). *Designing effective instruction: Applications of instructional design* (4th ed.).

Recall Strategies

When students must remember factual information, such as the four points of a compass or the state capital, recall strategies are used to help them recall the information. One common strategy is rehearsal—either covertly (e.g., saying the fact over and over "in one's head") or overtly (e.g., writing down the fact 10 times). Another rehearsal strategy is to create a song, such as the alphabet song. Mnemonics are memory devices for remembering lists of items such as "Every good boy does fine" and "FACE" for music terms or HOMES for names of the Great Lakes. Mnemonics also can be graphics that the learner constructs to help with remembering.

Integration Strategies

These strategies help students transform the information so that it is easily learned. One integration strategy is having the students paraphrase the information; that is, reading the information and then writing about it in their own words. Another strategy is to develop questions and new examples. For example, a student might create an electronic test board displaying questions and answers that causes a light to glow when the correct answer is selected. Students could also create "study" sheets for other groups or add examples of animals to a database on animal classifications.

Organizational Strategies

Students can use these strategies to group information into similar and dissimilar groupings. For example, they can create a database of food and complete fields regarding fat, protein, and vitamin content of each item. They could then group the food according to different levels of a characteristic such as high protein or low fat content. Another organizational strategy is the use of manipulatives. Students can create physical models such as a town, a mechanical device, or even computer graphics they can manipulate (Grabowski, 1996).

Elaboration Strategies

This strategy requires students to embellish the ideas presented in the instruction. Student activities can range from creating a drawing or diagram to writing activities. For example, students completing a science lesson on the geological development of their area might create a drawing depicting how their area might look in 200 years. Or, as a writing activity, they might list the steps describing how a bill becomes law. They might also list possible arguments others might offer for and against the bill's passage.

During this planning phase, develop a Think Sheet to guide the students' thinking. This sheet should include questions or other strategies that focus students' attention on the processes you expect them to develop (e.g., interpret a chart, make a prediction, etc.) that are specified in your objectives. Students also can create their own Think Sheet or modify yours as part of the instruction. Involving the students in the development of a Think Sheet will help them observe your critical thinking skills and provide them with extra motivation to think about their results.

SUMMARY

Careful planning and development of the lesson plan is essential for the success of an integrated lesson. These initial steps of understanding your learner, translating the standards into objectives, determining the topics and procedures to include, and planning your generative strategies provide the basis for beginning the lesson development. By determining this basic information, you will have the necessary information to design an appropriate learning environment for your students.

AT THE CLASSROOM'S DOORSTEP

Questions Teachers Ask

Does it take a lot of time to develop a lesson?

Lesson planning does take time; the amount varies depending on the scope of your unit and the existing resources. You should consider the time it takes to plan a lesson as an investment. If you teach the same grade again next year, you can use the lesson again. Thus your planning time is spread over 2 or more years. Good instruction takes an investment of time and effort.

Are there any shortcuts to developing a lesson plan?

You will become more efficient with the planning process as you gain experience. For example, your students will likely stay the same for a semester or year. Therefore you will not need to do a learner analysis for each lesson. Similarly, if your standards or benchmarks are carefully worded, they may suffice as your objectives.

Do I have to do all my lesson plans from scratch?

No. We recommend that you start with your existing teaching materials. Many of these lessons are easily adaptable to an integrated technology lesson. If you can adapt your existing lesson plans or those from your curriculum materials, you can save a lot of time. Another approach is to work with a team of teachers who share both their ideas and their lesson plans.

TECHNOLOGY INTEGRATION ACTIVITIES

To access the activities that connect the content of the text with the Companion Website and other technology, please go to the Activities module in Chapter 3 of the Companion Website at *http://www.prenhall.com/morrison.*

NTEQ PORTFOLIO ACTIVITIES

There are two parts to your portfolio for this chapter.

To begin, you will develop a manual that will help you complete the four tasks described in this chapter.

- First, prepare a two column chart. In the first column, list several characteristics of your learners (i.e., attention span, reading ability, age, etc.). In the second column, describe how this characteristic might affect your lesson development or teaching and learning in your classroom.
- Second, prepare a set of instructions that will help you write a behavioral objective and cognitive objective. Your instructions might include a table of observable verbs, or it might be a template in which you can substitute specific wording for each part of the objective. You might also include some questions that will help you test your objective.
- Third, prepare a similar set of instructions or guidelines for doing a topic analysis and procedural analysis. You might want to list a series of hints to help you do the analysis.
- Fourth, create a four-column chart and label the columns as Recall Strategies, Integration Strategies, Organizational Strategies, and Elaboration Strategies. In each column, list several examples of each strategy (e.g., mnemonic) that you can use in your lessons.

The second part of the portfolio is the organization of three lessons. First, prepare a learner analysis of a class you are teaching or for a class you hope to teach someday in the future. Next, select three standards from your district or state or a professional organization (see Check It Out 3-2 for URLs), for the class you have identified. For each standard, write one or more objectives that are appropriate for your class.

Now, select one of your objectives and create a topic analysis of the information students need to achieve this objective. This analysis might include the facts, concepts, and principles related to the objective. If you have an objective that involves a task or procedure, then complete a procedural analysis of the steps involved in completing the task.

Last, select three objectives and create a generative strategy that will encourage your students to engage in higher-level processing. Your strategy might include a series of questions about a graph, map, or piece of art that encourage the learner to examine the image. Another strategy might involve having them apply their new knowledge to a different context or write an essay or report using the information.

CHECK IT OUT 3-2

URLs for Standards

States: *www.educationworld.com/standards/*
Professional organizations:
Math: *www.nctm.org*
Social Studies: *www.ncss.org*
Science: *www.nsta.org*
Language Arts: *www.ncte.org*
Technology: *cnets.iste.org/*

Link to these resources and activities in the Check It Out module for this chapter of the Companion Website.

REFERENCES

Dunn, R. (1990). Grouping students for instruction: Effects of learning style on achievement and attitudes. *Journal of Social Psychology, 130,* 485–494.

Dunn, R. (1995). A meta-analytic validation of the Dunn and Dunn model of learning-style preferences. *Journal of Educational Research, 88*, 353–362.

Dunn, R., & Dunn, K. (1978). *Teaching students through their individual learning styles: A practical approach.* Reston, VA: Reston.

Grabowski, B. L. (1996). Generative learning: Past, present, and future. In D. H. Jonassen (Ed.). *Handbook of research for educational communications and technology* (pp. 897–918). New York: Macmillan.

Gronlund, N. E. (1985). *Stating behavioral objectives for classroom instruction.* New York: Macmillan.

Gronlund, N. E. (1995). *How to write and use instructional objectives* (5th ed.). New York: Prentice Hall.

Jonassen, D. H. (1988). Integrating learning strategies into courseware to facilitate deeper processing (pp. 151–182). In D. H. Jonassen (Ed.). *Instructional designs for microcomputer courseware.* Hillsdale, NJ: Lawrence Erlbaum Associates.

Jonassen, D. H., & Grabowski, B. L. (1993). *Handbook of individual differences, learning, and instruction.* Hillsdale, NJ: Lawrence Erlbaum Associates.

Mager, R. F. (1984). *Preparing instructional objectives* (2nd ed.). Belmont, CA: Pitman.

Morrison, G. R., Ross, S. M., & Kemp, J. E. (2004). *Designing effective instruction* (4th ed.). New York: John Wiley and Sons, Inc.

Park, O. K. (1996). Adaptive instructional systems. In D. H. Jonassen (Ed.). *Handbook of research for educational communications and technology* (pp. 634–664). New York: Macmillan Library Reference USA.

Wittrock, M. C. (1974a). A generative model of mathematics learning. *Journal of Research in Mathematics Education*, *5*, 181–197.

Wittrock, M. C. (1974b). Learning as a generative process. *Educational Psychologist, 11*, 87–95.

Wittrock, M. C. (1991). Generative teaching of comprehension. *Elementary School Journal, 92*, 167–182.

KEY TOPICS

Chapter 4

Teacher as Designer II: Teacher's Lesson Planning

Creating an integrated computer lesson using the NTeQ model (see Chapter 1) requires careful planning and designing of the lesson. Actually, any use of computer software for instruction requires planning. Unfortunately, we have observed many teachers who use computers only for drill-and-practice, tutorial, games, and simulations, with little or no planning or thought about how or *if* the computer activity will enhance student learning. This practice has led to rather disappointing results when using technology in the classroom. In this chapter, we explain the process for designing an integrated computer lesson. An integrated computer lesson is one in which the students use the computer to organize and manipulate data or information to solve problems while learning new content and skills. In an integrated lesson, students use the computer as a *tool* rather than as a delivery or teaching device. However, the computer is *not* the *only* form of instruction the students will use during the lesson.

GETTING STARTED

What Do I Know?

1. Do I have to use a different lesson plan when I want my students to use computers?
2. What is the relationship between objectives and computer functions?
3. How do you grade computer projects?
4. Can you use a computer for every objective or lesson?

Classroom Snapshot

Ms. Kuruk, the principal of Maple Leaf Middle School, has scheduled an observation of Mr. Arnista's social studies class and was to receive a copy of his lesson plan before observing the class visit. Mr. Arnista's class was studying climates and how they differ in the United States. One of Mr. Arnista's neighbors works at the county extension office and helped Mr. Arnista obtain data related to the required temperature needed to grow various plants. His neighbor also mentioned that farmers are aware of the temperature conditions needed for various plants to grow and suggested he add this data to the project. His class has been researching weather data on the Internet to determine the best location to grow various fruits and vegetables. Today is the fifth day of the lesson.

Ms. Kuruk had received a copy of the last lesson plan several days ago and was informed that what happened each day might vary depending on the students' progress with the research. When Ms. Kuruk visited Mr. Arnista's class, she found the groups working at different stages of the project. The first group was creating an elaborate spreadsheet to determine plants that require similar temperatures to grow. Another group was busy painting a three-dimensional landscape with colors to represent the various plants they had selected to grow. One group was having difficulty. It seems one student did not care to eat fruits or vegetables and wanted to focus on cows, one claimed to be a vegetarian, one was more interested in insects than plants, and the last student seemed to have no interest in the project beyond searching for a game on plants. The other groups were at various stages of conducting their research, preparing a report, or developing their presentations, which ranged from large plot maps to graphs to three-dimensional farm plots. Much to Ms. Kuruk's surprise, the activities appeared to support the objectives in Mr. Arnista's lesson plan—it just seemed that different groups were working on different objectives at the same time!

After the students had left the room, Ms. Kuruk discussed the lesson with Mr. Arnista. She was quite surprised *not* to see Mr. Arnista "teaching," but was very pleased with the level of engagement of the students. Her impression was that the class was organized chaos, but she had to admit that the students were involved in learning. When asked about the lesson plan, Mr. Arnista explained that he had spent a great deal of time thinking through the activities and that he was uncomfortable the first time he had tried teaching this way. The key, he found, was carefully planning the lesson and then being able to adapt as problems arose or students decided to venture in a different direction. Ms. Kuruk said she would like some of the students to present their projects at the next parents meeting.

DESIGNING AN INTEGRATED LESSON

An integrated computer lesson can vary in length from an hour, to a whole day, to one period a day for a week, to several weeks. The length of the lesson depends on the complexity of the problem, the specified instructional objectives, the content you intend to cover during the lesson, and the capabilities of your students. As you design a lesson that integrates the use of computers, you need to consider the following two factors. The first is the attention span of your students. How long, in minutes, hours, or days, can your students stay focused and interested in solving a problem? For example, a lesson for third-grade students might last 2 to 5 days, whereas a high school geography lesson might last 2 or 3 weeks or longer. Longer lessons, however, are not required because students have a longer attention span. You should plan a lesson that is appropriate for your students and your objectives or intentions.

Second, you *should not expect* to teach all of your objectives with a computer. Students should use other resources (e.g., books and videotapes) and other instructional activities (e.g., group and individual work). Historically, educators have viewed computers as an all-inclusive teaching machine that a student could learn from throughout the school day. Our approach views the computer as a tool rather than as a teacher. It is used by the students to solve problems rather than to deliver instruction. For example, a pencil and paper are considered tools and are used extensively in almost every class. However, we would not expect a student in a language arts class to write all period every day. Rather, we would expect the student to use other activities such as reading, conducting research, and discussing ideas in addition to writing. Thus each individual student does not need full-time access to a computer, as was needed with the computer-as-teacher model. We have observed several classrooms in which each student has a laptop computer. Often, we have seen a group of four or five students divide the tasks and each work independently on an aspect of the problem, whereas another group will all gather around a single laptop and work on a single task. It is nice when every student has a computer, but it is not necessary.

When students use a computer to help solve a problem, their motivation and engagement can increase. The initial motivation may come because using a computer is something new or novel (Clark, 1983). With time, however, the motivation stems from the computer being a useful tool. Students are motivated to use

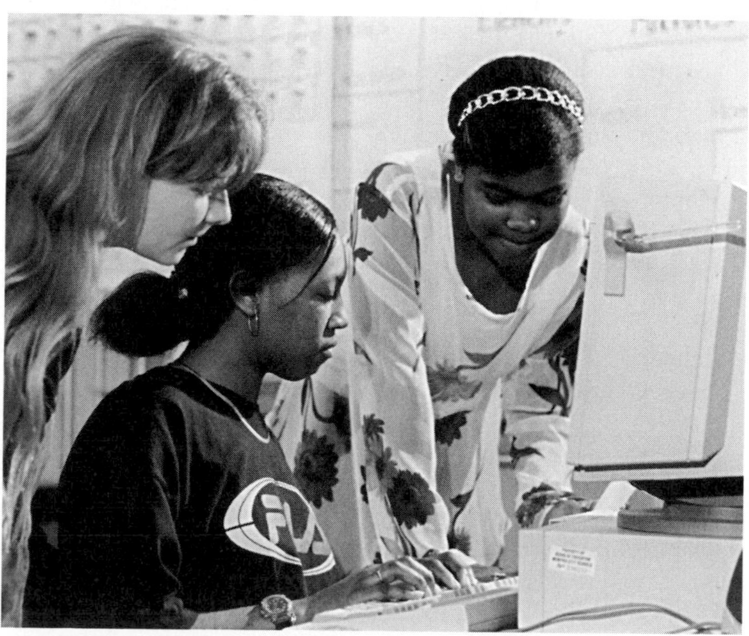

Time at the computer is more meaningful for students when they are well prepared.

FIGURE 4-1 NTeQ Model

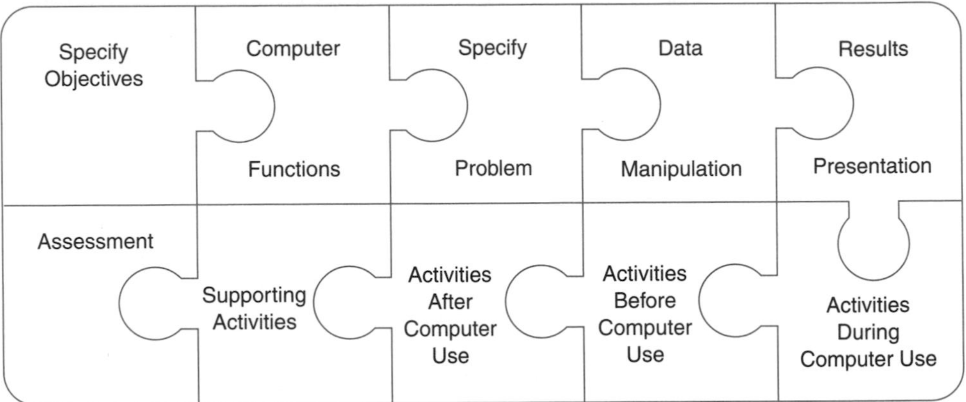

computers because the job gets done more easily and quickly than without it, just as we use a microwave oven because it is more efficient and quicker than a traditional oven. Or, to put it in a more realistic context, computers are not used in the workplace because they are fun and something new. But rather, the technology has become an integral component of everyday operations, again because of its efficiency and accuracy. The NTeQ model encourages use of computers as a tool in the classroom.

The NTeQ model consists of 10 steps (Figure 4-1) for *planning* an integrated computer lesson. Although you can complete the steps in any sequence, we have found that starting with objectives and working in a clockwise sequence is the most efficient. As you gain experience and expertise in developing integrated lessons, you will find that you may complete the steps in various sequences based on your ideas. This model is for *planning* your lessons. The sequence in which the lesson is implemented in your classroom will be much different; this sequence is discussed further in Chapter 11, Implementation: From Plan to Action. Let's examine the process for designing an integrated lesson that uses the computer as a tool.

Specifying Objectives

The lesson planning starts with specifiying your objectives (Figure 4–2). These objectives should cover *all* the instruction for the unit or lesson, not just the information related to the computer component. A lesson can also cross disciplines, either in your own classroom or as part of a team teaching project. For example, you might collect the data in a geography or a science class, analyze the data in a math class, and prepare the report or presentation in an English class. The objectives for the lesson should be inclusive of all the content.

Source of Objectives

One question teachers often ask is whether they are responsible for generating the objectives. In recent years, many districts have created objectives or benchmarks for

FIGURE 4-2 Specifying Objectives

Power Tip

Objectives

As you define your objectives and problems, you will probably find that your objectives cross one or more disciplines. For example, if you are using spreadsheets in a social studies class to analyze voting patterns, you will probably have objectives from both social studies and math. If you are teaching in a departmentalized class you may want to work with the math teacher to make a cross-disciplinary unit.

each content area and grade level. These objectives are sometimes derived from state mandates or guidelines developed by national organizations such as the National Council of Teachers of Mathematics (*www.nctm.org*). Some teacher editions of the textbooks include objectives relevant to the book's content.

A teacher, as the designer, can adapt existing objectives or write new objectives. Regardless of their source, the objectives should support the goals, benchmarks, or objectives of the district. Often, it is both easier and more efficient to adapt existing objectives than create new objectives from scratch. Please refer to Chapter 3, Teacher as Designer I: Teacher's Toolbox for specific guidelines regarding writing objectives.

Matching Objectives to Computer Functions

To create a successful integrated computer lesson, you must find a match between your objective(s) and one or more computer functions (Figure 4-3). Computer functions are tasks that computer software can assist with or perform. For example, spreadsheet software can *convert* fractions to decimals and decimals to percentages. A database can *match* or *select* specific items, whereas a spreadsheet can *calculate*

FIGURE 4-3 Matching Objectives and Computer Functions

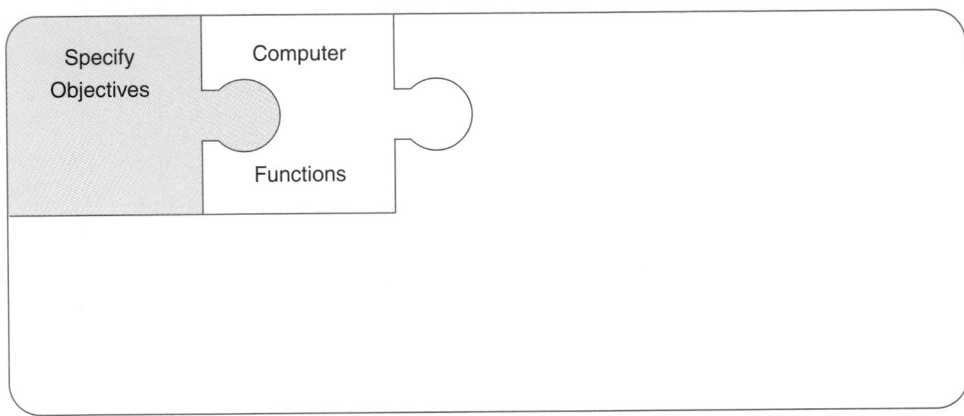

CHECK IT OUT 4-1

Computer Functions

Spreadsheets provide an easily accessible list to the available functions. Select Insert Formula or Function and you will see a complete list of spreadsheet functions.

Link to these resources and activities in the Check It Out module for this chapter of the Companion Website.

the area of a rectangle when the student enters the length and width. Draw and paint software is used to *create* diagrams and maps, and spreadsheet software can *plot* and *chart* data. A table of learning tasks (e.g., objectives) and related computer functions is presented in Appendix A.

Now that you have defined your objectives, you need to determine if there is a match between an objective and a computer function. Some objectives, such as calculate, draw, graph, and sort, are easy to match with a spreadsheet, drawing, or database application. Objectives describing such behaviors as plan, discriminate, evaluate, combine, infer, predict, interpret, judge, and evaluate require careful planning and thinking to match the process with a computer function. For example, an objective requiring the student to evaluate a story or data might use a spreadsheet or database to aid the analysis, a chart to evaluate the data, and a word processor to generate the report that explains the evaluation.

One approach to finding an appropriate match between your objectives and computer functions is to analyze how you would achieve the objective if you were the student. What processes would you need to perform to master the objective? For example, would you need to collect data, perform a calculation, and then graph it? Once you have identified the process or processes required to master the objective, you can select one or more computer functions for the student to use as part of the learning process. For example, to evaluate the best store to purchase a week's groceries, you might use a spreadsheet or database to help collect or organize the data, a spreadsheet to calculate the means and highest and lowest values, and a spreadsheet to chart the results. An objective might require only one computer function, such as calculate, draw, or sort; or it might involve several functions to arrive at the solution.

Specifying a Problem

The next step in the design of the integrated lesson is specifying a problem the students will investigate and solve as part of the instructional process (Figure 4-4). It is critical that this problem is highly motivating and interesting, because as students strive to solve the problem they will develop the thinking skills and gain the knowledge specified in the objectives. The three aspects of specifying the problem are identifying the nature of the problem, collecting the data, and using the data to solve the problem. These aspects of specifying the problem are examined in the following paragraphs.

Nature of the Problem

Problems in an integrated lesson are realistic, based on real-world events, issues, or phenomena. The problems need to come from the students' world so the students can relate to them in a meaningful manner. By using a realistic problem, the students can more readily manipulate the data needed to solve the problem and interpret the results in terms of the original situation (Hancock, Kaput, & Goldsmith, 1992). As the problem is being developed, it is important to make it as relevant as possible to the students by keeping the problem "real world" (Bransford, Sherwood, Hasselbring, Kinzer, & Williams, 1990; Bruner, 1996; Deal & Sterling, 1997; Petraglia, 1998).

FIGURE 4-4 Specifying the Problem

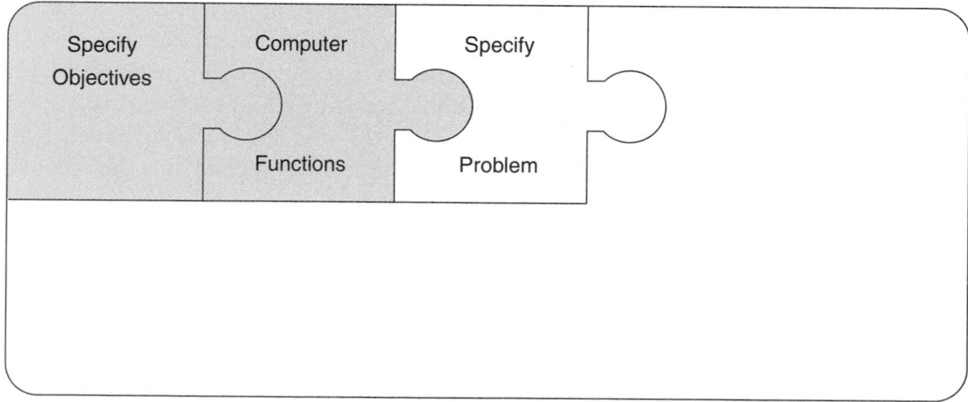

Using realistic problems requires you, the teacher, to take an additional step in the lesson planning process. For example, consider the teaching of frequency distributions in one of our advanced high school math classes. The problem was presented without any context or concrete data—it was simply a calculation we were supposed to complete with no purpose. Little did we realize then that this calculation is a central part of doing research! Today, if we were to teach this topic, we could easily present it as a problem in a realistic context for our students. We could construct a problem in which they survey how much their fellow students make an hour or week at work, the number and types of CDs they own, the number of hours of television they watch during the week, or the amount of time they spend on the telephone on a school night. Or, they could survey their neighbors on a topic such as how far they drive to work or their recycling practices. They could then construct a frequency distribution to determine the average, the mode, and the median. Of course, as a teacher you might have to deal with the parents of the students who place the greatest restrictions on television or telephone time! Presenting a realistic problem to which the students can relate increases both their chances of comprehending the content and their motivation.

When you define your problem, it is important to address the following four questions (Moursund, 1996):

- Do the students clearly understand the given problem?
- Do they know what the goal is?
- Do they know what resources are available to solve the problem?
- Do they have ownership of the problem?

There are several ways to ensure that students have a clear understanding of the problem they are solving. One way is to write the problem statement on the board or use a video projector. This problem can be an idea the teacher has developed or one that is generated by the teacher and students during class discussion. The teacher can also put the problem on a handout that has sections entitled: "Given," "Goals," and "Resources."

You can establish the goal in several ways. You can lead the whole class in a discussion that identifies the goal, cooperative groups can define the goal, or you can provide the goal as a separate part of the handout. If students define the goal of the problem they are solving, it will more than likely *not* be a statement of the objectives. Yet as they achieve the goals of the problem, they are also achieving the objectives. Through teacher facilitation skills, the students are able to "discover" the content or skills defined in the objective through a problem-based approach (Bruner, 1960; Collins & Stevens, 1983; Grambs & Starr, 1976; Mayer, 1987).

When possible, involve students in identifying the resources needed to solve the problem. Provide multiple sources so that students have some flexibility in reaching solutions to the problem. For example, students might use CD-ROM encyclopedias, the Internet, books, magazines, field trips, visits from experts, and survey or experimental data collected by the students.

Another approach is to start by having the students identify what they already know about the problem. Then ask them to identify what they want to know to solve the problem. Finally, after they have solved the problem, ask them what they have learned.

Student ownership of the problem is very important. Student ownership is easier to achieve in a student-centered learning environment than a traditional setting. The more involved students are in various aspects of solving the problem, such as identifying the goal, deciding what resources are needed, and determining how to configure the database, the more ownership they will feel. "We have known for years that if you treat people, young kids included, as responsible, contributing parties to the group, as having a job to do, they will grow into it—some better than others, obviously, but all benefit" (Bruner, 1996, p. 77). Ownership is also increased if the problem is relevant to the students. This relevancy is enhanced by having students generate their own data when possible or having them use real data collected from a survey, an experiment, the Internet, newspapers, or television. Another means of achieving ownership is by letting students define the initial problem. Present a rough idea of what you want to accomplish, then let them develop a clear problem. For example, you might tell the students, "Our school is doing a school-wide thematic unit on Native Americans. One of our objectives for this year is for you to identify different kinds of Native American art from the 1800s. If we have to create a display of this artwork, how can we approach this project?" The teacher can facilitate the discussion to guide the students in reaching a problem similar to the one he defined. However, because the students defined this problem, they will have more ownership and more involvement in reaching a solution.

Specifying a problem for the students typically begins by translating a problem or topic in the textbook or curriculum into a realistic problem, as illustrated with the frequency distribution problem. You might also let your students participate in the development of the problem by asking them to suggest ideas or problems. They can provide rich contexts that you can use to embed the problem.

Once you have identified the problem, you need to check that the problem-solving process will support the achievement of your objectives. For example, your objective for a unit might focus on the effect of the climate on the types of plants grown. Your problem, however, might have the students determine how to convert a Celsius reading to a Fahrenheit reading and to identify those countries that use the two forms of measurement. The problem does not support the achievement of your objective and needs to be revised.

Problem Data

To solve a problem, the students must have access to the appropriate data or information. There are three sources of data you can use for the lesson.

1. *You can provide the students with the data.* This approach is used when the instructional time is limited, the students have no feasible way of obtaining the data, or students lack the necessary search skills (e.g., Internet search). For example, consider a geography unit focusing on the type of crops grown in various countries. The students need to discover relationships between the weather and crops. Searching for the raw data is not a focus of this unit. You might provide the students with the necessary information so they can concentrate on manipulating the data and discovering relationships.

2. *Students can generate their own data through experiments or observations.* They can generate data through a laboratory experiment (e.g., chemistry, physics, or biology), a survey, or an interview or by observation, such as the number of students wearing seat belts as they arrive at school. A sixth-grade class, for example, could measure the height of a sampling of boys and girls in several grade levels as they study the relationship among physical growth, age, and gender.
3. *Students can search for data in a library, on CD-ROMs, or on the Internet* (see Chapter 9, The Internet in the Classroom). Computers create many opportunities for finding both useful and not so useful data. Student data searches should not be limited to just computer-based searches, but should include printed materials and other materials from the library, as appropriate. For example, an economics class studying organized labor might search the Internet for historical events in the labor movement and then search the local newspaper for information on strikes or other organized labor activity in their community.

As you plan the lesson, you will need to decide if students should gather the data or if you should provide them with it. If the process of gathering the data is part of the instruction, such as in a lab experiment or a survey, then the students need to collect the data. However, when the emphasis of the lesson is primarily on manipulating the data (e.g., calculations or probing the database), you may decide that it is a more efficient use of classroom time to provide the students with a template and the data, or even the finished database. You will need to determine the importance and value of the students collecting and entering data as opposed to using an existing data file. The tradeoff is one of instructional time and how it is used.

Collecting Data

If the students will be collecting the data, you will need to determine the type and amount of data they will need to collect. If the students are conducting a survey or an interview, how many individuals must each student survey? If they are collecting

Identifying Problems

The Problems Based Learning Clearinghouse at *http://www.udel.edu/pbl/* provides various resources, including sample problems and materials for instruction.

Another great resource is the IMSA.

Link to these resources and activities in the Check It Out module for this chapter of the Companion Website.

data from an experiment, how many observations does each student or group need to complete? You can also involve the students in this decision as part of the problem-solving process. If you need consistency in the data among students or groups, the class can create a data collection form to record their results.

Using Existing Data

When students will use a data set created by you or by others, you need to consider the following. First, are the data in a format (either on paper or on disk) that the students can use? If the data are not in appropriate formats, can you modify the format so the data are useful to the student? Second, are students allowed to modify, delete, or add data? Third, if the students are entering the data, must each one enter all the data or can they divide the work among groups and then merge the files? Fourth, where will the students save their data? Will they use their own disk(s), the hard drive, or the server? Careful consideration is needed to protect students from losing their data and becoming frustrated with the process.

Test the Data

We encourage teachers to try a test run of the data at this stage of the planning cycle. You can conduct this test with actual or random data to make sure your recording form and file template (e.g., database or spreadsheet) are designed correctly. This simple test run can save time and frustration if there is a problem. Also, consider the data you are using and make sure that it will help in solving the problem and help the students achieve the objectives. A step-by-step guide for implementing the problem-solving process planned in this section is found in Chapter 11, Implementation: From Plan to Action.

Planning the Data Manipulation

The fourth step in designing an integrated lesson is to plan how the learners will manipulate data (Figure 4-5). This decision is directly related to the computer functions and your objectives. Once the students have the data entered into a computer file such as a spreadsheet or database, what will they do with it? Similarly, how much instruction or guidance must you provide the students concerning the manipulation?

Providing Instructions

If your students are advanced in the use of the required application such as a spreadsheet or database, they may be quite capable of simply answering the questions either you or they have posed. Less advanced students may need step-by-step instructions on how to enter a formula or matching and searching criteria (Figure 4-6). Another alternative is to teach all the students how to do the data manipulation and then provide assistance on an individual basis. We have observed both good and bad examples of both approaches. One excellent approach was by a teacher who modeled the steps on a large monitor as the students created their own lists of steps. At the other extreme was a teacher who let four students at a time complete the process as she and the other students observed and commented. The students sitting at their desks could

FIGURE 4-5 Data Manipulation

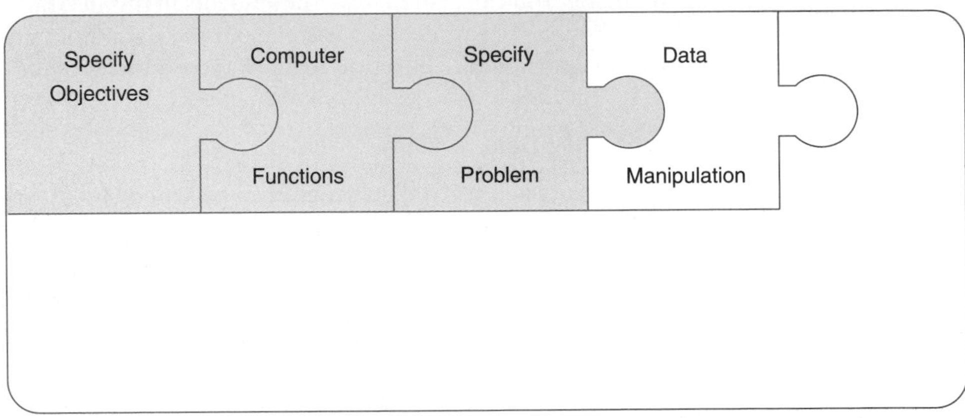

FIGURE 4-6 Sample Spreadsheet Calculation Instruction

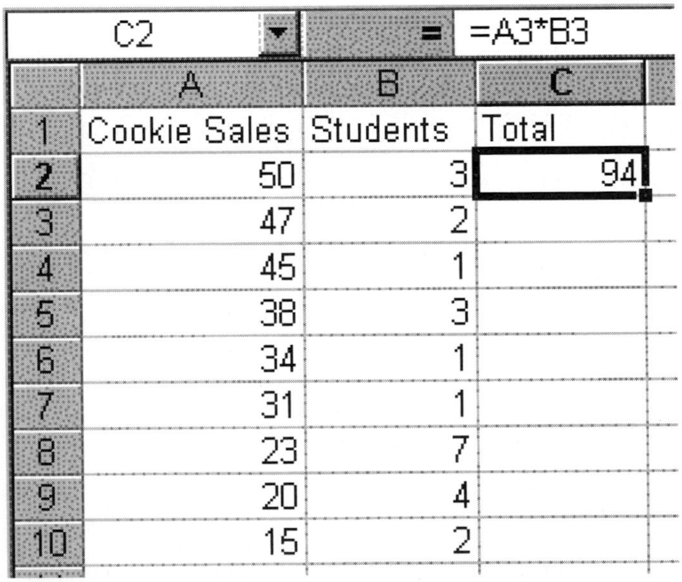

C2 = =A3*B3

	A	B	C
1	Cookie Sales	Students	Total
2	50	3	94
3	47	2	
4	45	1	
5	38	3	
6	34	1	
7	31	1	
8	23	7	
9	20	4	
10	15	2	

Calculating the number of packages sold.
1. Click in cell C2
2. Enter the following into the entry bar
   =A3*B3
3. Press enter and you will see the results of your calculation

FIGURE 4-7 Sample Think Sheet

Local Weather Think Sheet

Now that you have collected weather data for 3 weeks, think of these questions as you examine your database.

1. Does anything happen to the relative humidity as the temperature changes?
2. Look at the types of cloud formations that were present each day when you collected your weather data. Can you find any information in your database that might explain the changes that occurred (more humidity, lower barometric pressure, etc.)?
3. Use the information in your database to write "Weather Rules." For example, "When the temperature rises, the barometric pressure (*rises, falls, or stays the same*)."
4. Use the patterns you discover in your data to predict what would happen to the variables in your database if the temperature dropped by 20 degrees.
5. Using a weather map from the newspaper or from a Website, find a location that had the same weather as your area, one that was colder, and one that was warmer. What factors (e.g., atmospheric and geographic) affected the weather in each location?

not see the individual monitors, and there was little if any motivation to focus their attention on what the teacher was doing.

Think Sheet

Simply entering a formula, sorting data, making a graph, or creating a drawing is rather mechanical. Students can complete the steps to solve the problem, but fail to process or reflect on the results. A *Think Sheet* provides guidance to help students organize their thinking and probe the implications of the data manipulations. It helps them determine what to do once they have sorted the data, performed the calculations, or created a chart. Think Sheets can include generic information, such as which is the largest, which is the smallest, what is the most common, and what is the least common. Specific lesson Think Sheets can include probing questions asking the student about implications, interpretations, generalizations, and predictions using the data. Figure 4-7 illustrates a sample Think Sheet.

The questions in a Think Sheet should focus on higher-order questions that require the student to examine, analyze, and interpret the data. Bloom's Taxonomy for the Cognitive Domain provides a tool for checking your questions (Bloom, Englehart, Furst, Hill, & Krathwohl, 1956). The Taxonomy divides cognitive skills into six categories or levels (Figure 4-8). You can classify the verb or process in each of your questions into the appropriate category of the taxonomy. If most of your questions are at the knowledge and comprehension levels, you might need to reconsider your objectives or your questions. The knowledge and comprehension level questions are useful for orienting the learner to the data; however, they do not require the student to analyze the data.

FIGURE 4-8 Bloom's Taxonomy of Cognitive Objectives

Level	Description
Knowledge	Recall of information such as the capital of Indiana.
Comprehension	Learner understands the information and can make use of the information; for example, to understand an exaggeration.
Application	The ability to apply the abstractions presented such as applying a formula to calculate the area of a triangle.
Analysis	Ability to analyze information into elements such as analyzing a sales pitch, political speech, propaganda, or persuasive piece into its main arguments.
Synthesis	Putting the elements together to present a whole such as collecting data, analyzing the data, interpreting the results, and presenting the findings.
Evaluation	Ability to make judgments based on data and information, such as determining which dish soap product is the best, based on a series of tests.

FIGURE 4-9 Results Presentation

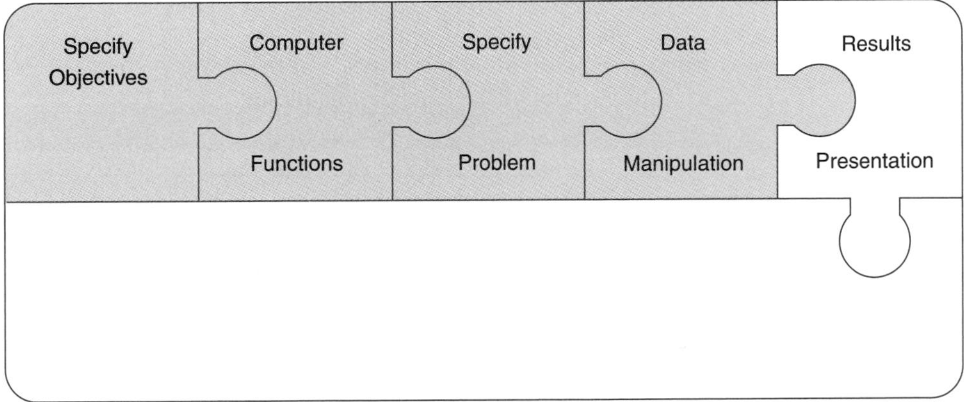

Planning the Results Presentation

The next step of planning the integrated lesson is presentation of the results (Figure 4-9). What type of product will the students produce to demonstrate they have achieved the objectives? Although these reports can take a variety of formats (see Chapter 8), there are four basic ways of presenting the results.

1. Each student or group of students can prepare a written report using either a word processor or paper and pencil. Using desktop publishing techniques, the students can prepare books, magazines, or newsletters and distribute their products to classmates, students in lower grades, parents, or possibly a government agency such as the city council. If the students have

worked on a problem of community interest, they might submit their story to a local newspaper for publication.

2. Students can prepare a poster or bulletin board display of their results. This type of presentation can take a variety of formats, from interactive displays to timelines, and can include both computer-generated and noncomputer-generated student products.
3. Students can publish their results on a Web page (see Chapter 8). This format is similar to a written report but is presented in a different format. The emphasis, however, should be on presenting the results, not learning HyperText Markup Language (HTML) or how to create a Web page.
4. Students can make a presentation to other students or parents. Students can present their findings in a scientific format using an electronic slide show. Or the presentation might take the format of a lesson (e.g., a HyperStudio stack) to teach other students. Other possibilities include a radio or television news show format.

Publishing the results encourages students to analyze their findings in a critical manner and draw appropriate conclusions, because their work will be viewed by others. This analysis was started with Think Sheets as students analyzed their data. The presentation component allows students to interpret their results and apply their findings to a solution.

As you plan the results presentation, you need to develop your criteria for what the students should include. For example, you might include a basic outline for a report similar to that used in scientific journals. A report of a survey the students have completed might use the outline in Figure 4-10. You can create similar outlines and

FIGURE 4-10 Sample Instructions for a Report

Format for Survey Reports on Students Who Wear Seatbelts

I. **Background information**
   A. Why you did the survey.
   B. Recent state law requiring seatbelts.
   C. Statement of the problem.

II. **Method**
   A. Who was surveyed?
   B. How were they selected?
   C. Describe the survey instrument.

III. **Results**
   A. What did you find?

IV. **Discussion**
   A. What do your findings mean?
   B. What are your conclusions?

criteria for Web pages, posters, and presentations. The criteria will help you assess the results presentation as well as let students know your expectations.

This step of the planning process requires careful thought to avoid problems such as computer access if *all* the students are required to prepare a written report. Students are easily frustrated if they have completed all the steps but cannot complete the final step because of the limited number of computers in the classroom. Thus a paper-and-pencil report supplemented with database reports or a spreadsheet chart may be a more efficient use of instructional time than requiring each individual to use word processing for the report.

PLANNING THE MULTIDIMENSIONAL ACTIVITIES

The next step is to plan the specific activities you will use in the classroom. There are two reasons for these activities. First, not all objectives are best taught with a computer. Second, many classrooms have only a limited number of computers; therefore, several activities are used to achieve the objectives. We can hardly expect each student in a class of 27 to have extensive computer time when there are only four computers in the classroom. There are also management and planning concerns in classrooms in which all the students have a laptop computer at their disposal. To address these two issues, the integrated lesson uses multidimensional activities. Activities are grouped into four time frames: before computer use, during computer use, after computer use, and supporting activities used anytime (the management of the classroom is discussed in Chapter 13, Managing the Classroom). Notice, however, that planning the *activities during computer use* is done before planning the *activities before computer use*. We reversed these steps for the planning process because you must know what your students will do while they are using the computer *before* you can determine what they must do before using the computer. Many of the data collection, data manipulation, and report presentation aspects of the lesson are included as part of these multidimensional activities. The following section describes each type of activity.

Planning: Activities During Computer Use

Now that you have identified your objective(s) and the problem the students will be solving and know how the students will use the computer to manipulate the data, the next step is to determine what the students will do while they are working with the computers (Figure 4-11). There are two factors to consider when planning the computer activities. First, identify the activities the students will engage in while using the computer. How will the students obtain information to find an answer or to solve the problem? If students are searching for information, will they search a CD, the Internet, a database on the hard drive, or all three? If students are using a database or spreadsheet, will they use a template you have created or make their own? Depending on your objectives, you might want the students to use your template and concentrate on entering and manipulating the data to find an answer. For other lessons, the emphasis might be on finding the correct solution by creating the correct formula. If students are

THE TEACHER'S DIARY

When I plan a literature-based thematic unit, I always look through my district's curriculum frameworks, classroom literature, and language textbooks. I use these frameworks to help define my instructional goals for the unit and review textbooks for ideas in the content areas. After I had reviewed the resources, I decided that the students needed to learn how to use an index and table of contents to find information, read for specific information, and summarize in writing what they had read. With these instructional goals in mind, I went to our school library and looked for books related to owls that would be of high interest and age appropriate to my students. I checked out a variety of books on owls and chose two as the basis for this unit. As I read these books, I began to formulate how I would use them to meet my instructional goals, and I made a list of activities.

The next day I asked my students to create knowledge charts about owls. On one side of their paper, they listed everything that they already knew about owls and on the other side those things that they would like to learn about owls. The class then discussed what they wanted to learn about owls. We made a list of questions about owls that they would like to have answered. We ended up with 34 excellent questions!

I recorded their questions and took them home with me that night. I used my list of instructional goals and activities and the students' questions to help me write the instructional objectives for this unit. After I had written the objectives, I checked my objectives against the list of state mandated objectives to ensure alignment with as many as possible.

Then I used the activity list and the students' questions to help me create a thematic activity web for this unit. I tried to include a variety of activities that would cross all curriculum areas and include the use of the computer in as many of the activities as possible. I wanted the students to use the computer in real-life situations and as a tool to help them accomplish their instructional goals.

I searched the Internet and found some excellent owl resources and brought in several different CD-ROM encyclopedias. The students used both the computer materials and books checked out from the school and public libraries to obtain information about owls. They then used this information about owls to create a database, write informative paragraphs, and create a multimedia report.

The final assessment for this unit was a group multimedia report about a topic related to owls. Considering student interest expressed in the questions, the topics for these reports were: (1) unusual owls, (2) feathers and flight, (3) special owl features, (4) owl habitats, (5) owl diet, and (6) owl babies. Each group was responsible for a topic. They searched for information on that topic using printed materials, the Internet, and the CD-ROM encyclopedias. The students kept individual notes and combined this information with that of other group members to create a group HyperStudio multimedia report. These reports were shared with other students in the classroom.

Fran Clark
Third-Grade Teacher

It is important for teachers to create a sample of student computer work prior to implementing a new lesson.

FIGURE 4-11 Activities During Computer Use

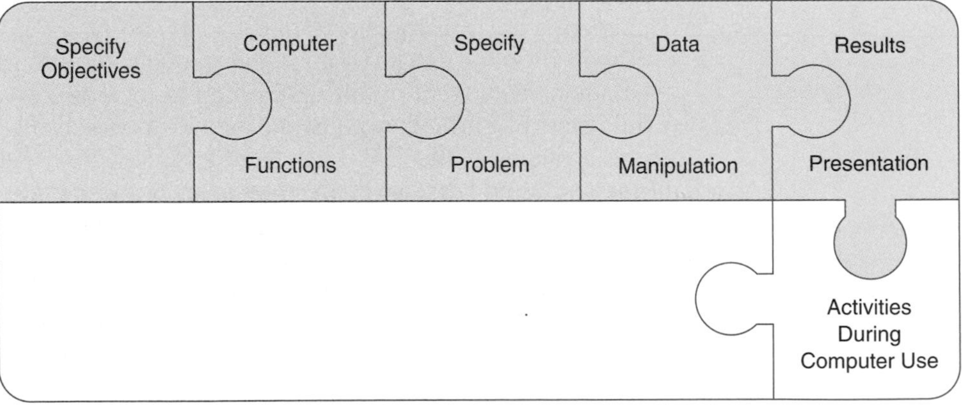

doing a report or drawing, can they use clip art or must they do original artwork? Similarly, do they need to show a graph of the results in their report? Students will need clear and precise instructions of what they are to do while working at the computer.

Second, will the students work individually or in groups? If you are using groups at the computer, assist students with identifying and assigning students to the different roles, ensuring that students have the opportunity to rotate through the different roles. When working in a group, one student can read the data, another can enter the

FIGURE 4-12 Activities Before Computer Use

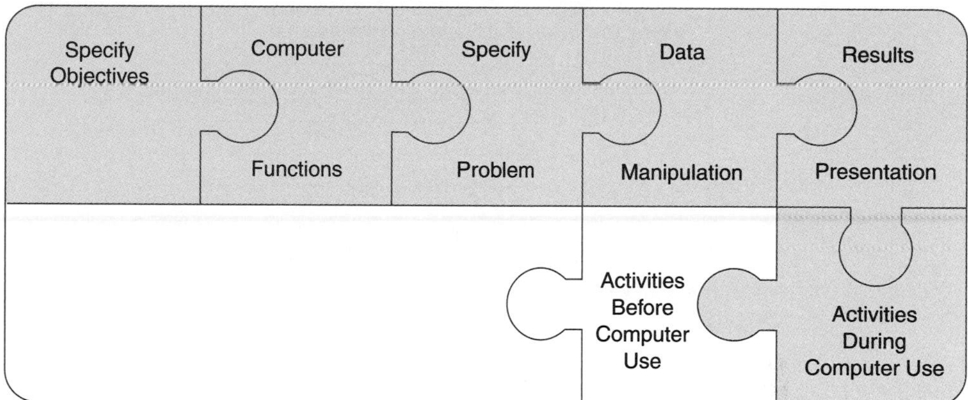

data, and a third can check the accuracy of the entry. Defining the roles before going to the computer can help you develop a rotation schedule so that students have a variety of experiences. More detail about using cooperative learning is found in Chapter 11, Implementation: From Plan to Action.

Planning: Activities Before Computer Use

Once you have determined the activities the students will engage in while at the computer and whether the students will work individually or in groups, then you can focus on the activities they *must* complete before using the computer. If you have limited access to computers because of time limitations or lack of computers in your classroom, it is essential to plan activities the students need to complete before using the computer (Figure 4-12). For example, if the students are entering data from an experiment or survey into a spreadsheet, they can collect the data and organize it before they start to use the computer. Similarly, if they are writing a report, they can create their outline and gather their materials before their computer time. Students who are searching a CD-ROM encyclopedia or the Internet need to plan their search by identifying the key words before they start using the computer. With proper planning, students can have efficient and productive use of their computer time.

In the previous planning steps you identified one or more ways students would use the computer and manipulate information. Think through each of these steps and identify what the student needs *to complete before* using the computer. You may find it easier to complete the steps and make notes as to what you did to complete the steps. This listing of information and steps to complete before using the computer is part of your lesson plan that you can communicate to the students with a handout, through a lecture, or with a poster or blackboard listing. For some students, a checklist with space for notes or blanks is helpful for organizing their thoughts and data (Figure 4-13).

FIGURE 4-13 Checklist for Work Before Using the Computer

Getting Ready to Do a Search on the Internet

What is your topic? ______________________

List at least three terms you can use to search for information on this topic:

____

____

____

____

____

List at least two other terms that mean the same as some of the above:

____

____

____

What are you searching for?

- ☐ Articles
- ☐ Pictures
- ☐ Movies
- ☐ Sound
- ☐ Software
- ☐ Other:

Planning: Activities After Computer Use

If students are using the computer to solve problems, their learning and work do not end with their computer time (Figure 4-14). While working at the computer, they have produced some results. Activities after using the computer should focus on exploring the results of the computer activity. If the students have analyzed the data of

FIGURE 4-14 Activities After Computer Use

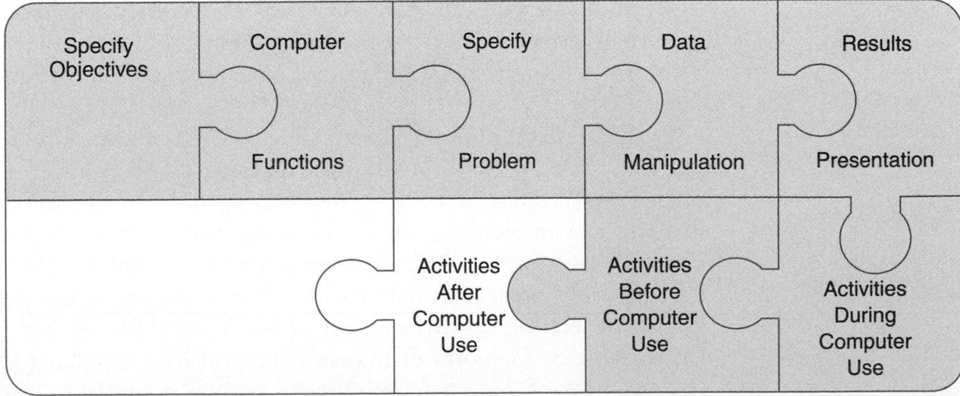

FIGURE 4-15 Supporting Activities

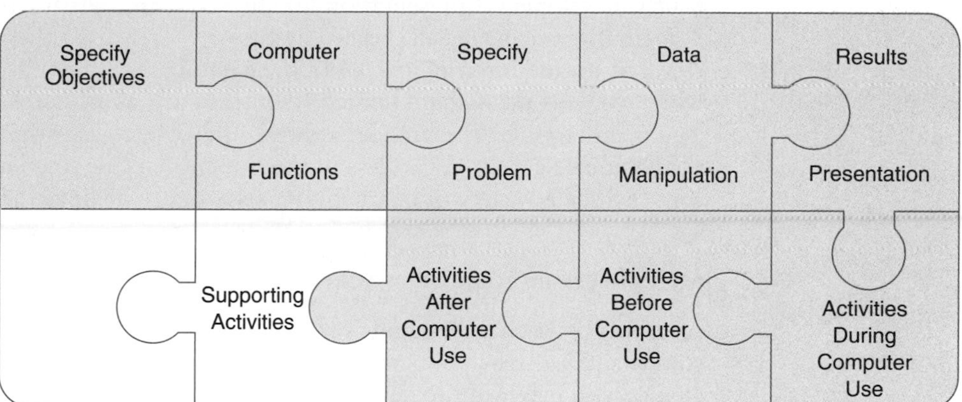

an experiment or study, they should focus on interpreting or explaining the results. Students who have searched for information can read, paraphrase, compare and contrast, and interpret the information in a written report.

The purpose of this activity is to use the information generated from using the computer as a tool. You might find a Think Sheet helpful for guiding the students' analysis and interpretation. This handout can include either generic questions such as "What is the writer's perspective in this news story?" or specific questions such as, "Using the graph you created, what happened to humidity as temperature increased?" Think Sheets can also include directions for how the students should read an article or story, including steps for what they should do (e.g., paraphrase or summarize the content) after they finish reading the material.

Planning: Supporting Activities

An integrated computer lesson incorporates a variety of instructional activities. Some require the use of a computer, and others rely on other forms of instruction (Figure 4-15). After you have designed the activities that are directly related to the computer activities, you will need to focus on the supporting activities that also help students achieve the objectives.

Lesson-Related Supporting Activities

The objectives for the lesson should cover a variety of skills and topics. Some require the use of a computer, whereas others require different student engagement activities such as experimentation, practice, and gathering information via multiple resources (reading, videotapes, teacher, and other content experts). Students engage in these activities as part of the instruction for the *total* lesson. It is often helpful to have a variety of activities that are not dependent on completing the computer activities, so that students can work on them at any time. We observed one classroom in which the students were using the computer to research a topic and build a database. The supporting activities included research and reading in several books, creating a poster, developing a presentation for the class, and writing test items for the topic. Students were engaged in these activities as they waited their turn to do additional research on the Internet and build their database. Similar strategies are often used when students must share limited resources such as a microscope or manipulatives. You must consider the broader context and objectives rather than just focusing on the computer aspect, regardless of the students' access to computers. Interesting lessons include a variety of instructional activities to achieve the objectives.

Multiple Lesson Supporting Activities

Another approach to designing supporting activities is to provide multiple units for the students. If you teach only one subject, such as math, science, language arts, or social studies, you may want to develop several units students can work on at one time. You do not, however, need to use a computer for each of the units. If you are teaching a geography class, for example, you might have the students working on units on reading maps, weather, and influences of technology on people and towns. Similarly, a math teacher might have students working on addition of fractions, comparing fractions with fraction strips, converting fractions to decimals, and doing fraction additions with a calculator. These units are independent and are not sequential; thus students can work on them at any time. All of the units provide instruction leading to the achievement of the objectives, although the objectives may be for different units of instruction.

Interdisciplinary Supporting Activities

An integrated computer lesson is an excellent approach to use across content areas. Such activities require a team-teaching approach if the students are not in a self-contained classroom. For example, students might collect data in science class or social studies class, make the calculations in a math class, and prepare the results presentation in a language arts class. Using this approach, students can work on various tasks related to the project in the different classes, with the goal of completing the project in a timely manner.

The supporting activities are often the most difficult to develop. These activities should provide instruction related to an objective(s) as opposed to "busy" work. If you are having difficulty identifying supporting activities, reconsider your objectives. You may need to broaden their scope or add additional objectives.

Assessment

The final step of the NTeQ model is the development of your assessment strategies (Figure 4-16). In recent years, educators have moved away from traditional forms of assessment, such as multiple-choice tests, and toward more authentic forms of assessment, such as portfolios, performance assessment, presentations, and experiments (Campbell, 2000; Marcoulides & Heck, 1994). Assessment of an integrated computer lesson will typically require more than a paper-and-pencil test. During lesson implementation, students can use a task list to guide productivity and assist with

FIGURE 4-16 Assessment

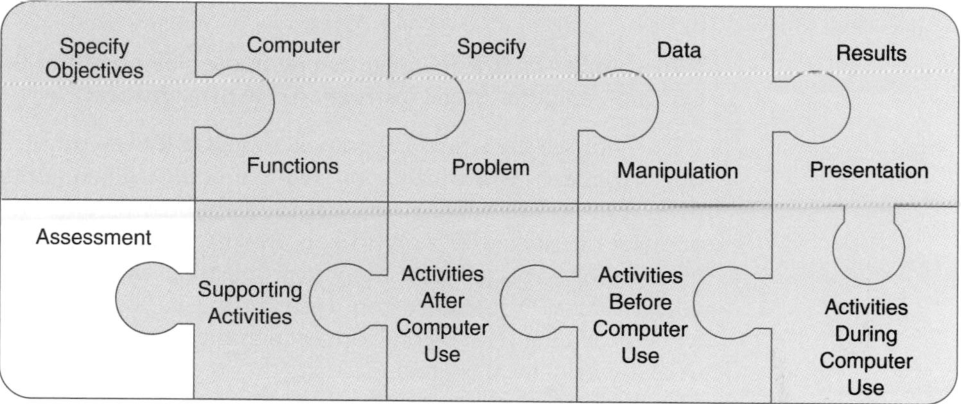

self-reflection on the quality of work being accomplished. At the conclusion of a lesson, we might use a traditional multiple-choice and short-answer test to assess the students' understanding of the concepts and principles. Then we might develop a rubric to assess student portfolios documenting their searches, the completion of the Think Sheets, and their presentation. We might also include an assessment of the group and individual work behaviors based on both a journal we kept and the students' personal journals.

Rubrics provide a means of rating student productivity on content standards according to predetermined performance standards (Danielson, 1997). Content standards define the subject knowledge and skills students should reflect. Performance standards indicate to what level a student presentation meets the content standard (Gandal, 1995). A complete discussion of assessment approaches is presented in Chapter 14, The Role of Assessment.

SUMMARY

Effective use of computers in your classroom requires careful planning to integrate their use into a lesson. The NTeQ model provides 10 steps to help you complete this lesson planning. The first 5 steps involve the planning of the content: specifying the objectives, identifying a match with the computer functions, specifying the problem the learners will seek to answer, planning how the source of the data and how they will manipulate it and, finally, planning how they will present the results of their research. The next 3 steps require you to plan how your students will use the computer(s) in the classroom. These three steps involve classroom management and planning for Think Sheets and job aids. The ninth step is the planning of supporting activities that can include support for objectives in the same unit or another unit that do not require the use of a computer. Last is the planning of assessment. The assessment of student learning when using an authentic task often requires more than a traditional paper-and-pencil test. This step will guide your planning of a rubric or other strategy to accurately assess student achievement.

AT THE CLASSROOM'S DOORSTEP

Questions Teachers Ask

Why should I create an integrated computer lesson rather than use some of the existing computer-based instructional (CBI) software?

We do not see the use of integrated computer lessons and CBI as an either/or question. Decide instead which approach will best help your students achieve the objectives. You may decide that the CBI can help provide the scaffolding (see Chapter 3) necessary to solve the problem you present in the integrated lesson. The integrated lesson allows you to create unique, problem-based units that are highly relevant for your students. You can custom tailor problems to meet your curriculum standards while providing a local context to which the students can relate. Providing this type of real-world, local context increases the meaningfulness of the instruction. Students see a problem that is concrete and easily understandable. The integrated lesson also helps construct a multidimensional learning environment incorporating a variety of instructional strategies rather than *just* focusing on the computer. As a result, "book" learning has as much importance as "computer" learning in the minds of the students.

I will never be able to create enough units for next year. Is there any reason to adopt this approach?

The first year of any new approach is the most difficult. We would not expect a teacher to develop enough materials in a year to cover every lesson of instruction for every class. Teachers that we have observed start with a few units the first year and add additional new units each year. There are also units that you can adapt and modify available from teachers on the Internet (*www.nteq.com*) and on the Websites for this text (*www.prenhall.com/morrison*). Teachers also are able to adapt some of their exisiting units to an integrated lesson by rethinking the problem and objectives.

One of the best sources of ideas for lessons is your old lesson plans and textbooks. It is often easier to adapt an existing idea to an integrated lesson plan than to generate a new lesson plan from scratch. Consider your objectives, standards, or benchmarks; then compare the behavior in those to the various computer functions. Teachers are often surprised at the number of possibilities they can generate for existing materials.

TECHNOLOGY INTEGRATION ACTIVITIES

To access the activities that connect the content of the text with the Companion Website and other technology, please go to the Activities module in Chapter 4 of the Companion Website at *http://www.prenhall.com/morrison.*

NTEQ PORTFOLIO ACTIVITIES

There are two parts to your portfolio for this chapter.

The first task is to complete the manual you started in Chapter 3. For this chapter, you will describe the steps you will need to complete for each of the steps in the

NTeQ model (see Figure 4-1). For example, for Specifying the Problem, you might list the various ways you could find a problem that is of interest to your students. You might also list the criteria of a good problem. This manual can then serve as a guide when you develop an integrated lesson because it will have guidelines and criteria that you have created.

The second task is to create an integrated lesson plan using the NTeQ model. You can use one of the ideas you started developing in the NTeQ Portfolio in Chapter 3. You can also take one of your existing lesson plans and adapt it to the NTeQ model.

REFERENCES

Bloom, B. S., Englehart, M. D., Furst, E. J., Hill, W. H., & Krathwohl, D. R. (Eds.). (1956). *Taxonomy of educational objectives: The classification of education goals. Handbook I: Cognitive domain.* New York: David McKay.

Bransford, J. D., Sherwood, R. D., Hasselbring, T. S., Kinzer, C. K., & Williams, S. M. (1990). Anchored instruction: Why we need it and how technology can help. In D. Nix & R. J. Spiro (Eds.), *Cognition, education, and multimedia: Exploring ideas in high technology* (pp. 115–142). Hillsdale, NJ: Erlbaum.

Bruner, J. S. (1960). *The process of education.* Cambridge, MA: Harvard University Press.

Bruner, J. S. (1996). *The culture of education.* Cambridge, MA: Harvard University Press.

Campbell, D. (2000). Authentic assessment and authentic standards. *Phi Delta Kappan, 81,* 405–407.

Clark, R. E. (1983). Reconsidering research on learning from media. *Review of Educational Research, 53,* 445–459.

Collins, A., & Stevens, A. L. (1983). A cognitive theory of inquiry teaching. In C. M. Reigeluth (Ed.), *Instructional design theories and models: An overview of their status.* (pp. 247–278). Hillsdale, NJ: Macmillan.

Danielson, C. (1997). *A collection of performance tasks and rubrics: Middle school mathematics* (pp. 247–278). Larchmont, NY: Eye on Education.

Deal, D., & Sterling, D. (1997). Kids ask the best questions. *Educational Leadership, 54,* 61–63.

Gandal, M. (1995). Not all standards are created equal. *Educational Leadership, 52,* 16–21.

Grambs, L. H., & Starr, I. S. (1976). *Modern methods in secondary education* (5th ed.). Fort Worth, TX: Holt, Rinehart and Winston.

Hancock, C., Kaput, J. J., & Goldsmith, L. T. (1992). Authentic inquiry with data: Critical barriers to classroom interpretation. *Educational Psychologist, 27,* 337–364.

Marcoulides, G. A., & Heck, R. H. (1994). The changing role of educational assessment in the 1990s. *Education and Urban Society, 26*(4), 332–337.

Mayer, R. (1987). *Educational psychology: A cognitive approach.* Boston, MA: Little Brown and Co.

Moursund, D. (1996). *Increasing your expertise as a problem solver: Some roles of computers* (2nd ed.). Eugene, OR: International Society for Technology in Education.

Petraglia, J. (1998). The real world on a short leash: The (mis)application of constructivism to the design of educational technology. *Educational Technology Research and Development, 46,* 54–65.

KEY TOPICS

Chapter 5

Word Processing

This chapter examines word processing and the many ways that students can use this software in the classroom. It begins with an overview of basic word processing functions and then discusses how students can use word processing as a tool. The chapter ends with a detailed description of how to create lesson plans that integrate the use of word processing.

GETTING STARTED

What Do I Know?

1. Did you know that most word processing functions could be completed if you know how to do seven simple computer tasks?
2. Did you know that word processing can be used to engage students in higher-level thinking?
3. Did you know that the individual needs of students are better met when their work is completed with a word processor?

Classroom Snapshot

WITHOUT COMPUTERS

Maria was happy about going to school today because the class was going to write their first "friendly letter" to someone special. Maria chose her grandmother in Mexico. Her teacher explained how to write the letter and emphasized that the draft copy was to be done in pencil to make it easier to correct mistakes. Maria wrote, erased, and rewrote the draft copy multiple times before taking it to her teacher. Upon approval to make the final copy, Maria took out a clean sheet of white notebook paper and a new ballpoint pen and began using her best handwriting to copy the letter. She very carefully added the date, address, greeting, and first paragraph; then, as her teacher recommended, she reviewed what she had done so far. She found a misspelled word in the second line, so had to get out another sheet of notebook paper. Maria took a deep breath and used her best handwriting to write the second copy of her letter. She was almost finished with the second copy, which was looking great, when Bobby "accidentally" bumped her arm. Her pen slashed across the letter, ruining it. After yelling at Bobby, she pulled out another clean sheet of notebook paper and began again. Although she didn't like having to start over, the writing went a little faster because she had most of the letter memorized.

Then her teacher reminded the class to once again proofread the letters. Maria was sure hers would be perfect because she had been so careful. But to her dismay, she realized that a complete sentence had been left out, so the last paragraph did not make any sense. She reluctantly pulled out yet another clean sheet of notebook paper. All of the elation was gone. In fact, she was beginning to dislike writing.

WITH COMPUTERS

Maria was happy about going to school today because her teacher said the class was going to write their first "friendly letter" to someone special. Maria chose her grandmother in Mexico. Her teacher explained how to write the letter and emphasized that a draft outline was to be done in pencil to make it easier to correct mistakes. Maria wrote, erased, and rewrote her outline copy a *couple* of times before taking it to the teacher. Upon approval to make the final copy, Maria goes to the computer to "write" her letter. Because her class finished the keyboarding lessons, she quickly used word processing to enter her draft. Using the outline as a guide, she carefully wrote each part of her letter to make sure it would make sense to her grandmother. She felt confident in her ability to write a good letter because she could easily correct errors and make changes with the copy, cut, and paste tools. She also changed the font to a larger size to make it easier for her grandmother to read. And, finally, she used the class digital camera to add a recent photo of herself with her teacher. She really enjoyed writing letters and asked the teacher if she could write another letter to her cousin in New York.

EXAMINING WORD PROCESSING

Word processing applications such as Microsoft Word, Microsoft Works, AppleWorks, or WordPerfect allow the computer user to create and enhance documents with the computer. This section presents the fundamentals of editing, formatting, and

FIGURE 5-1 Examining Word Processing

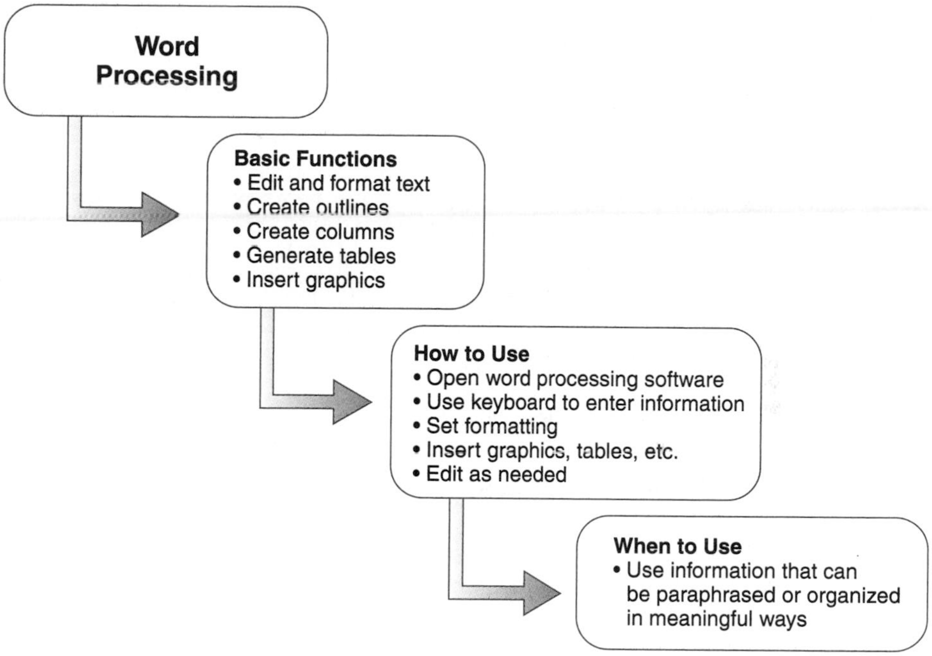

Word Processing

Basic Functions
- Edit and format text
- Create outlines
- Create columns
- Generate tables
- Insert graphics

How to Use
- Open word processing software
- Use keyboard to enter information
- Set formatting
- Insert graphics, tables, etc.
- Edit as needed

When to Use
- Use information that can be paraphrased or organized in meaningful ways

inserting. It also covers the basics for using the spelling, grammar, and thesaurus tools. If you are familiar with word processing, you may want to quickly review or skip this section and move forward to the Word Processing in the Classroom section.

BASIC FUNCTIONS

Word processing software is comprised of several key functions that can be used to enhance student learning, as illustrated in Figure 5-1. However, to use these functions, the first step is to enter information into the word processing application.

Entering Information

The most common way of entering information into a computer is through a keyboard. The information is displayed on the monitor as it is entered. Most keyboards are arranged in a way very similar to typewriters, although many are extended to include function (F) and directional keys and a 10-key number pad (Figure 5-2). Many of the keyboard functions used with word processing are similar to those used with a typewriter. The following list contains items that are used for both word processing and typing:

- Words are entered by pressing corresponding letter keys.
- Spaces between words are created with the space bar.

FIGURE 5-2 Keyboard

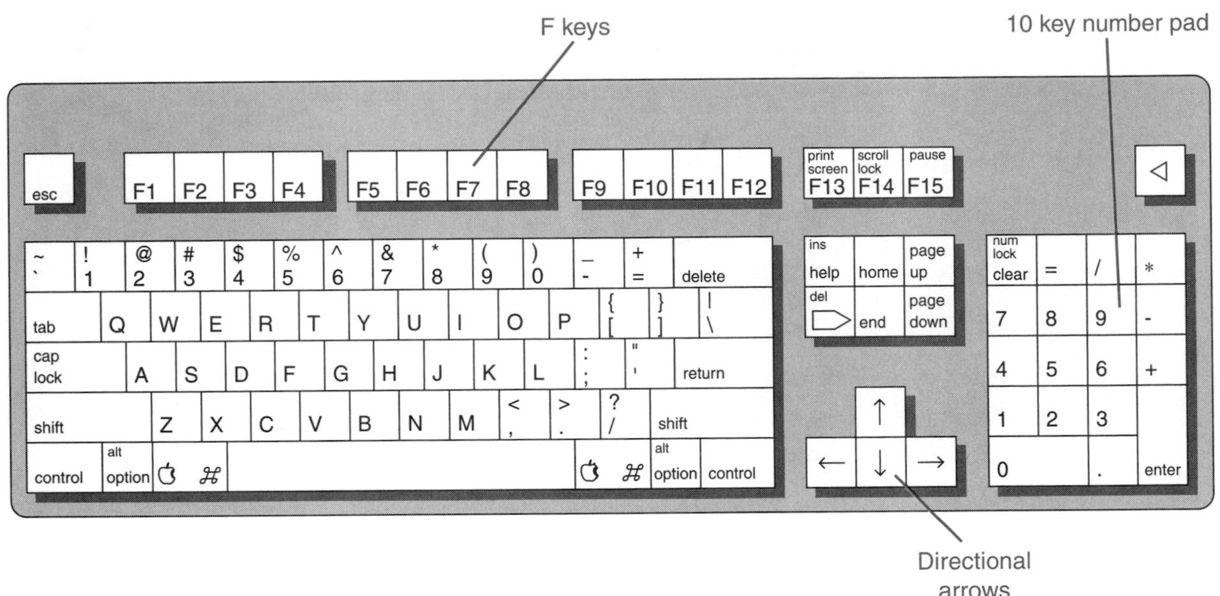

- Capital letters are created by holding down the Shift key as the letter is entered; all *caps* can be obtained by pressing the Cap Lock key.
- Characters displayed above the number and punctuation keys are entered by holding down the Shift key while pressing the desired key.
- Indents and tabs are created by pressing the Tab key.
- The Enter/Return key is used to move to the next line. (Word processing software will automatically wrap text to the next line, unlike the typewriter, which requires you to press the Return key at the end of each line.)

The similarities between using a word processing application and a typewriter basically stop with this list, because word processing provides many functions and features that go beyond the capability of a typewriter. The next few sections present some of those functions, such as being able to edit and format existing documents and to insert page numbers, dates, charts, graphs, and illustrations. Once the basics are mastered, you can add new and exciting things. Yet, even these basic functions make the word processor an excellent tool for students to use to expand their own "information processing" capabilities.

Editing

One of the most important functions of a word processing application is the ability to edit and change what has been entered. The editing process involves five basic

Power Tip

Digital Editing

Some word processing software applications have revision tools that highlight changes that are made to original documents. These tools mark each change that is made in the following ways.

Changing color of the text

~~Striking through the text~~

| Marking the margin of the line with a change.

- If you delete text, the revision tool changes the color, strikes through the text to be deleted, and places a marker in the margin.
- If you add text, the new information is displayed in a different color from the original text and a marker is placed in the margin.
- If you make changes such as adding or deleting spaces or lines, the change does not show, but a marker is placed in the margin.
- If students are working in teams of three or four, each student signs in as a reviewer and is assigned a different color automatically by the word processing application. Moving the cursor over an edit displays the name of the individual suggesting the edit. (*Note:* This identification feature is only available if the students have entered their name or initials into the User Information section of the Options dialog. To do this, select Options from the Tools menu and click on the User Information tab. You may not be able to use this option in a lab or classroom where there are limited computers).

functions that begin by either highlighting the text to be edited or inserting the cursor where changes are needed:

- DELETE a word, sentence, or paragraph
- REWRITE a word, sentence, or paragraph
- ADD a word, sentence, or paragraph
- MOVE a word, sentence, or paragraph to a new position in the document
- COPY a word, sentence, or paragraph to PASTE in a new position in the document

Formatting

Word processed documents are composed of various components that can be formatted in a variety of ways. The following section provides a description for formatting the entire document, fonts, paragraphs, and tabs.

Document

The primary function of document formatting is setting the page margins. Margin width is determined for the top, bottom, left, and right sides of the document. When

FIGURE 5-3 Page Layout

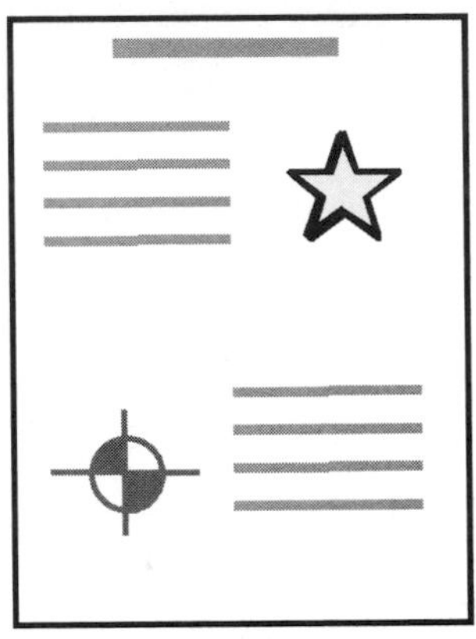

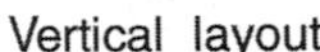

Vertical layout

Horizontal layout

determining the width of your margins, consider which page layout—portrait (vertical) or landscape (horizontal) format—to use (Figure 5-3).

Fonts

There are three basic ways to change the appearance of text in your document: Font, Size, and Style. Font refers to the type of letters used to create the text. Most word processing software comes with a variety of fonts that range from very simple, to ornate, to those that resemble handwriting. You can change the size of selected fonts from a size that is so small it is hard to read to sizes big enough to fill a poster. Font sizes are measured in "points," with 12 points being the most commonly used size for student work. The last basic way to change text is with the style function. Although there are a variety of styles to choose from, the three that are used most frequently are **Bold**, *Italic*, and <u>Underline</u>. These three functions, Font, Size, and Style, are typically found under the Format menu or as icons on the menu bar. The text must be selected/highlighted before selecting the desired formatting style. A sample of the various font formats is presented in Figure 5-4.

Paragraphs

The paragraphs within a document are formatted in a variety of ways; however, the two most frequently used functions are line spacing and alignment. The paragraph formatting for reports and research papers typically uses double-spaced lines that are left aligned. Details of these features are described below.

Line spacing. Three types of line spacing typically are found in most word processing applications: single (1), one and one half (1.5), and double (2) spacing. Many applications also allow the user to customize the amount of space by specifying the distance between the lines. Sample line spacing can be seen in Figure 5-5.

FIGURE 5-4 Text Variations

Type	Times New Roman	Arial	Zapf Chancery	Benguiat Gothic
Point Size	12	16	24	36
Style	Plain	Bold	Italics	Outline
Example	Text	**Text**	*Text*	Text

FIGURE 5-5 Line Spacing

Single Spacing

This is one of three sample paragraphs that are included to illustrate the difference among single, one and one half, and double line spacing. This paragraph is formatted with single spacing. Notice that the lines are spaced quite close together.

One and one-half (1.5) Spacing

This is one of three sample paragraphs that are included to illustrate the difference among single, one and one half, and double line spacing. This paragraph is formatted with one and one half spacing. Notice that the lines are not spaced quite as close together as the paragraph above.

Double Spacing

This is one of three sample paragraphs that are included to illustrate the difference among single, one and one half, and double line spacing. This paragraph is formatted with double spacing. Notice that these lines are spaced far enough apart that an additional line of information could be added between each line.

Alignment. There are four ways to align paragraphs within a document: left, right, center, and justified. Careful use of these different types of alignment can create interesting special effects in a document. Examples of the four types of alignment are presented in Figure 5-6.

Tabs

Tabs are useful for more than just indenting the typical half inch at the beginning of each paragraph. They are also used to create organized lists of material. Tabs, like paragraphs,

FIGURE 5-6 Alignment

Left Alignment

The content in this paragraph is left aligned. It is one of four sample paragraphs provided to illustrate the differences among left, center, right, and justified alignment. Notice how the left side of the paragraph is aligned together.

Right Alignment

The content in this paragraph is right aligned. It is one of four sample paragraphs provided as an illustration of the differences among left, center, right, and justified alignment. Notice how the right side of the paragraph is evenly aligned.

Center Alignment

The content in this paragraph is center aligned. It is one of four sample paragraphs provided to illustrate the differences among left, center, right, and justified alignment. Notice that neither the left nor right margins are evenly aligned.

Justified Alignment

The content in this paragraph has justified alignment. It is one of four sample paragraphs provided as an illustration of the differences among left, center, right, and justified alignment. In this paragraph both the left and right margins are evenly aligned.

FIGURE 5-7 Tabs

Nouns	Verbs	Adjectives
chair	sit	old
car	run	fast
baby	cry	little

are aligned to the left, right, or center. Tab formatting dialogue boxes are accessed in two ways: select Tabs from the Format menu or double click on a tab marker found on the ruler. These menus allow you to set the desired alignment and position of the tabs. Tabs can also be repositioned by using the mouse to "drag" them to a new position on the ruler. Figure 5-7 shows a list that has been formatted with tabs. Notice that the Nouns are left aligned, the Verbs are center aligned, and the Adjectives are right aligned.

When you are creating a list of numbered or bulleted items, such as test questions or a list of common elements, the list looks much better and is easier to read if the

FIGURE 5-8 Hanging Indents

With Hanging Indent

1. This is item number one, which is a sentence written long enough to wrap around to the second line to demonstrate the use of a hanging indent.
2. This is item number one, which is a sentence written long enough to wrap around to the second line to demonstrate the use of a hanging indent.
3. This is item number one, which is a sentence written long enough to wrap around to the second line to demonstrate the use of a hanging indent.
4. This is item number one, which is a sentence written long enough to wrap around to the second line to demonstrate the use of a hanging indent.

Without Hanging Indent

1\. This is item number one, which is a sentence written long enough to wrap around to
the second line to demonstrate the use of a hanging indent.
2\. This is item number one, which is a sentence written long enough to wrap around to
the second line to demonstrate the use of a hanging indent.
3\. This is item number one, which is a sentence written long enough to wrap around to
the second line to demonstrate the use of a hanging indent.
4\. This is item number one, which is a sentence written long enough to wrap around to
the second line to demonstrate the use of a hanging indent.

numbers or bullets are separated from the text. The key to creating this type of list is Hanging Indents. Figure 5-8 shows the difference between a list that has a hanging indent and one without a hanging indent. Word processing software will automatically create hanging indents by using the bullet or number icons.

Inserting

Most word processing applications provide a means for adding or inserting a variety of items such as page breaks, headers and footers, and graphics.

Page Breaks

When you are creating a word-processed document that is longer than one page, the application automatically adds a page break and continues adding the information on the new page. However, there are times that the text would be more meaningful, or the appearance more appealing, if the page break occurred earlier than what is set by the predefined margin. The preset margins can be overridden and a page break inserted at any desired location. To insert a page break, position the cursor at the place where you would like a new page to start, then select the appropriate page break command from the menu. If you insert the page break in the middle of a line or word, the page line or word will appear on two different pages.

FIGURE 5-9 Headers and Footers

Header

Final Report

The information that was collected verified Hypothesis I. The plants that were in the sun were much taller and greener than the plants that were in the shade or those that were kept in a dark location.

25
20
15
10
5
0
Plant Height
Sun
Shade
Dark

As can be seen in the chart, the plants in the sun grew 7 inches taller than those in the shade, and 15 inches taller than those kept in the dark.

Page 7

Footer

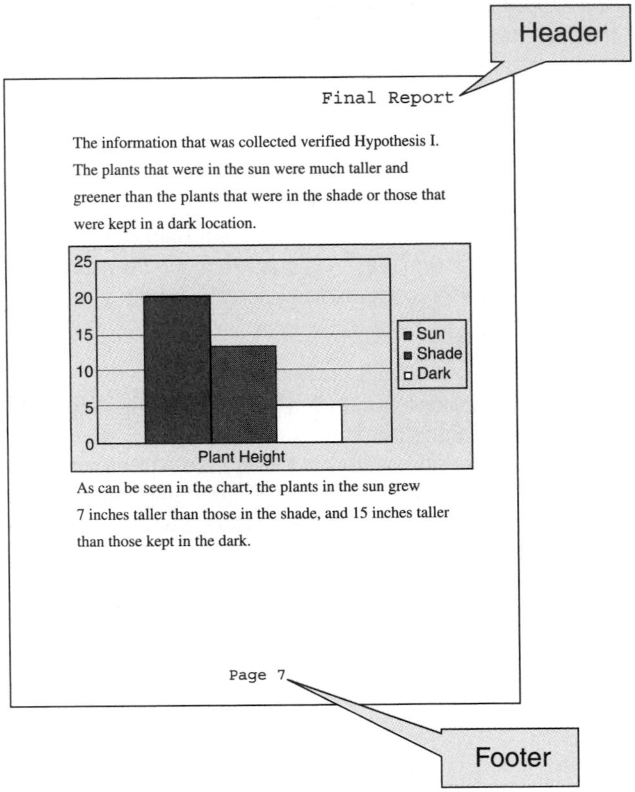

Headers and Footers

A header is at the top of the paper above the text, and, as you can guess, the footer is at the bottom of the paper (Figure 5-9). Headers and footers normally contain page numbers and the title and/or author of the paper. When you insert a header or footer, it automatically appears on every page of your document. Obviously, the page number changes with each page, but the chapter information stays the same for each chapter. This information also can be placed at the bottom of the page in a footer. To create a header or footer, select the Header and Footer command from the menu. The document will automatically shift to show the cursor inserted at the top of the page for the header or at the bottom of the page for a footer. At this point you can select the alignment. If the document is to be printed on one side of the paper only, a header is often placed at the right side of the margin.

Footers, on the other hand, are often centered at the bottom of the page. Once the alignment is selected, the information can be entered. If you want to include page numbers, select the Insert Page Number command from the menu. You can also add text to the header so that your page number reads Chapter 5-1, in which 1 is the page number. To add text, select the header, add your text, and then use the command to insert the page number. You may want to adjust the size of the information in the header or footer, because it is normally set at a default size of 12 points. The date and time can also be inserted, if desired. Most word processing applications provide a way to omit the header or footer from the first page (i.e., title page) of your document.

Inserting Pictures/Graphics

Inserting pictures or graphics is one of the most exciting features of word processing because it enhances students' ability to be creative and allows for the personalization of student work. There are two primary ways to insert graphics into a document. The first involves inserting graphics from clipart collections that come with the software, are found on the Internet, or are available on commercially prepared CD-ROMs. To do this, go to the menu item for inserting a picture, then locate and select the desired file to be inserted into your document. After inserting, you may need to format features of the object or picture, for example, text wrapping, position, and size.

The second way to insert a graphic is to copy and paste it directly into your word processing document. The object can be, for example, a picture created with a draw program, a spreadsheet chart, a database report, or a concept map. Begin by selecting the graphic to be placed in the word processing document by clicking on it with the mouse ("handles" appear at the corners) or selecting the area with a selection tool. Select Copy from the Edit menu. Then, move your cursor to the position where you want to insert the picture and click the mouse. Next, select Paste from the Edit menu. Chapter 8 provides guidance on choosing an appropriate format for the graphic. As mentioned, you may need to reformat the image once it is placed into the document, based on the desired effect of the graphic in the final product. These functions are performed from the Format menu.

Tools

Word processing applications provide students with tools to help them create their documents. In most applications there are spelling, grammar, and thesaurus tools that are easily activated or turned off if you want your students to work independently. Activating the spelling tool checks spelling in the entire document or in selected sections of text. When misspelled or unrecognized words (e.g., proper names) are identified, the student is presented with the word in question and a list of suggested word replacements. For example, as seen in Figure 5-10, if a student used the Spell Check function to check spelling in the following sentence: *The theem of the story involved courage and standing up for what you believe*, the word "theem" would be selected and several word choices given. The students are required to assess the word in question and do one of following: replace the word with one of the suggested words, ignore or skip the word, or add it to a customized dictionary if it is a frequently used word, such as the student's name. The Grammar tool is often included with the Spell Check tool. This tool offers suggestions regarding possible grammar errors, for example, punctuation, passive sentences, subject–verb agreement, possessives and plurals, and misused words.

FIGURE 5-10 Spell Check

Misspelled word:	**theem**
Word choices:	them
	theme
	thee
	teem
	thyme

FIGURE 5-11 Thesaurus

Dynamic	electrifying, thrilling, exciting, inspiring, active, alive, energetic, spirited, vibrant, vigorous, compelling, forceful, hardy, robust

The thesaurus works similarly to a paper-based version in that it is used when students wish to replace a word with one that has a similar meaning. To do this, students use the mouse to select a word they would like to replace with a synonym. The thesaurus dialogue box provides a list of synonyms associated with the selected word. For example, if a student had already used the term "dynamic" in a short story, yet needed to express that idea, the thesaurus provides the options seen in Figure 5-11.

WORD PROCESSING IN THE CLASSROOM

As seen in the previous section, word processing software is used to "process" information that has been entered into the computer. For example, word processing is used to prepare reports, letters, magazine and newspaper articles, legal documents, medical records, and anything else that contains text. Word processing is easy to learn and use, and it allows students to refine and personalize their work, promotes equity in final products, and better prepares students for the workforce. Because of these and other reasons, the National Education Technology Standards for Students suggests that students in all grades (K–12) use word processing at developmentally appropriate levels (NETS, 2000). The following section briefly describes how to introduce word processing to new users and discusses educational benefits when used by students.

Introducing Word Processing to Students

When you first introduce students to word processing, it is best to begin with just the essential basics. For example, when students understand how to do the following seven tasks, they can begin to create their work with the computer.

1. Press letter keys on the keyboard to enter words.
2. Press the Delete or Backspace key to "erase" entered information.

3. Hold down the Shift key to get a capital letter or the characters above the number and punctuation keys.
4. Use the Space Bar to add spaces between words.
5. Use the Tab key to indent a line or to align columns.
6. Position and click the mouse to insert the *cursor* and add new information.
7. Drag or double-click the mouse over text to *highlight* it so it can be changed or deleted.

Of course, many more sophisticated things can be done with word processing, but these seven steps are a good starting place. New tasks are added as the students' computer skills increase.

Educational Benefits

Word processing is the most commonly used software application in the classroom (Becker, 2000). Possible reasons for this level of use are presented below when discussing five educational benefits of students using it as a learning tool: ease of use, refinement of work, creativity and personalization of work, equity in final products, and building work place skills.

Ease of Use

The opening scenario demonstrated that word processing provides students with an easier way to complete their written assignments. Instead of using a pencil or pen, students "write" their papers using the keyboard to enter the text and numerical information. As the information is entered, it is simultaneously displayed on the computer monitor so students can continuously check or "monitor" their work. Initially, students need extra time to learn basic word processing functions. However, if they begin with simple tasks and are provided time for practice, the basics can be mastered even by those in primary grades.

Refinement of Work

When students use a word processor for their assignments, they are better able to actively engage in the learning process and higher levels of thinking. Thus students reinforce their learning and continue to build their knowledge and skills (McDaniel, McInerney, & Armstrong, 1994). As an example, word-processed rather than handwritten work better enables students to do the following:

- Use the computer's thesaurus to incorporate a broader range of descriptive terms
- Elaborate and add to what has been written
- Reorganize material
- Refine material by deleting less important information
- Spend more time on the task of the writing process rather than recopying to correct errors

THE TEACHER'S DIARY

Of all the computer applications, I use word processing the most in my classroom. The students use the computer for all of their writing activities—everything from creating lists to writing paragraphs and reports. Although many students have used word processing, they often lack basic keyboarding skills, which I teach during the first 6 weeks of school. The students catch on quickly and develop some word processing speed.

I guess what I really like about word processing is that I am able to create one word processing activity that can combine several curriculum areas and learning objectives. For example, the students created books on exercise for the culminating activity of a thematic unit. The book writing activity incorporated different types of exercises from the health curriculum, sequencing and identifying the parts of a book from the reading curriculum, identifying and using action verbs from the language arts curriculum, and creating a flow chart from the social studies curriculum.

Before the students began writing these books, they looked at examples of fiction and nonfiction books. They then created computer-generated Venn diagrams to compare and contrast the parts of a fiction and nonfiction book. Student groups then brainstormed to make a list of physical exercises. Each student picked one exercise and created a flow chart of the exercise steps. The students then exchanged flow charts and tried to do the exercises based solely on the flow chart, without input from the student who created it. It was a great learning experience for the students. They realized that their directions had to be very specific and that the steps to follow must be in sequential order.

At this point, the students were ready to begin writing their exercise books. As a class, they helped me develop the rubric that would be used to assess their exercise books. They decided that each book had to have an illustrated cover, a title page, a copyright page, a table of contents, and 10 exercise pages with illustrations.

It was interesting to watch them work independently. They decided to split up the tasks so that each student would be responsible for two exercise pages and an additional page. While working on their rough drafts, they always worked with a partner. One partner wrote and edited the directions as the other demonstrated the exercise. They also exchanged pages among themselves for an informal peer review.

By the time their rough drafts were completed, there was little that needed to be corrected. They took turns using the word processing program and usually worked in pairs. While one pair worked on the text, the other pair worked on the book cover or illustrations. Before the books were bound, they exchanged books among groups and tried out each other's exercises to make final edits and recheck for spelling and grammatical errors. The use of the word processing application made this task easy and quick.

Their books were fantastic! Each book was different. The students were proud of their accomplishments and their final products. These books were placed in the classroom library and were used quite often that year when the students could not go outside because of the weather conditions

Fran Clark
Third-Grade Teacher

Students writing drafts of their papers before going to the computer.

CHECK IT OUT 5-1

Title: Exercise Books [From "The Teacher's Diary"]

Grade: Elementary

Problem: *All of the exercises in the children's books required the exerciser to stand or lie on the floor. Your group needs to adapt three exercises so students who use a wheelchair for mobility can complete them.*

Activity: Download the exercise book and modify three lessons so students with mobility limitations can complete them.

Link to these resources and activities in the Check It Out module for this chapter of the Companion Website.

Creativity and Personalization of Work

As mentioned previously, most word processing applications have many fonts available for students to use when creating their work with the computer. Students can choose different fonts or change the appearance of some words by making them bold, italic, underlined, or outlined (Figure 5-12).

FIGURE 5-12 Sample Text Styles

Student Journal

September 3
Today we went to the botanical garden. I learned how to grow new plants by planting the leaf of another plant. I am going to try this when I go home.

Science Report

Investigation Title:	Effect of Heat on the Growth of Mold
Hypothesis:	Mold will grow faster in a warm environment.
Materials:	Four petri dishes
	One piece of bread cut into four equal parts
	One heat lamp
	One refrigerator
	One thermometer

Student Poem

Swimming is cool, refreshing and fun.
You slither and slink, then lie in the sun.

Color can be added if students have access to a color printer or if the teacher will assess the work from a computer. Students can personalize their work by including borders or drawings that they have created or imported from CD or online clip art collections from the Internet. Students also can add customized graphs and charts created in a spreadsheet. Another way to customize student work is to use the "columns" feature of word processing and add graphics to create products that resemble a newspaper or magazine article (Figure 5-13).

These functions help students personalize their work and demonstrate their creativity. The computer allows the students to immediately see how their work looks when displayed in a variety of fonts and colors. When they achieve the desired effect, they can save their work and print a copy. If student time at the computers is limited, students can print their word-processed material and draw their own illustrations. If students do not have access to a color printer, they can add illustrations and then color it after it is printed.

Equity in Final Products

When schoolwork is produced with a word processor, all students have an equal opportunity to create professional looking documents. An assignment completed using

FIGURE 5-13 Columns and Graphics

Monarch Butterflies:
The Metamorphosis

by
John Q. Student

Stages of Metamorphosis

There are four stages of metamorphosis for a monarch butterfly.

1. A monarch butterfly lays eggs.

2. A caterpillar hatches from the egg.

3. The caterpillar forms a chrysalis.

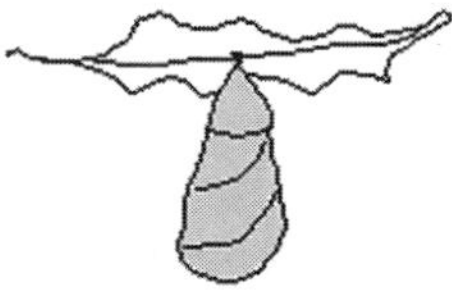

4. The monarch hatches from the chrysalis

Created by Mindy Morris

From the Butterfly's View Point

Hi! I am Shaina -the butterfly.
I am in search of a milkweed to lay my eggs on. We butterflies only lay our eggs on milkweed leaves because we can eat the leaves and get our nourishment. Great!! I spot a milkweed!! The eggs will hatch in a few days and out will pop my children. Oh, they won't look like me, they will be long, skinny, and furry. You guessed it, a caterpillar! Isn't nature amazing!! The caterpillar will eat the milkweed to grow and shed its skin four times. This is called molting. After a few weeks, it will spin a sticky thread around itself. The thread will harden around the caterpillar, like a hard shell. This is called a chrysalis. Inside the chrysalis, the caterpillar is changing into a butterfly. The chrysalis is very beautiful (if I say so myself!). About 7 days after the chrysalis stage, the skin of the chrysalis splits and out pops a monarch butterfly. Its wings are soft and mushy and it takes some short flights before it is strong enough to fly away. Think about me, Shaina butterfly, every time you see a monarch and all the stages that I went through to get here. Once again, isn't nature amazing!!!

a word processing program decreases student embarrassment over poor handwriting or biased teacher grading based on poor appearance. A word processing program allows students to concentrate more on what they write rather than what it looks like; therefore, all students can create documents that are legible and attractive. We have often heard teachers describe how they have discovered good writers in their class once they were able to read the students' work!

Another benefit is that teachers can more easily read student work, thus making the grading process more equitable. Because teachers no longer have to "guess" about what a student has written, the actual learning can be assessed. However, if students can choose to use the computer or write papers by hand, you must use caution when grading the two types of papers. Results of a study conducted by Roblyer (1997) indicated that teachers unknowingly tend to have higher standards for papers created using a word processing program than ones written by hand. One reason is that word-processed papers take up much less room on a page than a handwritten paper, thus appearing shorter. One way to address this concern is to consider giving word counts, such as a 500-word essay, rather than giving the number of required pages for assignments.

Workforce Tool

One of the primary reasons students attend school is to prepare them to become productive citizens in the workforce. Word processing is a common skill needed by many employees in numerous occupations. Some applications include entering medical histories of patients or names and addresses of customers at an auto repair shop, creating letters to people with overdue bills, writing newspaper and magazine articles, writing instruction manuals for audio equipment or new cars, or writing legal documents in an attorney's office. Therefore learning word processing in school will not only immediately benefit students with their schoolwork but also better prepare them for future careers.

DESIGNING AN INTEGRATED LESSON USING WORD PROCESSING

The basic components of the 10-step NTeQ Model for developing technology integration lessons were presented in Chapter 4 (Figure 5-14). This section describes the NTeQ components as they relate to creating lesson plans that have students use word processing as a learning tool.

FIGURE 5-14 NTeQ Lesson

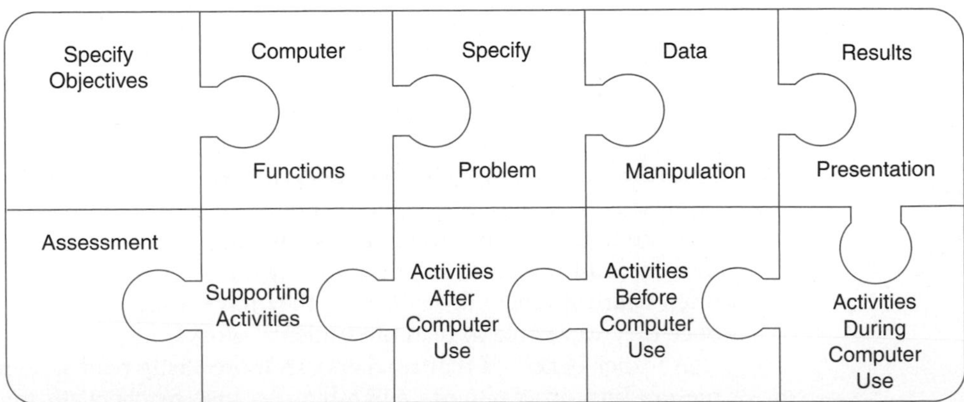

Specifying the Instructional Objective

Instructional objectives are what you want your students to know and do after they finish the lesson. These objectives are normally linked to the local curriculum guides and local, state, or national standards. Once you have identified the objective(s) for your lesson, you can then determine whether the use of word processing will help students with the learning process. Start by examining the functions of word processing and determining if they align with what the students are to learn. The following section describes this process.

Matching the Objective to Computer Functions

As seen in Figure 5-2, there are several basic functions that word processing software executes. The following list reiterates and expands on those functions:

- Enter text
- Edit text
- Format document, paragraphs, fonts, tabs
- Create tables
- Create outlines
- Sort lists of information—alphabetically or numerically
- Add descriptive headings
- Create columns
- Create bulleted or numbered lists
- Use thesaurus
- Use spell check
- Insert graphics

The objective(s) can be matched to various computer functions by comparing the learning tasks required by the objective with the functions of the computer, in this case, word processing. It is important to emphasize the "action" portion of the objective when aligning it with the computer. For example, if the objective is for students to compare and contrast the roles and responsibilities of a mayor and a governor, you would examine the "compare and contrast" part of the objective to see if it matches computer functions, rather than examining the content portion of the objective. The content, "roles and responsibilities of a mayor and a governor," could be any kind of content that would be compared and contrasted, for example, multiplication and division, French and Spanish pronouns, or Mars and Venus. Table 5-1 illustrates how word processing functions can be used to support achievement of the learning tasks. It also provides sample student activities to demonstrate the concept.

Specifying a Problem

When you have specified the lesson objectives and determined that the use of a word processor can be integrated effectively, the next step involves creating a

TABLE 5-1 Word Processing Functions, Learning Tasks, and Example Student Activities

Primary Word Processing Function(s)	Learning Task	Example
Edit, Cut, and Paste	Arrange	Arrange a scrambled list of procedures in sequential order
	Combine	Combine sections of a report that were written independently by different students
Edit—replace words	Alter, Change, Modify	Modify a paragraph by changing all the adjectives to different adjectives
Enter, Edit, Format	Assemble, Produce	Produce a report describing the findings of a study or experiment
	Collaborate, Cooperate, Contribute	Collaboratively write a poem
	Describe, Outline, Paraphrase List	Describe the *Declaration of Independence* Create a list of brainstormed ideas

problem for the students to solve. When possible, involve students in the NTeQ Problem-Solving Process, as presented in Chapter 4. As you guide the students through the problem identification process, keep the instructional objective in mind, because the stated outcome should be achieved as students proceed through the problem-solving process. The problem does not have to be elaborate, but it needs to be interesting enough to keep students engaged as they work toward reaching a solution. Table 5-2 contains objectives, associated curriculum standards, and sample problems that would involve the use of word processing to solve the problem. As seen, the information is presented at the elementary and middle/high school levels.

TABLE 5-2 Objectives, Curriculum Standards, and Related Problems to Solve

Elementary Level OBJECTIVE	STANDARD	PROBLEMS TO SOLVE
Students will classify items as liquid, solid, or gas.	NSES Grades K-4: *Standard B-1*	What do you have more of in your refrigerator—liquids or solids?
Students will compare and contrast New Year's celebrations between countries.	NCHS *Standard 1-B*	If you were a child living in Israel, how would your celebration of New Year's be different than a celebration in the United States?
Students will use specified criteria to evaluate written material.	NCTE *Standard 3*	Our class is going to create an online review site for children's books. You will each work on review panels that will summarize your individual book reviews into a final one to go on the Web.
Students will count money.	NCTM *Standard 4*	Your team must create a flow chart for giving change for purchases under $1.00.
Middle/High School Level OBJECTIVE	STANDARD	PROBLEM TO SOLVE
Students will describe the structure and movement of the earth's crust.	NSES Grades 5-8: *Standard D-3* Grades 9-12: *Standard D-1*	Your group will create a brochure that depicts how the Earth's continents might be configured in the year 7000.

Continued

TABLE 5-2 Continued

Students will list key events of the Civil Rights Movement.	NCHS Middle Grades: *Standard* 1-E High School: *Standard* 1-F	In honor of Martin Luther King Day, our class has been asked to create booklets for the library. Each booklet is to focus on three key events in the Civil Rights Movement. *Problem*: What are the important events of the Civil Rights Movement?
Students will conduct research on local events and synthesize it into a Letter to the Editor.	NCTE *Standard 7*	Our society has several issues that directly affect teenagers; yet their opinions are often not heard. Each team is to investigate an issue of your choice and share your opinions in a Letter to the Editor of our paper.
Students will multiply two three-digit numbers.	NCTM *Standard 1*	Fourth graders are having difficulty with multiplication. Which group can create the best "how to" sheet to help these students?

Manipulating Data

Once the problem is specified, you can then plan strategies for how students will manipulate the information. When using a word processing program, students can be easily engaged in the three types of generative strategies (see Chapter 3): integration, organization, and elaboration. For integration, students can manipulate the data by paraphrasing, writing questions, or generating examples. For example, students could integrate by the following activities:

- Writing a paragraph that summarizes one of William Shakespeare's sonnets
- Generating questions about a science experiment that is demonstrated

CHECK IT OUT 5-2

Title: Colorful Writing

Grade: Upper Elementary

Problem: *What makes something "Fun" to read? Why is writing sometimes described as being "colorful?" Are some authors more "colorful" writers than others are? Do you think your social studies textbook is as "colorful" as a story about Tom Sawyer?*

Activity: Download the "Colorful" Writing Sample, which has one paragraph from a social studies text and one from Tom Sawyer. Open it in word processing and use the highlight tool to color the primary parts of speech (e.g., nouns, verbs, adjectives, and adverbs) in both paragraphs. Use a different color for each part, but use the same colors for each sample. Write a paragraph that describes your thinking about the results.

Link to these resources and activities in the Check It Out module for this chapter of the Companion Website.

- Taking and importing digital pictures of objects that contain three-dimensional shapes into word processing, and then describing the shapes found in each object

Organizational strategies are accomplished by having students:

- Generate an outline of steps involved to multiply two 3-digit numbers
- Use the Highlight tool to color words by parts of speech
- Use "callout" autoshapes to identify key design elements used in Auguste Rodin's "The Thinker" sculpture

You can also have students process or manipulate the information they are to learn by using elaboration. Have students write a different ending to a story or historical event or generate new ideas as a way to manipulate the information. Student activities for elaboration could include writing a story that describes what life will be like in 10 years or discusses what could be done to improve the environmental protection initiatives. All of these strategies take the data or information that you want your students to learn and have them manipulate it in a meaningful way. Table 5-3 provides additional example activities by type of generative strategy.

Another consideration in planning your lesson is how students will present their results or solutions to the problems they are solving. Because this chapter focuses on word processing, the presentation of results will include some form of word-processed material. This presentation could be a traditional report including a description of the problem, hypothesis, procedures, results, and conclusion.

TABLE 5-3 Word Processing: Generative Strategies Examples

INTEGRATION *Paraphrase*	Rewrite the Preamble of the United States to a fifth-grade level.
Write questions	Write interview questions for a local seismologist who is investigating a recent earthquake.
Create examples	Create a list of words that could be used to describe life on an Iowa farm in the early 1800s.
ORGANIZATION *Outline*	Write a two-page outline of the Civil War.
Categorize	Create a table that categorizes animals as warm- or cold-blooded.
List key ideas	List the key ideas involved in buying three items with $5.00.
ELABORATION *New ending*	What would have happened if President Lincoln survived the shooting because he was shot in the leg?
New idea	You have been asked to create a new planet for our solar system. Please write a short description that includes the planet's name, where you would place it and why you chose that location, any life forms, and the climate.

The report could be enhanced by including spreadsheet charts (Chapter 6), database reports (Chapter 7), graphics (Chapter 8), or information from the Internet (Chapter 9). Students may also create a book or a display or write notes that are the basis for an oral presentation. Each of these methods requires the students to interpret their results and determine how to share the findings with others. In other words, students are engaged in synthesizing results that demonstrate their learning.

If students are to prepare a report as part of an NTeQ lesson or any lesson they must identify or locate specific information. If students are using library materials, they have a tendency to *copy* information from one or two sources. If they have access to the Internet or electronic encyclopedias, students often have a tendency to simply copy and paste a lot of information. Rather than requiring the students to prepare an informational report that basically consists of restating facts, we recommend that they prepare an *analysis* paper. The benefit of preparing an analysis paper is that students go beyond the facts by providing their interpretation of the information, rather than simply copying and pasting information into the document. Be sure to have the students help identify what should go in the analysis paper. The list of criteria can then be used to create the grading rubric for the assignment.

✓ CHECK IT OUT 5-3

Title: Seismologist Interview

Grade: High School

Problem: *Your neighborhood just experienced an earthquake that registered 5.5 on the Richter scale. Extensive damage occurred in several areas. The local newspaper wrote an article that blamed the Earthquake Research Center for not providing the community with enough advance notice of the disaster. Is the media justified in their accusations?*

Activity: Download the newspaper article that criticizes the Earthquake Research Center. Review the article to generate questions for interviewing the leading seismologist to determine if they could have done more to warn the community of the impending earthquake.

Link to these resources and activities in the Check It Out module for this chapter of the Companion Website.

MULTIDIMENSIONAL ACTIVITIES

When you plan multidimensional activities, you not only plan what the students will do but also how they will be grouped and what resources they will need. As you plan each activity, remember that students need to be actively engaged in processing the information (Jonassen, 1988). This information processing is enhanced when student groups work toward a common goal in a collaborative arrangement because students discuss decisions and possible solutions to problems, thus reinforcing the content (Jonassen, 1994).

When deciding which resources are needed for your activities, keep in mind that students can learn a great deal from finding their own resources. If students were to create the Civil Rights Movement booklets described in Table 5-2, they could brainstorm ideas about where to obtain the most up-to-date, accurate, and appropriate information. Their list would probably include the library, an Internet search, CD-ROM encyclopedias, and maybe some interviews. As they examine each of these resources, they actively process the information and determine if it will help solve the problem.

You begin planning the multidimensional activities by deciding what the students will do while using the word processor. For some lessons, you may want to create a sample student product to make sure your directions are clear, the planned resources

Student uses word processing to enter a report.

are suitable, and the time allotted is adequate. This sample can then be used as a model for the students. After planning what the students will do at the computer, you decide what they need to do before they go to the computer and after they finish their computer work. And, finally, you plan the supporting activities. Descriptions of how to plan these activities are given in the following.

Planning: Activities During Computer Use

As you plan the word-processing activities that students will do at the computer, realize that a lesson may involve more than one use of the computer. For example, consider another lesson from Table 5-2: "What do you have more of in your refrigerator—liquids or solids?" For this lesson, students could use the computer three times. During the first visit, students would use word processing to generate a description of each state of matter. The second visit would occur after students investigate what is in their refrigerators. At the computer the students would create a table with one column for solids and one for liquids, then enter items from their refrigerator into the appropriate column. If time permits, students could add clip art to their lists of examples. The final visit to the computer would be used to write a report describing the contents in relation to the type of matter. In planning the resources for this activity, students would need word processing software, student disks, clip art (if used), and a printer.

Another example of a lesson that would use word processing to assist students in achieving the instructional objective is the previously mentioned listing of key events of the Civil Rights Movement. The problem for this lesson is for students to determine three important events of the Civil Rights Movement. After these events are identified, groups of three students are to create memorial booklets for the library. Students could use word processing for several portions of this lesson. The first visit could involve creating a team-planning document that lists strategies for identifying the key events and how the booklets will be formatted. The next visit could be used to write an outline of the booklet content. Several computer sessions would then be used to write and edit the content drafts, remembering to rotate computer tasks among team members. Graphics could be added to the final copy, which can be printed in color if possible.

Planning: Activities Before Computer Use

After you have identified the types of word processing activities your students will do at the computer, you need to plan the activities that will prepare them for the computer work. This preparation can involve from one to several activities. These activities can include brainstorming sessions to clarify the problem they will be solving or to list information sources needed to reach the solution. Once the information sources are obtained, students can take handwritten notes on relevant information. These notes will be the basis for a draft outline of the final product, which is normally written by hand and then entered into the computer.

As mentioned, the lesson on states of matter involves three trips to the computer. The following example shows a sequential list of activities that would be completed before each trip to the computer:

- The first part of this lesson involves students working in pairs to create their own descriptions of solids, liquids, and gases. This activity requires students to do some research. The final descriptions might include citations from three references. Students could use their science textbook, the dictionary, and another resource book or the definitions provided by an adult. They could copy these definitions on a sheet of paper to use as a reference when writing a draft of their own description. They would then use this draft to create the final descriptions on the computer.
- The second activity is directly related to solving the problem "Does your refrigerator contain more solids or more liquids?" A class discussion will clarify why gases are not included. For their homework assignment, students should list the items in their refrigerator and classify them as liquid or solid.
- When students return to school with a classification list of the items in their refrigerators, student pairs can review each other's lists and discuss if some items need to be reclassified. Then they can combine their lists and sketch a draft table to be entered into the computer.
- The final activity before going to the computer will be for students to decide what kinds of illustrations should be added. For example, they could draw their own illustration of a glass of milk on the liquid page or use a clip art picture of a drink.

It may be helpful to create a matrix to plan the activities students need to complete before they go to the computer and what they do at the computer. Following is an example for the lesson on the Civil Rights Movement (Table 5-4). This lesson requires the students to visit the computer several times.

TABLE 5-4 Planning Activities Before Computer Use and During Computer Use: Civil Rights Movement Memorial Booklet*

BEFORE COMPUTER USE	DURING COMPUTER USE
• Brainstorm ideas: Plan of action for the project. Format for the booklet.	Create a proposed plan of action for determining how to identify the key events and how the booklets will be formatted.
• Review various resources containing information about the three key Civil • Rights Movement events selected by the team. • Take notes on items that may be included in the content. • Create a handwritten draft outline of the booklet content.	Enter outline of the booklet content.
• Write first draft of the booklet content by hand. • After draft is entered in the computer and printed, the team engages in "read and discuss" sessions to revise and edit the content until it meets the criteria established in the plan of action.	Enter and revise the content drafts.
• Generate list of graphics images that can be added to the final document. • Generate a list of search terms to be used to locate the needed graphics. • Create a storyboard to show placement of the graphics in the final booklet.	• Create final copy that has graphics added. • If possible, print with a color printer.

*Teams of three students working together.

Planning: Activities After Computer Use

It is a common classroom practice to finish lessons similar to the "States of Matter" and the "Civil Rights Movement" by simply having students turn in their completed work to the teacher. The teacher grades each assignment and gives it back to the stu-

FIGURE 5-15 Think Sheet for States of Matter

Answer the following questions in the space provided.

1. Which items in your refrigerator were the hardest to classify as either a liquid or a solid? Please explain why they were hard to classify.

2. Did you find any gases in your refrigerator? If your answer is no, please explain why.

3. What percentage of the items in your refrigerator were solid?

4. For your group, what was the average number of liquid items found in the refrigerator?

5. Do you think a child living in Kenya would have a similar amount of liquids and solids in his or her refrigerator? How could you find out?

dent or a group of students, who glance at the grade and teacher comments, then files the work in a portfolio, the desk, or the trash can.

An alternative to this approach is to engage the students in culminating activities after they have completed the computer assignments. As mentioned in Chapter 3, a Think Sheet is a critical component of this final activity. The Think Sheet questions should guide critical thinking about the information the students worked with or questions that have them predict what might happen if circumstances were different. Think Sheets also create links across disciplines. For example, the science lesson on states of matter could include math by having students calculate the percentage of foods that were liquid, or the average number of solid items for each food group. Or, you could move to social studies by having students find out if there would be any difference in the types of foods found in the refrigerator of a child in France or Kenya. Figure 5-15 provides a sample Think Sheet for the states of matter lesson. After students finish their computer work, a whole-class discussion can focus on the solutions the students found to the "problem" (Does your refrigerator contain more solids or more liquids?) that was introduced at the beginning of the lesson.

For the lesson on the Civil Rights Movement, student groups could be asked to explain why they chose the three key events selected for their booklets. The Think Sheet for this assignment could have students address the following items.

- What was the most startling fact or idea you learned?

  Why was this surprising?
- How does the Civil Rights Movement affect what is happening today?
- What still needs to be done?

Student journals are another way students can reflect on what has been learned. Before students write entries in their journals, you can facilitate a summary and review session with the whole class. During the session, you can clarify any misconceptions and also reemphasize the key objectives and why it is important for the students to have the identified knowledge and skills.

Assessment

When planning assessment strategies for lessons that integrate student use of word processing, the rubrics will probably have increased emphasis on the written components of each product. For example, criteria for this aspect of performance could include some of the following:

- Scope of description
- Consistency
- Clarity of expression
- Accuracy of information
- Sufficient detail
- Relevant information
- Logical organization

SUMMARY

Word processing is a commonly used application that is easily learned by students of all ages. It basically assists students with writing and thus can be integrated into almost any lesson. It also has functions that go beyond the basics of writing in that they support critical thinking activities. These functions include being able to easily cut, paste, move, and add to what has been written, thus fostering student ability to create documents that reflect their best work. Word processing also enables students to examine information in a table or list format to see patterns and groupings of concepts. Students can express their creativity by changing the fonts, sizes, and styles of text and adding graphics, diagrams, and color to further illustrate thoughts. When students work collaboratively to create a word-processed document, ideas can easily be intermingled, changed, and expanded. Plus, discrimination based on poor handwriting is eliminated because *all* students can produce a professional looking final product.

AT THE CLASSROOM'S DOORSTEP

Questions Teachers Ask

If my students use the spell check tool in word processing, will their ability to spell on their own be limited?

Let's imagine that your class has just completed a unit on Egypt. For one of your culminating activities, your students are required to write, with pen and paper, a paragraph describing an Egyptian pyramid. The completed papers are turned in to you for grading. You begin reading each paper and circle the misspelled words as they are encountered. You also write in the correct spelling above each word. For other assignments, you require the students to look up the misspelled words in the dictionary and turn in a list of correctly spelled words. Both of these methods require extra time on your part, but more importantly, the students receive delayed feedback. When students run a spell check on their papers, they receive immediate feedback on questionable words. In most cases, the spell checker will suggest more than one word, so students must still think about their error and select the correct spelling. They are also better able to see possible patterns of misspelling and how to correct them. Proofreading, however, is still necessary because spell checkers only identify misspelled words, not words out of context. For example, the spell check will not catch the misspelling of "pen" in the following example, "The author used a quill *pin* to write the letter." You might also want to turn off any options to correct/check spelling as the learner types. For example, some word processors will automatically correct a misspelling such as "teh" as it is typed. By turning off this option, the learner must then proofread the paper for *all* mistakes. Similarly, depending on your objectives, you may want to turn on or off an option that highlights misspelled words with an underscore or squiggly line.

I did not learn how to type until high school. How can my elementary students deal with using a keyboard?

Teachers can approach keyboarding by either providing some form of instruction or allowing students to develop their own approach. When students use their own approaches to enter information with a word processor, it takes about twice as long as when they write a paper by hand (Peacock, 1993; Wetzel, 1990). However, the students who wrote their papers using a word-processing program tended to write longer papers that were of slightly higher quality than those written in pencil (Peacock, 1993).

ISTE NETS FOR STUDENTS

When students use word processing software, two NETS for Students are specifically addressed: Standards 1 and 3. Basic word processing functions (e.g., enter, edit, format, insert) underlie almost every type of software; thus students reinforce the basic operations and concepts (Standard 1) of technology when it is used. The same is true when examining the effect of students using word processing as a means of achieving Standard 3, which recommends student use of technology productivity tools. Word processing is probably used more frequently than any other software because it is the means of transmitting the written word.

TECHNOLOGY INTEGRATION ACTIVITIES

To access the activities that connect the content of the text with the Companion Website and other technology, please go to the Activities module in Chapter 5 of the Companion Website at *http://www.prenhall.com/morrison.*

NTEQ LESSON PLAN

LESSON TITLE: Remembering the Civil Rights Movement

SUBJECT AREA: Social Studies

GRADE LEVEL: 6 to 8

Learning Objective

By the end of this lesson, the students will list and describe key events of the Civil Rights Movement.

Computer Functions

Word processing will be used to list and describe the key events of the Civil Rights Movement.

Specify Problem

In honor of Martin Luther King Day, our class has been asked to create memorial booklets for the library. Each booklet is to focus on three key events in the Civil Rights Movement. What three events of the Civil Rights Movement will your group choose as a focus for your booklet and why were they chosen?

Data Manipulation

Word processing will be used to edit and revise the information to be included in the final booklets.

Results Presentation

The final product will be the memorial booklets, which will be documents created using a word processing program and will include graphics.

Multidimensional Activities

Divide students into teams of three and have them follow the guidelines listed in the sections that follow.

Activities Before Computer Use

- Present the problem to students and, as a whole group, complete the first two sections of a KWL (what you Know, what you Want to learn, what you Learned) chart that lists what the students Know about the problem and what they Want to Learn.
- Divide students into teams of three and have them complete the remainder of the NTeQ problem-solving process (Chapter 4), which is embedded in the following activities.
- Create a draft plan of action that includes the following:
  - Where to obtain the best resources
  - How to choose three key events
  - How to format the booklets
- Create a list of search terms for the Internet and CD-ROM encyclopedia.
- Generate a list of questions for an e-mail interview.
- Collect resources from library and classroom.
- Review collected resources containing information about the Civil Rights Movement.
- Select three key events for the booklet.
- Take notes on items that may be included in the content.
- Create a draft copy of the outline to be written on the computer.
- As a team, write the first draft on paper. Then engage in "read and discuss" sessions with each printout to revise and edit the content.
- Determine which graphic images would best support the content and identify search terms for finding the images.

Activities During Computer Use

- Enter the draft plan of action.
- Conduct Internet and CD-ROM encyclopedia search.
- Use e-mail to correspond with either a Civil Rights expert or participant.
- Enter outline of the booklet content.
- Enter and revise the content drafts.
- Create final copy that contains the graphics.
- Print final copy on a color printer.

Activities After Computer Use

- Answer the following Think Sheet questions:
  - What was the most startling fact or idea you learned? Why was this surprising?
  - How does the Civil Rights Movement affect what is happening today?
  - What still needs to be done?
- The teacher facilitates a summary and review session with the whole class by discussing the Think Sheet responses. During the discussion, clarify any misconceptions that arise and reemphasize the key learning objectives and why it is important for the students to have an understanding of the Civil Rights Movement.

Supporting Activities

- Play "Can you Guess?" Create a set of note cards that lists the name of a Civil Rights Movement event or person on one side and descriptive details on the other side. Selected students randomly draw a card. Other students try to identify the person or event by asking questions that can only be answered with a yes or no reply. The student who correctly guesses the answer draws the next card.
- View videotapes of events related to the Civil Rights Movement.

Assessment

Create a rubric with items similar to the following for assessing the memorial booklets:

- The three events selected by the students represent key occurrences.
- Each event is presented with clarity.
- Appropriate graphics are included.
- The booklet is formatted in an appealing manner.
- The work is free of errors.

LESSON BYTES FOR WORD PROCESSING

The following list contains suggestions for word processing that can be created by elementary, middle, or high school students and a sample problem statement for each.

Rewrite . . .

Elementary Students

- Rewrite the *Ugly Duckling* story about a different animal that would have a similar story to tell.
- Some students find the descriptions of pictures in our history book hard to understand. Your team is to rewrite or simplify the picture descriptions for your assigned chapter.

Middle and High School Students

- The *United States Constitution* can be difficult for middle school students to understand. Your group is to use the online thesaurus to rewrite or simplify the *Bill of Rights: Amendments 1 to 10.*
- Rewrite a short version of *Robin Hood* so you are the hero and the story took place in your hometown.

Create "How-To" Descriptions . . .

Elementary Students

- Your new friend wants to come over to your home after going to the library, but doesn't know how to get there. You need to create a step-by-step guide that her mother can use to drive her from the library to your home.
- Which group can create the most concise list of steps needed to multiply two numbers?

Middle and High School Students

- The science lab just received new digital scales that people do not know how to operate. Your team is to create a step-by-step guide that explains how to use the scales.
- You are going to be given an "unknown" chemical to identify. List the steps you will follow to reach a solution.

Create a Description of . . .

Elementary Students

- The zoo is creating a new exhibit for its reptiles and would like to add student descriptions for each animal. Use your observation notes to write a one-paragraph description of your assigned reptile. Make sure to use the thesaurus to include a variety of descriptive words.
- Think about yesterday's history lesson and write a one-page description of a typical day for a Native American boy living in New Mexico.

Middle and High School Students

- Imagine that you are a tornado. Write a description of your life from beginning to end.
- Describe the components of an expertly written persuasive letter.

Generate Examples and Nonexamples for . . .

Elementary Students

- Create a table using a word processing program that provides an example and nonexample for basic shapes. For example, a cookie is an example of a circle, a sheet of paper is not an example of a circle because it is a rectangle.

- Create a plant classification table that has digital pictures and descriptions of local plants and downloaded photographs and descriptions of plants that could not be grown locally.

Middle and High School Students

- Use a table created using a word processing program to demonstrate examples and nonexamples of democratic governments.
- Create a document that displays examples of art created in the same year and describe how they are or are not typical pieces from that time period.

Generate Compare and Contrast Charts for . . .

Elementary Students

- Use tables created using a word processing program and clip art to show how animal cells and plant cells are similar and how they are different.
- Spanish is the primary language spoken in Spain and Mexico; demonstrate in a chart that there are other similarities and differences between the two countries.

Middle and High School Students

- If you had to choose the east or west coast of the United States as your future home, which would you choose and why? Write a three-page response that includes a chart demonstrating the comparisons.
- Shakespeare and Hemingway are well-known authors. Are there any key traits that are similar between the two? What are their greatest differences?

NTEQ PORTFOLIO ACTIVITIES: WORD PROCESSING

Please complete the following activities as part of the Word Processing section of your NTeQ Portfolio.

Reflections

The "Getting Started" portion of this chapter asked three questions that teachers might commonly ask. In this portion of your journal, a reflection question has been added to address how word processing could be used to resolve the problem. Please use information from this chapter to answer the questions.

1. Did you know that most word processing functions could be completed if you know how to do seven simple computer tasks?
   - *Reflection Question:* Describe how you could teach your students the seven basic word-processing functions.
2. Did you know that word processing could be used to engage students in higher-level thinking?
   - *Reflection Question:* List several examples of student activities that have students use word processing for higher-level learning.

3. Did you know that the individual needs of students are better met when their work is completed with a word processor?
   - *Reflection Question:* Teachers often have classes of students with a wide range of abilities and needs. List ways that student use of word processing can help to create equity in opportunities.

Lesson Ideas

Create a list of 10 word processing activities that would be meaningful for your students to create. You can use the Lesson Bytes from this chapter or your curriculum standards to help you generate ideas. Expand five of those word processing ideas by creating brief outlines, column and row titles when using a table, or a brief description of the final products.

Lesson Plan

The next step is to create a lesson plan that has students use word processing as a tool to enhance learning. The easiest way to do this is to select one of your favorite topics that is appropriate for integrating word processing and then complete an NTeQ Lesson Plan Template. After, or while you are developing the lesson plan, create sample word processing documents that are the same as the ones your students will create. By making the sample(s), you will be able to catch any areas of difficulty and make corrections. The sample product also can be shown to your students to give them an idea of what is expected.

REFERENCES

Becker, H. J. (2000). Internet use by teachers. The Jossey-Bass Reader on Technology and Learning. San Francisco: Jossey-Bass.

Jonassen, D. H. (1988). Integrating learning strategies into courseware to facilitate deeper processing. In D. H. Jonassen (Ed.), *Instructional Design for Microcomputer Courseware.* Hillsdale, NJ: Erlbaum.

Jonassen, D. H. (1994). Thinking technology: Toward a constructivist design model. *Educational Technology, 34*(4), 34–37.

McDaniel, E., McInerney, W., & Armstrong, P. (1994). Computers and school reform. *Educational Technology, Research and Development, 41*(1), 73–78.

NETS (2000). *National Educational Technology Standards for Students: Connecting curriculum and technology*. Eugene, OR: International Society For Technology in Education in cooperation with the U.S. Department of Education.

Peacock, G. (1993). Word-Processors and Collaborative Writing. In J. Beynon & H. Mackay (Eds.), *Computers into Classrooms: More Questions Than Answers* (pp. 92–97). Washington, DC: The Falmer Press.

Roblyer, M. D. (1997). Technology and the oops! effect: Finding a bias against word processing. *Learning and Leading with Technology, 24*(7), 14–16.

Wetzel, K. (1990). Keyboarding. In S. Franklin (Ed.), *The Best of the Writing Notebook* (pp. 46–48). Eugene, OR: The Writing Notebook.

KEY TOPICS

Examining the Spreadsheet
- Basic Components
- Entering Information
- Creating Calculations
- Creating Charts

Spreadsheets in the Classroom
- Using Spreadsheets for Learning

Designing an Integrated Lesson with a Spreadsheet
- Specifying the Instructional Objectives
- Matching the Objective to Computer Functions
- Specifying the Problem
- Data Manipulation
- Results Presentation

Multidimensional Activities
- Planning: Activities During Computer Use
- Planning: Activities Before Computer Use
- Planning: Activities After Computer Use
- Planning: Supporting Activities
- Assessment

Chapter 6

Spreadsheets

Much of the early success of both mainframe and personal computers is attributed to the ability of these machines to manipulate numbers quickly. Early personal computers such as the Apple II and the IBM PC allowed people to change numbers quickly and easily on a spreadsheet to portray a variety of scenarios. Thus it became easier to determine the effects of giving everyone in a company a 3% raise or having the company absorb a 5% increase in medical insurance cost. Over the past few years, educators have recognized that spreadsheets are powerful instructional tools with applications beyond the business environment. Spreadsheets can be used to solve time and distance problems or predict the weather based on wind data. In this chapter, we will explore the basic functions of spreadsheets and how and when students can enhance learning by using a spreadsheet to manipulate and analyze data.

GETTING STARTED

What Do I Know?

1. Can you identify three types of data your students could collect as part of a lesson?
2. How could your students manipulate the data to discover relationships or trends?
3. Can you identify three graphs or charts your students could make that would help them develop a better understanding of the content?

Classroom Snapshot

Susie teaches sixth-grade science in a school near Lake Superior and is struggling with the unit on friction. Although her students understand the basic concept, they are not able to apply the concept or principles to a real-world application. Last year, Susie obtained a 12-foot water test tank that has a pump causing the water to flow like a river so that students can test various boat designs. She also has purchased a ramp at a garage sale that was used for model car races. Students placed various types of flooring at the bottom of the ramp, ranging from vinyl flooring to low-to high-nap carpeting, and measured how far the cars would travel. The students' excitement about friction increased as they tested their cars and boats, but their scores on the statewide achievement testing in scientific reasoning did not increase.

This year, Susie's classroom received 15 laptop computers that caused her to rethink how she was teaching the unit on friction. Susie began by showing the students a series of pictures and videotapes of cars on the highway, race track, beach, gravel road, snow, and rain-soaked highway and even in the highway median. She asked the class about riding their bicycles and skateboards in each of these conditions and the benefits or hazards. Having piqued the students' interests, Susie began to ask why some surfaces are better than others. The discussion evolved into the design of an experiment. Groups of students would select a vehicle and collect data for three trials as they measured distance on several pieces of flooring placed at the bottom of the ramp. Each group would then calculate the mean for each piece of flooring and graph the results. Then Susie suggested that they run additional tests outside using a concrete walkway, blacktop, grass, and packed dirt. First, she had the students examine the characteristics of each surface. Second, she had them predict how far the vehicles would travel based on their existing data. Third, the students collected their data and graphed their results. Fourth, they interpreted their data and explained how friction affected the results. Fifth, they generated several ideas and scenarios on how they could use friction to control the speed of cars around their school to make it safer.

Susie is still waiting for the results of the state achievement test, but her own observations suggested the students were improving their scientific reasoning skills throughout the year.

EXAMINING THE SPREADSHEET

For those of us who use computers primarily for word processing or creating drawings, the spreadsheet may seem foreign. Spreadsheets are very powerful tools, and an examination of all the features is beyond the scope of this book. However, we will examine the basic features so that you can explore and use the functions of a spreadsheet. Let's begin by examining the basic components (See Figure 6-1).

Basic Components

A spreadsheet consists of a number of cells that form a grid (Figure 6-2). The letters across the top of the spreadsheet are labels for each column of cells. The numbers down the left side of the spreadsheet are labels for each row of cells. We can reference a cell with the column label and the row label (e.g., A5, B10, C1). Each cell holds

FIGURE 6-1 Examining Spreadsheets

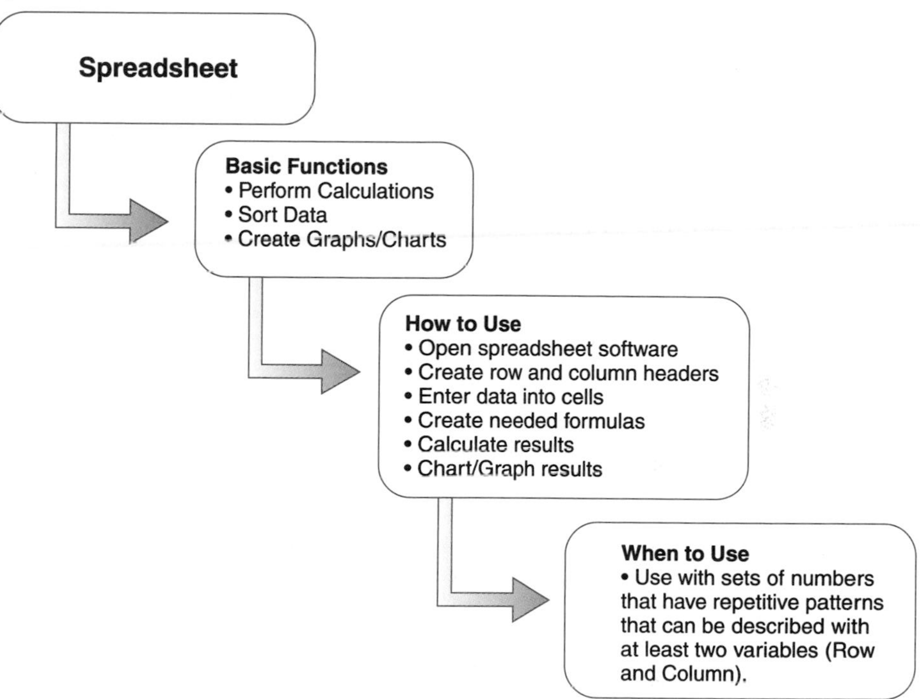

THE TEACHER'S DIARY

The spreadsheet was the one application that I did not use in the early years of my computer experience. I associated the spreadsheet with numbers, and math was not one of my favorite subjects in school. I did not use the spreadsheet application until I had to develop a lesson plan that incorporated a spreadsheet. I soon discovered that the spreadsheet could be a useful tool. I learned that it could be used for creating simulations, analyzing data, and exploring number concepts and mathematical relationships.

I decided that I would give the spreadsheet a try. For my first spreadsheet lesson, I adapted the AIMS M&Ms lesson to include the use of a spreadsheet. The students sorted and counted M&Ms by color. Instead of the students entering this data on a mimeograph sheet as we had done in the past, they entered it into a spreadsheet. I was able to teach them how to enter their data into a spreadsheet and how to calculate the total number of M&Ms in a bag by entering a simple addition formula. They even created a bar graph from this data. They loved this lesson because it was totally hands-on!

Continued

This experience gave me the confidence that I needed. I extended this lesson the next day by having the students analyze the percentage of each color in a bag. My students did not have the math skills to determine percentage, but this lack of skill did not stop us. I entered a formula in their spreadsheets that would determine the percentage of each color for them. The students made another bar graph showing the percentage of each color of M&Ms in their snack-size bags. They could visually analyze this numerical data. The students wondered if the percentages of each color would be similar in other sizes of packages of M&Ms and made some predictions.

I was able to extend this lesson again. I purchased various-size bags of M&Ms. The students sorted and counted these M&Ms by color. The students entered this data in another spreadsheet and repeated the process that was followed with the snack-size bags. I entered this new data into a master spreadsheet that included the percentages of color for each size of bag and created a bar graph. The students were easily able to analyze the percentages of each color in different-size packages. They were surprised to discover the percentages of color were not consistent across the bag size. This led to another question. Would this also be true of the other M&M candies such as M&M peanuts? This led to more spreadsheets, more graphs, more analyzing, and more candy. But they were learning and using those higher-order thinking skills!

They discovered that the percentages of colors were still not consistent across different-size bags. This finding led to the next question. Was this result due to something in the M&M manufacturing process? We discussed what might cause this to happen. I got on the Internet and found the Website for M&Ms. The students were able to take a virtual tour of the factory to see how these candies were made. We discussed what we saw and whether there was anything in the process that could explain why the percentages of colors were not consistent. With a little bit of questioning, they soon discovered that the bags were filled according to weight, not percentage of each color, and that the M&M colors are already mixed in huge containers before they are poured into the bags.

You can probably guess what the next question was. Would this also be true of other candies such as Skittles? We did not pursue this one in class, but we did come back to it later when we did a group science fair project. What started out as an hour lesson turned into a week's lesson! They entered data into a spreadsheet. They performed calculations. They created and interpreted graphs. They solved a problem. They learned a lot!

Fran Clark
Third-Grade Teacher

information such as numbers, dates, name, or titles (you can also add pictures to a spreadsheet, but not to a specific cell). When you click on a cell, it becomes active and is highlighted with a border. Cell A1 is the active cell in Figure 6-2. Note that the reference for the active cell is displayed in the upper left corner (e.g., A1 in Figure 6-2). The contents of the active cell are displayed in the data entry area above the cells.

FIGURE 6-2 Components of a Spreadsheet

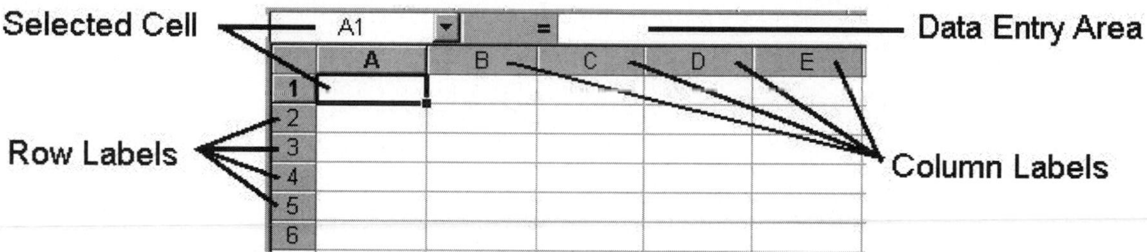

Entering Information

The following three steps illustrate how to enter data into a cell or edit existing data. Click in the cell where you want to place the new information or the cell in which you wish to enter data or edit. The cell becomes the active cell, and any contents of the cell are displayed in the data entry area. Type the information into the cell. The information is displayed in the entry bar. Use the delete key, highlight the text with the mouse, or use the left and right arrow keys to delete and navigate through the entry. Most spreadsheets will allow you to enter numbers, letters, or combinations of letters and numbers into the cells.

Once the information is entered, you must accept it. The simplest way to accept the information is to press the Return key. Or, you can also click the checkmark to the left of the entry bar. If you decide to leave the cell as is rather than accept the change, then click the X, or press Escape. After entering the data, you can format your spreadsheet to make it easier to read. The following section describes how to change the size of cells and how to format the text and numbers.

Changing Cell Width

When you create a new spreadsheet, the columns are all set to the same width. If a cell contains a name or multiple words, however, the column may be too narrow for all the characters. For example, the default column width in many spreadsheets is about 1 inch, which will display about 12 letters or numbers. You can change the width of an individual column or group of columns. To adjust the width of only one column, move the cursor over the dividing line in the column heading (Figure 6-3). The cursor will change to a vertical line with arrows on each side. Click and drag to resize the column. To change the width of several columns to the same size, move the cursor to the column heading of the first column, then click and drag across the other columns to select them. Select either cell or column width from the Format menu to display a dialog to change the columns' width. You can then enter the new column width for the selected columns (Figure 6-4). Row height is also changed by dragging the dividing line or with a menu item to adjust row height.

FIGURE 6-3 Changing the Width of a Single Column

C12 =

	A	B
1	Candy	Price/Ounce
2	Hershey Bar	$ 0.29
3	Hershey Bar Cookie & Mint	$ 0.29
4	Hershey Bar w/Almond	$ 0.31
5	Mamba	$ 0.17

FIGURE 6-4 Setting Column Width

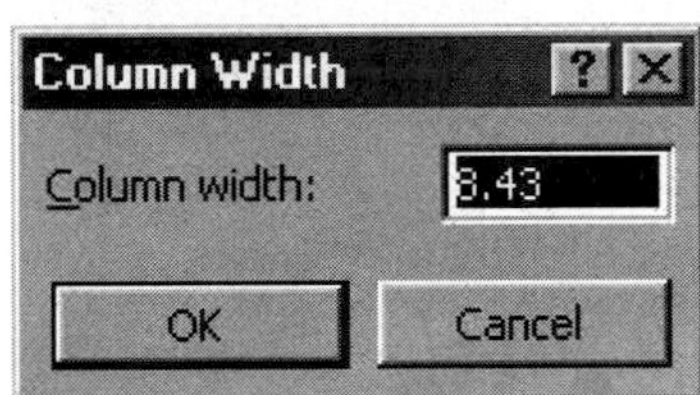

FIGURE 6-5 Candy Prices Spreadsheet

A7 =

	A	B	C	D
1	Candy	Price/Ounce	Weight (oz.)	Price
2	Hershey Bar	$ 0.29	1.55	0.45
3	Hershey Bar Cookie & Mint	$ 0.29	1.55	0.45
4	Hershey Bar w/Almond	$ 0.31	1.45	0.45
5	Mamba	$ 0.17	2.65	0.45

A cell filled with "########" or a question mark is a sign that you need to increase the column width to display all of the data in the cell. Some spreadsheets automatically adjust the column width to accommodate large numbers but display only a few of the characters of a word(s). Another option is to change the number format. For example, you might have a formula in the cell that produces a number with 10 decimal places. If you only need 1 or 2 decimal places, you can reduce the number of digits showing to fit the current width of the cell.

Changing Number Formats

Our candy prices spreadsheet (Figure 6-5) has three columns with numbers, one for the weight, one for the price, and one for the price per ounce. The numbers in the two columns look exactly the same, however. We need a way to distinguish the price

FIGURE 6-6 Formatted Numbers

	A	B
1	General	2.89391167445
2	Currency	$2.89
3	Percent	289.39%
4	Scientific	2.89e+0
5	Fixed	2.89

FIGURE 6-7 Shading a Cell

F10 =

	A	B	C	D	E	F
1	Cars	Monday	Tuesday	Wednesda	Thursday	Friday
2	Drivers with seatbelt on					
3	Passenger with seatbelt on					
4						
5	Trucks	Monday	Tuesday	Wednesda	Thursday	Friday
6	Drivers with seatbelt on					
7	Passenger with seatbelt on					

column from the weight column. Spreadsheets provide several ways to format numbers, dates, and time (Figure 6-6). To format the price column as a currency, we start by selecting cell D2 and dragging to cell D5. Select either the Cell item (Excel) or Number item (AppleWorks) from the Format menu to format the numbers. The price column in the spreadsheet will automatically format any number in the selected cells as currency (e.g., $1.45 or $0.45).

The first row illustrates how the number is displayed when General is selected. The remaining rows illustrate the other numerical formats for the same number when the precision is set to 2 (see Figure 6-6).

We also can change the formatting of a cell or cells using many of the features you have used in a word processor. For example, we can change the font, font size, color, and style (e.g., bold, italics, etc.) of individual cells or the whole document. We can also change the alignment of individual columns to left, center, or right. Finally, we can add borders and shading (Figure 6-7) to selected cells to set them off from other information.

Creating Calculations

The power of a spreadsheet is in the capability of manipulating data. For example, we can add, divide, subtract, and multiply numbers or columns. The spreadsheet also can determine the largest, smallest, range, sum, and average of a column or row. Spreadsheets include a number of functions that perform both common (e.g., average) and not so common (e.g., internal rate of return and standard deviation) functions. You can create your own formulas using the addition (+), subtraction (−), multiplication (*), and division (/) symbols.

Let's examine how to calculate the price per ounce in column B and the average weight of the items in our Candy Prices spreadsheet. We will start with the price per ounce for the first candy item by clicking in cell B2. The formula involves dividing the price of each item by the weight, or dividing column D (the price cell) by column C (the weight cell).

1. Start by entering an equal sign (=) to tell the spreadsheet that we are entering a calculation.
2. Enter the formula, which is D2/C2. That is, divide the contents of cell D2 by the contents of cell C2, which is the price, divided by the weight. The spreadsheet will display the results of our formula in the cell B2 (see Figure 6-5).
3. When the spreadsheet substitutes the values in the cells for the formula =D2/C2, the mathematical calculation is $0.45 divided by 1.55.

We could repeat the entry of this calculation for each row, but that would take time and allow for possible mistakes. A quicker and more accurate method is to use the Fill option of the spreadsheet to copy the correct formula into the remaining cells. We can select the cells from B2 to B5 in our Candy Prices spreadsheet, and then select Fill Down from the appropriate menu. The spreadsheet will automatically copy the calculation and change the reference cells (e.g., D2 and C2) for each row. You can also complete calculations for entries placed in a row by selecting Fill Right. Using the fill option can prevent simple typing errors that can create calculation errors.

Sometimes it is easier to use a function from the spreadsheet rather than entering a formula. For example, we could add all the weights together and divide by 4 to obtain the average weight of the candy. A simpler method is to use the *Average* function.

Spreadsheets include a Paste function item on the Edit menu, and Excel includes a Function item on the Insert menu. Selecting the appropriate item displays a dialog box (Figure 6-8) with a list of functions. The spreadsheet application will paste the selected function into the selected cell.

The Average function requires a set of values consisting of either a series of numbers (96, 97, 78, 63, etc.), a series of cells (B1, B2, B3, etc.), or a range of cells (B1 to C7). In most cases, you will want to enter a range of cells, because you are calculating the average of a column or row rather than listing each individual cell.

To calculate the average weight of our candy, we will enter a range of cells for values. We want to find the average of cells B2, B3, B4, and B5, so we can enter the range.

1. The range is entered by specifying the first cell and the last cell. Before entering the range, select the data inside the parentheses () and press Delete.
2. Type the range as B2:B5 (AppleWorks uses two periods to signify a range B2..B5).

FIGURE 6-8 Spreadsheet Functions

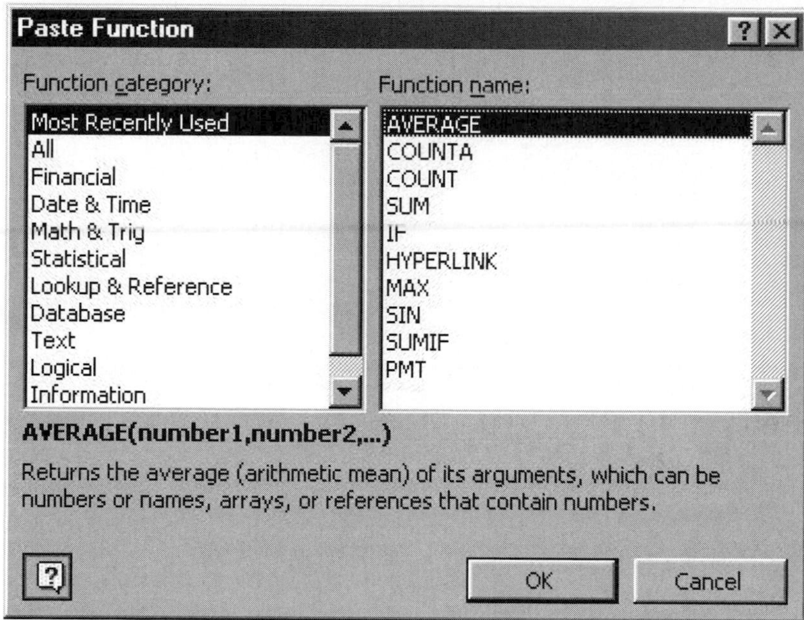

FIGURE 6-9 Average Function

B7 = =AVERAGE(B2:B5)

	A	B	C	D
1	Candy	Weight (oz.)	Price	Price/Ounce
2	Hershey Bar	1.55	0.45	0.290322581
3	Hershey Bar Cookie & Mint	1.55	0.45	
4	Hershey Bar w/Almond	1.45	0.45	
5	Mamba	2.65	0.45	
6				
7		1.8		

3. An alternative to typing the range is to click on the appropriate cells. Start by clicking the cursor between the two parentheses in the function and then click in cell B2 and drag to cell B5.
4. Click the checkmark or press Return to accept the function.
5. The average is displayed in cell B7 of our spreadsheet (Figure 6-9).

One last useful function is the summation function. You can highlight a series of numbers in a column or row and then click the summation button (Figure 6-10) to create a quick sum. Highlight the numbers you want to sum plus the cell where you

FIGURE 6-10 Summing a Column

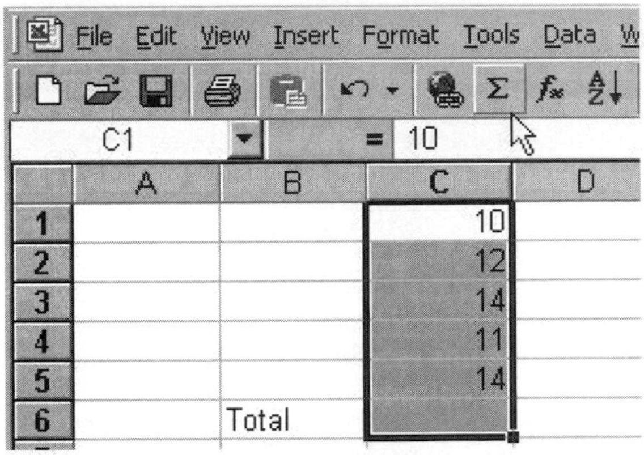

want to place the sum. Next, click the summation button. The sum will be placed in cell C6.

You can create and enter almost any formula or equation into a spreadsheet cell. For example, you can calculate the area of a rectangle where the two side measurements were entered into columns A and B (of Row1) with = A1 * B1. More complex formulas can be entered with parentheses to control the order of operations. Equations can use numbers (e.g., = 6*3.14) or references to cells (e.g., = B6*3.976) with numbers or formulas.

Creating Charts

Charts and graphs provide a visual means for representing numbers from data students enter into a spreadsheet. Students can create a bar chart illustrating the frequency count of their data to discover patterns and relationships. Similarly, a math student can graph a linear equation and observe the relationship between the variables as each changes. A teacher or student can create an interactive display between a graph and a spreadsheet, so the user can immediately observe the effects of changing variables. Let's examine how to create a chart using our candy prices spreadsheet.

The easiest way to create a chart is to have the data in contiguous columns or rows, although some spreadsheets will allow you to graph data that are not contiguous. It is usually easier to plan your spreadsheet so that the data are in adjacent rows or columns. If your cells or columns are not contiguous, you can cut and paste the data. First, you will need to insert a new row or column where you want to paste the data. Second, copy or cut the column or row you want to move. Third, paste the data in the new row or column you created. Fourth, check your formulas, because they may need to be updated. When pasting a column or rows with formulas, you will need to use Paste Special and select Value to display the numbers.

Let's examine how to create a graph of the price per ounce for each candy bar in Figure 6-11. First, select the rows with data in columns A and B. After selecting the cells, click the Chart button or select the Chart option from the appropriate menu to

FIGURE 6-11 Selecting Data to Chart

	A	B	C	D
1	Candy	Price/Ounce	Weight (oz.)	Price
2	Hershey Bar	$ 0.29	1.55	$ 0.45
3	Hershey Bar Cookie & Mint	$ 0.29	1.55	$ 0.45
4	Hershey Bar w/Almond	$ 0.31	1.45	$ 0.45
5	Mamba	$ 0.17	2.65	$ 0.45

FIGURE 6-12 Charting Options

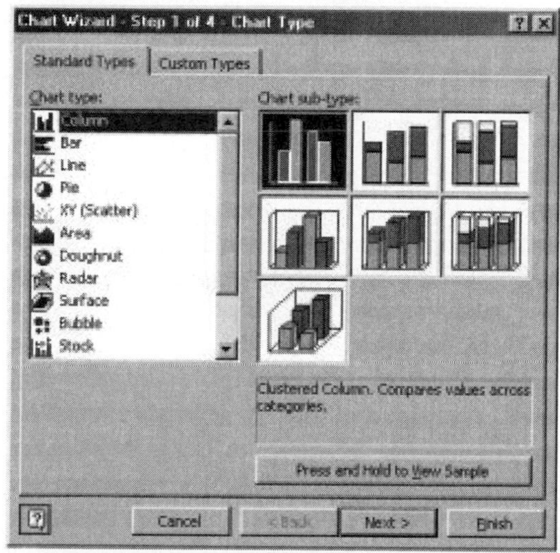

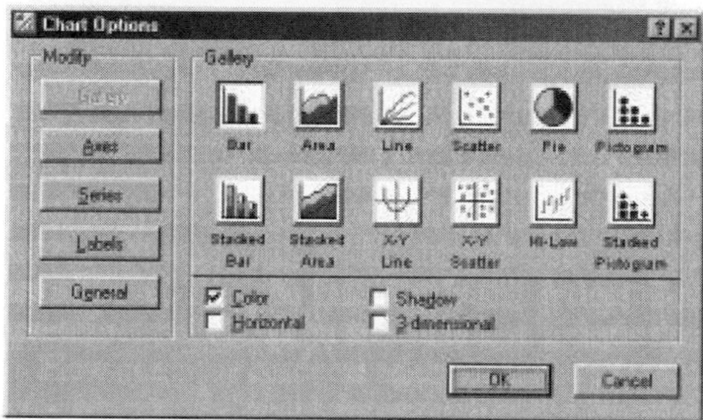

display the Chart Options dialog (Figure 6-12). There are a variety of charts available to graph the data. There are also options for creating color, horizontal bars (e.g., the bars on a bar graph go across rather than up), shadow, and three-dimensional charts. If you are printing to a noncolor printer, you may find that black and white charts using patterns such as diagonal lines produce the best results.

FIGURE 6-13 Labeling the Axes

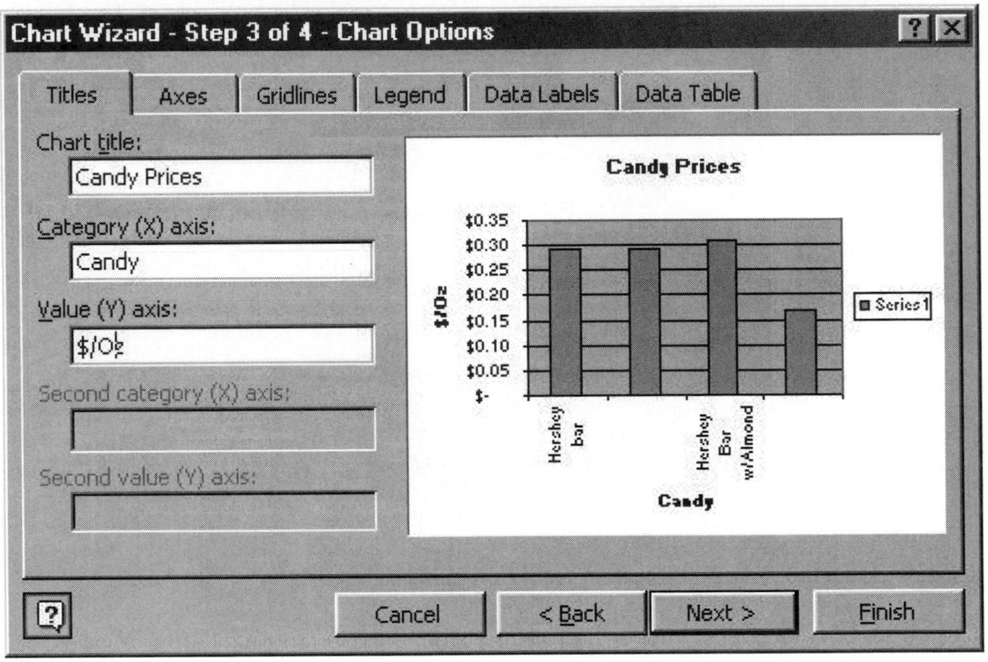

Next we need to label each of the axes (Figure 6-13). You can enter a label for the *x* and *y* axes, as well as a title for the chart. There are other options you can select to change the format of the graph. Once you have entered your options, click Finish or OK to create the graph.

If you are planning to use the chart in another document (e.g., word processing or drawing), you should drag it to the appropriate size while in the spreadsheet document. You can select various options to change the color or shading of the chart. You can also change the text by changing the font, style, color, or size. The chart can also be copied and pasted into a draw document. Once you have pasted the chart into a word processing document or other type of document, you typically can only change the overall size of the chart. It is important to save your original spreadsheet document so that you can make changes.

SPREADSHEETS IN THE CLASSROOM

Even for the expert user, spreadsheets can be an enigma. How many teachers have used one of the green-ruled worksheets we associate with accountants? Many teachers avoid spreadsheet applications on the premise that they have no need to work accounting problems. Yet, we have observed that teachers, professors, and information specialists use spreadsheets for a variety of tasks besides tracking finances. In the following section we will describe examples of how students can use spreadsheets as an instructional tool.

Using Spreadsheets for Learning

Spreadsheets are useful for more than accounting. They are a useful tool for creating simulations, analyzing data, and exploring number concepts and mathematical relationships. Spreadsheets are well suited for addressing standards and benchmarks on collecting and analyzing data, identifying relationships, and using mathematics in inquiry. The following paragraphs explain some of these applications of spreadsheets in the classroom.

Creating Simulations

Simulation software often conjures up images of expensive, complex software that is beyond the budget of many public schools. Teachers and students can create a simulation that demonstrates manipulation of one or more variables using a spreadsheet. These simulations are much simpler than a typical microworld that would include animation. However, they do allow the student to manipulate a variable and see the resulting numerical change or change in a graph.

Did you study the solar system and gravity in one of your science classes? A common illustration depicts a man on Earth weighing 160 pounds and the same man on our Earth's moon and other planets with the different weights. To a student who weighs only 60 pounds, the thought of weighing more than twice as much might be difficult to imagine. So, the instructional task simply involved memorizing on which planet a person weighed the most and on which he or she weighed the least, without developing an understanding of the effects of gravity. Using a spreadsheet, however, a teacher can create realistic examples and problems to help students understand and apply the concept of gravity.

For example, when students enter the classroom, they can weigh themselves and then enter their weights in a spreadsheet (Figure 6-14). Formulas in the spreadsheet then calculate the students' weight on the moon and other planets. Similarly, they can enter the weight of other objects such as a bag of sugar, a pair of boots, or a bicycle. Students can then use the graph function to determine where they or an object would weigh the most and the least in the solar system. In a math class, students could calculate how much a bag of sugar would cost on each planet based on a price per pound. Advanced students could use these weights to determine how much force a space shuttle would need to leave a planet's gravitational field. Using a spreadsheet, they can make adjustments in their supplies and personnel to achieve the desired load. Another use of spreadsheets is having students observe change over a period of time by graphing the results of mathematical models they have constructed of a real-world problem

It is helpful for students to work collaboratively on a spreadsheet.

CHECK IT OUT 6-1

Title: Outer Space Weight

Grade: Upper Elementary

Problem: *On which planet would you weigh the most; on which would you weigh the least?*

Activity: Use the spreadsheet to determine your weight and that of other objects on our moon and the other planets.

Companion Website

Link to these resources and activities in the Check It Out module for this chapter of the Companion Website.

(Walsh, 1996). Students can change different variables in the model to observe the effect on change. Similarly, students can use spreadsheets to model events such as population growth (Carter, 1999).

FIGURE 6-14 Using a Spreadsheet for a Gravitation Simulation

	A	B	C	D	E	F	G	H	I	J	K
1		Weight (Mass) in pounds									
2											
3	Object	Earth	Earth's Mo	Mercury	Venus	Mars	Jupiter	Saturn	Uranus	Neptune	Pluto
4	You	54	9.18	20.52	48.6	20.52	12.744	59.4	4806	61.02	3.78
5	Sugar	5	0.85	1.9	4.5	1.9	1.18	5.5	445	5.65	0.35
6	Bicycle	27	4.59	10.26	24.3	10.26	6.372	29.7	2403	30.51	1.89

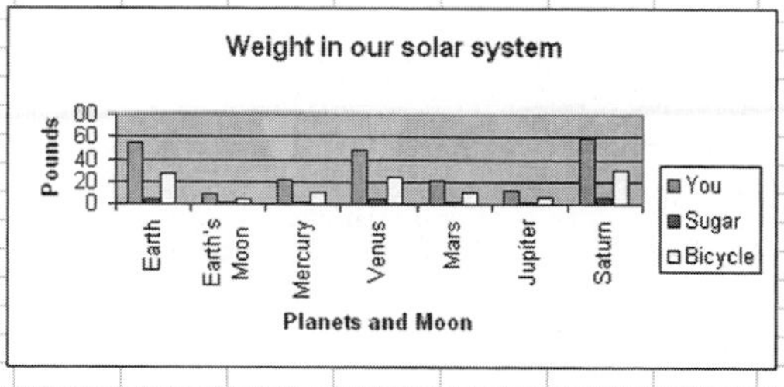

Weight in our solar system

Pounds

Earth, Earth's Moon, Mercury, Venus, Mars, Jupiter, Saturn

You, Sugar, Bicycle

Planets and Moon

Creating Discovery Spreadsheets

You can also create a spreadsheet simulation that allows students to manipulate variables and discover rules and laws. A chemistry teacher could design a spreadsheet to simulate the results of an experiment. For example, students could recreate the discovery of Charles' Law—a fixed quantity of gas at a constant pressure will increase linearly with temperature. Students enter various temperatures and the spreadsheet calculates the corresponding volume. After entering the data, the student can create a graph and then determine the relationship between temperature and volume (Figure 6-15). This type of spreadsheet also can be used to teach students how to make predictions based on the rules or laws they have discovered. For example, they can use atmospheric data to predict the weather (Niess, 1992) or predict the results of an election based on demographic and historical voting data (North Carolina State Department of Public Instruction, 1992). Murfin (1998) suggests that students collect data on seismic activity from various sites on the Internet and make predictions concerning possible earthquakes. The students then monitor the activity over several weeks to determine the accuracy of their predictions. These examples can be extended to the foreign language classroom by having the students enter the labels in the foreign language (North Carolina State Department of Public Instruction, 1999).

Exploring Math Concepts and Rules

Another example of spreadsheet use is to let students explore mathematical relationships. Either the student or teacher can create a spreadsheet to both calculate and plot the relationship between an unknown (x) and its coefficient and constants. As students change the values, the equation is solved for x, and the relationships among the coefficient, constants, and x are displayed in a graph that is automatically updated with each change (see Figure 6-16). Spreadsheets are useful

FIGURE 6-15 Using a Spreadsheet for Charles' Law Simulations

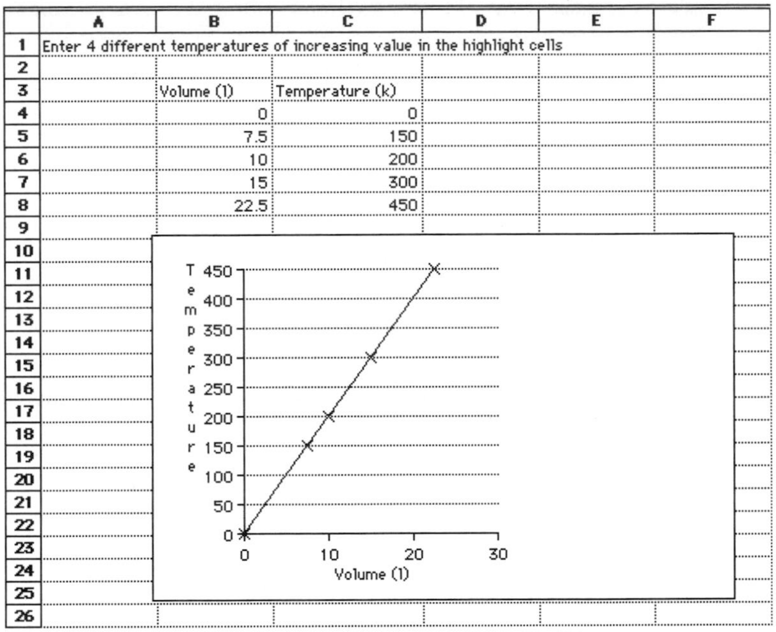

	A	B	C	D	E	F
1	Enter 4 different temperatures of increasing value in the highlight cells					
2						
3		Volume (1)	Temperature (k)			
4		0	0			
5		7.5	150			
6		10	200			
7		15	300			
8		22.5	450			
9						
10						
11						
12						
13						
14						
15						
16						
17						
18						
19						
20						
21						
22						
23						
24						
25						
26						

for teaching math concepts such as surface area and volume problems (Verderber, 1992) and polynomial problems (Timmons, 1991). Teachers can use spreadsheets to teach math concepts in classes such as economics (Adams & Kroch, 1989; Smith & Smith, 1988). Spreadsheets also can be used to illustrate graphically the solving of simple and complex equations (Niess, 1998). Another example is using a spreadsheet to explore probability problems such as the probability of two people in the room having the same birthday (Lesser, 1999) or to collect and analyze data on penny tossing (Reese & Monroe, 1997). We can use spreadsheets to track nutritional information, voting trends, population trends, and word or phrase usage. The use of spreadsheets is not limited to mathematics classes; they can be used in many disciplines in which students analyze data to identify trends and solve problems.

Solving Problems

Our last example requires students to use a spreadsheet to solve a specific problem. For example, the class has collected $47.83 for a party. They have decided that they want to serve candy at the party. The problem, then, is what type of candy can they purchase so that they get the most for their money? The class can list all the various types of candy they might purchase and enter these items in a spreadsheet (Figure 6-17). After completing their list, individuals check the weight and prices of the various items. The price and weight are then entered into the spreadsheet, and the price per ounce is calculated. Students can create a chart from the data to identify the most expensive and

FIGURE 6-16 Solving Linear Equations

Spreadsheet2 (v4.0) (SS)

B5 x

Solving Linear Equations in One Unknown
How does x change as its coefficient and the constants change?

	A	B	C	D	E	F	G	H	I	J
1	Change only the numbers in row 5.									
2	Use only positive numbers ≤ 200.									
3										
4										
5	10	x	+	35			=	200		
6	10	x	+	35	-	35	=	200	-	35
7	10	x					=	165		
8	10	x	/	10			=	165	/	10
9		x					=	16.5		

Changes in x

200
100
0
Coefficient Constant 1 Constant 2 x

100 Page 1

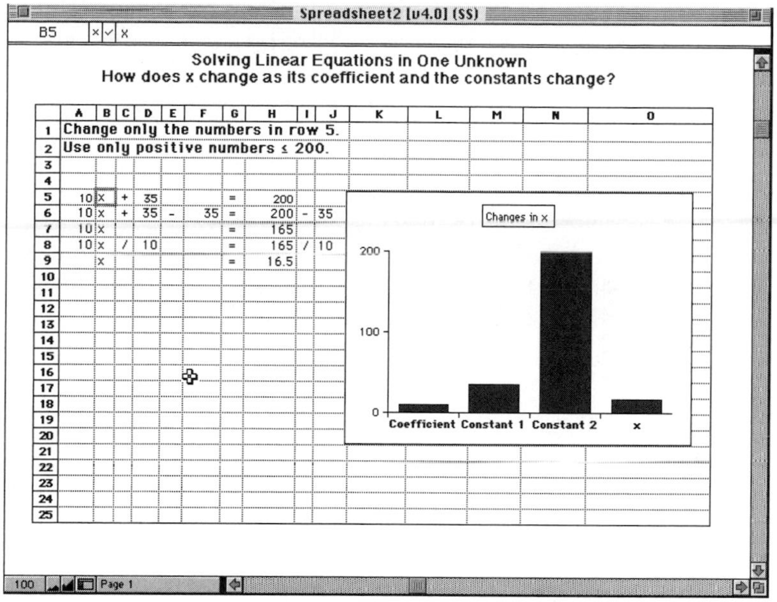

Adapted from a unit by Katherine Abraham. Used with permission.

FIGURE 6-17 Spreadsheets as Tools

A7 =

	A	B	C	D
1	Candy	Price/Ounce	Weight (oz.)	Price
2	Hershey Bar	$ 0.29	1.55	0.45
3	Hershey Bar Cookie & Mint	$ 0.29	1.55	0.45
4	Hershey Bar w/Almond	$ 0.31	1.45	0.45
5	Mamba	$ 0.17	2.65	0.45

least expensive candies. For advanced students, you might ask them to determine a mix of "good" and "average" tasting candy based on the price per ounce.

A more complex problem is one of planning a pizza party that requires the students to calculate the area of various cheese pizzas and then determine the price per square inch. Spreadsheets can play an important role in solving real-world problems such as studying the quality of river water (Mihich, 1996) or redistricting a school district. Students in a language arts class can track types of novels they have read and produce graphs to help them determine what genre they prefer. Students in a communications or social studies class can compare the column inches in newspapers or the minutes a television or radio station devoted to a story to study patterns of news coverage. Students can conduct a contextual analysis of speeches, political speeches, short stories, or books by analyzing the use of imagery, appeal to ethos, appeal to logos, appeal to

CHECK IT OUT 6-2

Title: Best Candy Price

Grade: Elementary

Problem: *Which candy gives you the most for your money?*

Activity: Use the spreadsheet to determine the price per ounce for various candies.

Link to these resources and activities in the Check It Out module for this chapter of the Companion Website.

pathos, or verb tense and other grammatical structures. Once the data are collected, they are entered into a spreadsheet and analyzed to identify differences and trends.

Spreadsheets are excellent tools for students to use for problem solving, inquiry, and discovery learning. In each of the previous examples students manipulated data to find an answer. They manipulated the data and constructed new charts and graphs or sorted the data to identify patterns. These opportunities to explore numerical relationships provide a laboratory for problem solving and inquiry. Learners make discoveries through active learning as opposed to passively reading a text or listening to a lecture. For example, rather than reading that they will weigh less on the moon and Mars and more on Jupiter, students can enter their weight and graph it (see Figure 6-14). Then they can calculate the weight of common objects such as a bag of sugar or a carton of cola. Students can try various options and obtain an answer as quickly as they can press the Return key. This immediacy of response provides more motivation to explore different possibilities. Spreadsheets can remove the burden of completing tedious calculations by hand or calculator and allow the learner to focus on analyzing the patterns and results. This use of the spreadsheet as a tool not only enhances learning but also improves the likelihood of the learner transferring the use of the tool to other situations (Salomon, 1993).

DESIGNING AN INTEGRATED LESSON WITH A SPREADSHEET

Now that you have a basic understanding of how to use a spreadsheet, let's examine how to integrate this tool into your lesson. The next section of this chapter describes how to develop an integrated spreadsheet lesson using the iNtegrating Technology for inQuiry (NTeQ) model.

Specifying the Instructional Objectives

The first step in integrating a spreadsheet activity into a lesson is to identify the lesson's objectives. You should list *all* of your objectives, not just those related to computer tasks. Objectives can be written as behavioral or cognitive, or a mix of the two forms. If you are modifying an existing unit, you may be able to use the objectives for the unit. You also can add or expand the objectives from the unit to create a better lesson plan. Your objectives can come from the textbook or from the standards or benchmarks your district is using.

Matching the Objective to Computer Functions

If there is a match between the objective(s) and the functions of a spreadsheet, you can plan to integrate the spreadsheet activity into the lesson. If there is not a match between the objective(s) and the spreadsheet's functions, you should consider another strategy rather than the spreadsheet. For example, we observed a teacher recently who had the class enter data about classical music composers, their compositions, and the style of music into three columns of a spreadsheet. She then wanted the class to sort the items by composer and then later by style of music. When one of the students attempted to sort the list, only one column was selected. As a result only that column was sorted; thus the links were lost with the composer. A database would have been a more appropriate tool for this activity. Think carefully to select the best tool for the task. This selection should reflect the tasks you want the students to perform and the cognitive skills you want them to master. Let's examine the relationship between the functions of a spreadsheet and instructional objectives.

We can categorize the functions of a spreadsheet into three broad categories: manipulation of numbers or data, creation of charts and graphs, and discrimination and interpretation. The first, manipulation of numbers, includes the capabilities to add, subtract, multiply, divide, sum, sort, convert, find the highest and lowest numbers, and calculate the average, to name a few. Spreadsheets can do a number of mathematical calculations ranging from simple addition to geometric calculations to financial calculations. The second grouping of functions is the creation of charts and graphs. Once students have entered their data, they can create a variety of charts and graphs to display the data visually. The third category is discrimination and interpretation, which includes inferring, discriminating, interpreting, and generalizing. Students can analyze the results of a sort, selection, calculation, or chart to make inferences, predictions, generalizations, or to interpret the data to make a decision.

There is a very close relationship between objectives and functions. Both are verbs (e.g., sort, add) and both are observable actions. For example, an objective might state that the learner will determine the average number of people in the five largest cities of Ohio. One of the functions of a spreadsheet (actually, a built-in function) is the capability of averaging a row or column of numbers. Thus there is a match between the objective and a spreadsheet function. Similarly, an objective in a nutrition unit might require students to interpret the results of a taste test using a bar chart.

Power Tip

Protecting Data

Students have a long history of changing files both by accident and as a challenge. Consider the time you might spend creating our sample candy prices spreadsheet by entering the names of 20 to 30 types of candy and creating the formulas to determine the price per ounce for each. Then, 5 minutes into the lesson, one of your students deletes the column of candy names and saves the file before you can leap to the aid of your spreadsheet. The only safe procedure is to keep several backup copies of your spreadsheet at home, in the principal's office, your safety deposit box, and under the sink; you can make it more difficult for the adventuresome student to ruin your file!

Let's examine how we can protect our candy prices spreadsheet (see Figure 6-17). We want the student to enter the price of the candy bar (column D). Thus we want to protect or lock all the data except for column D. The following illustrates the steps.

Protecting an Excel Spreadsheet

1. Select the cells to leave *unlocked* (e.g., D2 to D5).
2. Select the Cells item from the Format menu. Then, click the Protection tab.
3. Unselect the Locked option and click OK.
4. Select the Protect Sheet from the Tools menu.
5. Check all the items.
6. If students or others will be using the spreadsheet, you can enter a password to keep them from unprotecting your work.
7. To unprotect the cells, select Unprotect Sheet from the Tools menu.

Protecting an AppleWorks Spreadsheet

1. Select the cells you wish to lock.
2. Select Lock from the Options menu.
3. To unlock the cells, select the cells and then select Unlock from the Options menu.

Again, there is a match between the objective, interpret, and the charting function of a spreadsheet. Some objectives related to spreadsheet functions are listed in Table 6-1. Although this is not a complete list, it provides several examples related to manipulation of numbers (e.g., alter, convert, combine), charting and graphing (e.g., chart, graph), and discrimination and interpretation of numbers (assess, discriminate, differentiate, infer). (See Appendix A for a more complete listing of objectives and tool functions.)

Once you have specified the objectives for the lesson and found a match between your objectives and an appropriate computer tool, you are ready to design the lesson.

TABLE 6-1 Spreadsheet Functions, Learning Tasks, and Example Student Activities

Primary Spreadsheet Function(s)	Learning Task	Example
Perform Calculations	Add, Divide, Multiply, Subtract, Sum, Average	Enter a formula to calculate the temperature range on the hottest and coldest days of the year.
	Alter, Change, Vary	Determine the the effect on profit if the fixed price increases.
	Deduce, Infer, Generalize, Estimate, Predict, Formulate	How much will the force on a billboard increase if the wind increases from 12 mph to 20 mph.
Sort Data	Analyze	Determine which city had the greatest rainfall in June.
	Compare, Contrast, Differentiate, Discriminate, Relate, Assess	Compare the voting record of young voters in a rural and urban environment.
Chart/Graph	Interpret, Interpolate, Extend	Which region of the country the country has the most rain per year?
	Solve, Determine	Based on the per capita income for the surrounding counties, which would be the best for a mid-value car dealership?

Specifying the Problem

After you have specified your objective(s) and found a match with one or more computer functions, the next step in designing the lesson is to specify a problem for the students to solve or investigate. Individual units of instruction might have only one problem; for example, what agricultural products could we grow in this area if the effects of global warming were to raise our average temperature by 10° Fahrenheit? Other units might require the learner to solve several smaller problems that have a narrower focus. For example, you might pose the problem of identifying voting precincts in the city or county that students could use to accurately predict the presidential election. Or they could determine on which planet they would weigh the most and on which planet they would weigh the least. Once a problem statement is developed, identify alternative ways of stating the problem.

Problem statements should focus on issues students feel are relevant and worthy of solving (Table 6-2). The problem context should be anchored in a realistic setting that has meaning for the students and motivates them (Cognition and Technology Group at Vanderbilt, 1990). For example, a math unit or a psychology unit might focus on frequency distributions and measures of central tendency. One approach is to define a problem in the context of a scientist collecting data in a lab. A more realistic setting would cast the student as a researcher hired by the local grocery store to conduct a taste test of five new brands of crackers. Although both contexts allow for developing a data collection strategy, the grocery store context provides a realistic setting that students could use to collect data in their school.

Data Manipulation

Once you have identified the problem, you need to identify the data the students will use to solve the problem. Will they collect all or part of the data or use data you provide? If the students are collecting the data, you will need to plan for the collection process. For example, if they are doing an experiment, they will need equipment and materials. If the students are working on designing a new size of can for a soup company, they will need at least one appropriate-size can to calculate the needed volume, or you will need to provide the volume data. Similarly, if the students are searching for information on a CD or the Internet, you will need to develop guidelines to help their search. If you are providing the data, you will need to organize the data and prepare either handouts or files with data. Giving careful consideration to the data the students will use can help solve problems as the students work on the unit.

After the data and collection methods are identified, you need to plan the specific data manipulation. The alignment of spreadsheet functions with the learning objectives was completed in Step 2. Now, you need to describe specifically how the students are to manipulate the data. Do students need to multiply the area of the face by the height, find the best interest rate, or determine the rate of growth? Do students need to see the data displayed to help them understand the calculations? If yes, which chart(s) or graph(s) is best? It is often helpful to create a sample spreadsheet with data similar to what the students will use to ensure it works and to find shortcuts that may make the task easier. When using a spreadsheet to manipulate data, students can be engaged in the three types of generative strategies. Specific examples for integration, organization, and elaboration are provided in Table 6-3. These generative strategies are used to create the Think Sheet that helps the students analyze the data and understand the relationships and content.

TABLE 6-2 Objectives, Standards, and Related Problems to Solve

Elementary Level OBJECTIVE	STANDARD	PROBLEM TO SOLVE
Students will evaluate books by author and story type.	NCTE *Standard 3*	Do female authors write different types of books or longer books than male authors?
Students will explore the relation between sides of a rectangle and the area and perimeter.	NCTM *Standard 5*	You must create an advertisement for the paper that is 6 square inches. How many different-size rectangles can you create for the advertisement?
Students will draw upon data in historical maps.	NCHS *Standard 2F*	Find the shortest route from our school to our state capital building.
Students will compare and contrast the planets of our solar system.	NSES Grades K–4 *Standard D*	On which planet would your weight have the greatest difference from your current weight?
Middle/High School Level OBJECTIVE	STANDARD	PROBLEM TO SOLVE
Students will describe different language structures	NCTE *Standard 6*	Both President Kennedy and President Lincoln were noted for their persuasive speeches, but did they use similar approaches? Create a chart that compares and contrasts the language structure of a key speech given by each one.
Students will calculate interest rates.	NCTM *Standard 6*	Is it better to finance a loan for a short period of time at a higher interest rate or longer period of time at a lower interest rate? Is there a pattern that can be described?
Students will explain dew point.	NSES *Standard D-1*	Using recent weather data, determine what days are most likely to have dew, frost, or fog.
Students will explain the relationship between supply and demand.	NCHS *Standard VII* NCTM *Standard 6*	What would be the effect on the demand for gasoline if the price increased by 50¢ per gallon? What would be the effect on the price of gasoline if everyone decided to purchase an extra tank of gasoline per week?

TABLE 6-3 Spreadsheets: Generative Strategies: Examples

Strategy	Example
Integration	
Write questions	Create a list of five questions that you could answer with information from the Natural Disaster line graph.
Create examples	Use the data in our weather spreadsheet to show examples of global warming.
Organization	
List key ideas	Examine the bar graphs showing characteristics of our state's governors and list the most common features.
Categorize	Review the spreadsheet showing data from our recycling survey and group the people into three categories. List reasons for forming each group, then choose a descriptive name for the category.
Elaboration	
New information	Create a timeline for U.S. residents to transfer from using fossil fuels to using alternative forms of fuel for automobiles. Use data from the Current Supplies of Fossil Fuels as a basis for your plan.
New idea	We need new flowers in our school's front flower bed. We want half of the flowers to match colors that are already there, and the other half needs to be two new colors. Plus, we want the flowers to not be shorter or taller than any of the current flowers. Review the spreadsheet data from our Flower Investigation and the Internet to help you choose the new flowers.

Results Presentation

After the students have solved the problem, they will need to present their work and solution (see Chapter 8). Their results can take the form of numerical answers on the spreadsheet or a chart or graph generated by the spreadsheet application. For most reports, the students may want to include parts of either the spreadsheet or graphs in their written report or oral presentation. You will need to determine some basic guidelines and expectations for the report before the students start the lesson. For example, will they make a slide show, a multimedia presentation, a poster presentation, a written report, or some combination of these? Will the students organize all the papers and produce a magazine, book, or newsletter?

MULTIDIMENSIONAL ACTIVITIES

The next step of the NTeQ lesson design is to plan the various instructional activities that will engage the learner and lead to mastery of the objectives. A number of carefully planned activities that support the objectives are needed to successfully integrate the lesson. The following paragraphs describe four types of strategies you need to plan before implementing the lesson. These activities include those during computer use, before computer use, after computer use, and supporting activities.

Planning: Activities During Computer Use

What will the students do when they work at the computer? For example, if they are entering information, will they use a template you have created or will they create their own? If they are doing calculations, will they use your formulas or must they create their own? You can create spreadsheet templates that include the formulas and the students need only enter their data. Students also can use a spreadsheet template that already has the data; they add the formulas and calculations to answer questions and solve problems. Another alternative is to allow the students to create the complete spreadsheet using data they have gathered and then create the necessary calculations. For example, the designing a soup can problem might have students in a lower grade enter various heights and radii to calculate the volume, whereas a high school class might create the formula for the calculation. Proper planning for the computer activities will help you determine the materials and instructions that you must provide for efficient computer time. After you have identified what the students are going to do with the data, you can design any necessary spreadsheets and protect the cells. If the students are unfamiliar with the computer task, you may need to develop a step-by-step instruction sheet for creating and using a spreadsheet.

Planning: Activities Before Computer Use

As you plan the lesson, consider how you can make each student's time at the computer efficient and effective. For example, if students are searching a CD-ROM or the Internet for information, they could generate a list of key words or terms to use *before* they start searching. Similarly, if students are entering data they have collected from observations, experiments, or other research, they can organize the data before they have an opportunity to enter the data. Thus, if students must enter their own formula for calculating the volume of a can, they should have instructions to determine the formula *before* using the computer. If they must also create the spreadsheet, they can plan for the labels, columns, and rows. Careful planning of these activities will help students have adequate access to the limited computers to complete their work. When planning these activities, you may need to complete each step of the process yourself to identify what the students must do. Working through these steps can help you identify organizational and planning activities that are not readily apparent.

Careful planning prior to creating spreadsheets can ensure successful results.

Planning: Activities After Computer Use

Once the students have manipulated their data in a spreadsheet, what should they do with the information? As a teacher, you may need to help them interpret the data or charts so that they can solve the problem. Guidance for exploring the spreadsheet data or charts can take different forms. For example, if your chemistry class has entered data from a series of experiments, you might prepare a Think Sheet (Chapter 3) with questions that will focus the students' attention on the salient points. In their quest to find an appropriate-size can, you might have them create models from construction paper and collect data from others as to which can is most appealing. They might also determine which can appears to hold the most and why. A Think Sheet might ask questions such as the following:

- How many of each can design can you place on a grocery shelf that is 24 inches wide by 18 inches deep and 13 inches high?
- Which can is most likely to tip over? Which is least likely to tip over? Why?
- Which can design is most appealing to a buyer and which to a grocer? Why?
- How many different can designs can you find that hold the same amount?
- Does a change in diameter or height have a greater effect on the volume?

As each group works through their analysis and interpretation, you can facilitate their efforts by asking questions and modeling the behaviors you are teaching. Once the students understand the process for analyzing and interpreting the data, they will need less and less direction from you.

Planning: Supporting Activities

The last learning activities to plan are the additional activities that support the achievement of the objectives. Students are engaged in these activities when they are not working on computer-related tasks. We can group these activities into three categories. First, students can review prior learning and pursue areas of interest related to already learned ideas. Second, students can do additional readings or research on the current topic or they can pursue related topics of interest. Third, students can explore enrichment activities that further enhance their learning or develop their critical thinking skills.

Review of Prior Learning

Review activities are designed to help students prepare for the current lesson and may not be needed by every student. Review activities can include reading either old or new materials, completing a tutorial, or working practice problems. For example, students working on the can design problem might practice some problems on calculating the area of a circle before working on the formula for calculating the volume of a cylinder. Similarly, younger students might measure the amount of sand in various shaped cans (of the same volume) to understand volume and how differently shaped objects can hold the same amount.

Required Research/Reading

The second type of supporting activity is for all students; however, you can adapt your classroom environment to provide different forms of delivery. Students might have the choice of completing additional readings, participating in an experiment, watching a videotape, or listening to an audiotape to gain the same information. The activities can also be on different, but related, topics that support the objectives. Students can then strengthen their various learning skills rather than relying exclusively on their favorite form of learning.

If you want to promote transfer of the students' knowledge, you can provide additional practice activities that illustrate how they can apply their knowledge to different problems. For example, students might extend their calculation of a cylinder's volume to calculating the optimum shape of a barrel that will be transported on a truck. They must consider the size of the trailer and the maximum height they can stack the barrels (or containers) so the trailer will pass safely under overpasses.

Enrichment Activity

The last type of supporting activity is enrichment that is available to all students once they have demonstrated mastery of the skills and knowledge for the unit. These activities broaden students' understanding beyond the content of the unit. A student completing the can design example might do additional reading on advertising while another explores the process of making cans, either in print, from a CD-ROM, or on the Internet. Another student might study the recycling of cans and develop an interest in alternative forms of packaging. If your students need a more concrete activity, you can have them create model cans by using bases and tops cut from cardboard and heavy construction paper for the side.

As you design the multidimensional activities for a unit, keep in mind that they should support the objectives for the unit. You should avoid creating "busy work." If you plan to use a unit in the future, you can add one or two additional activities each year. You will likely consider including some of the ideas students generated for additional learning.

Assessment

The assessment for an integrated lesson using a spreadsheet will focus on several objectives. An assessment will include spreadsheet skills such as entering data, creating formulas, and creating graphs. Another aspect of the assessment will probably focus on the results presentation. The results presentation might include assessment of a report (see Chapter 8) but, more importantly, it should also focus on the higher-level thinking skills involved in interpreting and applying the results generated from the analysis of the data. Criteria to include in a rubric might include the following:

- Ability to enter data
- Ability to enter a formula
- Presentation of data
- Selection of appropriate chart
- Explanation of results
- Appropriate conclusions

When students are working in collaborative groups, it is important to explain your expectations for each student. For example, if you are requiring the students to enter or develop a formula for a calculation, must only one person on the team know how to do it? Or must each team member demonstrate how to create a formula?

SUMMARY

Spreadsheets are a versatile application that you can easily adapt as a tool for learning at most every grade level. First, spreadsheets are excellent for demonstrating and testing "what if?" scenarios. You can create a template with formulas and graphs that allow students to simply input data and see the results. After entering several data points, they can analyze the results and begin to discover relationships. The results are displayed immediately as numerical values and changes to a graph or chart. Second, students can create their own spreadsheets to analyze and display results based on their data collection. This approach allows the students to focus not only on the results but also on the mathematical operations needed to solve the problem. Both approaches address NET Standards for Students for using technology tools to process data and report results, problem solving, and decision making.

Spreadsheets are organized into columns that are identified by a letter and rows that are identified by a number. You can reference a specific cell in the "grid" with the column and row reference, such as C6. Data are entered into each cell in the data entry area. Spreadsheet functions (i.e., formulas) perform both simple and complex calculations on the data. Once you have entered data into a spreadsheet, you can create a variety of graphs and charts to visualize the data. Data from a spreadsheet, as well as charts and graphs, can be integrated into word processing documents, slide shows, and Web pages.

AT THE CLASSROOM'S DOORSTEP

Questions Teachers Ask

My students are having trouble using a spreadsheet. What can I do?

One approach is to prepare a template complete with instructions. For example, you can include the instructions and spreadsheet in a single document. You can take screen shots, or screen captures, of parts of a spreadsheet and include them in a document along with simple step-by-step instructions. We have found that several short instruction sheets explaining a single task are better than longer sheets that address several different tasks.

My students have a tendency to lose, modify, or erase the formulas that I include. Is there any way to keep them from modifying my spreadsheet?

There are two solutions. First, you can save your spreadsheet as a stationary or template file. When they try to open it, the spreadsheet application will open an exact copy of your original spreadsheet. Second, you can select the cells with your data and formulas and lock or protect them. Students will not be able to change the cell. By protecting selected cells of the spreadsheets, you can keep students from modifying or deleting critical information or formulas (see Power Tip for specific instructions). You can thus limit their data input into specific cells and reduce the chances that they will have to start all over with a new copy of the template.

How can I tell if my students are old enough to use a spreadsheet?

We have seen first graders use a spreadsheet to enter data and copy calculations. Younger students often need more hands-on directions, as do many inexperienced learners. A spreadsheet provides a virtual playground for the inquisitive student who is interested in discovering mathematical concepts and relationships. As a teacher, you must keep in mind both the students' developmental readiness and their computer skills.

What can I do if my students do not know the formula for calculating the needed information?

Let's consider two scenarios. First, consider the problem we have introduced with redesigning the soup can. For younger students, you might create a spreadsheet where they enter the diameter and height of their proposed can. The spreadsheet would then calculate the volume. Second, consider a unit in which students are exploring the relation between the sides of a rectangle and the area. Again, you could create a template where students enter the length of each side and the area is calculated. In both instances, the students can explore the relationship between the numbers by graphing their data. Then, when they understand the relationships, you can introduce the formula and repeat the exercise as they do the complete calculation.

How can I get my students to examine a spreadsheet to discover new information?

Suppose you are teaching the concept of a prime number. You might create a spreadsheet that has the numbers 1 to 15 in the first column. In the next columns you label and display the results of the numbers divided by 1, 2, 3, and itself (format so only two decimal places show). Each of the columns is color coded by selecting a background color for the columns. You can then turn the task into a game. Students are directed to examine the columns and describe the differences among the numbers. If they need help, they can ask you for a hint card that directs their attention to specific information. However, for each hint card they lose five points or 15 seconds are added to their problem-solving time. The winners are all rewarded with a Nobel Prize in mathematics for discovering a new math concept.

ISTE NETS FOR STUDENTS

Integration of a spreadsheet activity in your lesson plan can address three ISTE Standards. When your students use a spreadsheet, you are addressing ISTE Standard 3 related to the use of productivity tools. If your students are manipulating data, then you have addressed Standard 5, which deals with using technology research tools. Last, when your students solve a problem or make a decision or recommendation based on their data, you have addressed ISTE Standard 6.

Most likely, you will also address Standards 1 and 2 in your lessons. As the students use the tools, they will become more proficient in their use of technology (Standard 1). Similarly, the learner environment that you create will address Standard 2 because it relates to responsible use of technology, collaboration, and addressing various issues. If your students are publishing their results, then you are addressing Standard 4.

TECHNOLOGY INTEGRATION ACTIVITIES

To access the activities that connect the content of the text with the Companion Website and other technology, please go to the Activities module in Chapter 6 of the Companion Website at *http://www.prenhall.com/morrison.*

NTEQ LESSON PLAN

LESSON TITLE: Product Testing Lab

SUBJECT AREA: Math

GRADE LEVEL: 5 to 8

Learning Objective

By the end of this lesson, students will collect and use data to complete a compare and contrast analysis of a product (e.g., paper towels).

Computer Functions

- Spreadsheets will be used to calculate strength and absorbency.
- Word processing will be used to write a report for the school newsletter.

Specify Problem

We have all seen the various television advertisements for paper towels showing their strength and absorbency. But, which is really the best when tested in our lab?

Data Manipulation

- Students will use a spreadsheet to determine the average weight a paper towel can hold.
- Students will use a spreadsheet to determine how much water a paper towel can absorb in 15 seconds.
- Students will use word processing to edit and revise a report on the results of the tests.

Results Presentation

The final product will be a word-processed report that contains graphs supporting the final recommendation for the best paper towel.

Multidimensional Activities

Small groups of students complete the following activities.

Activities During Computer Use

The following computer tasks are divided among group members:

- Create spreadsheet columns and rows.
- Enter formulas.
- Enter testing data.
- Create a graph that effectively depicts the results of each test.

Activities Before Computer Use

- Decide on a plan of action for solving the problem.
- Conduct three trials of each product to test the strength by securing a stretched piece of paper towel over a coffee can with a rubber band. Add weights (e.g., pennies) until the towel breaks.

- Conduct three trials of each product to test the absorbency. Place a paper towel in a container with 6 ounces of water for 15 seconds. Remove the towel and measure the amount of water remaining in the container.
- Determine how to set up the spreadsheet (i.e., column and row names, formulas for calculating the average weight held and for calculating the average amount of water collected).

Activities After Computer Use

- Answer the Think Sheet items:
  1. List the supporting reasons for the final selection.
  2. Which product holds the most weight? Which product absorbed the most liquid? Please explain why.
  3. How did you select the best product?
  4. What was the most difficult aspect of this lesson?
     - As a large group, have the reporters from each group share their findings.
     - Facilitate a summary and review session with the whole class by discussing the Think Sheet responses. During the discussion, clarify any misconceptions that arise and reemphasize the key learning objectives.
     - Prepare a report describing the results and select the best product.

Supporting Activities

- Study how paper is made.
- Investigate how paper is recycled.
- Look for ways paper is used and how it is made stronger.

Assessment

Create a rubric for assessing the following:

Spreadsheet

Columns and rows named appropriately.

Data entered accurately.

Formulas are accurate.

Manipulation of data is evident.

Graph

Depicts the final selection.

Displays information in easy-to-read manner.

Appropriate graph is used.

Report

Supporting arguments are reasonable.

Format is appropriate.

Report is free of errors.

LESSON BYTES FOR SPREADSHEETS

Following are different spreadsheets that can be created by elementary, middle, and high school students and a sample problem statement for each.

Elementary Students

Growth of Bacteria

- In which conditions does bacteria grow the fastest?

Amount Read

- Who reads more paragraphs per week—boys or girls?
- Athletes or nonathletes?

Genetic Traits Tendencies

- Do girls tend to have different observable genetic traits than boys (e.g., curling tongue, attached ear lobe)?

Counting and Measuring

- Do bigger pumpkins have more seeds or just bigger seeds?
- Which foods affect your heart rate?
- How many more steps would it take for the shortest person in your class to walk the length of the hallway compared to the tallest person in your class?
- Can the height of a person be predicted by knowing his or her arm span?

Calculating Food Costs

- Which pizza place has the best price per square inch of pizza?
- Find three examples of a larger size item being more economical than a smaller size item, then find the reverse where the smaller items cost less.

Middle School and High School Students

Change in Motion

- Which factor has the greatest impact on how high a ball will bounce?

Determining Mileage

- Determine the *shortest* route from your school to the state capital and the *fastest* route if driving a car.
- Does the distance flown by North American migratory birds differ based on where they reside?

Plant Growth

- Demonstrate how the chemical balance of soil affects plant growth.

Voting Patterns

- How have the voting patterns for your state changed over the past 50 years?

Recycling

- Based on a sample of your home's recycling, how much glass, paper, and metal does your community recycle each year?
- Determine how many trees can be saved each year in your community by the amount of paper recycled.

NTEQ PORTFOLIO ACTIVITIES: SPREADSHEETS

The following activities are designed to help you build your NTeQ Portfolio with regard to students using spreadsheets as a tool to foster deeper learning.

Reflections

Redesigning the Past

Think back to some courses you had in elementary, middle, or high school or in college in which you had difficulty understanding some of the content; or maybe you can identify a lesson you have taught. Can you identify a way the instructor or you could have used a spreadsheet to help you better grasp the content? Describe your experience and how a spreadsheet could have been used.

Preparing for an Integrated Lesson

Integrating technology into a problem-based lesson requires careful planning on the part of the teacher to create a successful lesson. Create a checklist of steps that you will use to make sure your lesson and spreadsheet template are ready for your students.

Lesson Ideas

For this activity, we want you to identify five potential lesson plans that you can create or modify as an integrated lesson. There are two general sources for ideas. First, you can review benchmarks or standards for a source of ideas. These standards can come from a national organization (e.g., NCTM) or from your state or local school districts. You can find many of these standards on the Internet (see *www.nteq.com*). Second, you can modify existing lesson plans to create an integrated lesson. The lesson plans can come from your own resources, or you can search the lesson Internet for existing lesson plans.

For each Lesson Idea, create a three-to five-sentence description of the lesson including the problem for your NTeQ Portfolio.

Lesson Plan

Create an integrated lesson plan that uses a spreadsheet as the tool. Your lesson plan can be for a single discipline, or it can go across two or more disciplines. Add the lesson plan to your NTeQ Portfolio.

REFERENCES

Adams, F. G., & Kroch, E. (1989). The computer in the teaching of macroeconomics. *Journal of Economic Education*, *20*, 269–280.

Carter, A. (1999). Using spreadsheets to model population growth, competition, and predation in nature. *American Biology Teacher*, *61*, 294–296.

Cognition and Technology Group at Vanderbilt. (1990). Anchored instruction and its relationship to situated cognition. *Educational Researcher*, *19*, 2–10.

Lesser, L. M. (1999). Exploring the birthday problem with spreadsheets. *Mathematics Teacher*, *92*, 407–411.

Mihich, O. (1996). Computing the water index: The Hudson River Project. *Learning and Leading with Technology*, *24*, 27–31.

Murfin, B. (1998). Seismic studies. *Science Teacher, 65*(2), 34–37.

Niess, M. L. (1992). Math: Winds of change. *Computing Teacher*, *19*, 32–35.

Niess, M. L. (1998). Using computer spreadsheets to solve equations. *Learning and Leading with Technology*, *26*, 22–24, 26–27.

North Carolina State Department of Public Instruction. (1992). *Voteline: A project for integrating computer databases, spreadsheets, and telecomputing into high school social studies instruction*. Raleigh, NC: North Carolina State Department of Public Instruction. (ERIC Document ED350243).

North Carolina State Department of Public Instruction (1999). *Technology: The common language. A guide for integrating technology in the foreign language class.* Raleigh, NC: North Carolina State Department of Public Instruction. (ERIC Document ED445554).

Reese, P., & Monroe, M. (1997). The great international penny toss. *Learning and Leading with Technology, 24,* 210–231.

Salomon, G. (1993). On the nature of pedagogic computer tools: The case of the writing partner. In S. P. LaJoie & S. J. Derry (Eds.), *Computers as cognitive tools.* Hillsdale, NJ: Lawrence Erlbaum.

Smith, L. M., & Smith, L. C. (1988). Teaching macroeconomics with microcomputer spreadsheets. *Journal of Economic Education, 19,* 363–382.

Timmons, T. (1991). A numerical and graphical approach to Taylor polynomials using an electronic spreadsheet. *Primis, I,* 95–102.

Verderber, N. L. (1992). Tin cans revisited. *Mathematics Teacher, 85,* 346–349.

Walsh, T. P. (1996). Exploring difference equations with technology. *Learning and Leading with Technology, 24,* 28–32.

KEY TOPICS

Examining Databases
- Basic Components
- Defining Fields
- Reports

Databases in the Classroom
- Engagement in Critical Thinking

Designing an Integrated Lesson Using Databases
- Matching Objectives to Database Functions
- Data Manipulation
- Results Presentation

Multidimensional Activities
- Planning: Activities During Computer Use
- Planning: Activities Before Computer Use
- Planning: Activities After Computer Use
- Assessment

Chapter 7

Databases

This chapter will guide you through the key components of a database and how to develop lesson plans that have your students use them as learning tools. Specifically, we will look at how students can use databases to critically examine information in new and meaningful ways to solve problems, answer questions, and conduct investigations that lead to a greater depth of understanding.

GETTING STARTED

What Do I Know?

1. Have you ever worried because lessons often result in students just memorizing facts?
2. Have you wondered how to get your students engaged with the trends and patterns that are embedded in the content they are to learn?
3. Have you wished there was an easy way to have your students examine information from a multitude of perspectives?

Classroom Snapshot

Mr. Martinez has been teaching social studies for 15 years and has always included a unit on U.S. presidents. He really likes this topic, so he makes the lectures very lively and adds video clips of presidential speeches. His students are required to create a set of presidential note cards and memorize key facts, answer the chapter questions, and write a final report about a favorite president. As a result, most of his students perform well on a unit test that has students list the presidents by the year in which they served. But recent national emphasis on student engagement in higher-order thinking caused Mr. Martinez to question whether or not his students are learning the most critical information about our country's leadership. As a result, he explored the possibility of using technology to make his teaching more meaningful.

After careful consideration, he decided to have his students create a presidential database, because it is more efficient and accurate than the non-digital note cards and allows students to examine the stored information from different viewpoints. Students could now collect presidential information such as date of birth, birthplace, height, religion, interests, political party, marital status, number of children, age at election, occupation before presidency, highest degree obtained, number of terms, age at death, and cause of death. The database could also contain other details such as important presidential accomplishments and world events during the term(s). Once the information is entered into the database, the students can use it to solve problems posed to them by Mr. Martinez or student-generated questions. These include questions such as the following:

- What, if any, patterns exist between the religion and/or birth state of a president and his choice of political party?
- What characteristics would a presidential candidate possess if he were to have the most common traits of past presidents?
- What type of work did most of our presidents do right before taking office? Did this previous work seem to influence key accomplishments once in office?

Mr. Martinez discovered that the new database unit takes about the same amount of time as the note card one, but student learning is greatly improved. His students now know much more than the names and years in office, in that they are able to discuss key issues related to the presidents, to depict trends, and ask meaningful questions.

EXAMINING DATABASES

Database applications are used to store, manipulate, and retrieve information. In fact, the majority of information in our society (medical records, Social Security records, inventories, military records, etc.) is kept in very large databases. When information is stored in a database, it can be efficiently and effectively retrieved in a variety of formats—from a single record to a report of all data in specified fields. It is these functions that make databases very useful learning tools in K-12 classrooms (Figure 7-1). The following section discusses the basic components of a database and how to define fields, enter information, and create new layouts and reports. The subsequent section contains suggestions and guidelines for having your students use databases.

FIGURE 7-1 Examining Databases

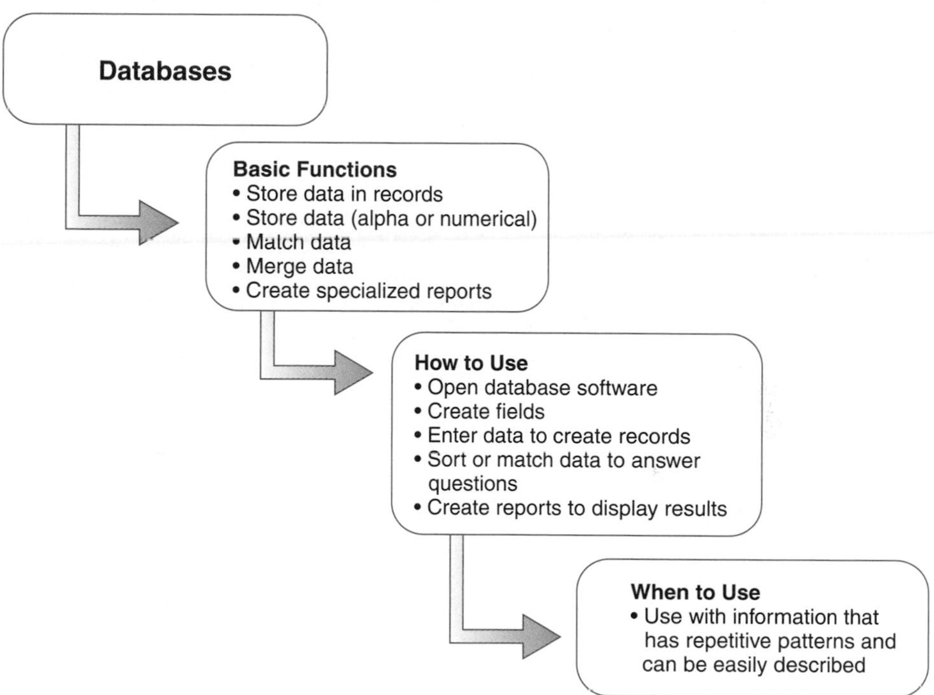

Basic Components

A computer database electronically stores sets of related information in *data files*. Within a data file, there are individual *records* that all contain similar types of information stored in *fields* (Figure 7-2). The field entries typically contain either text or numerical data; however, in some database applications the fields can also contain pictures, dates, and times. Once the fields have been defined and the information has been entered for each record, queries or computer searches can be conducted to answer particular questions. For example, if a data file were created for the 50 states in the United States, the fields for each record might include state name, flower, and bird; population; and average yearly rainfall, for a start. Once students have a complete database of information about the states, they can answer a variety of questions. Which states, if any, have the same state bird or flower? What are the five most populous states? Which three states could you live in if you wanted very low humidity and a small population? If you wanted to examine a specific set of data, you could use the match feature to identify states that joined the United States between 1800 and 1850.

Defining Fields

The first step in creating a database is to define the fields of information that will be stored in each record. Start by carefully describing the problem to be solved and identifying the information needed to solve the problem. Use the NTeQ Problem-Solving Process to involve students in brainstorming possible fields and

FIGURE 7-2 Basic Database Component

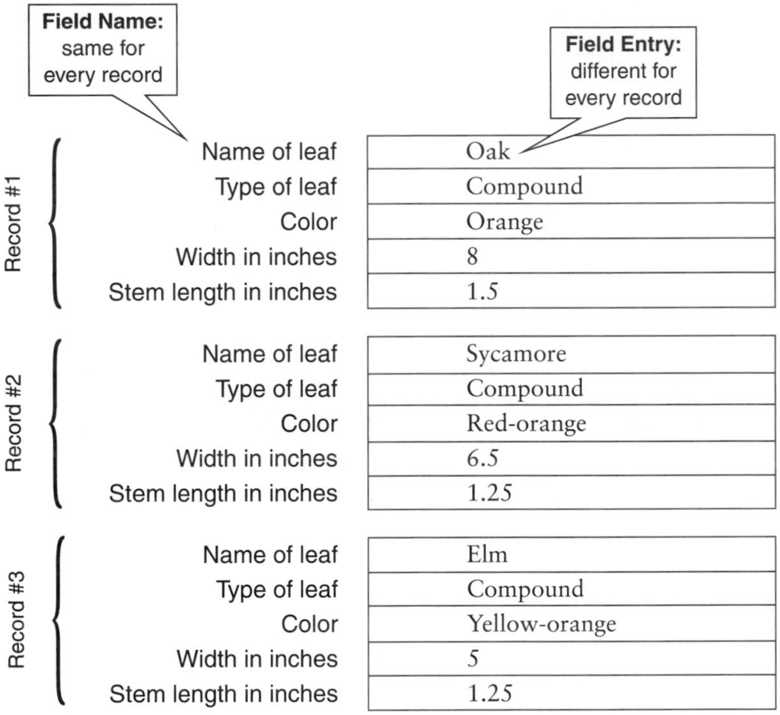

Field Name: same for every record

Field Entry: different for every record

Record	Field Name	Field Entry
Record #1	Name of leaf	Oak
	Type of leaf	Compound
	Color	Orange
	Width in inches	8
	Stem length in inches	1.5
Record #2	Name of leaf	Sycamore
	Type of leaf	Compound
	Color	Red-orange
	Width in inches	6.5
	Stem length in inches	1.25
Record #3	Name of leaf	Elm
	Type of leaf	Compound
	Color	Yellow-orange
	Width in inches	5
	Stem length in inches	1.25

then defining the purpose and meaning of the fields selected for the final database. The following example demonstrates one way to have students participate in defining the fields of a database. Imagine a fourth-grade class with the following problem to solve: "Why were some dinosaurs much bigger than other dinosaurs?" The teacher writes "Dinosaur Name" on the board, then tells the students, "If we are going to use a database to solve our problem, we need to know the name of each dinosaur. What other information about dinosaurs is needed to solve the problem?" The students will probably suggest things such as how tall they were, how much they weighed, where they lived, what they ate, who their enemies were, how long they lived, and during what time period they lived. After a list is generated, the teacher leads a discussion about each field and the information it would contain to determine if the field is needed to help solve the problem. This discussion would focus on the following two primary considerations for defining fields:

- Fields need to be limited to one type of data or information.
- Vocabulary for each field needs to be predetermined.

Fields Need to Be Limited to One Type of Data or Information

It is important to limit each field to one type of data or information because it makes the database more useful. For example, if one of the fields in the dinosaur database

FIGURE 7-3 Using Field Guidelines

Without Guidelines		With Guidelines		Tallest to Shortest	
Dinosaur 1	8 Ft.	Dinosaur 1	08	Dinosaur 2	12
Dinosaur 2	12'	Dinosaur 2	12	Dinosaur 3	10
Dinosaur 3	10	Dinosaur 3	10	Dinosaur 1	08
Dinosaur 4	5 feet	Dinosaur 4	05	Dinosaur 4	05

was "Dinosaur Size," a student might enter, "12 ft. tall by 15 ft. long." The data would be more useful if it were entered in two fields: "Dinosaur Height" and "Dinosaur Length." This enables students to compare dinosaurs by either height or length. It is also useful to choose field names that are concise and easily understood, such as "Diet" rather than "What the Dinosaurs Ate."

Vocabulary for Each Field Needs to Be Predetermined

Once the fields are determined, the specific vocabulary for each field needs to be established. This helps to avoid student use of a variety of descriptive terms within each field. For example, if the height information for four dinosaurs was entered without guidelines, the data entries might resemble what is seen in the "Without Guidelines" column in Figure 7-3. However, if guidelines such as "height will be entered as two-digit numbers, and the numbers represent feet" are used, the data are entered in a consistent manner, as seen in the "With Guidelines" column in Figure 7-3. When data are entered with specific, predetermined vocabulary, they can more accurately be sorted or matched with other information, as seen in Figure 7-3, the "Tallest to Shortest" column.

When the entries for a field will always consist of a small number of responses (e.g., male/female; yes/no; carnivore/herbivore/omnivore), it is best to use predefined lists displayed in pop-up menus within the fields (Figure 7-4). Use of a predefined list helps eliminate possible typing errors or the use of similar but inexact words that hinder searching and sorting capabilities (e.g., entering "Apt.," "apart.," or "apartment").

Entering Information

After the fields are defined, the database is ready for information to be entered. The information for each field is typically classified as one of the following: text, numbers, dates, times and, sometimes, graphics. When using dates or times, most software can automatically enter the date or time the record was created. When the information being entered is names, definitions, or descriptions, for example, it is considered text. The entries are classified as numbers only when totals or averages are going to be calculated from the entries, not when the entries are numbers such as dates, times, or phone numbers.

FIGURE 7-4 Predefined Lists

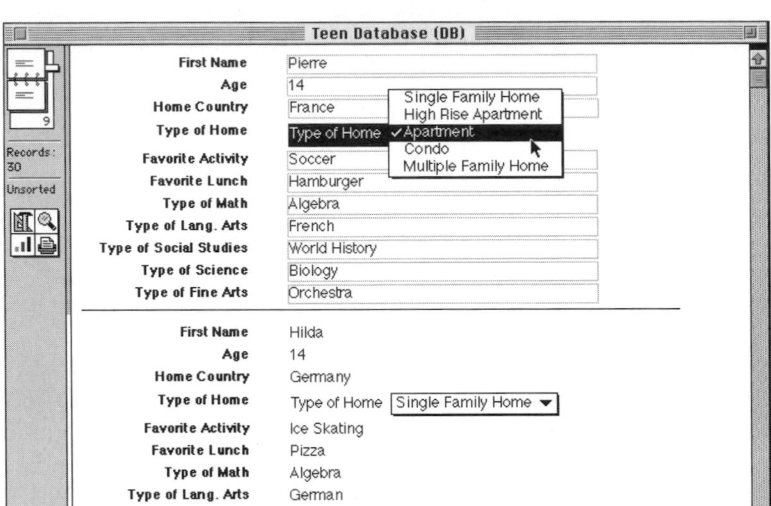

To enter information into a field, use the Tab key or mouse to position the cursor within the field. Once the cursor is in the proper field, either type in the information or select it from a predefined list if the field has one. Information in the predefined list is selected by using either the Arrow key to move to the desired selection and then pressing Enter, or using the mouse to double-click on the selection. The information within each field can be changed by using word processing functions such as delete, copy, paste, bold, and underline. After the information has been entered into a field, use the Tab key or mouse to move to the next field. Again, it is very important to use consistent terms and to check spelling to aid in conducting accurate queries.

Database Layouts

Most databases have more than one way to view the entered data. One is a ***standard*** layout that presents all information from each field in an individual record in a scrolling list. Another typical layout is a ***list*** or ***table*** layout that displays the data in a table format (Figures 7–5 and 7–6). The table or list layout is useful when examining data in several fields.

Customized layouts can be created for most databases. To create these, select the appropriate layout mode for your software. In this mode, the field names and fields become objects that can be resized or moved to any location. A field must be selected, or clicked on with the mouse, before it can be moved or resized. The selected field becomes highlighted, which means a box with "resizing handles" at each corner is placed around it. The selected field can be changed in the following ways: drag it to a new location, make it smaller or larger by dragging one of the corner handles, delete it, or change the text by selecting a different font, size, style, or color. The layout mode also allows the user to add graphics such as clip art, lines, borders, or colors (Figure 7-7).

FIGURE 7-5 Standard Layout

Name	New York
Flower	Rose
Bird	Bluebird
Population	18,119,416
Square Mileage	47,224

Name	Texas
Flower	Blue Bonnet
Bird	Mockingbird
Population	17,655,650
Square Mileage	261,914

Name	California
Flower	Golden poppy
Bird	California Valley quail
Population	30,866,851
Square Mileage	155,973

FIGURE 7-6 List or Table Layout

Name	Flower	Bird	1992 Population	Square Mileage
New York	Rose	Bluebird	18,119,416	47,224
Texas	Blue Bonnet	Mockingbird	17,655,650	261,914
California	Golden poppy	California Valley quail	30,866,851	155,973

Power Tip

Using Real Data from the "Net"

The Internet contains a vast amount of information that is constantly being updated—a true advantage over print materials. Current information can be copied and pasted into databases created by your students. The instructions for retrieving information from the Internet are as follows. As an example, we will use statistics from the U.S. Geological Survey regarding earthquakes in California.

1. Search the Web for the information to be placed in a database. The information should be in a list format with columns and rows, even though lines may not be dividing the data. For our example, we did a search for California earthquakes (Power Tip Figure 7-1).

Continued

POWER TIP FIGURE 7-1 Online Data File of California Earthquakes

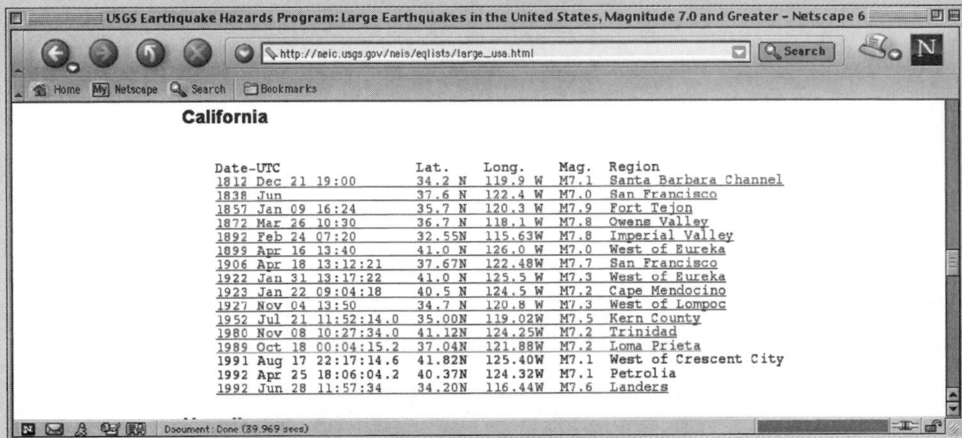

California

Date-UTC	Lat.	Long.	Mag.	Region
1812 Dec 21 19:00	34.2 N	119.9 W	M7.1	Santa Barbara Channel
1838 Jun	37.6 N	122.4 W	M7.0	San Francisco
1857 Jan 09 16:24	35.7 N	120.3 W	M7.9	Fort Tejon
1872 Mar 26 10:30	36.7 N	118.1 W	M7.8	Owens Valley
1892 Feb 24 07:20	32.55N	115.63W	M7.8	Imperial Valley
1899 Apr 16 13:40	41.0 N	126.0 W	M7.0	West of Eureka
1906 Apr 18 13:12:21	37.67N	122.48W	M7.7	San Francisco
1922 Jan 31 13:17:22	41.0 N	125.5 W	M7.3	West of Eureka
1923 Jan 22 09:04:18	40.5 N	124.5 W	M7.2	Cape Mendocino
1927 Nov 04 13:50	34.7 N	120.8 W	M7.3	West of Lompoc
1952 Jul 21 11:52:14.0	35.00N	119.02W	M7.5	Kern County
1980 Nov 08 10:27:34.0	41.12N	124.25W	M7.2	Trinidad
1989 Oct 18 00:04:15.2	37.04N	121.88W	M7.2	Loma Prieta
1991 Aug 17 22:17:14.6	41.82N	125.40W	M7.1	West of Crescent City
1992 Apr 25 18:06:04.2	40.37N	124.32W	M7.1	Petrolia
1992 Jun 28 11:57:34	34.20N	116.44W	M7.6	Landers

2. Retrieve the data. This can be done in the following two ways:
   - Use the Save As command from the File menu. Save the text as "text only," then open it in a word processing application.
   - Use the mouse to highlight the information to be placed in the database, then copy and paste it into a word processing document.
3. Once the information is in a word processing application, replace the space between each different type of information with a tab space. Highlighting the space then pushing the Tab key (Power Tip Figure 7-2) can do this. Please note that the information may also need some

POWER TIP FIGURE 7-2 California Earthquake Data: Reduced and Tab-Separated

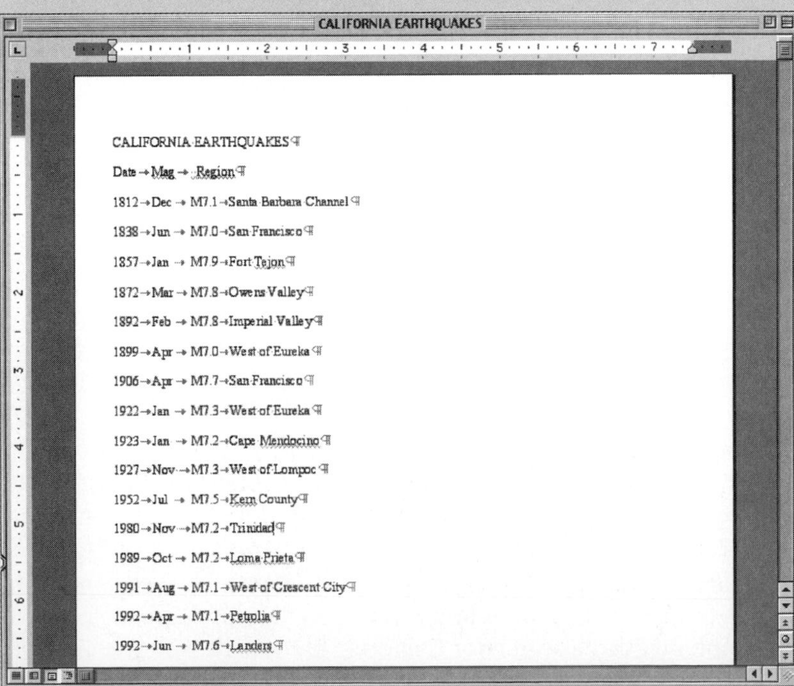

CALIFORNIA EARTHQUAKES

Date → Mag → Region

1812 → Dec → M7.1 → Santa Barbara Channel

1838 → Jun → M7.0 → San Francisco

1857 → Jan → M7.9 → Fort Tejon

1872 → Mar → M7.8 → Owens Valley

1892 → Feb → M7.8 → Imperial Valley

1899 → Apr → M7.0 → West of Eureka

1906 → Apr → M7.7 → San Francisco

1922 → Jan → M7.3 → West of Eureka

1923 → Jan → M7.2 → Cape Mendocino

1927 → Nov → M7.3 → West of Lompoc

1952 → Jul → M7.5 → Kern County

1980 → Nov → M7.2 → Trinidad

1989 → Oct → M7.2 → Loma Prieta

1991 → Aug → M7.1 → West of Crescent City

1992 → Apr → M7.1 → Petrolia

1992 → Jun → M7.6 → Landers

"cleanup" because the text may have extra spaces before or after words that need to be deleted. To do this, highlight then delete the unwanted items.

4. Open a database program and create fields for each set of information. For the California Earthquake data, we created fields for Year, Month, Magnitude, and Region. Place the fields in the same order as the information is set up in the word processing document.
5. Return to your word processed information and highlight just the information that will be placed in the database. Copy the information, then open the database that has been created.
6. In the database, make sure the cursor is not in any of the fields. In AppleWorks this is done by pushing the Enter key. When the cursor is not in any fields, select the paste command and the information will automatically be placed into the fields. It will create a record for each set of data (see Power Tip Figure 7-3).

POWER TIP FIGURE 7-3 California Earthquake Data in a Database

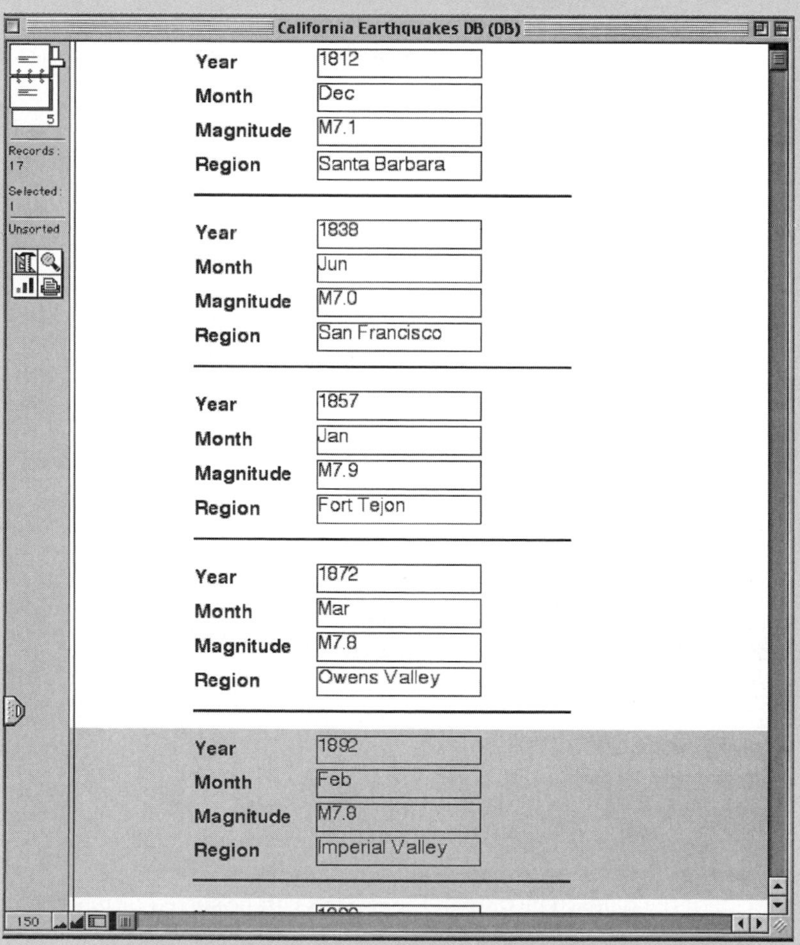

FIGURE 7-7 Customized Layout

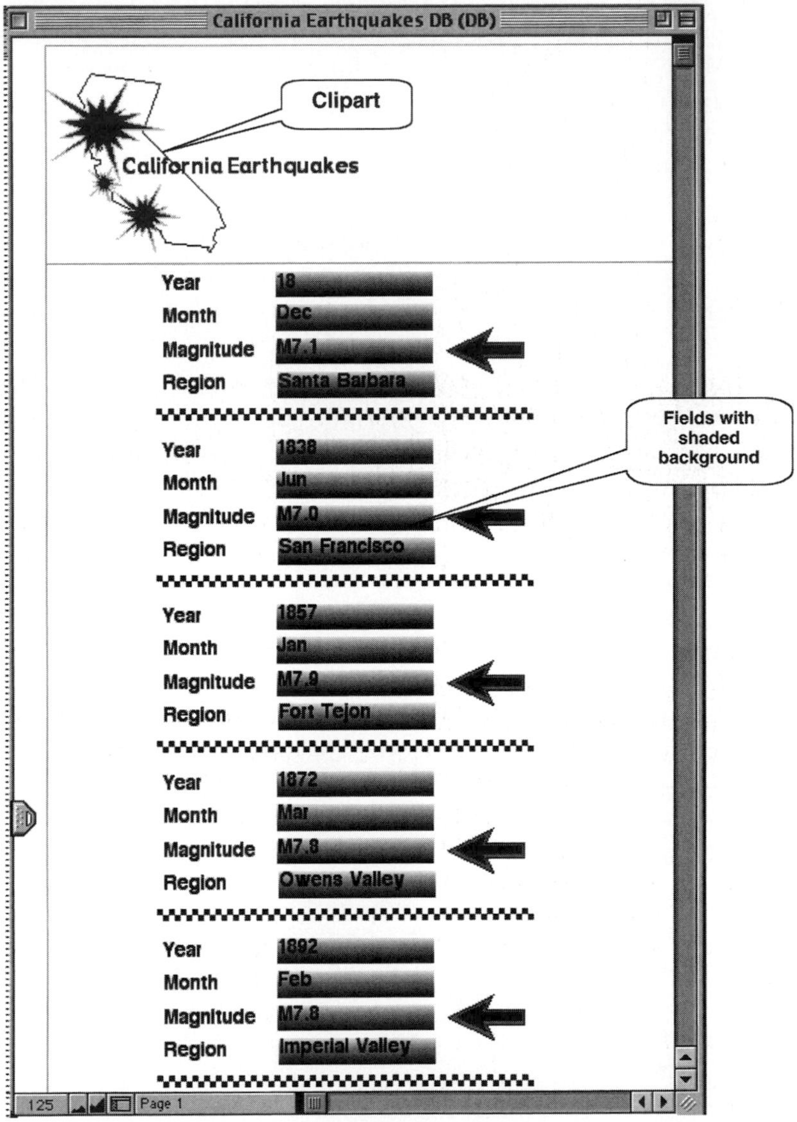

Reports

After creating the database and entering the information, there are a variety of ways to examine the data. Students can create reports that include data from a single field to data from all of the fields. The data in the reports can be sorted or matched to specific criteria. Students can also customize the layout for each report or use one of the default layouts, such as the List or Table layout.

Student pairs can help each other enter data into a database.

The Sort function in a database allows the information in fields to be arranged in either an ascending or a descending manner. A student working with the differences between American and European teenagers could sort the list of favorite activities in an ascending list that would start at the beginning of the alphabet. For example, all the students who listed Bike Riding as their favorite activity would be listed together. This reinforces how critical it is to use a common language when entering data. If someone entered Riding Bikes, it would not be grouped with the other bike riders. A field that contains numerical data sorted in ascending order starts with the smaller digits, and data sorted in descending order begins with the larger digits. For example, the chart with dinosaur heights mentioned earlier had data in the last column sorted in a descending order from tallest to shortest. All numerical data should have the same number of digits to ensure proper sorting. If a student sorts the following list in ascending order 23, 18, and 7, the order would be listed as 18, 23, and 7, because the computer thinks 7 is 70. To avoid this, a zero should be added to make the number "07."

Specific searches can be conducted to find answers to questions. If students want to know how many presidents served two or more terms, they can match records with the following formula: Terms>="2." Some of the more common matching computations include: = (EQUAL); > (GREATER THAN); < (LESS THAN); AND; and NOT. If students wanted to examine the number of presidents who served as governor before becoming president, the "Job Before Term" search term would be =governor. To examine traits of presidents during a specific time period, for example the 1800s, the search would be: 'Terms' >1799 or <1900.

The next section demonstrates how databases can be used in the classroom and how to design integrated lessons that have students use databases.

DATABASES IN THE CLASSROOM

Our experiences have revealed that database software is readily available and easily integrated into K-12 lesson plans. Regarding access, database software is included with integrated packages such as AppleWorks and Microsoft Works that are loaded onto most school computers. In addition, the easy-to-use format helps students manage and manipulate information because it automatically keeps related information within records. Database information is also very flexible, because new information easily can be added to or deleted from the records. When students are ready to examine the information they have entered, they can create reports that show from just one type to all the information in the record. For example, all of the information about George Washington stays in his record and all of the information about Ronald Reagan stays in his record, no matter how many different ways the information is organized or sorted.

Even primary-grade students can create a simple database and do sorting, matches, and searches to find the answers to problems. For example, Betty Lindhardt has her second-grade students use a database to solve the following problems: "What is the most common type of fall leaf in our area?" and "What differences are there in our fall leaves?" This lesson could begin with students collecting leaves while taking a "Fall Walk." After the leaves are collected, students return to the classroom and use a field guide to identify the specific names for each leaf. They also record the following information for each leaf: color, type of leaf (simple or compound), and the measurement of both the widest part of the leaf and the leaf stem. The students enter the descriptive information about each leaf into a database (Figure 7-8). They then sort the information in a variety of ways to answer the questions posed at the beginning of the lesson.

FIGURE 7-8 Leaf Database

Name of leaf	Oak
Type of leaf	Compound
Color	Orange
Width in inches	8
Stem length in inches	1.5

Name of leaf	Sycamore
Type of leaf	Compound
Color	Red-Orange
Width in inches	6.5
Stem length in inches	1.25

Name of leaf	Elm
Type of leaf	Compound
Color	Yellow-Orange
Width in inches	5
Stem length in inches	1.25

CHECK IT OUT 7-1

Title: Fall Leaf Database

Grade: Primary

Problem: *What type of fall leaf is most common? How are our fall leaves different?*

Activity: Use the online database to answer these questions and others you may have.

Link to the resources and activities in the Check It Out module for this chapter of the Companion Website.

Engagement in Critical Thinking

The entire process of creating and using a database involves students in several critical or higher-order thinking activities (Resnick & Klopfer, 1987). To create a database, students must carefully define what information is needed to answer questions, solve problems, or conduct investigations. The database provides students with an excellent means of examining the collected information because of its sorting and searching capabilities. Databases allow students to sort information in either an alphabetical or numerical manner; thus patterns emerge as similar items are grouped or as values change.

Let's look at an example of middle school students solving the problem "How is the lifestyle of teenagers in Europe different from the lifestyle of teenagers in the United States?" The students might begin the lesson by determining underlying factors in the lifestyle of teenagers that can be compared. These factors would be the basis for designing the database. Some of these factors might include types of housing, subjects studied in school, favorite school lunch, and favorite activity (Figure 7-9).

Students could gather the information by sending a survey via e-mail to students in a variety of countries. Once the surveys are returned, students would need to critically analyze each response to determine whether it is valid or really answers the question. After the information is verified, students enter it into the database. Critical thinking skills are required again as students begin to generate reports of the database information. Each report focuses on answering some aspect of the problem introduced at the beginning of the lesson. Students may begin by creating general descriptions of teenage lifestyles from each location. This information could be followed by observations of similarities and differences and explanations as to why the differences occur. The explanations would probably require the students to conduct further research to determine the impact of things such as political influences, culture, and geographic resources. Students can expand the database to include this new information.

FIGURE 7-9 Teen Database

Name	Country	Age	Type of Home	Favorite Activity	Favorite Lunch	Math	Science	Lang. Arts
Pierre	France	14	Apartment	Soccer	Hamburger	Algebra	Biology	French
Hilda	Germany	14	Single-family home	Ice skating	Pizza	Algebra	Chemistry	German
Jose	Mexico	14	Multiple-family home	Soccer	Tacos	General	Physical	Spanish
Mary	England	13	Condo	Chess	Lamb stew	Geometry	Physical	English
Shiji	China	13	High-rise apt.	Computer	Stir fry	Algebra	Chemistry	Chinese and English
Francis	Canada	13	Single-family home	Baseball	Pizza	Algebra	Biology	French
Jonathan	Israel	14	Single-family home	Basketball	Pizza	Algebra 2	Chemistry	English

CHECK IT OUT 7-2

Title: Teen Database

Grade: Middle School

Problem: *How is the lifestyle of teenagers in Europe different from the lifestyle of teenagers in the United States?*

Activity: Use the online database to answer these questions and others you may have.

Link to the resources and activities in the Check It Out module for this chapter of the Companion Website.

DESIGNING AN INTEGRATED LESSON USING DATABASES

This section describes the five key components of the NTeQ model that specifically need to be addressed when creating lesson plans that have students use databases as a learning tool. The remaining NTeQ components, which are discussed in the first three chapters, remain consistent across all lessons.

THE TEACHER'S DIARY

Our school is located in an area where there is a lot of growth, and we get many students new to the school system. I moved many times as a child and remember how traumatic going to a new school can be. I want my students to make a new friend in the classroom before the end of the first day. I begin working on this goal before the first day of school by creating a "Getting to Know You" database template on a classroom computer. Many parents bring their children to the school before the first day, so I have the students (with help, if needed) enter data about themselves into the database.

The remaining students who come in the first morning add their data. I then put the database on the server in the computer lab and reserve a time to take my class to the computer lab during the first day of school. That morning we begin a unit on friendship and brainstorm to list those things that make a person a friend—leading them to the idea that friends usually have similar interests, likes, dislikes, and so on. I then ask them to write a short paragraph that describes their idea of a "perfect friend." After they have written their paragraphs, I ask them if the computer could help them find their "perfect friend" and, if so, how? I take the class to the computer lab and reintroduce them to the "Getting to Know You" database. I demonstrate how to do simple sorts to find all the students who like the same thing. Student pairs then use the database to complete a "Getting to Know You" activity sheet to find classmates that have similar likes (Figure 7-10). I use information from the activity sheet to pair the students who, later in the day, work together to introduce each other to the class.

I have found this to be a very good activity. The students are introduced to a database and learn how to sort and analyze data in a fun and meaningful way. They are introduced to the idea that the computer is more than a word processor or a game machine. They learn that the computer is a tool that can help them solve problems. In addition, the students have found others in the classroom that have similar likes, and the beginnings of friendships have been formed.

Fran Clark
Third-Grade Teacher

Matching Objectives to Database Functions

The functions of a database can be compared to how a person processes information. Obviously, a computer can process the information much faster and more accurately. This efficient processing allows the learner to concentrate on learning rather than on physically organizing sets of information. If you examine a database to determine its primary functions, the following capabilities would emerge:

- Sort lists of information alphabetically
- Sort lists of information numerically

FIGURE 7-10 Getting to Know You Activity Sheet

Getting to Know You

Name ______________________ Date ______________

Complete the sentences in each box with your favorite. Then open the "Getting to Know You" database. Use the sort function to find classmates that have the same favorites as you. Write their names in the boxes below.

My favorite color is ______________.	My favorite subject is ______________.
My favorite sport is ______________.	My favorite food is ______________.
My favorite holiday is ______________.	My favorite game is ______________.
My favorite pet is ______________.	My favorite snack is ______________.

Look at the names in the boxes. Does anyone have many of the same favorites as you? Write that person's name. ______________________

- Match information
- Create standard reports
- Create customized reports

To determine if a database can be effectively integrated into a lesson, examine the lesson objectives to see if any of the database functions align with or support achievement of the objective. As seen in Table 7-1, some learning tasks will have a direct correlation to the database functions. In other instances, the teacher may want to modify an objective that requires only simple rote recall to one that requires the students to engage in more critical thinking. This modification often can be accom-

TABLE 7-1 Learning Tasks and Associated Database Functions

Primary Database Function(s)	Learning Task	Example
Sort	Arrange	Arrange states by year of entry into the Union.
	Choose, Select, Categorize	Categorize a list of animals by their eating habits.
	Classify, Identify, Isolate, List	List 19th-century artists by type of work.
	Solve, Determine	Determine which state has the lowest cost of living and low crime rate.
	Synthesize	Synthesize a list of foods by common elements.
Create standard or customized report	Assemble, Produce	Assemble information about your community.
	Collect, Gather	Collect daily observations of a crystal formation.
	Compare, Contrast, Differentiate, Discriminate, Relate	Compare male and female reading preferences.
	Report	Report differences in types of environmental protection laws by country.
Match information	Combine, Match, Sequence	Match agricultural products with region where they are grown.

plished through integrating the use of databases or other computer applications. For example, rather than have students memorize properties of elements listed on the Periodic Table of the Elements, have them create a database of the properties and then create new ways to group the elements. By doing this, student engagement with the content to be learned goes beyond recall and rote memorization by requiring the application of higher-order thinking skills. For the students to create new ways to group the elements, they must carefully consider the properties of each element and the relationships they have to other elements. This requires integration, organization, and elaboration skills and will result in a deeper understanding of the elements.

Data Manipulation

As previously mentioned, a database can manipulate information with the following functions: sort lists of information, match information, and create standard or customized reports. The types of answers needed to solve the problem determine the type of data manipulation selected. Each type of manipulation, though, engages students in higher-level thinking skills. As seen in Table 7-2, the three types of generative strategies and the six levels of learning are all required when using a database to manipulate data.

When a list of information is sorted, similar items are grouped together, thus enhancing students' ability to identify patterns and trends within the information. For example, students could use the information in the presidential database to answer the question "Do presidents who have previous military experience tend to focus more on national security issues than on education or health-related issues?" Students would answer this question by creating a new layout that included the following fields: presidents' names, past employment, and major presidential accomplishments. The students could sort the list by type of accomplishments. This sort would allow an analysis of whether or not those who served in the military were more involved in military-related accomplishments such as a war or enlarging the military forces during their term(s). When numerical data are sorted, the sorted information can depict groups of similar items as well as show trends found within information. Examples of trends include more money spent on business subsidies than on education, less rainfall in the southwest region of a state, or more fat grams eaten by American teenagers than by European teenagers.

A problem may need to have specific fields of information matched with information in other fields to determine a solution. When this is the situation, the selection criteria are specified and then information in the database is matched to the criteria. Examples of these criteria include American cities with populations larger than 500,000; endangered species with fewer than 1,000 animals remaining; or buildings that have more than five shapes used in their construction. Other specific examples, grouped by generative learning strategies, are seen in Table 7-3.

TABLE 7-2 Databases: Bloom's Taxonomy by Generative Strategies

		Generative Strategies		
Bloom's Taxonomy	To Use a Database, Students Must:	Integration *Students write questions, generate examples to:*	Organization *Students list key ideas and categorize to:*	Elaboration *Students extend beyond original information to:*
Knowledge	know the information.	write questions about it or generate examples from the database records.	list the key ideas needed to create database fields and then categorize the data for placement into the appropriate field.	elaborate on it.

TABLE 7-2 Continued

		Generative Strategies		
Bloom's Taxonomy	To Use a Database, Students Must:	Integration *Students write questions, generate examples to:*	Organization *Students list key ideas and categorize to:*	Elaboration *Students extend beyond original information to:*
Comprehension	understand the information.	write meaningful questions or to generate representative examples.	organize or sort it in a meaningful manner.	extend it in a meaningful way.
Application	be able to generalize the information.	write questions or find examples.	create the appropriate fields (list the key ideas), then correctly categorize information to place into the records.	use it as a basis for the extension, or to ask the "What if?" questions.
Analysis	be able to analyze the database information.	determine if the right questions are being asked or the right examples have been created.	determine if the fields are appropriate and if the information pertinent	determine which components are appropriate for an elaboration.
Synthesis	be able to use the results of the analysis.	synthesize questions or examples from the database information.	synthesize a database that has key ideas as fields and categorized information in each record.	synthesize new ways of looking at the information.
Evaluation	be able to assess.	determine if the questions or the examples are representative of the original information. Be able to assess the questions or the examples . . .	determine if the database accurately represents the target information. Be able to assess if the database . . .	the addition or elaboration to determine if it is plausible.

TABLE 7-3 Database: Generative Strategies Examples

Integration	
Write questions	Create a list of 15 questions that you could answer with information from our U.S. Presidents database.
Create examples	Use the Endangered Species database to create a map that displays the countries with the highest number of endangered species.
Organization	
List key ideas	Investigate poetry written during the last decade (1990–1999) and determine what fields would be needed to create a Poetry of the '90s database.
Categorize	Now that we have created our Animal Groups database, your teams need to enter each animal from our Animal Alphabet into the database.
Elaboration	
New information	Your team is going to open a restaurant just for kids, but it needs a name and a menu that is healthy but fun. Use your Food Groups database to create five Kids Kombo meals that meet the Healthy Eating guidelines.
New idea	The class database of Our Oldest Cities is very good, and we are just about ready to use this collected information to create the final products. Before we finish, each team is to research and find one unique category that can be added to your group's database.

Results Presentation

After the data manipulation plans are determined, a means of presenting the database results and problem solution can be selected (see Chapter 8). As noted earlier, data reports can be presented in any type of layout desired because all of the information can be moved or reformatted and graphics can be added to the final presentation. The type of data layout should be determined by the type of final product the students will be creating. If the final product is a report, the data should be kept in a format similar to the report format, that is, same font and borders. If the students are going to create a display, the data can be presented with color backgrounds and graphics that relate to the data. When the final product is going to be a hypermedia stack, the results need to be presented in smaller groups because the screen size can accommodate only a limited amount of information.

MULTIDIMENSIONAL ACTIVITIES

Please remember that the following steps are for *planning* the lesson rather than for implementing the lesson. Therefore the Activities During Computer Use are

CHECK IT OUT 7-3

Title: Presidential Database

Grade: 7-12

Problem: *Do presidents who have previous military experience tend to focus more on national security issues than on education or health-related issues?*

Activity: Write two more questions that can be answered with the presidential database.

Link to these resources and activities in the Check It Out module for this chapter of the Companion Website.

Students collecting data to be placed in a database.

planned before the Activities Before Computer Use. Once the computer activities are planned, the activities needed to prepare the students for computer use can be planned.

Planning: Activities During Computer Use

One of the best ways to plan for student use of a computer database is to actually develop a sample of what the students would generate during the lesson. This task involves deciding which fields are needed in the database, actually collecting some data from the resources the students will use, entering the information into the fields, and generating sample reports required to reach a solution. This database can serve as a prototype when showing the students how to build their databases. When students become more familiar with the database structure, they can begin to design their own databases. Please keep in mind that the student databases may not have exactly the same fields or layouts as the teacher prototype. In addition, the students may possibly reach different solutions than the teacher expected, yet their engagement with the information will still help them achieve the lesson objectives (Resnick & Klopfer, 1987).

Once a workable prototype of the database is developed, the teacher needs to decide how to group the students at the computer. Will individual students go to the computer and complete various activities, or is it more beneficial to have students working collaboratively? In developing a database, it is sometimes helpful to have two students involved in creating and entering the data into the fields. With students paired at the computer, one student can enter the data and one can read the information to enter. When students are manipulating the data in an effort to answer questions, small groups of students gathered at the computer is often an arrangement that generates many possible responses to the questions. Group members can all make predictions, suggest new ways to organize the information, and describe what they think the various results mean. The synergism created from these small-group activities can increase the amount of meaningful learning that takes place.

To promote equity among student opportunities, the number of computer tasks needs to be estimated and divided among the students. This strategy gives all students opportunities for keyboarding and other computer experiences. The student groups may need to be monitored to ensure that the more computer-literate student does not do the majority of the computer work because it is easier than letting the less proficient member struggle through the required steps.

Planning: Activities Before Computer Use

After the computer activities are planned, the next step is to determine what students need to do as preparation for their computer time. These preparations can include both whole-class activities and small-group activities, depending on the instructional approach used. In some instances, the students may determine the fields without using any resources. For example, high school students could probably figure out the major fields to include in a database of American presidents without looking at an encyclopedia or textbook. However, students creating a database of Native American art may need some resources to help determine how the artwork can best be described and thus what fields will be needed.

If students are going to be sharing database files, it is important that all groups have exactly the same database fields and configure their data in the same manner.

However, if students are approaching the instructional problem from a small-group perspective, the need for consistent fields and data is not as important. After the fields are identified, either as a whole class or as small groups, students can create the fields and begin gathering data to enter in the identified fields.

As students progress through their research and data entry, they may realize that the database would be more functional if it were modified by adding new fields, deleting existing fields, or adding predefined pop-up menus to fields. This process of identifying database fields involves the students in the generative learning strategies of organization and categorization. The research needed to find the required information for each field engages the students in reading, analyzing, categorizing, organizing, and paraphrasing activities (Jonassen, 1988). If computer resources are available, the research also helps develop student computer search skills on CD-ROMs and the Internet.

When students first start using databases, it is helpful to develop a sheet for students to record the information that will be entered into the database (Figure 7-11). As students become more proficient using a database, they can develop their own means of recording the collected information.

FIGURE 7-11 Database Record Sheet

Database Information Sheet

Name of Database ____________________

Name of Group Members ____________________
____
____
____
____

Database Fields	**Database Information**
Record 1	
____________	____________________
____________	____________________
____________	____________________
____________	____________________
____________	____________________
____________	____________________
Record 2	
____________	____________________
____________	____________________
____________	____________________
____________	____________________
____________	____________________
____________	____________________

Planning: Activities After Computer Use

Once the data are entered and reports generated, students then use the Think Sheet to analyze the information and solve the driving question or problem. During this time, students often go back and forth between their group area and their assigned computer. This activity is the most engaging portion of the lesson because students begin to discover or synthesize new information. This discovery process often leads to the development of new questions and further analysis of the collected information and a need for additional research. When students use databases in this manner, they are modeling information processing tasks performed every day in the workforce. For example, teams of engineers, retail merchants, architects, biologists, and many other professionals routinely collect and analyze data to solve problems and guide decision-making processes.

It is a good idea to have students participate in some kind of culminating activity that requires them to reflect on the learning that has occurred. This culminating activity can involve writing a group report that includes reports printed out from the database or reports created from placing database results into a spreadsheet and generating graphs of the results. Or students could create a multimedia presentation using a program similar to HyperStudio (see Chapter 8). Again, all of these activities actively engage the students in multiple generative learning strategies.

Assessment

When planning assessment strategies for lessons that integrate student use of databases, the rubrics will probably have increased emphasis on organization, classification, and synthesis. For example, criteria for this aspect of performance could include some of the following:

- Relevance and thoroughness of fields
- Accuracy of data entries
- Sufficient detail
- Logical organization
- Meaningful reports

SUMMARY

Databases are an easy and efficient means of storing, organizing, and manipulating information or data. They can be integrated into numerous lesson plans because their functions emulate many learning objectives that focus on developing critical-thinking skills. When students create a database, they are actively engaged in reading, analyzing, categorizing, organizing, and paraphrasing. When students use databases, they are able to manipulate information to solve problems, answer questions, and conduct investigations that promote meaningful learning. If students are placed into groups to solve problems, they can collaboratively generate predictions and ask "What if?" questions that lead to additional database queries as they search for solutions. As a result, students are able to critically examine bodies of information to detect trends and commonalities. The database skills that students acquire in school will be used throughout their lives, because databases are used for information management throughout our society.

AT THE CLASSROOM'S DOORSTEP

Questions Teachers Ask

Will it really be beneficial for my students to spend the extra time it takes to build a database that is only used for a couple of lessons?

Building a database can be very beneficial for students because it requires a great deal of information processing. However, you probably do not want to use a database for every lesson. If your lesson objectives involve a rich set of information, the use of a database will extend the processing abilities of the students and promote active engagement with the information (Derry, 1990). Another option is to create databases from downloaded information, thus saving setup time, but allowing student manipulation and examination of the information. This could be done for commonly studied topics such as planets in the solar system, endangered species, U.S. states, and so on.

Creating and using a database seems to be a complicated process. How can younger students do this?

Students should be able to read before they create and use a database. You can start young students with very simple databases that only have two or three fields. You may want to begin with a database that you have created. You can even have all the fields as pop-up menus so the students do not have to enter any words. An easy way to start would be with a birthday database to familiarize your students with a monthly calendar. Students could enter their name and date of birth and then select their birth month from a pop-up menu.

ISTE NETS FOR STUDENTS

When students engage in the development and use of databases to more closely examine and learn subject area content, four NETS for Students are directly addressed. The first is Standard 1 (basic operations and concepts) in that students work directly with the databases from initial development to creating final reports, which results in increased knowledge and understandings of basic database functions. Next is Standard 3, which recommends student use of technology productivity tools, of which databases are one of the most commonly used tools in today's workforce. Following this are Standards 4 and 5, technology research tools and problem-solving/decision-making tools; both are directly correlated to the NTeQ approach, which has students use databases and other tools to support research targeted toward solving meaningful problems.

TECHNOLOGY INTEGRATION ACTIVITIES

To access the activities that connect the content of the text with the Companion Website and other technology, please go to the Activities module in Chapter 7 of the Companion Website at *http://www.prenhall.com/morrison.*

NTEQ LESSON PLAN

LESSON TITLE: Our Fall Leaves

SUBJECT AREA: Science

GRADE LEVEL: 2 to 3

Learning Objective

By the end of this lesson, the students will classify leaves as simple or complex.

Computer Functions

- Database will be used to organize information collected about the fall leaves.
- Word processing will be used to write a final report about the fall leaves.

Specify Problem

"What is the most common leaf shape in our playground?"

Data Manipulation

- Students will use a database to examine descriptive information about the leaves they collect (name of leaf, color, type, shape, etc.).
- Students will use word processing to edit and revise a report describing how they determined the most common shape of leaf found on the playground.

Results Presentation

The final product will be a word processed report describing the fall leaves on the playground.

Multidimensional Activities

Activities Before Computer Use

- Teacher introduces the problem and guides the class through the beginning problem-solving steps.
- Students are placed into small groups.
- Student groups decide how they will collect leaves and how they will record their observations of each leaf.
- Students go outside and collect leaves.
- Students return to class and begin recording observations of each leaf on "Leaf Data Sheet" (color, size, edge patterns, type, etc.).

- Students plan computer tasks
  1. Define fields for database.
  2. Choose common words for data entry (e.g., Leaf edge = smooth or jagged; not smooth and wavy).
  3. Decide how data will be sorted.
  4. Determine what database reports will be printed.
  5. Select what will be included in report prepared with the word-processing program.
- Students plan what to include in the final report.

Activities During Computer Use

The following computer tasks are divided among group members:

- Create database fields.
- Enter data—each student enters data.
- Sort data—sorting tasks are equally divided among the students.
- Print results—sorts that resulted in answering questions are printed.
- Each student enters a portion of the final report.

Activities After Computer Use

- Answer the Think Sheet questions
  1. What is the most common shape of fall leaf in our playground?
  2. What differences are there in the sizes of our fall leaves?
  3. What differences are there in the colors of our fall leaves?
- As a large group, have the reporter from each group share the group's findings.
- Discuss the characteristics of a simple and compound leaf. Facilitate a summary and review session with the whole class by discussing the Think Sheet responses. During the discussion, clarify any misconceptions that arise and reemphasize the key learning objective.

Supporting Activities

- Make leaf rubbing of both a simple leaf and a compound leaf.
- View videotape on fall leaves.

Assessment

Create a rubric for assessing the following:

- Database.
- Fields named appropriately.
- Data entered accurately.
- Sorts are accurate.

- Printed reports contain appropriate information.
- Report.
- Meaningful problem solution is presented.
- Information is clear and easy to understand.
- Information is accurate.
- Format is appropriate.
- Report is free of errors.

LESSON BYTES FOR DATABASES

The following list contains suggestions for databases that can be created by elementary, middle, and high school students, and a sample problem statement for each.

Elementary Students

Active volcanoes

- Where could you live if you wanted to avoid volcanoes? Study an active volcano? Study the oldest volcano?

Classification (Shapes, Parts of Speech, Animals, Plants)

- Your team is to choose plants for three flower beds at your school, one in full sun, one next to the water sprinkler, and one inside the front entrance. Which plants can be placed together in the same flower bed?

Endangered Species

- If you were given a grant to "save" three endangered species, which three would you choose and why?

Food Groups

- How healthy is the cafeteria food in your school?

Planets

- Do bigger planets have more moons or rings?

Survey Information

- Who is more likely to recycle—males or females? Which item is recycled the most? Why? If you had to choose five items to recycle, which would you choose and why?

U.S. Cities or States

- How does weather influence the population size of cities? Of states? Which factors have the greatest impact on the population size of cities? Of states?

Middle School and High School Students

Authors and Their Works

- Which factors may have influenced the type of writing completed by American authors?

Careers

- Which careers would be a good choice if you really enjoy science?

Character Portraits from Stories

- Which character traits influenced the outcome of the story?

Current or Past Government Representatives

- What characteristics of our presidents have changed over time and which have remained the same?

Historical Landmarks

- Has our state chosen the "right" historical landmarks to depict its past?

Observation Data

- Can the types of clouds that occur be predicted if you know the temperature, barometric temperature, and humidity?

Wars

- When examining the causes of major European wars, what are the most common reasons for the conflicts? Does length of a war affect the number of casualties or the final outcome?

Weather Patterns

- What differences are there in weather on the east coast versus weather on the west coast of the United States?

NTEQ PORTFOLIO ACTIVITIES: DATABASES

Please complete the following activities as part of the Database Section of your NTeQ Portfolio.

Reflections

The "Getting Started" portion of this chapter asked three questions that teachers might commonly ask. In this portion of your journal, a reflection question has been added to address how databases could be used to resolve the problem. Please use information from this chapter to answer the second question.

1. Have you ever worried because lessons often result in students just memorizing facts?
   - *Reflection Question:* Provide an example of how student use of a database can result in students going beyond memorization to deeper learning.
2. Have you wondered how to get your students engaged with the trends and patterns that are embedded in the content they are to learn?
   - *Reflection Question:* Use either the Fall Leaves or Teen Database from this chapter as a basis for writing Think Sheet questions that would have students identify trends and patterns that could be discovered within the chosen database.
3. Have you wished there was an easy way to have your students examine information from a multitude of perspectives?
   - *Reflection Question:* Describe the different types of sorts that could be conducted if students created a Presidential Database.

Lesson Ideas

Create a list of 10 databases that would be meaningful for your students to create. You can use the Lesson Bytes from this chapter or your curriculum standards to help you generate ideas. Expand five of those databases ideas by creating possible field names and sample data entries for two records for each of the five databases. You can use a format similar to the one used for Fall Leaves to display each sample database. After the fields and sample entries are created, write a problem statement similar to the ones found in this chapter's Lesson Bytes.

Lesson Plan

As a final demonstration of your understanding of how to have students use databases as a tool to enhance learning, select an appropriate topic and follow the NTeQ Lesson Plan Template to create a Database lesson. Make sure to create a sample database and print the various reports that students would submit with their final product.

REFERENCES

Derry, S. J. (1990). *Flexible cognitive tools for problem solving instruction.* Paper presented at the annual meeting of the American Educational Research Association, Boston, April 16–20.

Jonassen, D. H. (1988). Integrating learning strategies into courseware to facilitate deeper processing. In D. H. Jonassen (Ed.), *Instructional design for microcomputer courseware.* Hillsdale, NJ: Erlbaum.

Resnick, L. B., & Klopfer, L. E. (1987). Toward the thinking curriculum: An overview. In L. B. Resnick & L. E. Klopfer (Eds.), *Toward the thinking curriculum: Current cognitive research.* Alexandria, VA: ASCD.

KEY TOPICS

Why Present the Results?
Tools for Publishing
- Basic Layout
- Rules
- Headers and Footers
- Using Pictures and Graphics

Paper Reports
- Newspapers and Magazines
- Books

Electronic Reports
- Multimedia Presentations
- Creating Web Pages
- Radio and Television

Chapter 8

Publishing and Presentation

Once a researcher finishes a project, he or she will present the results for others to read. It is appropriate then that our student researchers also present the results of their work. The audience for their presentation can include other students in their class, students in a different grade or school, parents, or the community.

One process that computers have made much easier is publishing, including paper and electronic formats. Anyone who has a computer can publish a paper, newsletter, newspaper, book, Web page, or CD-ROM. Some schools now have access to television and radio studios where students can produce their own programming. Publications such as newspapers and books that we have always viewed as printed on paper are now published on a Website or sent to readers via e-mail. Twenty-five years ago we might have viewed the information explosion as limited to a finite supply of paper and ink. Today the information explosion is limited only by electronic storage capacity that seems to grow at an even faster rate than the information! Although we do not want to clutter the world with trivial information, we do believe that students of all ages can produce knowledge that is both of interest and helpful to others. For example, we once heard an astronomy teacher describe how scientists from around the country have commented on his students' astronomy papers published on the school's Web page. Now that your students have solved a problem, it is appropriate for them to present their results to share with their classmates, other students, parents, and maybe the rest of the world.

GETTING STARTED

What Do I Know?

1. Why present the results?
2. What are the various ways my students can present their results?
3. What tools can they use?

Classroom Snapshot

The last 2 weeks in Mr. Hines' tenth-grade classroom have been quite hectic, or so it would seem to anyone passing by in the hall. There were even rumors that Mr. Hines was the new slave driver at Leatherwood Creek High School. His students have not been seen in the lunch room for some time—it seems they are all bringing their lunch and eating at their desks. Often, 10 to 15 students stay after school for 30 to 45 minutes. Can social studies be that engaging?

Mr. Hines created a unit that would take 6 weeks to complete. The students are actually working on several units at the same time, because this unit on the election process has several components. After the introduction, the students decided to survey voting-age residents in their school district to determine if they voted in the last local and national elections. If they did not vote, they were asked to answer several questions as to why they did not vote. For example, less than 6% of those eligible voted in the last school board election. The students analyzed their data and identified the most common reasons for not voting.

Then the students suggested that they develop a plan to address this problem. One group created a Web page for the city indicating how to register and where to vote. They also found that there were a lot of new residents in the area, so they developed a pamphlet with information similar to that on the Website that could be distributed by realtors and the city. To implement their plan, Mr. Hines made arrangements for the students to make a presentation at the city council meeting. The students created a PowerPoint presentation, as well as a report on their project. They also selected two students to make the presentation. The council was amazed at the students' research and recommendations. They passed a resolution directing the mayor to place the students' Web pages on the city's site and to make copies of the brochure for new residents. Mr. Hines and his class were invited to make another presentation in the future to see if voting behaviors had changed as a result of their work.

WHY PRESENT THE RESULTS?

If your students have completed an integrated computer lesson, they have learned new content, solved problems, and maybe discovered new relationships among ideas that you had not anticipated. A final step in an integrated lesson is for each student or team to present their results. This publishing process can help students synthesize ideas as they work through their data and determine what they want to tell others (Brookes, 1988; Corbine, 1995; Johannessen & Kahn, 1991) and to become active and involved in the learning (Keys, 1999). The process of writing or elaborating on ideas can help students discover ideas and relationships (Corbine, 1995) from their data analysis. Students can also respond to provocative questions from the teacher and their peers, which helps focus their writing and improve their understanding of the content (Brookes, 1988). This approach addresses the problems of school Web pages focusing primarily on school information rather than using the pages to help students synthesize their knowledge (Ivers & Barron, 1999).

Preparing a report of a study conducted in a science, social studies, math, or language arts class provides the students with an opportunity to generate meaning for the lesson concepts (Wittrock 1974, 1990). Writing allows the students to expand their ideas in a report. This expansion can include defining or explaining an idea (elaboration), making a new connection between two ideas (extension), and supporting or qualifying an idea with additional information (enhancement) (Halliday, 1985). There are several ways that students can publish their results as part of the *Results Presentation* step of the NTeQ model. Writing can include traditional reports, but it can also include television and radio style programs (Welsh, 1994), as well as Web pages and multimedia presentations.

If you are using portfolios to collect a longitudinal record of your students' progress, a published report adds another dimension to portfolio assessment. Middle and high school teachers, as well as elementary teachers in departmentalized (e.g., different teachers for different subjects) schools, can use the publishing step as a cross-disciplinary project that integrates language arts classes (e.g., writing across the curriculum) with the other disciplines. The spreadsheet and database components of integrated software such as AppleWorks and Microsoft Works (or stand-alone applications) provide opportunities to enter and manipulate data and generate charts to show results. The word processing component or application allows learners to synthesize and report what each has learned from the data manipulations. The following sections of this chapter illustrate how to create reports, books and newsletters, slide shows and presentations, and Web pages.

TOOLS FOR PUBLISHING

Basic Layout

Layout refers to how the report looks on the page or computer screen and includes the margins, font, and text styles (we will use the term "page" to refer to both paper reports and computer screens). The margins determine where the text will print on the page. Pages with a margin that is too narrow or with too little white space appear cramped and may dissuade some readers. Fonts are used to create emphasis and communicate a feeling about the report. The following sections provide general guidelines for designing a report that is printed, presented, or published on the Internet.

If multiple students are planning to contribute to the same publication, they will want all their contributions to have a similar look and format. For example, if your class is working on a newspaper, then all the pages should have a similar overall appearance. You can help your students achieve this look by creating or helping them create a template or stationery. This template has predefined margins, fonts, and styles so that each student's paper is similar to all the others. The following sections describe some of the considerations to include in your template.

Margins

Word processors have a default template or stationery that is used each time you create a new document. For your own personal computer, you might want to customize these settings to fit your needs (e.g., double spacing and a 12-point font). Classroom

CHECK IT OUT 8-1

Typography for Publications

There are several Websites devoted to typography. You can download a variety of materials and information from these sites, including free fonts.

http://www.microsoft.com/typography/links/default.asp
http://www.redsun.com/type/
http://www.mcu.org.uk/articles/acc

Link to these resources and activities in the Check It Out module for this chapter of the Companion Website.

and lab computers, however, should all use the same default page. For class projects such as a newspaper, the students should avoid making modifications to the default template's margins. However, you can provide the students with a template for their newspaper that has different margins.

Margins for a printed document are limited by the duplicating and binding. For example, most word processors require a minimum margin of approximately ½ inch to print. Using *all* the paper for printing is seldom wise because it makes the document look cluttered and unappealing. If you are planning to bind the document or documents, appropriate space is needed on the left side or top. Materials that are placed in a three-ring notebook must have space for the holes. If you are using a thermal binding such as those available at copy stores, you must allow enough room for the binding and fold of the pages so you can read the words against the left margin. Longer documents will require a wider left margin to allow for the space taken by the folded pages.

Printed documents can vary in size. Most documents are printed in a **portrait** format on an 8.5- × 11-inch piece of paper so that it measures 11 inches from top to bottom. You can also print in **landscape** format so that the page measures 8.5 inches from top to bottom (select Page Setup from the File menu). You can also select smaller (e.g., 5.5 × 8.5) and larger (e.g., 11 × 17) sizes of paper if you have a printer capable of printing these sizes. Another option is to lay out the document so that two or more columns are printed on a page. If you decide to use columns, make sure there is adequate space between the columns and the columns are wide enough to make the text readable.

For 12-point type, the column should be approximately 3 inches wide, because a narrower column will be difficult to read. Another option is to use a landscape format and create either two larger columns or three small columns (Figure 8-1).

Guidelines for margins in a multimedia presentation such as PowerPoint, AppleWorks, or HyperStudio slide shows are similar to those for a printed page. You can

FIGURE 8-1 Column Layout

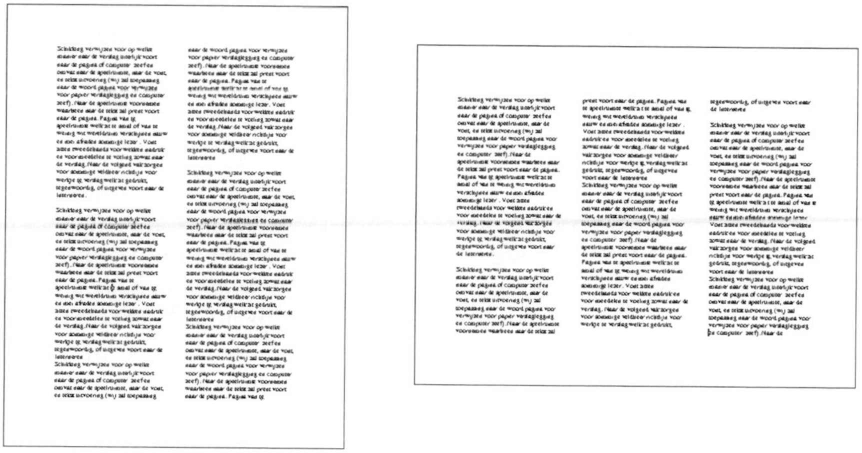

change the size of the text boxes in which you display your information, but avoid making the text area as wide as the actual slide, for esthetic purposes. Margins on Web pages have a different meaning. Web pages are of two types. The first type allows the text to expand and contract as the width of the Web page changes. For example, view *http://www.cfsan.fda.gov/~dms/fdfats.html* in your browser. Note how the width of the page varies as you change the width of your browser window. The second format is illustrated by *http://www.yahoo.com/*. Note how the text on the main page stays the same width as you change the width of your browser window.

Fonts

Most computers have fewer than a dozen different fonts. We have found computers that still have only three or four fonts, and we have found computers that have a hundred or more fonts. You can download fonts from the Internet, you can purchase CD-ROMs with fonts, and you can also receive free CD-ROMs with fonts when you purchase some magazines and books. Our advice, however, is to keep only a few fonts on your computer. If you look at a book or magazine, you will find that most use only two or three fonts throughout the entire document. Good designs typically use only one or two fonts rather than a "ransom note" approach!

How can your students select an appropriate font for a report or newsletter? First, on a Macintosh, avoid fonts that are names of cities, such as Geneva or New York. These fonts are specifically designed to work on the screen and were not meant for printed documents. For all but graphic design classes, we suggest that you have your students select only *one* common font for a report, such as Helvetica, Times, Palatino, or New Century School Book. Selecting a font installed on all of your computers makes it easy for students to work on different computers. One font, however, does not mean the reports will look plain. The secret is to use many variations.

Students can use different sizes of type for headings. They can use bold, italic, shadows, small caps, or outlines for emphasis. They can combine font sizes with bold and italic to create variety. By using one font with many variations as opposed to multiple fonts, the students can produce a more professional-looking document while avoiding the disorganized, ransom note look.

Styles

Styles are predetermined formatting selections that students can apply to their documents. For example, if your class is creating a book consisting of a chapter from each of four groups, you might want each chapter to have a consistent look. That is, the chapter heading might be 36-point Times and centered and the body of the report 12-point Times. Headings in the chapters might be 14-point Times in bold. You can add these styles to your template or stationery document so that the students can produce similar-looking documents. You also can create a template for research papers. Students can then gain experience in using consistent styles for their papers that follow a published style guide, such as the *MLA Style Guide*.

Most popular word processors allow you to define styles. You can create styles for the body text, headings, bulleted lists, titles, picture captions, and so on. If you want your students to use the styles, you can save them as a template once they are defined. When creating a new document, the students need to select the template or stationery you have created. Once the new document is open, they will have access to the styles. Without the styles, the student would need to center the text, select a size of 16 points, select bold, and then type the text. If the styles are available, the student can type the text, select it, and then select the appropriate style from a menu or palette. There are several advantages to using styles. First, you can change the appearance of *all* instances of a single style such as Heading 1 with a single task. Simply change the font, size, and so on of the style, and the word processor will update all instances of the style in the document automatically. Second, if you combine documents from several students who have used the same styles, the students can easily change the styles to create a more pleasing look. They only need to change the style's definition, and the word processor will update each instance. If they had set each heading by making it bold, then changing to 16-point type, and finally centering the text; they would need to make changes to *each* instance. Thus the use of styles makes it easier to change the appearance of a document and provides a way to produce consistent-looking documents.

The ability to produce consistent document styles is useful if you are creating a single book based on reports or projects created by different groups. Creating and using styles is an advanced feature of a word processor that could be confusing for less experienced computer users. Although styles can make the task of formatting a document much easier, they may introduce an additional complexity that frustrates some users. Therefore you may want to introduce your students to styles by using only one or two choices, for example, Report Title and Section Headings. You can add additional styles as students become more familiar with using styles. Students can help decide which other elements of the report would be easier to format if a designated style were created.

Rules

Rules are thin or thick lines used to separate text. Books often have a rule near the top of the page to separate the chapter heading or page number from the text. Newspapers use rules to separate stories or quotes in a story or to highlight a table. Students can use rules to add flair to their written documents. Related to rules are borders that you can apply to all four sides of a paragraph or section, or to only selected parts (Figure 8-2).

Rules and borders can help emphasize and highlight the text in a word processing document, newsletter, or book, or in an Internet Web page. However, caution should

FIGURE 8-2 Rules and Borders

Styles

Styles are predetermined formatting selections that students can apply to their documents. For example, if your class is creating a book consisting of a chapter from each of four groups, then you might want each chapter to have a consistent look. That is, the chapter heading might be 36 point Times and centered while the body of the report is 12 point Times. Headings in the chapters might be 14 point Times in bold. You can add these styles to your template or stationery document so that the students can produce similar looking documents. Similarly, you can create a template for research papers. Students can then gain experience in using consistent styles for their papers that follow a published style guide, for example, the *MLA Style Guide*.

Most popular word processors allow you to define styles. You can create styles for the body text, headings, bulleted lists, titles, picture captions, and so on. If you want your students to use the styles, then you can save them as a template once they are defined. When creating a new document, the students need to select the template or stationery you have created. Once the new document is open, they will have access to the styles. Without the styles, the student would need to center the text, select a size of 16 points, select bold, and then type the text. If the styles are available, the student can type the text, select it, and then select the appropriate style from a menu or palette. There are several advantages to using styles.

Styles

First, you can change the appearance of *all* instances of a single style such as Heading 1 with a single task. Simply change the font, size, and so on of the style and the word processor will update all instances of the style in the document automatically. Second, if you combine documents from several students who have used the same styles, the students can easily change the styles to create a more pleasing look. If they had set each heading by making it bold, then changing to 16 point type, and finally centering the text; then they would need to make changes to *each* instance. Thus, the use of styles makes it easier to change the appearance of a document and provides a way to produce consistent looking documents.

Styles provide a way to produce consistent documents that are very useful if you are creating a single book based on reports or projects created by different groups. Creating and using styles is an advanced feature of a word processor that could be confusing for less experienced computer users. While styles can make the task of formatting a document much easier, they may introduce an additional complexity that frustrates some users. Therefore you may want to introduce your students to styles by using only one or two choices, for example, Report Title and Section Headings. You can add additional styles as students become more familiar with using styles. Students can help decide which other elements of the report would be easier to format if a designated style were created.

Styles

First, you can change the appearance of *all* instances of a single style such as Heading 1 with a single task. Simply change the font, size, and so on of the style and the word processor will update all instances of the style in the document automatically. Second, if you combine documents from several students who have used the same styles, the students can easily change the styles to create a more pleasing look. If they had set each heading by making it bold, then changing to 16-point type, and finally centering the text; then they would need to make changes to *each* instance. Thus the use of styles makes it easier to change the appearance of a document and provides a way to produce consistent looking documents.

be used to guard against overuse. Using too many rules or boxes can result in the text looking choppy and less appealing to the reader.

Headers and Footers

Headers and footers are used to place the same information at the top and bottom of every page or group of pages in a document. They are particularly useful when assembling a portfolio or a document with contributions from several students. Students can use headers and footers to identify individual contributions or sections and to add page numbers to each page. Word processors have an automatic function for including the page number in the header or footer. There are many variations on how to display the page numbers. For example, you might want to add the child's name to the pages—Jenni-1, Jenni-2, Jenni-3, Keegan-4, Keegan-5, and so on. Similarly, you could add a title to the header, or simply "dress up" the number: —5—, —6—.

To create a more attractive header, you can use a rule or underscore below the text of the header or above the text of the footer to separate it from the text. You can enter a carriage return on the first blank line of the footer and underline the blank line to create the same effect. Adding an extra line after a header or before a footer will separate it from the text, creating a polished look.

Using Pictures and Graphics

The final aspect of creating a report is to add pictures or graphics to illustrate the text. Often students (and teachers) want to include a graphic with their report. A graphic can illustrate an idea such as a cell nucleus or a graph of the results entered in a spreadsheet. A graphic could also just serve as a decoration for the report. Most word processing and desktop publishing applications allow the user to include graphics with the text. Students can use graphics that they have created with a draw program, photographs from a digital camera, scanned pictures, and clip art in their reports. When using the graphic with text, the student will need to make a decision concerning how the text is wrapped around the graphic. Figure 8-3 illustrates some of the options for text wrap.

Ways of Drawing

There are two basic ways to draw pictures with a computer. Each method has strengths and weaknesses. One method is often referred to as drawing or drawing objects, and the other is referred to as painting. The following section provides a brief description of the two approaches to help you select the method that is best for a project.

One of the major differences between paint and draw programs is how they draw on the computer screen. Let's consider a drawing of a spotted leopard. We would probably start by drawing an outline of the leopard. Then we would add spots to the leopard. We could use either a draw or paint application to draw the leopard—the computer will follow our instructions exactly. The application, though, will store the information differently, and that is the source of the difference between the two documents.

FIGURE 8-3 Text Wrap Around a Picture

The final aspect of creating a report is to add pictures or graphics to illustrate the text. Often students (and teachers) want to include a graphic with their report. A graphic can illustrate an idea such as a cell nucleus or a graph of the results entered in a spreadsheet. A graphic could also just serve as a decoration for the report. Most word processing and desktop publishing applications allow the user to include graphics with the text.

Students can use graphics that they have created with a draw program, photographs from a digital camera, scanned pictures, and clip art in their reports. When using the graphic with text, the student will need to make a decision concerning how the text is wrapped around the graphic. Figure 8-3 illustrates some of the options for text wrap. There are two basic ways to draw pictures on a computer.

Each method has its strengths and weaknesses. One method is often referred to as drawing or drawing objects and the other is referred to as painting. The following section provides a brief description of the two approaches to help you select the method that is best for a project. One of the major differences between paint and draw documents is how they draw on the computer screen. Let's consider a drawing of a spotted leopard. We would probably start by drawing an outline of the leopard. Then, we add spots to the leopard. We could use either a drawing or paint application to draw the leopard—the computer will follow our instructions exactly. The application, though, will store the information differently, and that is the source of the difference between the two documents.

As we drag the cursor over a pixel (a scientific name for an off and on switch the size of a small dot on the computer screen) to draw our leopard, the computer turns the pixel on so that it is black or the color we selected. Think of your computer screen as a grid of 640 × 480 pixels that we can turn on or off with the cursor. The computer remembers which pixels are on and which pixels are off using a map of the screen grid. A paint document, then, is a map of the complete image with an indication of which pixels are on and which are off.

As we drag the cursor over a *pixel* (a scientific name for an off and on switch the size of a small dot on the computer screen) to draw our leopard, the computer turns the pixel on so that it is black or the color we selected. Think of your computer screen as a grid of 640 × 480 pixels that you can turn on or off with the cursor. The computer remembers which pixels are on and which pixels are off using a map of the screen grid. A paint program treats a word you have typed the same as a circle—both are described as pixels that are on (e.g., black) in that part of the map. When you save your file, the computer writes this map of the entire image with the on and off position of each pixel to the disk. When you open the file, the computer reads the map and turns the pixels on or off to recreate your illustration. It is somewhat like playing chess or checkers with someone at a distance. You tell them where you moved, and they make an appropriate mark on their map or board. When they send you information about their move, you update your map. If your dog or cat knocks the board off the table, you can recreate the image by placing the pieces according to your partner's board. A paint document, then, is a map of the complete image with an indication of which pixels are on and which are off. Paint documents are often referred to as bit-mapped graphics because they are a map of the bits on the computer screen.

In comparison to a paint program, a draw program is a mathematical wonder. A draw program also "paints" the screen like a paint program. However, a draw program creates *objects* such as lines, squares, circles, and text that are described by mathematical equations that are literally used to draw the object. For example, a draw program might describe a circle as having an origin at grid location 200,145 on the screen and a radius of 78. The draw program uses a formula to draw the circle. Thus each object drawn is stored as a mathematical formula or function rather than as a map of the screen. Draw programs will save information for each object to a disk when you save the file and then use this information to redraw each object when the file is opened. Thus a paint document sees the whole painting space as a single map with off and on switches. A draw document uses a mathematical formula to keep track of every object—its location on the screen, its size, and so on—much like written directions to a location rather than a map of the roads.

Making the Choice

Selecting a draw or paint document depends on your objective. Table 8-1 describes the advantages and disadvantages of each.

Selecting the type of document to use is based on what you want to do and your level of skill. For example, if you want to create an illustration such as a still life, then you will probably want to use a paint document. If you are creating a layout for a poster that uses objects and text, then you would probably select a draw program. Some tasks, such as editing a picture taken with a digital camera, are best accomplished using a paint program. We have found that individuals who have well-developed drawing or painting skills are very adept at using a paint program. Lacking such a skill, we prefer to use a draw program, which allows us as much freedom as possible to correct our mistakes!

These procedures for using styles, headers and footers, and graphics can give your students' reports a professional appearance. One problem we have observed with desktop publishing is that there is more emphasis on the desktop publishing aspect of the report than on the actual research and writing aspects. We are reminded of an old computer phrase, GIGO—garbage in results in garbage out. In other words, a pleasing appearance will not improve the information in a poorly written and researched report.

PAPER REPORTS

Sometimes, you or your students may want to do something more than just create a report. A book, magazine, or newspaper might provide a more appropriate method for disseminating their new knowledge. For example, a class that has created a number of reports on animals might prepare a book for a lower grade. If a class has completed a project identifying plants in a park or school, the group might want to create a book for the library or the park commission. Similarly, the class might want to prepare a newspaper or magazine to report their findings. This section describes the tools students can use to create newspapers, magazines, and books.

TABLE 8-1 Comparison of Draw and Paint Capabilities

TASK	DRAW	PAINT
Drawing circles, squares, lines, etc.	Easy to do with tools	Easy to do with tools
Moving an object such as a circle	Click on object and drag it to new location	Difficult to select if overlapping another object Will leave an image on other object if moved
Resizing an object such as a circle	Select the object and drag handles to resize	Can resize, but image is often distorted and has jagged edges
Selecting part of an object	Cannot do, must select whole object	Can select and move any part of image
Changing parts of the drawing or object	Cannot change the parts of a circle	Can use various tools to change individual pixels of image
Layering objects	Easy to layer objects and then change them	Can layer objects, but cannot move individual layers once they are drawn
Overlapping objects with transparent mode (when top object is filled with a color)	Can do only when object is drawn	Can make objects opaque, transparent, or tinted

Newspapers and Magazines

Another alternative for students to use when publishing the results of their work is a newspaper or magazine. They can use newspapers as a means of publishing their work as it progresses or as the final product of their work (Figure 8-4). Most word processors can create multiple columns of text and even present templates for creating newsletters.

A magazine and newspaper require some initial planning to reduce the effort needed to assemble the edition. First, help your students create the basic layout. The layout includes the heading or masthead that appears at the top of the first page. Next, determine if the publication will have one or two columns. Finally, you might

FIGURE 8-4 An Example Student Newspaper

Project News

Lincoln Elementary's Fifth Grade Team Reports

Tree Mapping Team

We are making a map of all the trees at the school. We draw a picture of each tree on our map. The picture is what a bird sees when flying. One of us prints the name of the tree in the picture using the computer. We glue the name on the picture.

Next week, we will color each of the trees. We need to select colors for the

Plant Identification Team

Our team is naming all the plants at the school. A woman from a nursery came to school this week. She helped us use a book to find the plant names. We found many types of bushes.

We are going to name the different types of flowers. Some flowers only bloom one time. Other flowers bloom every year.

Determining the type of final product should be a group decision.

want to determine how you will number each edition if you plan to publish your newspaper or magazine on a regular basis. Second, you will need an editor for each edition. This student or students will determine the order of the stories, the headlines, and the pictures to include. Third, you will need to provide each student with a template so everyone uses the same styles when preparing their articles.

Newspapers and magazines are excellent formats for publishing the results of studies the students have conducted. For example, in a science class, students might test different household products such as household cleaning products or breakfast foods each month. They could use a newspaper format to report their results to help parents decide which products to purchase. A class that is studying an environmental problem or voting behaviors might select a magazine format for a special issue to report their results.

If your class decides to create a realistic-looking publication, you may need to use a desktop publishing application such as Adobe's PageMaker or Microsoft Publisher. These applications allow you to create and print a variety of formats.

THE TEACHER'S DIARY

What I really like about using computers in the classroom is that they allow my students to publish their work in a variety of formats. Students are limited only by their imagination as to what they can publish in the classroom.

We study communities in our social studies curriculum. One of our thematic units is the study of our own community. We spend 4 weeks learning all about our community and its history. As a culminating event, we take a walking field trip to visit the town square, post office, police station, fire station, and several of the historic buildings. The students always enjoy this field trip. They especially like to see things such as the mail carriers sorting the mail before putting it on the mail trucks, the police dispatcher's desk where the 911 calls are answered, the inside of a police car, the rescue fire truck, and so on. In the past, the students returned to school and wrote paragraphs using a word processing program about something that they had seen on the field trip.

One year the students decided to write a book about their community. They wanted to take what they had experienced and learned on the field trip and add to it. The field trip was not the culminating activity that year, but rather the beginning activity for a book publishing project.

The students wanted to learn even more about the community. So, we invited some community business and civic leaders to come into our classroom to tell us about our community: its past, present, and future.

We learned a lot, and we wanted to pass this knowledge on. Many of us were new to the community and had recently experienced a move, so we thought it would be a good idea to write a book about the community. This book would be written specifically for children, and it would portray the community from a child's perspective. The students hoped that this book might introduce children moving into the area to our community and convey the message that our community was a great place for kids to live!

The students were divided into groups of four. Each group was given a historic place, school, or community building to research. They had to draw a picture of

Continued

the building, research its history, and interview people associated with it. This activity was completed after school and on Saturday mornings. After collecting their information, the students worked in their groups to write a page about their assigned building. These pages were prepared using a word processing program and the drawings were scanned to make up the body of the book. We added another section because we had learned so much interesting information. We created a "photograph" section, Looking at Our Community Through Our Eyes. Each student drew a picture of somewhere special in the community and wrote a caption to go under the picture. We scanned these drawings, and each student handwrote the caption.

I helped them put everything together and printed a copy of the book. They were so excited! They all wanted the book. I felt like each student had to have a book. They had worked so hard. I didn't know what I was going to do, but my prayers were answered! A local business had heard about our project and volunteered to print copies of our books. In fact, they were going to print 1,000 copies so that the Chamber of Commerce could put them in the packets that are sent to people wanting information about the community.

The company that printed our books invited us to their printing facility. They had a complete graphic arts department and printing press. We visited the graphic arts department, and the director put the computer disk that had the student's book on it into his big-screen computer and showed the students how he could manipulate their drawings and text. There were a lot of oohs and ahhs! He then took us into the printing shop and showed us the equipment. As we stood watching the printing press, the pages of our book began to come off the press. I will never forget the looks on the students' faces. It was so exciting! We also got to watch the books go through the machine that folded and stapled the pages together.

The students got to take their books home that night. Not only did they have a book published, but they also got a once-in-a-lifetime experience. They got to see a project develop from the conception of an idea to the finished product. They also learned a lot about their community and developed a sense of community pride. Best of all, they were able to give a little of themselves back to the community by writing this book.

Frank Clark
Third-Grade Teacher

Books

Many of the techniques used to prepare a newspaper or magazine are applicable to creating a book. There are three additional considerations for a book. First, you must allow a larger left margin for binding the book. Second, you must plan for a table of contents. Third, you need to print the book to create facing pages. Often, you can use a word processor to create the book layout and use the copy machine to print back-to-back pages.

Book Margins

Extra space is needed on the left margin for binding the book. The amount of space needed will increase for larger books (100+ pages) to accommodate the fold of the paper. A variety of options are available for binding at copy stores that provide a pro fessional touch.

Table of Contents

The table of contents provides a listing of the major chapters or sections of your book. Your students may want to study the table of contents from a variety of books to find a style they wish to use. A table of contents should provide the reader with a quick overview of the book. A brief table of contents includes just the title of the chapters. A more detailed table of contents would include the chapter titles and the first levels of headings. Some word processors will automatically generate a table of contents.

Facing Pages

When creating a book, you will print on both sides of the paper (or at least copy on the front and back if you are making multiple copies). Thus, if you were to open the book to page 4, which should be on the left side (Figure 8-5), page 5 would be on the right side. The left margin on page 4 would be on the *outside* (thumb) of the book, while the left margin for page 5 would be on the *inside* (gutter) near the binding. When printing a book, the larger margin should always be nearest the binding edge.

Most word processors and desktop publishing tools have a way to adjust the pages so the "left" margin prints in the correct position—closest to the binding. The margins of facing pages will mirror one another when they are printed, making it easy to assemble a book with the wider margin on the binding side.

Books are useful for publishing a collection of student reports on a similar topic. For example, if students are doing research on the history of their community, the collection of reports could be published as a book. Similarly, a collection of poems, drawings, or creative writings could also be published as a book.

FIGURE 8-5 Illustration of Mirror Margins

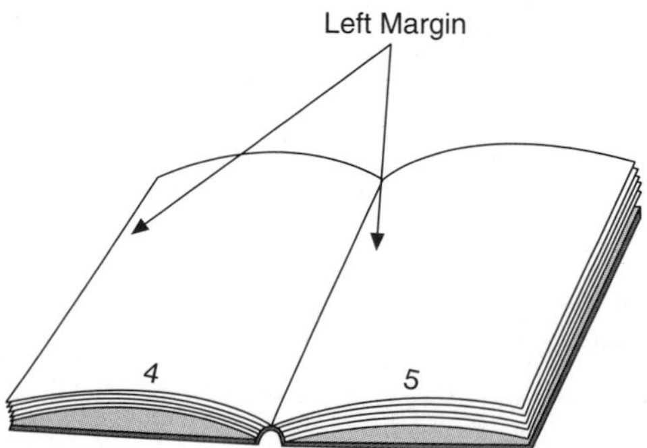

ELECTRONIC REPORTS

Today, students are not limited to just handwritten or word-processed reports. Students can publish their reports on the Internet as Web pages, make presentations using multimedia tools, or broadcast their ideas in a classroom, to the school, or to the local community using radio and television. This section will describe the use of other media for publishing results.

Multimedia Presentations

Sometimes printed materials are not suitable for presentation of student results even when printed with a color printer. An alternative to printed communication is a multimedia presentation that can incorporate sound, graphics, animation, video, and text. Students can create these presentations as electronic slide shows or hypermedia stacks. Although multimedia presentations provide a number of "bells and whistles," consider the reason for developing such presentations. We have often encountered teachers who simply teach their students how to develop a multimedia presentation for the sole purpose of creating the presentation. We encourage you to consider the purpose of the assignment and to develop a clear rationale for including such a project.

Students should complete two tasks before creating an electronic slide show or hypermedia stack: (1) plan the structure and (2) create a storyboard. When planning the structure of the project, the students need to address the following:

- Who is the intended audience?
- What is the project topic?
- What information will this project share?
- What is the actual purpose or goal of this project?

Next, students need to create a storyboard of the project. Storyboards are sketches of each card or slide in the presentation. Students can draw storyboards on a piece

PowerPoint Backgrounds

Several Websites in addition to Microsoft offer free backgrounds and templates for PowerPoint. The following is a list of some of our favorites.

http://www.powerpointart.com/index.html
http://www.powerpointbackgrounds.com/freesample.htm
http://powerpointsolutions.com/

Link to these resources and activities in the Check It Out module for this chapter of the Companion Website.

Production of a quality final product takes time and careful planning.

of notebook paper divided into four sections, or use note cards. Drawing only one card per page makes it very easy to reorder the cards. Careful planning before going to the computer results in less student frustration and more meaningful presentations (McBride & Luntz, 1996).

There are several applications for creating electronic slide shows or multimedia presentations. Some, including PowerPoint, are designed specifically for creating electronic presentations. Drawing programs such as AppleWorks and Canvas have a slide function. One advantage to using PowerPoint is the ability to print handouts and lecture notes.

Hypermedia Presentations

Sunburst's HyperStudio and Microsoft's PowerPoint are easy to use tools for creating hypermedia and multimedia presentations. Hypermedia and hypertext allow students to navigate through the content in different ways and explore the information based on their needs. A hypermedia unit incorporating sound, graphics, animations, or digital video is referred to as multimedia. Multimedia provides students with unique ways of communicating their ideas via the computer. An advantage of hypermedia and multimedia over an electronic slide show is that the user can select the sequence rather than following a set sequence of slides. There are also players you can install on any computer to run your presentation when the software application is not installed. In addition, you can also publish your presentations on your Website.

Power Tip

Time Frames

Students often want to spend their time adding animations, sound, graphics, and transitions to the slide shows at the expense of presenting well-organized content. One approach is to set a time frame for creating the content and one for adding the bells and whistles. For example, you allot 45 minutes for preparing the content on the slides and 15 minutes for adding graphics, animations, transitions, and so on.

Creating Web Pages

Printed materials and multimedia presentations reach a relatively small audience and are typically limited to times the student or author is available to present or distribute the information. The World Wide Web offers the advantage of making student research available to others beyond the classroom (see Chapter 9). Software applications such as Netscape Composer, DreamWeaver, and FrontPage make Web page creation as easy as writing a report with a word processor. Students can create Web pages to present their results that others with Web access can link to and read. A search of the Web will produce many K–12 school sites that publish materials on specific themes (e.g., astronomy, mammals, comets, ecology, etc.) and add to the sites each year with new materials produced by students. Sites that contain unique information, such as information on ancient mathematicians or scientists researching AIDS, can provide valuable information not only to other students but to other Web surfers.

Web Page Terminology

Web pages are created using special tags that tell the browser, for example, Netscape or Internet Explorer, how to display the text, graphics, animations, movies, and other features. These tags are referred to as HyperText Markup Language or, more commonly, HTML. Fortunately, you can design a Web page without knowing this language by using one of the applications described in the previous paragraph. A basic understanding of the features of HTML, however, can help you better design your Web page. Let's examine some of the features related to text, tables, graphics, color, and links.

Text

There are several options for displaying text on a Web page. You can select the size of the font and styles such as bold and italic (Figure 8–6); however, you should not specify a font (e.g., Times or Helvetica). If you specify a specific font and the user

CHECK IT OUT 8-3

Web Page Design

You can find several tutorials and guidebooks on the Web for Web page design. The following are some of our favorites:

Style Guides and Tutorials

http://www.webstyleguide.com/index.html?/contents.html
http://www.utoronto.ca/webdocs/HTMLdocs/NewHTML/intro.html
http://archive.ncsa.uiuc.edu/General/Internet/WWW/HTMLPrimerAll.html

Link to these resources and activities in the Check It Out module for this chapter of the Companion Website.

FIGURE 8-6 Text for a Web Page

Text Examples

Heading 1

Heading 6

Users can also use **bold** and *italic* for emphasis.

A numbered list:

1. Apples
2. Oranges
3. Grapes

A bulleted list:

- Apples
- Oranges
- Grapes

Definition and Term:

HTML
: A collection of tags for creating text documents that World Wide Web browsers can display according to standard formats.

does not have access to the font, the browser may not display the page as you intended. There are also six different preset heading levels you can select when creating a Web page. Heading 1 is the largest and heading 6 is the smallest. These headings are used much like the headings in desktop publishing—to indicate different sections of the content. You can also use different colors for your text and links, but remember, most links are in blue before accessing them and then turn to purple once you have followed the link. Changing the standard colors may confuse your visitors.

There are several ways of formatting different types of text. For example, if you have a list of items, you can use either a bulleted or numbered list. Most browsers will format these lists by identifying them and adding a number or bullet before each item. If you need to create a glossary or dictionary of terms, you can use the HTML term and definition tags to create a unique layout.

Tables

If you need to display information in a row and column format, you can create a table to align the data. Each cell of a table can hold text and/or a graphic (Figure 8-7). You can also adjust the width of the table border from no border to a very thick border.

Graphics

You can use clipart, digital or scanned photos, your own drawings, and rules in a Web document. Clipart and pictures that you draw are typically saved as GIF files,

FIGURE 8-7 A Table from a Web Page

Group	Example
Fats, Oils, & Sweets	Cake
Milk, Yogurt, & Cheese	Skim milk
Meat, Poultry, Dry Beans, Eggs, & Nuts	Omelet
Vegetable	Carrot
Fruit	Apple
Bread, Cereal, Rice, & Pasta	Brown rice

whereas photographs are saved as JPEG files that allow for more colors. Some Web page creation applications allow you to paste a picture into a Web document, and the application automatically converts it to a GIF file. Another "graphic" that is part of the HTML tag is a rule that is used much like a rule in desktop publishing (Figure 8-8). Remember, the use of graphics in your Web pages can slow the loading of the page and cause some users to skip your site.

Color

Web page documents allow you to specify the color of the background (the part of the window where the text is printed), color of the text, and the color of links. Although different colored backgrounds and text may look very appealing on your

FIGURE 8-8 A GIF Image and Rule from a Web Page

Our Pets

Lady Gaelin

My dog is an Irish Setter and is a year old. She likes to play ball and chase squirrels.

Nike

My cat likes to sleep on my bed all day long.

monitor, they may appear unreadable on another computer monitor because of the way the computer displays the selected colors. Most experienced Web masters test their color schemes on several different computers and monitors to make sure all the information is readable. We have found that simple color schemes with plenty of contrast between the background color and the text are easily read on most computers.

Links

The greatest feature of Web pages is the ability to link a word or graphic on one page to another page either on your server or another server halfway around the world. This process of linking documents is another example of **hypertext**—the ability to jump from one idea to another with a click of a mouse. A link is created by providing a Uniform Resource Locator (URL) or File Transfer Protocol (FTP) address to another page (URL) or file (FTP).

Many books and Web resources can guide you in designing a Website and Web pages (see Resources at the end of this chapter). Good Web pages and sites are user friendly—they are designed for the person *reading* the page and not the person *creating* the page. We recall one Web master who had designed several pages that our students could not read in the lab. When informed of this problem, the designer simply stated that the pages were readable on his computers. Rather than reading a poorly designed page, our students found another site with the same information. If you want Web surfers to visit your site and return to it many times, then focus on making your pages user friendly.

Considerations When Creating a Web Page

FrontPage and Netscape Composer have many similar features for designing a Web page. Creating a Web page is very similar to creating a word processing document. A Web page that uses the standard styles (e.g., headings, normal text, lists, etc.) will appear more consistently in your visitors' browsers than creating your own styles or conventions.

A poorly designed Web page can prove useless to its author and frustrating to users who choose to visit the site. Before spending time creating a Web page, first consider the goal of the page and the content, graphics, and layout (Snyder, 1996).

Goal. Why are your students going to publish? What do you want the Web page to accomplish? How does it tie in with your objectives for the project? These are all important questions to consider before students create their own Web pages. Once you or your students have clearly and specifically articulated the goal, make sure the design supports the goal. For example, a page designed solely to provide educational information will look much different from a page designed to be interactive.

Content. Nothing is more frustrating than surfing through a series of links only to find a final link that says, "Under Construction!" Content is everything on the web. Be sure that your site has something to say, says it, and leaves overused options, such as counters, guest books, and feedback buttons, to other sites (unless these options support your goals).

Graphics. Learn to be conservative in your use of graphics. They often can be distracting to readers, and they require a lot of memory, which makes it time-consuming for users trying to link to your page. We have often stopped a connection to a link because it was taking too long to download. If you want users to stay connected, make graphics useful.

Layout. Help users locate information quickly on your Web page by giving an overview up front. Many teachers create wonderfully extensive sets of Web pages, but lose those readers who just don't have the time to leisurely browse through many pages. A table of contents, an introductory paragraph, or a mini-search engine built into the top of the page will help users find what they want fast. Also, make the title succinct and as descriptive as possible. This will help when your page comes up as a hit in a search engine. Users can determine quickly whether they want to visit your site or not.

Once you have finished your Web pages, you must make them accessible to others. You will need to move them to your Web server. Depending upon your setup, you can either drag the files to the server or use an FTP program to transfer the files. There are several Websites that offer free Web space for publishing your pages if you cannot use a school server.

Radio and Television

The last type of publishing is the use of radio and television programs to publish student results. Students can use either real or mock broadcasts to report their findings. A radio program could be combined with a multimedia presentation to provide a narrated slide show to view in the classroom or place on the Web. Similarly, a television broadcast could be taped in the classroom, broadcast from the school's studio, broadcast on the local educational or local access channel, or converted to digital video and distributed on the Internet. Let's examine how to produce a program.

The Script

Radio and television programs start with a script. A radio script includes the narration and sound effects. A good radio script recreates a scene for the listener by using sound effects. For example, if a group of students is creating a radio program to report on traffic problems around the school or the use of seatbelts, they might use a tape recorder to capture the sounds of cars passing through the school parking lot. This recording is then used as a sound effect to make it appear the reporter is standing on the street corner while giving the report.

A radio script has two columns. The left column is narrow and indicates who is speaking (Figure 8-9). The right column includes the sound effects and narration.

CHECK IT OUT 8-4

Sound Effects

Sound effects can add depth to your radio programs or to a multimedia presentation. You can find examples of how sound effects are used to enhance a story on the National Public Radio (NPR) (*www.npr.org*) Website.

You can also search the Internet for free sound effects by using the search term "sound effects" at *www.google.com.*

Link to these resources and activities in the Check It Out module for this chapter of the Companion Website.

FIGURE 8-9 Sample Radio Script

Narrator:	In just a moment, we will have a report from Keegan on the current weather. Keegan just stepped out to check the snow accumulation and temperature.
	Sound Effect: Door Closing
Narrator:	Ah, there is Keegan now. Can you give us some updated information on the weather?
Keegan:	We now have 8 inches of snow near the school's flagpole. The temperature is 18 degrees.

A television script is also in two columns. The left column includes information about the video, and the right column is the narration. In a radio script, sound effects are used to create a vivid picture for the listener. In a video script, the students need to illustrate the narration with picture or live video. Figure 8-10 is a sample video script for the weather broadcast. This script has a host, Jenni, rather than a narrator.

The radio and television programs can use different formats to present the students' results. One format is a news broadcast in which the students read short scripts describing their results. If students have related, but different, topics such as reports on different countries or tests of different laundry detergents, then a talk show format could be used. A radio show variation would be a listener call-in format in which the listeners (i.e., other students) ask the expert (i.e., student presenting the report) questions. If you have the editing equipment or the ability to

FIGURE 8-10 Sample Video Script

Video	Narration
Jenni, the host, is sitting behind a desk.	Jenni: In just a moment, we will have a report from Keegan on the current weather.
Cut to video of Keegan measuring snowfall.	
Camera cuts to door where Keegan is entering.	
	Keegan just stepped out to check the snow accumulation and temperature. Ah, there is Keegan now. Can you give us some updated information on the weather?
Keegan walks to our weather map. Medium shot of Keegan and map.	Keegan: We now have 8 inches of snow near the school's flagpole. The temperature is 18 degrees.

produce digital videos, the students could use a magazine format like *60 Minutes*, in which they could use both still pictures and video they shoot to create their report presentation.

SUMMARY

The presentation of results step of the NTeQ model is an important part of the learning process. First, the action of creating the presentation provides an environment for the learners to reflect and make connections with the new content and ideas. It provides a means for the learners to construct or generate new knowledge by actively processing the information. Second, it provides the students with an opportunity to communicate their findings to others. Students can interact with other students in the school or elsewhere or with adults. They can practice and refine their communication skills, as well as receive recognition for their work.

Students can publish their work in a variety of formats. They can use a traditional written report, or they can transform the report into a magazine or newspaper type of publication. Reports also can take the form of a multimedia presentation or a radio or television show. If students have access to a Website, they can publish their findings on the Internet so others can benefit from newly acquired knowledge.

AT THE CLASSROOM'S DOORSTEP

Questions Teachers Ask

What is the value of letting students publish their results?

Publishing results is a strategy to help the students synthesize what they have learned by solving a problem. The answer to the problem might be very simple, such as the "I would weigh more on Jupiter than on the Earth." Students probably learned more than where they would weigh the most. They gained an understanding of gravity and the solar system, as well as related concepts such as revolution, rotation, and day and night. The publishing strategy provides a means for them to go beyond the answer to the question and elaborate on their findings and observations.

Will anyone read my students' publications?

To paraphrase a famous line, if they write, others will read. There are four potential audiences for your students' publications. First is their classmates, who might use the publications for learning or reference information. Second is students in lower-level grades, who can use the materials for learning or reference. Third is parents, who could benefit from the research from such projects as the cost per square inch of pizza that might be published in either a classroom or school newsletter. Fourth is anyone who surfs the Web, visits the class Web page, or reads the materials.

Should I encourage my students to produce multimedia projects because other teachers are doing it in their classes?

The answer depends upon both your objective and your students' objectives. If you have an objective that specifies the development of multimedia materials, such a project is appropriate. For example, if you are teaching a high school speech class, it may be appropriate for your students to develop an electronic slide show as part of one or all of their speeches. If a hypertext document with links best communicates the information the students have generated, a HyperStudio stack may be appropriate. Requiring students to create multimedia materials because the software is on the computer is as logical as requiring first graders to learn the history of computers before they learn keyboarding skills. The learning tasks should have a purpose and support the achievement of an objective.

ISTE NETS FOR STUDENTS

When students publish and present their work, five of the six NETS for Students are specifically addressed: Standards 1, 2, 3, 4, and 5. Students reinforce the basic operations and concepts (Standard 1) of technology, the use of productivity tools (Standard 3) by using a variety of software to present the results of their investigations, as specified in Standard 5—Technology as a research tool. Standard 2, Social, Ethical, and Human Issues, is addressed as students are taught how to "practice responsible use of technology" when preparing information to be shared with others.

Finally, Standard 4, Technology Communication Tools, is achieved because the primary purpose of this chapter is to enable students to use technology to share, or communicate, the new information learned when completing the NTeQ lesson.

TECHNOLOGY INTEGRATION ACTIVITIES

To access the activities that connect the content of the text with the Companion Website and other technology, please go to the Activities module in Chapter 8 of the Companion Website at *http://www.prenhall.com/morrison.*

NTEQ MODEL

Publishing can be part of the results presentation step in most lesson plans (Figure 8-11).

LESSON BYTES

Publishing can be a part of most lessons developed with the NTeQ model; therefore, we will describe some examples of how other lessons have incorporated publishing.

Books for Younger Students

A by-product of your students' research might be a book for younger students. For example, students who have researched animals might create an alphabet book for younger students that includes an animal for each letter and a brief description of the animal based on their research. Similarly, students in a science class might create a series of science experiments for younger students based on class projects or science fair projects. Students can also create multimedia presentations for their classmates and students in lower-level grades to share their results.

FIGURE 8-11 NTeQ Model

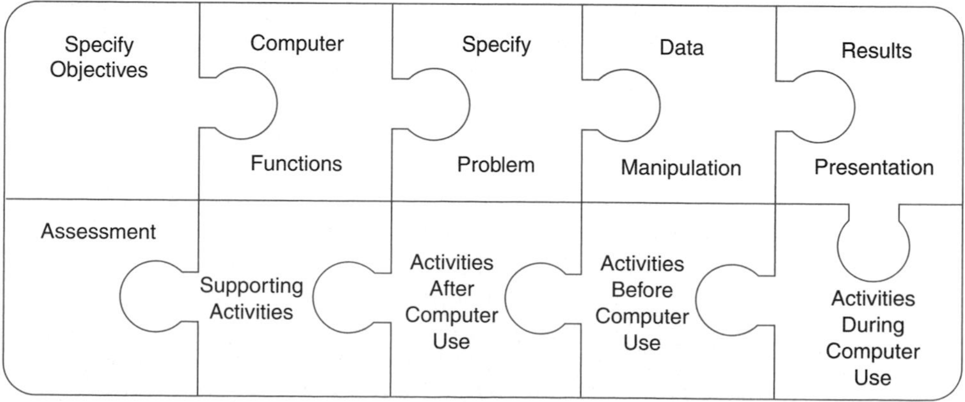

Reports for Parents

One theme for a classroom might be to produce a *Consumer Reports* style magazine during the year to report the results of their product testing. Students can conduct research incorporating math and science principles and report the results in their special bulletins or magazine. One example mentioned is calculating the cost of a square inch of pizza, which uses calculation of the area of rectangles and circles. Other projects might include the evaluation of paper towels, price per ounce of selected types and sizes of laundry detergent, capacity of trash bags, and effectiveness of dishwashing liquids. Students who have conducted surveys or studies such as the number of individuals wearing seat belts or the varieties of trees in a park might submit their reports to appropriate government agencies.

Web Publishing

Students can also publish their work on the school's Website. A visit to K–12 Websites will reveal various approaches to publishing student projects. Some schools publish a mixture of papers related to different grade levels and a variety of topics. Other schools focus on a specific theme for their papers. One secret to increasing the visibility and number of visitors to a Website is to provide information on related topics. Focusing on one theme or related themes allows students to both benefit from and build on the work of other students, creating an additional advantage to the publishing activity.

NTEQ PORTFOLIO ACTIVITIES

The portfolio activity for this chapter involves the identification of resources you can use to help your students present their findings. Create a two-column table with 25 rows using a word processing program. Label the left column as Resource and the right column as URL. Search the Internet for resources using a search engine such as *www.google.com*. When you find a useful resource, enter a brief description in the left column and then cut and paste the URL into the right column. Try to find the following types of resources:

- Templates or backgrounds for PowerPoint or Hyperstudio
- Clipart for the Web or print materials
- Guidelines for producing a radio or TV program
- Collections of fonts for print materials
- Templates for newsletters, books, or other print materials

REFERENCES

Brookes, G. (1988). Exploring the world through reading and writing. *Language Arts, 65*, 245–253.

Corbine, M. (1995). The effective use of student journal writing. *ERIC Digest*, Bloomington, IN:ERIC/REC [ED378 587].

Halliday, M. A. (1985). *An introduction to functional grammar*. Baltimore, MD: Edward Arnold.

Ivers, K. S., & Barron, A. E. (1999). The presence and purpose of elementary school Web pages. *Information Technology in Childhood Education Annual, 10,* 181–191.

Johannessen, L. R., & Kahn, E. A. (1991). *Writing across the curriculum.* Paper presented at the Teachers' Institute, Summit, IL.

Keys, C. W. (1999). Language as an indicator of meaning generation: An analysis of middle school students' written discourse about scientific investigations. *Journal of Research in Science Teaching, 36,* 1044–1061.

McBride, K. H., & Luntz, E. D. (1996). *Help, I have HyperStudio® . . . now what do I do?* Glendora, CA: McB Media.

Snyder, J. (1996, April). Good, bad and ugly pages. *Internet World, 7,* 26–27.

Welsh, S. (1994). Students and television: Anything but a passive role. *Middle School Journal, 25,* 52–53.

Wittrock, M. C. (1974). Learning as a generative process. *Educational Psychologist, 11,* 87–95.

Wittrock, M. C. (1990). Generative processes of comprehension. *Educational Psychologist, 24,* 345–376.

KEY TOPICS

Internet Components
- The World Wide Web
- Browsers
- E-mail
- Mailing Lists
- Newsgroups
- Chat Forums

Internet Policies
- District-Level Policies
- Classroom Policies

Copyright Issues

Using the Internet as a Tool
- Standards

Integrating the Internet
- The Internet as an Information Source
- The Internet as a Collaboration Tool

Using the Internet with an Integrated Lesson

Chapter 9

The Internet in the Classroom

The Internet—the greatest innovation in information technology since Johannes Gutenberg's moveable type, or is it a technological fad soon to go the way of opaque projectors and ditto machines? What started as a mechanism for a group of university researchers to communicate with one another now affects information access worldwide. How big is the Internet? In April 2002 it was estimated that there were over 165 million Internet users in the United States and 605 million worldwide (*http://www.nua.com/surveys/how_many_online/n_america.html*).

The actual size of the World Wide Web is more difficult to measure. Zakon (2003) reports that the number of Websites (not Web pages as reported by Google) on the World Wide Web has grown from 10 million in December 1999 to over 3 billion pages in June 2003. Google reported in July 2003 that they had indexed 3,083,324,652 Web pages (*www.google.com*). With approximately 60% of the U.S. population connected to these 3 billion pages, we can say the Internet is quite large and growing exponentially each day.

Opponents and proponents are still debating the issues of access, rights, and security, but the benefits and uses of the Internet for education continue to grow. Owston (1997) shows convincing evidence that the Internet can make education more attainable for more people, promote improved and new types of learning, and do both while containing the costs of education. The number of schools connected to the Internet grows each week. In 1993, only 3% of the classrooms in the United States had an Internet connection. By the fall of 2001, 99% of the public schools in the United States were connected to the Internet. In 1998, only 51% of the individual classrooms were connected to the Internet, allowing students to have ready access; however, in 2001, the percentage of Internet-equipped classrooms had increased to 77% (National Center for Educational Statistics [NCES], 1998, 2002).

As educators and parents, we might be very excited about the growth of connectivity to the Internet or wonder why our own district has not made the connection. Gaining access to the Internet is just the first step. Although the Internet has many features and serves many needs, many of us tend to think of only a few of the features. We tend to view the Internet as a communication tool that allows us to instantly communicate with colleagues and friends. Second, we view part of the Internet as a *very large* database of information that varies in accuracy and timeliness from immediate to outdated. To use the Net successfully, a teacher must carefully plan for its use. Very few teachers would send their students to the local university's library with no direction. Yet, we have often seen students given free reign of the

Internet with no planned purpose. This chapter provides some of the basics necessary to begin integrating the Internet into your curriculum.

GETTING STARTED

What Do I Know?

1. What is the Internet and how does it differ from the World Wide Web?
2. How do I manage students' use of the Internet in my class?
3. How can I use the Internet as a tool in an integrated lesson?

Classroom Snapshot

At first glance, an outsider might wonder why Ms. Aldrick's students had laptop computers. All 27 laptops were on the desks, but they were closed. The students were plotting information provided by Ms. Aldrick to connect various locations on a map. It would seem the students could have produced a much cleaner map by using their laptops.

Finally, a pair of students raise their hands in excitement and show Ms. Aldrick something they have written on a sheet of paper. After she gives her approval, the students begin working on their laptop. Their excitement, however, only lasts for about 45 seconds, and then they close the laptop. The pair return to their map. Ms. Aldrick gives another excited group approval and they open their laptops and begin typing. After about a minute, they excitedly raise their hands. Again, to the casual observer it appears the students are hardly using their computers.

Let's see what Tameka and Brianna are doing. The class is studying a unit on water and are focusing on how cholera is spread. Ms. Aldrick has given each pair of students a map and list of people who have contracted cholera. The students then map the location of those infected, as well as places they have visited. Once the information is entered on the map, the students try to determine the source of the cholera by finding a common location all those infected have visited. Once they have identified the location, they enter the location in *www.google.com*. If they have entered the correct location, the first Website returned by Google is the correct answer! In this case, if the students enter "Broad Street pump" as the search terms, they will find a description of a cholera outbreak in London in 1859 written by John Snow.

Students in Ms. Aldrick's class are using the Internet to *confirm* their answers rather than to conduct research. They are still learning to think like a scientist as they have undertaken the role of an epidemiologist in trying to determine the source of the cholera outbreak. Rather than using their laptops to research epidemiology, they are using traditional paper and pencil to determine the source of the problem and then using their laptop to verify their answers. Ms. Aldrick required each team to have their search terms approved by her. If they used the wrong search term, they had to go back to their map and use a different strategy to locate the source.*

*This scenario is based on a strategy developed by Ryan Ossenmacher.

INTERNET COMPONENTS

What exactly is the Internet and how does it differ from the World Wide Web (WWW)? Think of the Internet as "the mother of networks." Linking computers together with a telephone line, cables, radio signals, or infrared signals is known as a network. The Internet is the largest network, and all single computers and networks can connect to it. In Figure 9-1, we see that the Internet encompasses many components, including the WWW, e-mail, File Transfer Protocols (FTPs), mailing lists, newsgroups, chat forums, instant messaging, and text messaging.

The WWW is part of the Internet. Web browsers such as Netscape Navigator and Internet Explorer have grown in sophistication so that they manage most of the Internet components. Just a few years ago, you needed separate software to access each Internet component separately; it was not very user friendly. You can now use a Web browser to navigate the Web, send e-mail, download files, engage in Web groups, access a site via FTP, and chat with others. Some of the early Web components such as gophers have all but disappeared because of the text and graphics available on Web pages. Let's examine a few of the more common components.

The World Wide Web

The WWW began as a means for a group of scientists to "converse" with one another. It has now developed into the largest public forum for disseminating all kinds of information. It is easy to see why the WWW has become the number one source for the latest information on almost any topic.

The WWW consists of pages (Figure 9-2) containing links that allow you to jump from one page to another with a click of a mouse. Many pages contain graphics, sound bites, video clips, streaming video, and animations. Web sites offer exciting educational opportunities for teachers and students.

FIGURE 9-1

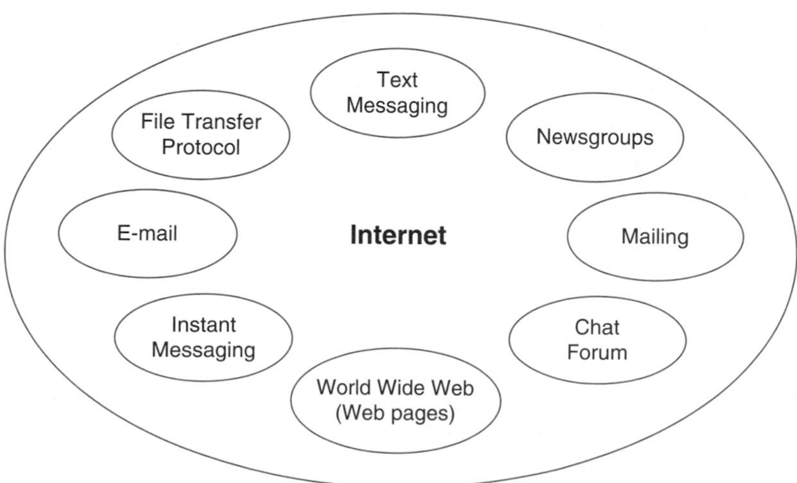

FIGURE 9-2 WWW Page

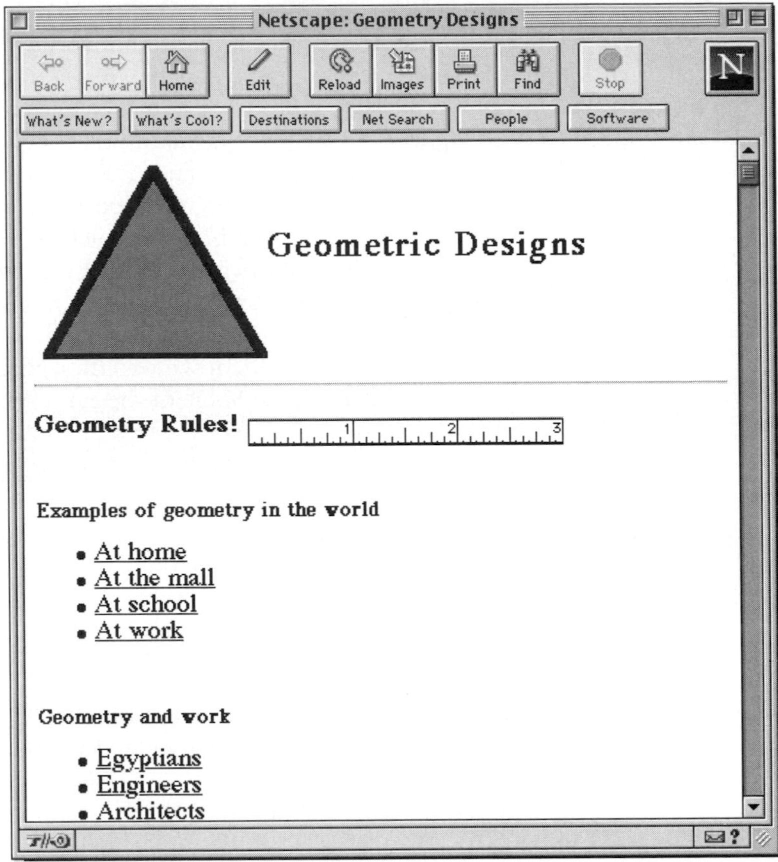

FIGURE 9-3 Netscape's Navigation Buttons

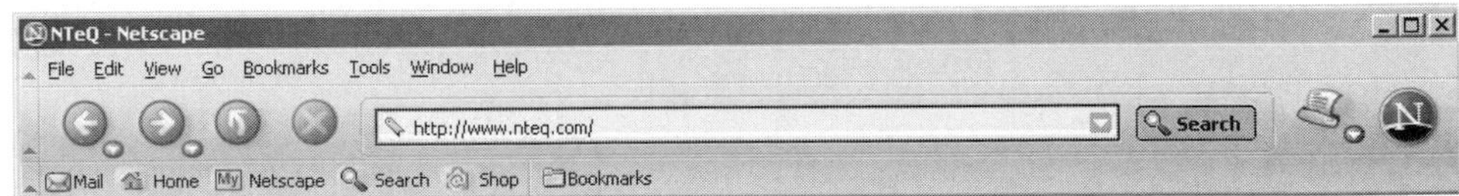

Browsers

The Web is accessed with a software application known as a browser. Netscape Navigator and Microsoft Internet Explorer are two of the most popular browsers. Let's examine Netscape's buttons to see how a browser operates (Figure 9-3).

Clicking on the **Back** button (left arrow) takes you to the previous Web pages you accessed, one page at a time. Similarly, **Forward** (right button) works in the same manner, taking you forward along a path of pages you have visited in the current session. Clicking **Reload** (up arrow) refreshes the page you are viewing. For example, if you were viewing a news page, such as one showing stock prices for the second time today, you might need to reload it with new information rather than the information from the cache. (*Note*: Browsers store images and data on your hard drive in a cache. Sometimes, the browser loads data from the cache rather than from the Internet.) The **Home** button takes you to the first page that loads each time you start the browser. You can set your home page to any URL that you want to appear each time your browser is launched. If you click the **Search** button, you are directed to a search page—usually one at Netscape's site. The **My Netscape** button takes you to a page you can customize to display various types of information. When you click **Print**, the browser will display the printer dialog so that you can print the page. **Stop** (X button) is definitely one of the most useful buttons on the tool bar. You can click Stop during a search or download, and the browser will quit downloading or searching at that moment. You can also click Stop to stop the sound or music playing on a Website. This feature is most useful when your computer seems to get stuck trying to find a location, or you decide you don't want to wait for an entire page to download.

Plug-ins are small applications that you download to your computer to view special effects on Websites with your browser. You can watch and hear a video interview, interact in three dimensions, or take advantage of special color effects. Some of the more popular plug-ins include Shockwave (view animations), Acrobat Reader (view portable documents), RealOne Player (listen to audio), and QuickTime (view digital movies). Once you have taken the time to download a plug-in to view a particular Website, you need only download it again when there is an update. If your browser detects the need for a plug-in, it will prompt you and then direct you to an appropriate Website where you can download it.

E-mail

Most computer users are now familiar with the concept of electronic mail (e-mail). E-mail software allows users to send messages electronically via the Internet to another recipient. Again, most popular Web browsers have the ability of sending and receiving e-mail. Most users, however, prefer to use a dedicated application such as Eudora, Outlook, or Netscape e-mail to send and receive their e-mail. To send a message using e-mail, you must have an e-mail account. These accounts can be obtained through Internet Service Providers (ISPs) such as America Online, Road Runner, and AT&T WorldNet or your school district. Free accounts are available at several different locations on the Internet, for example *www.hotmail.com* and *http://www.yahoo.com*. Some universities also provide their alumni with free mail accounts. You can also create kid-safe e-mail accounts for your students at places like *http://www.gaggle.net* and *http://www.epals.com*.

Mailing Lists

A mailing list provides a forum for a group of people to exchange e-mail about a particular topic. Lists are social, educational, or informational in nature. Lists are open (available to the general public) or closed (open only to specific members). There are lists specifically for teachers and lists available only to students.

All participation in lists is handled via e-mail, although it is possible to find and subscribe to lists over the Web. When you send a message to the list server, the message is then sent to *all* the subscribers. For example, we needed the URL for one of the Websites mentioned in this chapter. A message was sent to a mailing list, and we had an answer in less than 10 minutes! Mailing lists sound great, except for one problem. You might see a message from a friend posted to the list. Without thinking, you hit reply and send some juicy gossip. About 2 minutes after you send the message, you suddenly realize that you sent the gossip to everyone on the list rather than to just your friend! Take care when replying to a mailing list and make sure you know to whom you are replying.

Newsgroups

Newsgroups also provide a forum for exchanging ideas on a multitude of topics. However, they differ from lists in that messages sent using e-mail are posted to an electronic bulletin board rather than received via e-mail (Figure 9-4). These bulletin boards are accessible only through the Web or by using a newsgroup software application.

FIGURE 9-4 Example of a Newsgroup

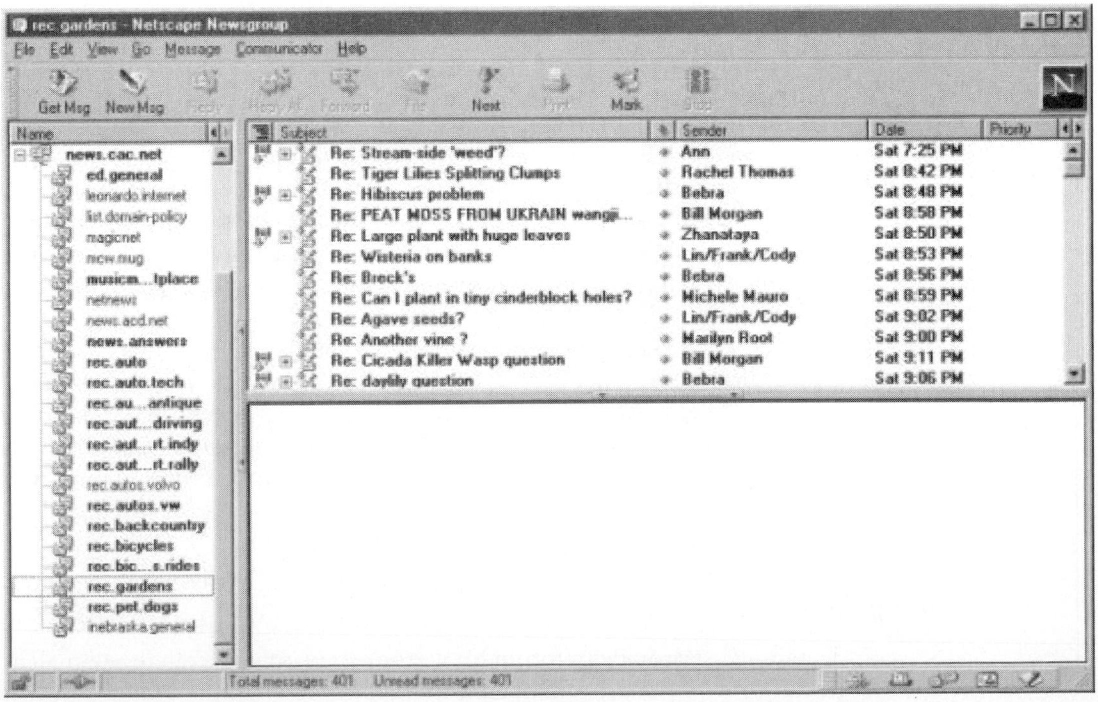

Power Tip

Mailing Lists

One of the most confusing terms related to the Internet is the mailing list. One term that is often used to describe these lists is Listserv. Listserv is a registered trademark for software distributed by L-Soft (*http://www.lsoft.com/*). The term Listserv is often used like the term Kleenex is used to refer to facial tissues. The term Listserv is misused when referring to *all* mailing lists. Listserv is correctly used to refer to mailing lists that are run on the Listserv e-mail list manager software. If you belong to a mailing list that uses Majordomo, Macjordomo, Listprocessor, or ListGuru, the correct term is "mailing list," not Listserv.

Caution is needed when using any synchronous (i.e., real time) communication with students. Once connected to the Internet with a chat, you lose some if not all control of with whom the students can converse. Chat software is an excellent way for teachers to talk with other teachers and exchange ideas in real time; however, careful planning and monitoring is needed if you plan to allow your students to use the software. In addition, you should check your district's policy concerning the use of chat software in your classroom or lab.

Most chat software is text based. That is, two or more individuals communicate by typing information, much like e-mail, but it is done synchronously so there is no delay between sending and receiving the conversation. Other software such as CU-See Me and NetMeeting allow text, audio, and video communication.

Chat Forums

Chat forums differ from e-mail, newsgroups, and mailing lists in that the "chat" or talk occurs synchronously or in real time. Similar to a telephone call, chat forums provide users the opportunity to "talk" with users who have compatible software on their computers. After text is entered by a participant, it is sent to the other participants, where it is displayed almost immediately on their screen. Once another individual has read the message, she can respond immediately. There are several different means of chatting using the Internet. Some of the more popular chat applications are AOL Instant Messenger (AIM), ICQ, and Internet Relay Chat (IRC). There are also chat applications that use your Web browser. Older Telnet-based chat applications such as MUDs and MOOs are still used by some individuals and groups. Both NetMeeting, and CU-See Me are specialized collaborative software that include shared whiteboards, video, and audio.

INTERNET POLICIES

The Internet creates many interesting and exciting possibilities for classroom instruction, but it also provides opportunities for new problems. One of the problems received a great deal of publicity when Fortune 500 Companies started firing individuals for abusing the company's e-mail system by sending inappropriate materials (e.g., sexually oriented, violence, etc.) or using sexually explicit, profane, or other types of unacceptable language (in e-mail). School districts are not immune from these abuses or problems. The focus of this section is on how to address these problems.

District-Level Policies

Many states suggest or require each school district to develop an acceptable use policy concerning the Internet. This policy provides guidelines concerning the use of the Internet by faculty, staff, and students. An acceptable use policy establishes guidelines for appropriate use of the Internet, as well as outlines conditions for its use. There are several Websites devoted to information on what to include in a policy. The following sites provide excellent guidelines and samples of existing policies:

- A legal and educational analysis of K–12 Internet acceptable use policies: Indiana's Department of Education guidelines: *http://www.doe.state.in.us/olr/aup/aupreq.html*
- Links to several other sites with guidelines for acceptable use policies: *http://www.monroe.lib.in.us/~lchampel/netadv3.html*
- Guidelines provided by the Virginia Department of Education: *http://www.pen.k12.va.us/go/VDOE/Technology/AUP/home.shtml*

What should an acceptable use policy include? A review of several policies and guidelines produced the following list of items. This list should not be considered complete, but rather a starting point.

- *Uses of the Internet:* The policy should describe the educational value of the Internet and how it will be used for instructional purposes. For example, the policy might describe how it can be used for communication via e-mail and for gathering information to support instruction or research.

CHECK IT OUT 9-1

Searching for Acceptable Use Policies

We found a number of acceptable use policies on the Web. If you would like to see some model policies, go to *www.google.com* and search with the following terms.

"school acceptable use policy guidelines"

Link to these resources and activities in the Check It Out module for this chapter of the Companion Website.

- *Responsibilities:* The policy should explain the responsibilities for administrators, faculty, staff, and students when using the Internet. This section might include reference to user accounts, privileges, and system security. One common theme is that Internet access is a privilege, not a right, and this privilege can be revoked if abused.
- *Acceptable and unacceptable behavior:* It is very important that the policy explain in simple language what is acceptable and what is not acceptable Internet use for all. Many policies explicitly state that it is a violation of the policy to download or send sexually oriented materials or to use sexually explicit language. Other unacceptable behaviors include using the Internet to access another individual's account or files or distributing copyrighted material.
- *Consequences:* The policy should provide guidelines for dealing with violations of the policy. For example, what action is taken against a student who distributes copyrighted material or accesses another student's account?
- *Parent notification:* Some states or districts require parents be notified that their children will have access to the Internet. The policy should address this issue and provide an alternative to students whose parents do not want them to have Internet access.
- *Access:* The policy should describe the procedures for students to access the Internet and school resources. For example, this policy statement might describe how one obtains an individual account or password if needed.

One of the primary concerns with student Internet access is the availability of sexual, racist, violent, and other unacceptable Websites. Many districts use filtering software, but it is not always effective in preventing or limiting access. The acceptable use policy should clearly define what types of sites are unacceptable and the consequences of accessing unacceptable sites. A clearly defined policy *and* filtering software can provide an initial strategy to help students learn appropriate behaviors.

Classroom Policies

The school's acceptable use policy will define appropriate uses of the Internet and each individual's responsibility. It is the teacher, however, who must implement the policy in his or her classroom. As a teacher, how can you help your students find appropriate Websites and use e-mail responsibly? This section will present strategies on how to use the Internet in your classroom.

Web Access

Having access to the Internet in a classroom can enlighten any conversation. We observed a classroom in which a student asked a question about the gestation period of a mammal they were studying. No one knew the length of time. Immediately, three or four students connected to the school's wireless network using their laptop and did a search. Almost immediately, one of them had an answer! The same day, we saw a few students visiting Websites that discussed their favorite idols while they listened to the latest hit songs with earphones and were off task as they searched for new music files.

First, let's consider classroom management. How do you manage a classroom or lab in which each student has a computer? If you are using an integrated lesson plan, your students are probably working in small groups or individually and are spread about the room if not in more places. This problem is more pronounced when each student has a laptop that allows him or her to sit almost anywhere, or at least within distance of an electrical outlet. One strategy we have observed is to place the teacher's desk at the back of the room. This vantage point allows you to easily view the computer screens so that you can recognize students who are off task. Another strategy is to place the chairs or tables in a U shape. When the students are working on their laptop computer, they move to the inside of the U. The teacher can then easily move around the room in an open area of the U and view each student's computer screen.

Before computers, it was said that teachers had eyes in the back of their heads (we swear it was true of our fifth-grade teachers). Today, you have to be able to read minds and intercept packets of information as they flow from the Internet to the students' computer and from student computer to student computer. If you have created a student-centered learning environment, you are probably working with individual students or groups as they are located around the room, which makes it more difficult to find students who are off task. If your students are using PCs, you can glance at the task bar at the bottom of the screen to see which applications they have open. Similarly, you can check the Mac's application menu on the far right of the menu bar to determine what applications the student is running. If you find something suspicious, you can ask the student to explain how they are using the application or information to solve the problem.

Second, when students are doing Internet searches, "accidents" happen. They may type in the wrong URL or click the wrong link, resulting in accessing a site that is inappropriate. It is not a matter of *if* it will happen, but *when* it will happen. You need to develop a strategy that you can explain to your students *before* they start using the Internet. One effective strategy we have observed is to have the student either turn off the monitor or close the laptop when they arrive at an inappropriate site. The student then goes to the teacher and explains what happened. The teacher can then deal with the problem. You might want to determine how the student got to the site by clicking the back button. A student should not be punished for accidentally arriving at an inappropriate site. For example, we typed in the URL for our bank the other day, but left off the last letter of the bank's name. As a result, we were directed to an inappropriate site.

Third, how can you determine if a student has been accessing inappropriate Websites? Both Netscape Communicator and Internet Explorer keep a history of sites visited. You can display a list of all sites visited by reviewing the history file. In the newer versions of Netscape Navigator, you can click on Go and select History. In older versions, click on Communicator, then Tools, and select History. In Internet Explorer you can click the History button. A list of URLs that were visited by the user or users of the computer is displayed (Figure 9-5).

E-mail

The second important component of the Internet is e-mail. Many school districts, however, do not provide students with e-mail accounts because of the potential problems. There are several Internet sites that offer kid-safe, filtered e-mail. These sites allow a teacher to create e-mail accounts for students that are accessible through a Web

FIGURE 9-5 Browser History Window

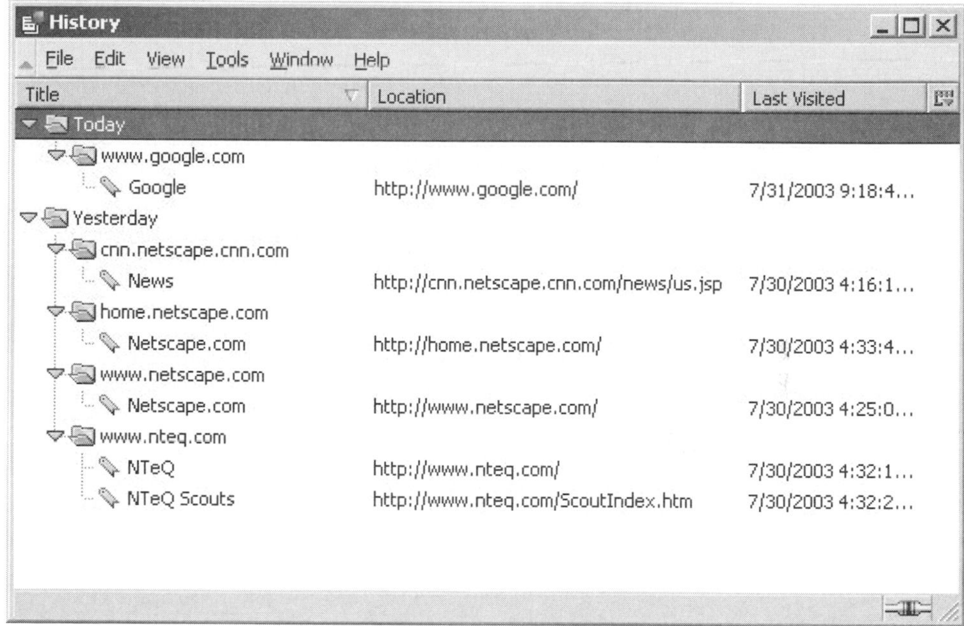

Power Tip

Who Accessed the Adult Site?

Bob is a fifth-grade teacher in a classroom in which each student has a laptop he or she takes home every day. Each Friday, Bob reviews the browser history files on each laptop to make sure the students are not accessing inappropriate Websites. Bob was surprised when he saw Terry's history file. Terry had been visiting quite a few adult sites while at home. Bob immediately called Terry's mother and explained the situation. Terry's mom thanked Bob and assured him she would have a talk with Terry when he came home that evening. The next morning, Bob had a voice mail message from Terry's mother. It seems Terry's dad was the one who had been visiting the sites.

browser. Two sites offering this service are *www.gaggle.net* and *www.epals.com*. When the filters on these sites identify inappropriate words, the e-mail is forwarded to the teacher for action.

Facilitating Web Access

Access to the WWW is often limited in a classroom; thus efficiency in finding information is a critical issue. One strategy for finding information is by accessing search engines such as *www.google.com*, *www.altavista.com*, and *http://www.ask.com/*.

CHECK IT OUT 9-2

Kid-Safe Search Engines

You can find a list of kid safe search sites at:

http://www.searchenginewatch.com/

Link to these resources and activities in the Check It Out module for this chapter of the Companion Website.

One problem with these search engines is that they do not filter or provide kid-safe content. For example, we were searching for a drawing and a photograph of a heart to use in a lecture. Our search term was "heart." Many of the listed Websites would not pass the scrutiny of even the broadest acceptable use policy! How, then, can you provide your students with access to information that is acceptable?

One approach is to use a kid-safe directory or search engine. One popular search engine is *www.yahooligans.com*. This site, among others, provides filtered content that would pass the acceptable use policy. Students can use a bookmark to go directly to the site and search for information.

A second approach is for the teacher to create a list of approved Websites. Students can submit a site to the teacher. Once the teacher has verified the site, it can be added to a list of acceptable sites. Some schools also require teachers to approve Websites before using them in class. Although this policy helps prevent the display of inappropriate sites, it also prevents spontaneous research. For example, a class might be studying space exploration and a question is raised about the number of space missions conducted by the United States. It would seem logical, then, to visit *www.nasa.gov* and search for a list. Under some policies, the teacher is vulnerable if he did not check the site out before using it in class.

The next problem is providing the students with a list of acceptable sites, or even a single link you want them to use. Most of us have found that often we cannot accurately type a URL regardless of its length. Plus, there is an inherent danger in typing in a URL. For example, suppose you wanted your students to access *www.rstuvwxyz.com* (a fictitious site at the writing of this book). But, one student mistakenly enters *www.rstuvwxyz.net* rather than *.com*. This mistake might direct the student to an adult-oriented site because the *.net* and *.com* URLs are owned by two different individuals. For example, *www.ford.com* is for the Ford Motor Company while *www.ford.net* is for an Internet company.

How, then, can you help your students reach the correct Websites? There are four methods. First, if you have created e-mail addresses for each student, you could e-mail them the URL(s). Most e-mail applications make it very easy to simply click the URL to link to the site. Second, you can create a word-processed document that lists one or more links. You can show the actual URL or enter a name (i.e., Ford Motor Company) and make it a hyperlink so the URL is "hidden." The word processing file can be distributed to students with e-mail or on disk. They would open the word processing file and then click a link to access the site. For special projects, you can create an instruction sheet using your word processor and then embed the links in the directions. Third, you can create a list of bookmarks and then replace the bookmark file on each computer. This method will destroy existing bookmarks unless you rename the file. Fourth, you can create a Web page with your links that is posted on the school or classroom's Website or given to the students on disk.

You can direct your students to your bookmarks on a Website, attach the file to an e-mail message, or distribute it on disk.

COPYRIGHT ISSUES

As with any medium that is in the public domain, copyright of Internet material is an issue. Copyright protects an author's work from being stolen by someone else or being used in a way that the author is uncomfortable with, such as using a graphic in curriculum materials. All information published on the Internet is technically copyrighted, even though the copyright notice may not be visible with the work. So, what can be copied off the Internet freely? When do you need to obtain permission of the author?

The law allows for "fair use" of copyrighted material (Crawford, 1993). Educational uses and newsworthy uses are likely to be considered fair use. Factors considered in determining fair use include the following:

1. The purpose and character of the use, including profit.
2. The character of the copyrighted work.
3. How much of the work is used: not more than one copy per student; 250 words or less of a poem; a complete article or 2,500 words or less; excerpts of 500 to 1,000 words; one illustration per publication.
4. The effect of the use on the market value of the work.

The following guidelines also apply to classroom use:

1. The copies may be used for only one course in the school.
2. Same author copies may not exceed more than one article or two excerpts, or more than three from a collection of works.
3. Multiple copying for one course is limited to a maximum of nine instances during the term.
4. Copying may not be used to substitute for collections of works.
5. You may not copy "consumable" materials such as workbooks.
6. Students may not be charged for the copied material, other than photocopying costs.

The issue of copyright and the Internet is often confusing. If you want to use something from a Website, put yourself in the author's place. How would you feel

CHECK IT OUT 9-3

Fair Use in the Classroom

Check out the following sites for information on fair use in the classroom:

http://www.umuc.edu/library/copy.html
http://www.groton.k12.ct.us/mts/pt2a.htm
http://www.dpi.state.nc.us/copyrig

Link to these resources and activities in the Check It Out module for this chapter of the Companion Website.

if someone used your materials? In most cases, you should e-mail either the owner of the materials or the web master and ask permission to use the materials. You should also consider the following guidelines when using shareware, icons, and graphics.

Shareware is software that individuals and companies market on the Internet. You are often allowed to use the software on a trial basis. However, if you continue to use it, you are obligated to pay the cost of registration or purchase. Examples of shareware are compression and graphic utilities and games.

Some icons and graphics are specifically offered for downloading. Several sites offer free clip art that you can download and use.

The following would be examples of copyright infringement:

- Placing another person's graphic or photograph on your Web page.
- Copying text and including it in curriculum materials from which you or others gain profit.
- Copying icons not specifically created to be shared publicly.

To obtain permission to reproduce copyrighted material, contact the author (easy to do because most authors give e-mail addresses on their Web pages), indicating how the material will be used and asking what credit they would like to be given and what payment they would like, if any. Getting a signature should avoid problems with future legal actions (see Crawford, 1993, for further guidance). The following Websites also offer guidance related to copyright issues.

Myths about copyright
http://www.templetons.com/brad/copymyths.html

U.S. Copyright Office
http://lcweb.loc.gov/copyright/

PBS guidelines for fair use
http://www.pbs.org/teachersource/copyright/copyright_fairuse.shtm

Power Tip

Creating a Bookmark File

You can easily create a bookmark file for your students from your browser. If you use Netscape Communicator, use the following:

1. Click Bookmarks and then Edit Bookmarks.
2. Select Save As from the File menu and save the file to a folder.
3. Select Composer from the Communicator menu.
4. Select Open from the File menu and open the bookmark file you created.
5. Make any changes you want to the title of the file, and delete any irrelevant bookmarks.
6. Publish the file to your Website or select Save from the File menu.

If you are using Internet Explorer, use the following steps.

1. Organize your bookmarks so the bookmarks for your students are in one folder under the favorites list. Otherwise, you will export *all* of your bookmarks.
2. Select Import and Export from the File menu.
3. Select Export Favorites from the list and click Next.
4. Select the folder to Export and click Next.
5. Select Export to a File or Address.
6. Click Browse and then select a place to save the file.
7. Click Next.
8. The wizard will complete the process.

USING THE INTERNET AS A TOOL

Just a few years ago, only teachers who were techno-wizards would have considered integrating the Internet into their curriculum. Now, as schools and classrooms gain access to the Internet, the next step after becoming acquainted with the various components of the Net is to use it effectively as a part of the learning process. There are several ways teachers can begin using the Internet in their instruction, as follows:

1. Obtain ready-to-use Internet curriculum materials.
2. Rework existing lesson plans to incorporate aspects of the Internet.
3. Develop Internet curriculum materials from scratch.

As more teachers gain access to the Internet, many companies are offering lesson plans and strategies for using the Internet as a part of instruction. Although these materials may not be specific to your grade level or particular topic, they offer an excellent starting place for creating an integrated lesson plan. You can adapt many of the lesson plans to your particular context. You will find Internet lesson plans available in several places—published books, curriculum guides, columns in teacher's

Students gathering information for their Internet search.

journals such as *Instructor*, and online. *Classroom Connect* specializes in Internet curriculum.

As you expand your use of the Internet and its potential use in your classroom, we'd like to offer some helpful hints for reworking some of your existing lesson plans. First, there are particular types of lessons that lend themselves to incorporating the Internet, such as the following (Classroom Connect, 1997):

- Comparing and classifying
- Inducing/deducing
- Analyzing errors
- Abstraction
- Analyzing perspectives
- Information gathering
- Team building

Standards

Integrating the Internet into your classroom will also help you address the NET standards for students. You can develop lesson plans that address standards related to social, ethical, and human issues through the responsible use of information and data. If your students are using e-mail, chats, or Web pages, you can address the standards related to communication tools. Last, you can address the technology research tools standards if your students are collecting or searching for data on the Internet. As students use the technology, they will also gain competencies and skills related to the first standard on operations and concepts. With more creative uses you can also address the remaining standards on productivity tools and problem solving. (See ISTE NETS for Students at the end of the chapter for more detail.)

INTEGRATING THE INTERNET

In the following section, we describe two ways for teachers to think about the Internet as a potential part of their curriculum: as a source of information and as a means of collaboration and communication.

The Internet as an Information Source

Many users would agree that the greatest strength of the Internet is the amount and types of information available at the touch of a mouse button. This information can influence a teacher's thinking about a given topic, provide a handout for a class, or serve as a source of data for students. The possibilities for using this information are limitless. The key question, however, is how to find the information in an efficient manner.

Searching the Internet

We think of the Internet as a gigantic database. Over the years, we have learned that we can look in the index of a book for key words and then turn to the correct page. With an encyclopedia, we learned to again select the volume with a key term. And, when we received our first CD-ROM encyclopedia, we immediately felt comfortable typing our keyword into a field and clicking on the search button. The Internet, though, does not have one search button; it has several. Let's examine how we can search the Internet (Figure 9-6).

First, let's consider three common ways to search the Internet. The first is the search engine. Search engines such as *www.google.com* have developed software that crawls through the Internet collecting information from various sites. For example, if you created a page on your integrated lesson plan and posted it on the Internet, it would likely show up in a search engine and be indexed. The second method is a directory. Directories are created by people, usually called editors, who compile a list of Websites on a specific topic. For example, if you visit *www.yahoo.com*, you will see a directory. On Yahoo's main page there is a directory entry for Education. If you click on the Education link, you will see a directory listing of Education information. Some of the links are additional directories for such topics as conferences, instructional technology, and ERIC. The advantage of directory searches is that all the links are researched and checked by a person, and the search engines rely on software to classify the links. For example, a reference to chili might end up in travel, music, or recipes with a search engine because it depends on the keywords on the Website to catalog the site. If you recall our earlier example of searching for a heart, the search was done with a search engine. If we had used a directory and accessed clip art, we probably would have found our artwork much quicker because an editor would have accepted only pictures of a heart for the clip art directory. Third is a metasearch engine such as *www.metacrawler.com* and *www.search.com*. These metasearch engines

FIGURE 9-6 Searching the Internet

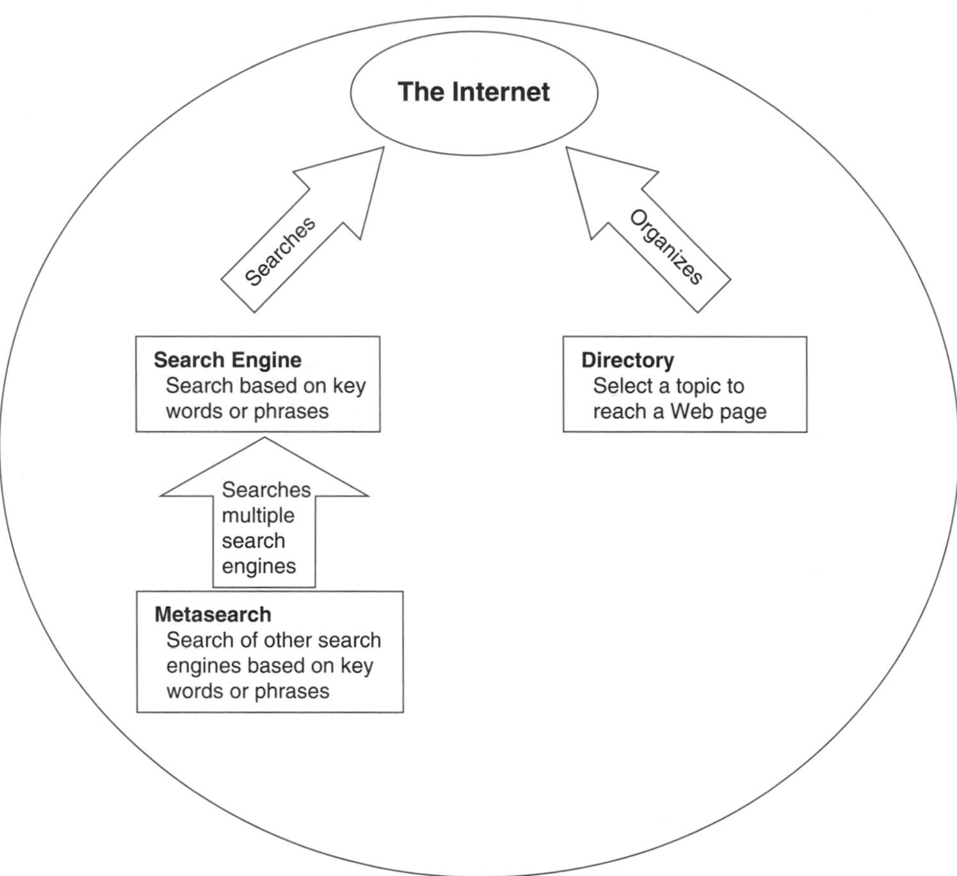

do not collect information like Google does, but rather search the search engines. If we were to do a search at Metacrawler for NTeQ, it would send the search query to such engines as Google, AltaVista, and Infoseek. Which method do you use? The best strategy is to have all three methods available. If you know the search terms, start with your favorite search engine. If you are not happy with the results, try a metasearch engine. If you are not familiar with the key terms, you might start with a directory. Similarly, if you want very focused information, you should start with a directory such as *www.yahoo.com* or *www.about.com*.

Search Strategies

Each search engine, directory, and metasearch engine has specific syntax or formats for entering search terms. You can use special words such as AND, OR, and NOT to create a more specific search. Figure 9-7 lists some of the more common terms you can use in your searches. Although these seem somewhat universal in application, you should consult the help or advanced search section of your favorite search engine if you do not receive the results you expected.

FIGURE 9-7 Search Terms

TERM	FUNCTION	EXAMPLE	RESULT
AND (Sometimes + is used in place of AND)	Finds Web pages that have all terms connected with AND. The terms, however, do not have to be contiguous. For example, a search for fire and truck might turn up a Website of an old hot rod truck that has fire shooting out the exhaust.	President AND Congress	Returns only pages that mention both President and Congress. Would ignore a senator's pages that had only the word Congress but would include another senator's page that had the words Congress and President anywhere on the page (e.g., maybe a meeting with members of Congress and the President).
OR	Finds pages that have either of the terms connected with OR.	Congress OR President	A senator's Web page that mentions Congress as well as the student body president of the local high school would be returned.
NOT (or -)	Excludes term following NOT.	Animals NOT Cat	Would return all pages mentioning animals that *do not include* the term cat.
" "	Use to find a phrase. Use if you want the words in exact order like "fire truck."	"John Smith"	Finds pages with the phrase John Smith; that is, the two words are contiguous rather than some place in the page.
*	Use to indicate the missing letters of a word.	Learn*	Would find pages with learn*er*, learn*ing*, and any other words starting with learn.
Domain:	Finds Web pages in a specified domain.	Domain:ca Domain:org	Finds pages in Canada. Finds all .org sites.
Like:	Finds all Web pages that are similar.	Like: Wayne.edu	Finds pages of other universities.
Link:	Finds pages that are linked to a particular page.	Link:www.nteq.com	Finds Web pages that have a link to www.nteq.com Website.
Title:	Finds pages with the text in the title.	Title: Voting	Finds pages that have Voting in the title.

THE TEACHER'S DIARY

When I was introduced to the World Wide Web, I fell in love with it. It was so exciting to think that with a few simple commands, I could surf the world! I entered a Cybersurfari contest and spent many hours on the World Wide Web searching for hidden treasures. I would get up early in the morning and drink my cup of coffee at the computer as I surfed. I had so much fun and it was so interesting that I hated to have to stop. I'd go to school and think about all the places that I had visited. I could see how the World Wide Web could be integrated into the curriculum and wished that I had access at school. As soon as I would get home from school, I'd turn on my computer and try to surf while I cooked dinner. I became obsessed! The more places that I visited in my search for treasures, the more excited I became. Luckily for my family, the contest only lasted 2 weeks.

I had a wonderful time participating in the Cybersurfari contest and surfing the World Wide Web. I got far more from this experience than I ever expected. I was introduced to a new and powerful tool.

I was also taking a class at this time that dealt with using the Internet in education, and I was required to do a final project. I could see the potential of using the Internet in the classroom, and I wanted to share what I had found. I decided to write an Internet activity book for children for my final project. I wanted this book to be something that could be used by teachers and parents to introduce children to the World Wide Web in a safe environment. I wanted to be able to take children to the Websites that I had found and give them something to do that would allow them to use the information found at that Website. This book became a children's Internet ABC activity book.

I made some copies of the book and sent them home over winter break with some students and teachers that had Internet access. I wanted to get some feedback about the Websites and activities from a student's, parent's, and teacher's point of view. I got very positive reviews. Unfortunately, I was not able to use these books that year in my classroom, because I did not have access to the Internet at my school. I put them on my shelf and hoped that I would be able to use them someday.

Having an Internet connection in my classroom became number one on my wish list! After the winter break my principal asked me if I would be interested in writing a grant proposal for the State of Tennessee's ConnecTEN Project. If we received this grant, our school would become connected to the Internet that spring. Of course I said yes! I wrote the grant proposal, and our school was chosen to become one of the ConnecTEN Schools.

We were connected to the Internet in March. Our project for this grant was to create a virtual field trip that would be exchanged with that of a partner class in East Tennessee. We decided that our virtual field trip would be a visit to our town's historic square and railroad display.

Continued

In preparation for this project, the students researched information about trains using library and Internet resources. They invited resource people into our classroom to share the history of our town square and information about trains. The students e-mailed information about their community back and forth with their partner class.

Students went on a field trip to the town square and railroad display. They took the digital and video cameras with them and took photos and videos of the old log cabin, the Civil War monument, the gazebo, the town square clock, the historic buildings that surround the square, and the insides of the different railroad cars. They even recorded the sound of the town square clock striking and playing "Amazing Grace" and a train coming through town.

The students took all the information, photos, videos, and sounds they collected on their field trip back to school and created a virtual field trip. Their virtual field trip began as they walked out of the school to a waiting bus, continued as they walked around the historic town square and through the railroad display, and ended as they got off of the bus and walked back into the school building. They used HyperStudio to create this virtual field trip.

They exchanged their field trip with their partner class. Their HyperStudio stack was compressed and sent as a Eudora Mail attachment through the Internet. It was a very exciting process. It was amazing to the students that they could send their HyperStudio stack from our school to another school across the state in such a short amount of time!

This was a great learning experience for the students. They learned to use a very powerful communication tool. They began to understand that through e-mail communication they could not only make new friends but also share their community with another class without ever having to leave their classroom.

As you can see, my experiences with the Internet built slowly, one upon another. I have encountered many frustrations along the way, but the benefits my students receive almost always outweigh the negatives.

Fran Clark
Third-Grade Teacher

The Internet as a Collaboration Tool

One of the greatest strengths of the Net is the ability to extend learning beyond the four walls of a classroom. Teachers and students can connect with their community, other schools, experts, and people and sites around the world. Through these collaborations, students become more aware of the global nature of information, and discover the importance of connecting with others in the pursuit of knowledge.

Connecting with the Community

To connect yourself and your students with the local community, consider how different Internet tools can help. For example, does the mayor have an e-mail address? Is there a local newsgroup for your city? What types of information do local businesses

Teacher assisting students with an Internet publication.

provide over the Web? What types of information or services can your school offer to the community through a school Website? The more you explore local Internet resources, the more your thinking will be stimulated about how to connect with the community through cyberspace. For example, your students might create a Website on historical buildings near the school or in the community.

Connecting with Other Schools

Students get *excited* when they have the opportunity to connect with students from other schools. Whether they are collaborating for the purposes of knowing more about each other's geographic location, for sharing student work, to learn more about a specific culture, or to participate in a larger online project, getting connected with other kids is fun for teachers and students alike. If you are hesitant to collaborate with another school, start by communicating one-on-one with a teacher who might be posting in a newsgroup. Once you get a sense of one another, you might find a possibility for some type of online collaboration.

If you have a project in mind and would like to find another teacher who's interested in working with you, try the following suggestions:

1. Determine whether you want a local or long-distance collaboration. If local, check the school district's Website. Many school districts now have Web pages and may include a section for teachers wanting to collaborate.

If you are seeking a long-distance collaboration, determine the grade level and geographic location and post a message on a K–12 bulletin board. You can also check Websites such as *http://www.gaggle.net* and *http://www.epals.com* for other classroom teachers interested in collaborative projects.

2. Check publications such as *Classroom Connect*. They have a section devoted to teachers seeking collaborative partners. Other resources for online projects include the following:
   http://www.educationplanet.com/
   http://quest.arc.nasa.gov/

Connecting with Experts

The Internet provides an easy means of bringing experts to your classroom. The simplest method is for students to e-mail an expert. Addresses for experts are found at various Internet sites. For example, if you are studying space exploration, your students can submit a question to U.S. astronauts at *http://nauts.com/*. When sending letters to experts, the students should develop a well-written e-mail that is direct and to the point. The e-mail should provide some brief background information such as "I am in Ms. Jones's third-grade class in Walled Lake, Michigan." If the expert understands that the question is asked by a third grader as opposed to a twelfth-grader, he or she will be able to provide a more appropriate response. You should also review the e-mail with the question to make sure it is concise and well stated. The shorter the e-mail and more precise the question, the better your chances are of obtaining a response. Once you receive a response, a reply with a "thanks!" is appropriate.

Reconsider who counts as an expert. Look beyond professionals and individuals with a Ph.D., and don't forget to include people who have first-hand experience with the subject matter. For example, if you're studying the Civil Rights Movement, check with the Civil Rights Museum in Memphis, Tennessee, to locate an expert who may have been present the day Martin Luther King, Jr. was assassinated.

Videoconferencing for Collaboration

One of the most exciting tools for collaboration is desktop videoconferencing. With broadband Internet connections, it is now possible to have a live video and audio of the expert in your classroom. Your classroom and the expert need an inexpensive video camera. You can use the software that comes with the camera or you can use software such as Microsoft's NetMeeting or First Virtual Communication's CU-SeeMe.

You can use different formats for the videoconference. For example, you could show the expert's image to the whole class using a large monitor or video projector and then let students listen and ask questions. Small groups of students or individual students in two or more locations could hold meetings using videoconferencing. The quality of the sound and video are affected by a number of factors. First is the speed of the Internet connections between the two sites. If your school computers are connected to the school's network, you probably have a fast connection and will be able to send and receive good-quality images and sound. If one of the connections is using a modem, the sound and video quality may not be suitable for lengthy or large group conferences. Second is the speed of the Internet. Some days, there is a lot of traffic and information will travel slowly (*http://www.internettrafficreport.com*). Internet speed seems to be slow in the afternoon, which could hamper the quality of your videoconferencing. Third, if your whole class is participating, the student who is speaking should move close to the microphone to improve sound quality. If the software you are using allows keyboard entry, a teacher or student can type the question.

USING THE INTERNET WITH AN INTEGRATED LESSON

The Internet is a tool, like a spreadsheet, database, or word processor. It provides another source of information, a way to communicate, and a place to publish the results. The following steps provide guidelines for using the Internet in an integrated lesson plan:

- ✓ Determine the problem the students are to solve.
- ✓ Identify ways they can use Internet resources to help solve the problem.
- ✓ Provide clear directions on how they are to use the Internet. For example, if they are to search for information on psychologists to create a psychology Website, your instructions should provide a description of the type of information they need, as well as how much information they need.
- ✓ Teach students to interpret, summarize, and cite information they are using from the Internet (as well as other resources). We have observed many classrooms in which the students simply copied and pasted information for their reports rather than processed the data. Written directions and Think Sheets can help the students accomplish this task.
- ✓ Either provide the students with some initial URLs or keywords or help them develop a list of search terms to get started.
- ✓ If the students are contacting an expert, discuss etiquette for contacting the individual and the criteria for a good e-mail (see Connecting with Experts in a previous section).
- ✓ When using videoconferencing, try to make a connection preferably with the other location at least a few days before the actual conference time. You can then test the software and the equipment. Remember, the video image and sound requirements are different when one or two individuals are conferencing versus a presentation to the whole class. If you are planning a presentation to the whole class, test the equipment to determine the quality of the image and sound from near the back of the room.
- ✓ Have an alternative planned if *and when* the equipment or Internet fails!

SUMMARY

The Internet is another tool students can use to solve problems. Activities can range from searching for information, to collecting data, to collaborating with other students and experts both far and near. Having Internet access in the classroom also adds another level of classroom management complexity. As a teacher, you will need to monitor your students' use of the Internet and make sure they are aware of and follow the guidelines established in your district's acceptable use policy as well as your classroom guidelines.

AT THE CLASSROOM'S DOORSTEP

Questions Teachers Ask

I'm totally unfamiliar with the Internet and feel intimidated about using it with my students. Where should I start?

Start slowly. Skip the online projects for now. Rather, begin by browsing the Web. Locate information that can help inform lessons you are currently teaching. Keep a record of the sites you visit. Or, get involved by reading some of the postings on the K–12 newsgroups. You don't have to respond until you feel comfortable. Finally, you may be inspired by checking Websites specifically developed for teachers (some were mentioned in this chapter). There are a variety of lesson plans available for using the Internet in a classroom setting. Most current textbooks list URLs of sites related to the subject area of the book.

I'm concerned about publishing students' photographs or work on the Internet. Do I need parental permission?

Most school districts have now set policies regarding usage of the Internet. Some require parents to sign permission slips, others do not allow the publishing of photographs, and some publish photos but leave off the student's name. Find out the school and district policy.

Do I have to use the Internet in my classroom?

No. The Internet is a tool. If it is appropriate, you should use it in your classroom. There are many resources and experts in your school and local library that you can use to either build your own skills in using the Internet or invite into your classroom to help your students.

I am afraid my students will abuse the Acceptable User Policy for the school. What can I do?

Someone once said rules were made to be broken, and, as former students, we tend to agree. You should discuss the policy with your students before their use of the Internet and then again at various intervals. The students should understand that Internet access is a privilege, not a right. They must demonstrate that they are responsible citizens if they want to continue to access the Internet. Then be prepared for problems. Ask other teachers how they have dealt with problems and then develop a plan of action. We have found that successful teachers have handled the problems quietly. One teacher described an instance in which a student created a PowerPoint presentation of sexually explicit images at home. The presentation was then circulated among some of her friends. When the teacher discovered the problem, the computers were confiscated.

Each student who participated attended a conference with his or her parents, the teacher, and the principal. The student then showed the presentation to his or her parents. The school revoked the students' access to the Internet. We assume that the parents imposed additional constraints on the students.

Another approach is to have the students and parents sign an agreement indicating they have read and understand the acceptable use policy. Some districts have a simplified version for students to make sure they understand the policy and consequences for violating the policy.

ISTE NETS FOR STUDENTS

The content in this Chapter supports four NETS for Students: Standards 1, 2, 4, and 5. The use of the Internet involves a basic understanding of how computers and Internet browsers work, thus reinforcing Standard 1. The Social, Ethical, and Human issues addressed in Standard 2 were covered when discussing Internet policies and copyright issues. As discussed, when students use the Internet as an information source, Standard 5, Technology Research Tool, is being met in that they "use technology to locate, evaluate, and collect information from a variety of sources." As with Chapter 8, Publishing and Presentation, student use of the Internet as a collaboration tool fulfills Standard 4, Technology Communication Tools. Specifically, students "use telecommunications to collaborate, publish, and interact with peers, experts, and other audiences."

TECHNOLOGY INTEGRATION ACTIVITIES

To access the activities that connect the content of the text with the Companion Website and other technology, please go to the Activities module in Chapter 9 of the Companion Website at *http://www.prenhall.com/morrison.*

NTEQ PORTFOLIO ACTIVITIES

Your NTeQ portfolio for this chapter involves the identification of Internet resources for you and your students. Let's start with the resources for you. Create a word processing document that has a two-column table and 25 rows. Label the left column as Resource and the right column as URL. Using one or more search engines, identify Internet resources that you can use for developing integrated lessons. Possible resources might include sites that allow teachers to create Web pages, sites offering student e-mail accounts, sites for establishing collaboration or e-mail pen pals, sources of data students can manipulate (i.e., government and professional sport sites), sites with lesson plans, and search engines.

Create a similar document for the student resources. Using one or more search engines, identify resources your students can use as part of a lesson. The resources might include kid-safe search engines, kid-safe e-mail, sources of graphics or pictures, dictionaries and encyclopedias, and sources of data (i.e., government Websites).

Lesson Ideas

- To study severe weather, students can visit the Storm Prediction Center (*http://www.spc.noaa.gov/*), the National Hurricane Center (*http://www.nhc.noaa.gov/*), or the Weather Channel's Website (*http://www.weather.com/*) to gather information. They can gather data from one or more weather sites and track hurricanes or storms across the United States.
- Integrate math and social studies by having students participate in a "Dream Vacation." Assign groups to a continent and assign a budget. Students must plan airfare, hotel, and food costs and calculate currency exchange rates. They also have to plan the sights they want to visit, they have to know the language and customs of people, and they have to know what to expect in terms of weather. Have them present their findings in a multimedia tour created with information and graphics downloaded from the Internet (Serim & Koch, 1996).
- Set up an "Internet News Bureau" where students can work in groups to track the latest local, national, and international news online, and then report the findings by creating an online classroom newspaper. They can also do a weekly news broadcast over the school's P.A. system (Cotton, 1997).

REFERENCES

Classroom Connect. (1997). *The Internet curriculum planning system.* Lancaster, PA: Author.

Cotton, E. (1997). *The online classroom: Teaching with the Internet.* Bloomington, IN: EDINFO Press.

Crawford, T. (1993). *Legal guide for the visual artist.* New York: Allworth Press.

National Center for Educational Statistics [NCES]. (1998). *Internet access in public schools and classrooms: 1994–1998.* Retrieved July 30, 2003, from http://nces.ed.gov/surveys/frss/publications/1999017/#.

National Center for Educational Statistics [NCES]. (2002). *Internet access in public schools and classrooms: 1994–2001.* Retrieved August 9, 2003, from http://nces.ed.gov/pubs2002/internet/3.asp.

Owston, R. D. (1997). The WWW: A technology to enhance teaching and learning? *Educational Researcher, 26*(2), 27–33.

Serim, F., & Koch, M. (1996). *NetLearning: Why teachers use the Internet.* Sebastapol, CA: Songline Studios, Inc.

Zakon, R. H. (2003). *Hobbes' Internet timeline v6.1.* Retrieved August 1, 2003, from http://www.zakon.org/robert/internet/timeline/#2000s.

KEY TOPICS

Choosing the Right Software
- Types of Educational Software

Software Evaluation
- Software Evaluation Criteria
- Software Reviews
- Two Types of Software Evaluation

Educational Software and NTeQ
- Five Key Components
- Computer Functions
- Meaningful Integration

Chapter 10

Educational Software

Recent research indicates that most teachers tend to rely on drill and practice or computer games when using educational software (Becker, 2001). However, by following a well-thought-out integration plan, such as the NTeQ lesson plan, educational software can become an integral component of a lesson. This chapter provides an overview of the types of software, ways to evaluate the software, and how to meaningfully integrate the software into an NTeQ lesson.

GETTING STARTED

What Do I Know?

1. I just did a Web search for fourth-grade mathematics software, and the results showed 44,700 Websites. How do I decide which software to use?
2. I'd like to use some of the educational software we have in the library, but most packages have a lot of information that is not covered in our curriculum standards. What do I do?
3. NTeQ emphasizes using the computer as a tool in ways that are similar workplace uses. How does educational software "fit" into a student-centered, problem-solving approach?

Classroom Snapshot

TRADITIONAL APPROACH

Let's go to "High Marks Elementary School," the technology showcase of the district. Every classroom has three to five computers, and the library has numerous software programs in all content areas. Ms. New-Trend, the principal, enthusiastically encourages all teachers to integrate technology into their lessons. In an effort to "be current" and on the good side of the principal, Mr. Exemplary, the lead fifth-grade teacher, regularly goes to the library to select just the right software for each lesson. This week, he begins by scanning titles in the social studies section to find something about U.S. agriculture. A box covered with brightly colored vegetables and fruit titled *Farmland* catches his attention. After quickly reading the software box to see if it looks like it will be fun for the students to use, he decides that *Farmland* is his computer integration selection for this week. He writes Farmland in the "technology integration" section of his weekly lesson plan, loads the software on Computer 2, and adds time to the weekly schedule for pairs of students to "use" the software. As Mr. Exemplary introduces the lesson on U.S. agriculture, he indicates that the technology portion of the lesson will be for the students to "use" the Farmland software on Computer 2. He tells the students that they begin by clicking on the ear of corn and spend 20 minutes exploring the various aspects of the program, then spend 10 minutes writing a journal entry telling about what they learned while using the computer. At the end of the 30 minutes, the next pair of students visit Computer 2 and explore *Farmland.*

NTEQ APPROACH

Now, let's visit "Exceptional Elementary School," also a technology showcase of the district. Classrooms are well equipped with three to five computers, and the library has a large selection of educational software. Mr. Informed Leader, the principal, enthusiastically encourages all teachers to integrate *meaningful* uses of technology into their lessons. In an effort to meet the curriculum and technology needs of his students, Mr. Facilitator, the lead fifth-grade teacher carefully plans how best to integrate the use of computers and educational software. This involves reviewing his lesson plans, student work, and journal entries to identify the most appropriate goals and how technology can assist students to achieve those goals. He then goes to the library to select the software. He begins by scanning titles in the social studies section to find something about U.S. agriculture. A box covered with brightly colored vegetables and fruit titled *Farmland* catches his attention. He carefully reads the software description and determines that it has potential for his lesson. He returns to his class and loads the software on his computer to examine the different lessons. He discovers that Lessons 3 and 6 cover information required by the district standards and that the lessons are presented in a fun manner—so he adds *Farmland*, Lessons 3 and 6 to his lesson plans. As Mr. Facilitator introduces the lesson on U.S. agriculture, he indicates that the technology portion of the lesson will be for the students to complete *Farmland's* Lessons 3 and 6 on Computer 2. He then provides a brief overview of the new information they will be learning from the software. He tells the students to carefully read all the content and complete all the activities. When finished, they are to reflect on their learning by answering the questions he provides. At the end of the day, when all students have completed the two lessons, Mr. Facilitator engages the class in a review discussion of the *Farmland* material and shows how it fits with the rest of the information they have been learning about U.S. agriculture.

CHOOSING THE RIGHT SOFTWARE

One of the key features of computer-based instruction is the ability to provide feedback. In other words, the computer can be programmed to "tell" the user if their answer is correct or incorrect. This feature has been the impetus for the development of a neverending supply of educational software packages that "guarantee" to teach children everything from basic math skills to advanced physics for only $19.99 to $599.00 per computer. And, of course, no "guarantee" would be complete without a knowledgeable salesperson to convince you of the software's credibility and value. When you combine the sheer number of available educational software programs with the skillful tactics of salespersons, it is obvious that educators need some basic guidelines to assist them in making wise purchase decisions. This section begins with a review of the types of software, criteria for assessing software, locations of software reviews, and two approaches to software evaluation.

Types of Educational Software

If you examine the Educational Software Preview Guide published by the International Society for Technology in Education (ISTE), you will find over 800 software programs that have been "favorably reviewed . . . by knowledgeable computer-using educators" (Educational Software Preview Guide Consortium, 2000, p. vi). Those that would fall into the category of educational software, as defined in this text, would be the programs that present the student with content, activities, and/or process tools focused on increasing a particular type of knowledge or skill. Within this framework, there are five main types of educational software (Table 10-1).

SOFTWARE EVALUATION

There is a wide variety of software available to teachers; thus it is critical to evaluate the educational soundness of the software, preferably before it is purchased. To determine the educational value of software, begin by determining which criteria should be used to judge software effectiveness, then determine how to use the criteria as a basis for selecting software reviews or conducting software evaluations.

TABLE 10-1 Types of Educational Software

Type of Educational Software	Descriptions
Tutorials	Tutorials present students with new information to be learned and provide interactive practice and feedback.
Drill-and-Practice	Drill-and-practice software provides students with interactive practice and feedback of information for which students have already received instruction.
Learning Games	Most learning games provide drill and practice of previously learned material, although some teach new information. The difference between games and drill and practice is the competitive and motivational nature of the software. Competition can be provided with time constraints, points earned, and/or computer characters.
Problem Solving	Problem solving software presents students with situations that require the use of higher-order thinking skills to achieve the intended outcome(s). Many problem solving programs involve simulations of "real-world" situations and often are game-like.
Process Tools	Process tools software provides students with a set of tools to assist them with completing a designated process such as concept mapping, writing, graphing, or designing. The tools can be divided into two groups: those with prompting and those without. *Prompted:* The ones with prompting go beyond basic application software such as word processing because they provide prompts to engage students in specific steps required to complete a process, such as writing a book report. *Not Prompted:* Those without prompting provide just the tools to complete a designated process, such as shapes and connector lines to create concept maps.

Software Evaluation Criteria

When examining the criteria used to evaluate educational software, as seen in Figure 10-1, four primary types of evaluation criteria are consistently recommended (Gill, Dick, Reiser, & Zahner, 1992; Hannafin & Peck 1988; Hubbard, 1992; Rickenberg, 1996). It is important to keep these criteria in mind when ex-

It is important for teachers to carefully evaluate educational software before having students use it during a lesson.

FIGURE 10-1 Software Evaluation Criteria

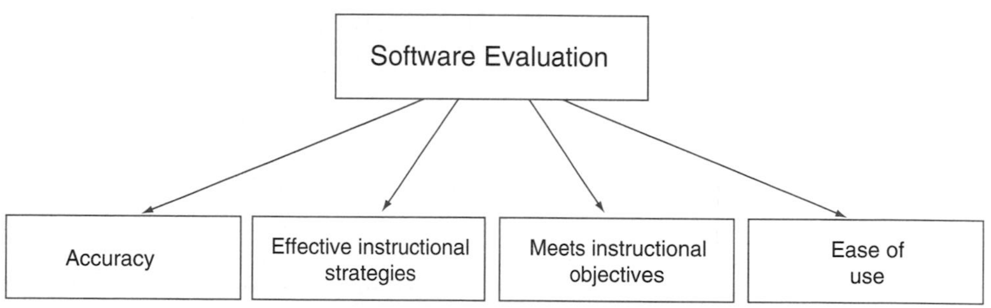

amining software reviews or choosing an evaluation format to use when selecting software to use with your students.

1. Accuracy (information is correct and consistent)
2. Effective instructional strategies
   - Learner control of various program features (sound, pace, sequence, etc.)
   - Variety of appropriate feedback (instructional feedback given when appropriate)
   - Maintains student interest

3. Meets instructional objectives
4. Ease of use
   - Technical quality
   - Precise and consistent directions

Software Reviews

You can find reviews of educational software on the Internet, in educational journals, and as separate printed documents, for example, the *Educational Software Preview Guide* (2000). When selecting a software review, it is important to determine who reviewed the software and the criteria used to assess the software. Reviews are conducted by a variety of people, including professional reviewers, teachers, parents, children, university faculty, and graduate students (Gill et al., 1992; Rickenberg, 1996).

Begin by determining which type(s) of reviewer(s) will provide the most useable information, then select software reviews by your selected group. It is often helpful to examine reviews that have included a variety of reviewers to obtain a broader perspective. The next area to consider when selecting software reviews is the criteria used to evaluate the software. First determine if the criteria address the Software Evaluation Criteria listed above, and, second, determine if they address other items that may be of specific interest to the particular needs and interests of your students.

Two Types of Software Evaluation

Software reviews and evaluations obtained from numerous Websites can provide useful background information about a piece of educational software and its perceived effectiveness. However, for you to be confident that the software will meet the needs of your particular students, you may want to conduct your own evaluation.

Teacher-Conducted

Teachers can use two approaches when evaluating software. The first approach uses your own experience and expertise to evaluate the software. This evaluation examines the type of software, subject area, grade level, and intended learning objectives. After these items are identified, the evaluation asks you to rate items related to the criteria listed above: accuracy, effectiveness of the instructional strategies, amount of learner control over variables, if it is easy to use, and if it will interest your students. The form ends with a description of the best and worst features of the software and a place to add any notes that may help when the software is used. A form for conducting this type of software evaluation is seen in Figure 10-2.

Student Performance and Attitudes

The second approach is proposed by Reiser and Dick (1990) and determines whether or not students actually learn from the software. This approach takes more time and teacher involvement than completing an evaluation form. However, the benefits of

CHECK IT OUT 10-1

Fair Use in the Classroom

Title: Software Review Sites

Grade: Any

Problem: *You have been chosen as Chair of your school's technology committee and provided with a budget of $4,000 to purchase educational software that has been highly reviewed. How can you find the best software review sites to use when making software selections.*

Activity: Download the Software Review Site Evaluation Sheet. Complete one Evaluation Sheet for three to five of the listed Software Evaluation sites. Choose the top two sites and write a brief rationale for your decision.

Link to these resources and activities in the Check It Out module for this chapter of the Companion Website.

collecting student performance and attitude data outweigh the effort when considering the purchase of an expensive educational software package to integrate into your curriculum. The criteria for software selection and the evaluation steps for this approach can be seen in Table 10-2.

EDUCATIONAL SOFTWARE AND NTEQ

The process for integrating educational software into a lesson is similar to integrating other types of computer use into a lesson, except that the software should be evaluated or selected from trusted software reviews before considering it for inclusion in lessons. The following section describes how to use the NTeQ model to meaningfully integrate educational software into your curriculum.

Five Key Components

All 10 components of the NTeQ lesson plan (Figure 10-3) are addressed when integrating *educational software* into a lesson, but only 5 differ from an NTeQ lesson plan that integrates *applications* as a tool. These five are discussed in the section below:

1. Computer Functions
2. Data Manipulation

FIGURE 10-2 Software Evaluation: Teacher-Conducted

Software Evaluation Form

Title: ______________________

Type of Software: ❑ Drill-and-Practice ❑ Tutorial ❑ Simulation
❑ Game ❑ Other ____________

Subject Area: ______________________

Grade Level: ______________________

Instructional Objectives:

____

____

____

____

Rating..

Accuracy	❑ High	❑ Medium	❑ Low
Effective instructional strategies	❑ High	❑ Medium	❑ Low
Learner control of various features (sound, pace, sequence, etc.)	❑ High	❑ Medium	❑ Low
Variety of appropriate feedback	❑ High	❑ Medium	❑ Low
Maintains student interest	❑ High	❑ Medium	❑ Low
Meets instructional objectives	❑ High	❑ Medium	❑ Low
Ease of use	❑ High	❑ Medium	❑ Low
Technical quality	❑ High	❑ Medium	❑ Low
Precise and consistent directions	❑ High	❑ Medium	❑ Low

Best Features ______________________

____

____

Worst Features ______________________

____

____

NOTES ______________________

____

____

3. Activities During Computer Use
4. Activities Before Computer Use
5. Activities After Computer Use

Computer Functions

You still start planning your lesson by specifying the instructional objectives. Once these are identified, you then move to the second step of the NTeQ lesson planning, which determines if attainment of any of the objectives would be enhanced by integrating student use of the computer. Just as with the computer tools, the basic func-

TABLE 10-2 Software Evaluation: Student Performance and Attitudes

CRITERIA FOR SELECTING SOFTWARE

Software that is to be evaluated with this process needs to meet the following two criteria:

- Highly rated by commercial or educational sources
- Has identifiable instructional objectives

EVALUATION STEPS FOR THE TEACHER

- Reviews software with a form similar to the one in Figure 10–2

1. Develop the following tests to measure attainment of instructional objectives
    - Pretest
    - Posttest
    - Retention test
2. Develop student attitude survey that measures:
    - Enjoyment
    - Recommendation of software to other students
    - Description of what was to be learned
3. Administer pretest to whole class to identify a high, medium, and low achiever for the field test.
4. Field test the software with the three identified students.
5. Administer the posttest and attitude survey to the three students.
6. Administer the retention test 2 weeks after the posttest.
7. Review the results, preferably with colleagues, and make decision.

Adapted from the Evaluating Instructional Software Model (Reiser & Dick, 1990)

tions of educational software are identified to see if they align with the objectives (see Appendix A). This step, however, is often a two-part process because most educational software not only has functions but also a content area and grade levels that will need to align with the objectives. When you examine educational software, the functions primarily fall into three main categories: providing content, providing practice and feedback, and providing process tools.

Providing Content

The function of providing content includes such things as descriptions, definitions, examples and nonexamples, diagrams, photographs, maps, or any type of information to be learned by the students. For example, the content area of a software program could be metamorphosis or The Pony Express. The content can be provided as text to be read by the student or the computer, as animated or static graphics, or as narration that does not have the script provided on the screen.

FIGURE 10-3 NTeQ Model

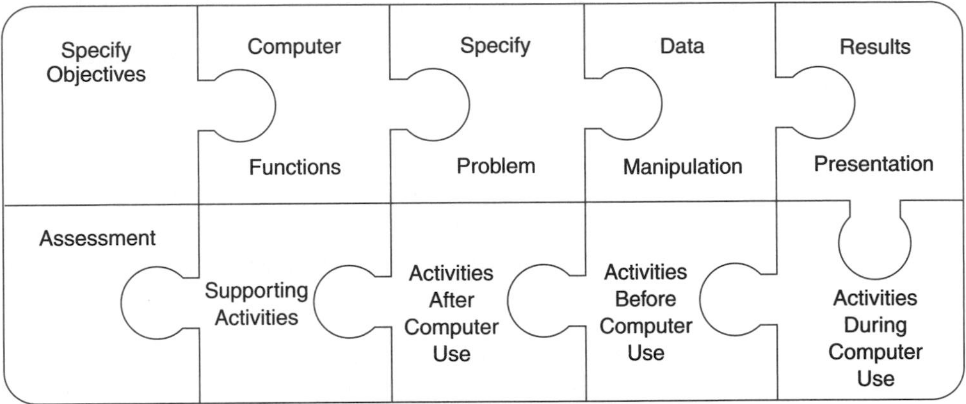

Providing Practice and Feedback

The next main function of educational software is the provision of practice and feedback. This consideration is the most unique aspect of using computers and what enables them to be considered *interactive*. Computers can be programmed to provide "individualized" feedback to students. This feedback is available in the following forms (Morrison, Ross, Gopalakrishnan, & Casey, 1995):

- Correctness of response (right or wrong)
- Answer until correct
- Review of material, if wrong answer is given
- Branching to next material based on performance
  - Advancement
  - Reinforcement
  - Remediation

The practice and feedback function is what separates educational software from digitized reference materials, such as CD-ROM encyclopedias, that primarily provide content. Although some of the newer reference materials have added some interactivity into the programs, it is typically limited to only a portion of the material.

Providing Process Tools

The final primary function of educational software is providing process tools. The tools can include prompts or they can be stand-alone tools. The tools that provide prompts are different from basic application tools in that the learner is given tips or guidance at varying stages of the process that is being learned. For example, if students are using educational software that provides them with tools that help with the writing process, they might receive prompts similar to the following, if learning to write a book review:

- Write a sentence that describes the main character.

- Choose the drawing that best shows how the main character felt at the beginning of the story; then write one sentence to describe the feeling.
- Choose a drawing that shows how the main character felt at the end of the story, and write two sentences to describe the feeling.

Process tools that would not include prompts include those used to create concept maps, create calendars or timelines, graph information, create shapes, and so on. Most of these software programs have underlying, preformatted templates that allow for some creativity, but offer less freedom than basic application tools. The preprogramming of process tools allows students to concentrate on the process that is being learned rather than computer skills. For example, when students use *Inspiration,* a concept-mapping tool, they do not have to worry with using a draw tool to create shapes, the text box tool to add information, and the line tool to connect them. Use of a process tool like *Inspiration* frees student thinking for developing connections between concepts and ideas.

Software Selection

Once you have determined that integrating one or more of the functions of educational software will enhance student attainment of the lesson objectives, you then need to select the appropriate software. If the functions that align with your objectives are to provide content and practice with feedback, you will need to consider the content area, the grade level appropriateness, and the quality and appropriateness of the activities. If the function that aligns with your objectives is providing process tools, you will need to match the type of needed process skills with those provided by the software.

The selection of software can often be made easier because much of the needed information is provided by software reviews or product descriptions. For example,

THE TEACHER'S DIARY

My students use a drill-and-practice software program called Speedway Math. I put a speedway track on the bulletin board. Each student designs a racecar. At the beginning of the week, the students put their racecars on the starting line. The students compete individually as I set the number and difficulty of the problems for each student, based on ability. They use this program as many times as they want during the week and move their car one space for each time they use the program. Their short-term goal is to get to the finish line by the end of the week. Their ultimate goal is to make it to the Hall of Fame, which shows that they have mastered all of the multiplication facts. This is a great motivator to get the students to practice the facts.

Fran Clark
Third-Grade Teacher

ISTE's *Educational Software Preview Guide* (2000) provides the following information for each reviewed program: subject area, grade level, platform/operating system, and instructional mode, for example, drill-and-practice, simulation, tutorial, and education game.

Data Manipulation

The data manipulation portion of the NTeQ lesson varies based on the function being emphasized. In this case, because educational software is the focus, the basic functions are providing content, providing practice/feedback, and/or providing process tools. When the needed function is providing content and/or providing practice/feedback, the data manipulation would involve identifying the specific sections or portions of the software that align with the objectives. For example, a piece of software may have 15 practice lessons for identifying parts of speech or 10 lessons about volcanoes. Unless the entire software package addresses your lesson objectives, you will need to select only the portions that are directly related to and will support student achievement of the objectives. The volcano software may include the history, impact on humans, and location and formation of volcanoes, as well as other lesson topics. Your lesson objectives are for the students to understand the formation of volcanoes; therefore only these sections should be assigned. The remaining sections can be covered as enhancement activities if time permits.

When the educational software is needed to provide process tools, the data manipulation will involve students working with the tools to learn the designated process. This typically involves two steps: choosing the data or information that will be used (manipulated) when learning the process and the specific process tool. For example, software that teaches and supports the writing process may have lessons on several different types of writing projects, for example, book reviews, friendly letters, or persuasive arguments. If your lesson is to have students learn how to write friendly letters, in order to plan the data manipulation you will need to determine the recipient and the content of the letters (even if the content is "free choice" of the students). The second step is choosing the friendly letter lesson of the writing process software.

Activities During Computer Use

Planning what students do at the computer while using the selected educational software is fairly well designated by the time you reach this portion of the lesson planning. When students use application tools, you must plan for students to set up the format, enter data, and complete a variety of manipulations. The use of educational software requires less planning in that the software is already programmed. To plan the computer time, you will need to determine how many computers will have the software, how you will let students know exactly what sections or lessons they will be completing, and whether they will work alone or with other students. It might be helpful to "cue-up" the software before each student comes to the computer if the designated lesson is not easily accessible.

THE TEACHER'S DIARY

One of the most memorable moments this year was watching my students working together on a project I put together about Dr. Martin Luther King, Jr. I researched to find several excellent Internet sites about Dr. King, obtained the Timeliner software, then put together some project ideas.

The groups began by creating a timeline of key events in the life of Dr. King. Students then worked in groups of two, and I assigned them a project topic. Some topics were much more advanced than others, so I assigned the more difficult topics to students who have demonstrated the ability to handle higher-level thinking tasks.

Most of the assignment topics were given to two groups of students. The class became deeply involved in research and discussion. I wandered around the classroom, stopping to answer questions and monitor the progress of each group. Watching the groups do their work and noting the direction that each group intended to go made me feel thankful to be a part of these young people's lives. Even groups assigned to the same topic were attacking the project in different ways, which I always encourage.

Two groups were given the task of finding a movement similar to the Civil Rights Movement that exists today. Both groups were frustrated at first. "Help us, Mrs. Shoemaker. We have no idea how to even research this!" I hinted to both groups to think of current event issues that we've been discussing in social studies class, but didn't say more. The frustration continued for about 15 minutes, as these two groups watched other groups around them, feeling like they were way behind the progress of other groups. However, both groups came to me when they thought of the direction they intended to go with the project. One group decided to research the events that happened recently in Kosovo. The other group decided to focus on women's rights. Both groups were so proud of themselves for coming up with the project idea on their own. The discussion that I overheard was fascinating. The students became more and more involved as they became more aware of other injustices in the world. One of the students became so involved in the study of women's rights, I told her she might be the first woman President.

What was so enjoyable to me was seeing how involved the students were. The projects turned out so much better than I ever imagined, and they all looked very different. I believe that every one of my students now has a whole new outlook about the significance of Dr. Martin Luther King, Jr. and what he did for our country. These projects were meaningful to each and every one of my students, and the computers made this possible.

Pam Shoemaker
Sixth-Grade Teacher

Activities Before Computer Use

When planning activities to get students ready to use educational software, the activities will again vary based on the functions that are being emphasized. If the software will be providing new content or practice and feedback, students may need to complete activities that will provide reinforcement of prerequisite skills required to complete the assigned lessons. If the lesson is primarily practice and feedback for remediation, it again is useful to have students review the rules and procedures for skills that are to be practiced. If students are learning or reinforcing a process skill, such as concept mapping or writing, students will need to prepare or collect ideas and information that will be used at the computer.

Activities After Computer Use

When educational software is used to provide content and practice and feedback, students do not have products to work with when they finish their computer time. You could, however, plan time for students to discuss what they learned or have them enter reflections of the learning into their journal. Students do have final products when they use educational software that provides process tools. If each student or small group of students produces a product, students can complete a compare/contrast activity to determine similarities and differences in how the process was completed. For example, if students are using a tool that helps them to create a timeline of events leading up to the Civil War, they can see what each team included and how it was described. If students created concept maps to describe geometric shapes, again students can compare the final products and decide how they might create the concept map if two groups combined their map to create one.

Meaningful Integration

Educational games and drill-and-practice are too often the emphasis of technology integration in today's classrooms. It is not that educational software, in and of itself, does not provide effective instruction, but rather that teachers often do not plan for its meaningful use. It is easy to think that a software program is "complete" and self-explanatory, that students must begin with lesson one and go through all lessons, and that the software will show students what is important and guide their learning activities as they progress through each level. In reality, the only difference between educational software and books is the degree of interactivity. Teachers typically carefully review material students will be covering in the textbook. They typically even choose which chapter questions should be answered or which map should be copied. Yet these same teachers may not carefully review software and determine which portions best support the learning objectives.

To meaningfully integrate educational software into a lesson, teachers need to review the content and activities to carefully select the appropriate portions to support the intended learning. Teachers should also provide support activities that reinforce material and skills being taught with the software. The fact that the information and

With careful planning, NTeQ lessons can be enhanced by integrating appropriate educational software.

activities come in a computer-based format that may appear sophisticated and professionally produced does not mean that your careful judgment and planning are not needed. You, as a teacher, are still the best judge of what your students need to achieve successful learning.

SUMMARY

As seen in this chapter, educational software is the most prevalent type of software used in today's classrooms. Some of the reasons underlying this use are that numerous packages are available for every grade level and subject area and most are very easy to use. However, this vast array of choices makes it challenging for teachers to know which type of software to choose (tutorials, drill-and-practice, learning games, problem solving, or process tools) and how to determine if the software is of high quality. Therefore this chapter recommends that teachers solicit credible software reviews and/or conduct their own evaluations. These evaluations need to examine the software's accuracy of content, use of effective instructional strategies that result in attainment of the targeted objectives, and ease of use. When a software package meets these standards, it can then, with careful planning as seen in the NTeQ model, be meaningfully integrated into classroom instruction.

AT THE CLASSROOM'S DOORSTEP

Questions Teachers Ask

There are so many software programs to choose from; I do not have the time to review each one. Is there a quicker way to see if the software will work with my students?

There are a couple of approaches you can take. You could start by working with other teachers in your school to divide up the software programs that seem interesting and then share your reviews. Another approach is to join a teacher's e-mail list and ask for comments and suggestions about a particular software package that you are considering or ask for recommended software for topics of interest.

We have quite a large selection of software in our school and I have reviewed several packages, but I am finding it difficult to keep track of the information. Is there a way to make this information easier to use?

It would be helpful to keep a database of information that you have collected about the software. This could include software title, subject area, specific skills being taught, alignment with district performance standards, number of copies available, sections to use, and so on. If a server is available at your school, or a common computer is available in the library, the database could be used and updated by more than one teacher.

TECHNOLOGY INTEGRATION ACTIVITIES

To access the activities that connect the content of the text with the Companion Website and other technology, please go to the Activities module in Chapter 10 of the Companion Website at *http://www.prenhall.com/morrison.*

NTEQ PORTFOLIO ACTIVITIES: EDUCATIONAL SOFTWARE

Please complete the following activities as part of your NTeQ Portfolio on Educational Software.

Reflections

The "Getting Started" portion of this chapter asked three questions that teachers might commonly ask. In this portion of your journal, a reflection question has been added to address how you would answer each question. Please use information from this chapter to answer the questions.

1. I just did an Internet search for fourth-grade mathematics software, and the results showed 44,700 Websites. How do I decide which software to use?
    - *Reflection Question:* Imagine that you write a technology column for your school district's monthly newsletter and you received question 1 above. Use information from this chapter to write a response to this teacher.

2. I'd like to use some of the educational software we have in the library, but most packages have a lot of information that is not covered in our standards. What do I do?
   - *Reflection Question:* Prepare a checklist that you can use when examining an educational software package to determine if sections of it might be appropriate for your students to use during a lesson.
3. NTeQ emphasizes using the computer as a tool in ways that are similar to workplace uses. How does educational software "fit" into a student-centered, problem solving approach?
   - *Reflection Question:* Review the Educational Software and NTeQ section of this chapter and write a response to this question.

Select a previously developed lesson from your NTeQ Portfolio and locate at least one educational software package to integrate into the lesson. Modify these sections to show how it would be integrated:

Teacher-Conducted Software Evaluation

Locate educational software that is available to you either through your personal collection or the school's and find one that seems to be age-appropriate for your students and covers a topic that you teach. Review the software to find specific lessons that you would like to evaluate for possible use with your students. Use the Software Evaluation: Teacher-Conducted form found in Figure 10–2 (download from *http://www.prenhall.com/morrison*) to evaluate the selected lessons. Include the final review in your portfolio.

Educational Software and NTeQ

✓ Computer Functions

✓ Data Manipulation

✓ Activities During Computer Use

✓ Activities Before Computer Use

✓ Activities After Computer Use

REFERENCES

Becker, H. J. (2001, April). *How are teachers using computers in instruction?* Paper presented at the meeting of the American Educational Research Association, Seattle, WA. Retrieved July 8, 2003 from http://www.crito.uci.edu/tlc/FINDINGS/special3/.

Educational Software Preview Guide Consortium (2000). *Educational software preview guide*. Eugene, OR: International Society for Technology in Education.

Gill, B. J., Dick, W., Reiser, R. A., & Zahner, J. E. (1992). A new model for evaluating instructional software. *Educational Technology, 32*(3), 39–44.

Hannafin, M. J., & Peck, K. L. (1988). *The design, development, and evaluation of instructional software*. New York: Macmillan Publishing Co.

Hubbard, P. (1992). Software evaluation guide. [Online]. Available at http://www.owlnet.rice.edu/~ling417/guide.html.

Morrison, G. R., Ross, S. M., Gopalakrishnan, M., & Casey, J. (1995). The effects of feedback and incentives on achievement in computer-based instruction. *Contemporary Educational Psychology, 20,* 32–50.

Reiser, R. A., & Dick, W. (1990). Evaluating instructional software. *Educational Technology Research and Development, 38*(3), 43–50.

Rickenberg, D. (1996). Software evaluation and selection page for educators. [Online]. Available at http://www.sp.utoledo.edu/~lelsie/StudF96/dricken/software.html. Accessed July 14, 2003.

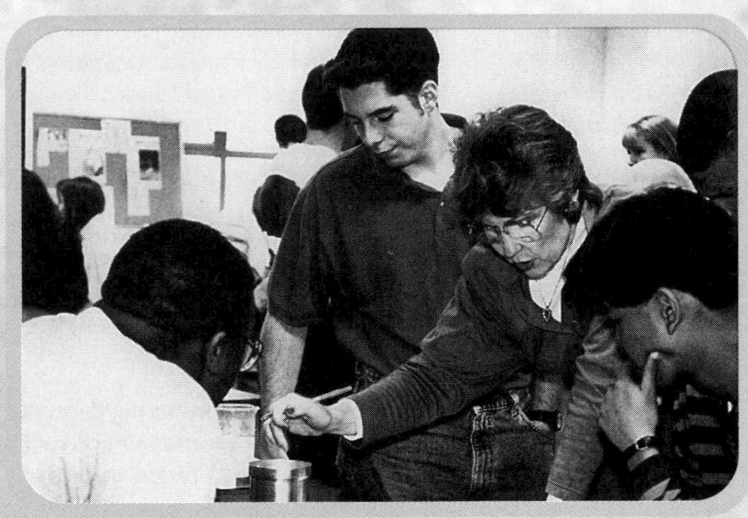

KEY TOPICS

Before Classroom Implementation
- Make Handouts and Assignment Sheets
- Tech Prep

During Classroom Implementation
- Five Elements of Effective Instruction
- The Five Elements of Instruction and NTeQ
- Implementing the NTeQ Problem Solving Process
- As-Needed Activities

Chapter 11

Implementation: From Plan to Action

As mentioned in Chapter 3, the 10-step NTeQ Model is a *planning* model that guides you through the development of problem-based lessons that integrate student use of computers. Developing a well-thought-out lesson plan is an imperative component to achieving effective instruction. However, additional preparation is necessary to go from the lesson plan to successful implementation in the classroom. This chapter discusses both the preparation needed before lesson implementation and guidelines for using the NTeQ Problem Solving Process *during* classroom implementation of an NTeQ lesson.

GETTING STARTED

What Do I Know?

1. What can I do to "get ready" for a lesson that has my students using computers?
2. Where does the "computer part" come when I am teaching a lesson?
3. I've never used an inquiry-based approach, much less computers, so how is a teacher supposed to do both of these at one time?

Classroom Snapshot

MY FIRST NTEQ LESSON JOURNAL

WEDNESDAY, OCTOBER 15

I'm very excited because I have my first NTeQ lesson developed and am going to use it next Wednesday! The lesson problem is: Do states get bigger when moving from the East to the West Coast? The students are going to do Internet searches, create a spreadsheet with information from the Internet, and then create a final PowerPoint presentation to share the results. I need to make samples of the student products and make sure to find some Internet sites to help make the searching easier.

THURSDAY, OCTOBER 16

I reserved the laptop cart today. It has 15 computers, so I plan to have two children per computer. It has a wireless connection to the Internet, so I don't have to worry about wires. The cart comes with a printer and a digital projector, so the students can show their presentations to the whole class.

FRIDAY, OCTOBER 17

Today, I used my planning period to find Internet sites that would be appropriate for the students to use. I had a notebook next to me to jot down each URL. I'm glad I did this because it took me a long time to find just the right sites. I am a little concerned, though, because some of the longer URLs may be hard for the students to copy.

MONDAY, OCTOBER 20

Only 2 days left till the lesson. I am very excited. I made a sample spreadsheet to make sure it would work, then printed a copy of the final chart so students can see what their spreadsheet should look like. Tomorrow I am going to make a PowerPoint presentation—the final thing.

TUESDAY, OCTOBER 21

I made the sample PowerPoint presentation today. It was so much fun. I added lots of cute graphics and some fun sounds. The students will love doing this. I printed the slides on a handout with three slides per page to save paper. I had 15 copies made of the spreadsheet and presentation to share with the student pairs.

WEDNESDAY, OCTOBER 22

What a disaster!! I had no idea that so many things could go wrong. I started out by presenting the problem to the students. They were very interested in finding the answer. I put students into pairs and handed out the laptops and the handouts with the completed spreadsheet and presentation. I then wrote the URLs that I found on the whiteboard and told students to collect information and then create a spreadsheet and a presentation of the results using the handouts as a guide. All of the students knew how to use the laptops from lessons completed in the lab, so they quickly opened the computers and started to work. However, in a short amount of time the students began asking a million questions: Can you tell me the problem again? Why are we doing this lesson? How do we create a spreadsheet chart? Do our slides have to look just like yours? Can we add animation? Where do we save our work? What do we call the documents? How can we find the presentation we started before lunch? Is this good enough to get a good grade? Why don't some of the URLs work? What do we do when we get to the Internet site? Why is Hector doing all the computer work? What formulas do we use in the spreadsheets? How do we choose the best solution? Our laptop's battery is dead—what do we do now?

THURSDAY, OCTOBER 23

I know there has to be a better way to implement a technology lesson. Where can I find some tips and guidelines that will make the process easier?

BEFORE CLASSROOM IMPLEMENTATION

Preparing a lesson that integrates student use of computers, use of multiple resources, and a variety of activities, takes additional preparation time compared to preparing to implement a more traditional lesson. The amount of time required, however, decreases as you and your students become more experienced with using technology in a classroom setting. Things that you can do before implementing your NTeQ lesson include the following:

Make Handouts and Assignment Sheets
- Think Sheets
- Technical step-by-step guides (i.e., job aids)
- Resource guides
- Rubrics

Tech Prep
- Create folders
- Create templates
- Load specialized software
- Bookmark Internet sites
- Turn on computers and open applications

Make Handouts and Assignment Sheets

As with most lessons, students will need information and instructions to guide them through the various activities. Handouts have proven to be a very successful means of transmitting this information to students. Below are guidelines for creating Problem Sheets, Think Sheets, technical step-by-step guides, resource guides, and rubrics.

Problem Sheet

Regardless of how well you explain the focus of the lesson, students tend to either lose focus or forget the task at hand. Maintaining the focus with an integrated lesson is often made more difficult because the lesson may take more than one class period to complete. A Problem Sheet can provide enough information to motivate the student and explain the purpose of the lesson.

Problem Sheets start by creating a context for the lesson (you may need to develop or refine this section later if the students are helping to identify the problem). You can increase the motivation by creating an uneasiness in the student by either showing conflicts with their knowledge or presenting data suggesting there is a problem. The context should provide a basis for their understanding the problem by framing it in a context they can understand.

The Problem Sheet can also include directions or suggestions for one or more tasks. You might decide to prepare several Problem Sheets to create small steps for the students. When the students complete one step, you can give them a sheet with the next step. Using this approach can help the students stay focused on the lesson.

Think Sheets

As seen in Chapters 2 and 3, Think Sheets are the stimulus for engaging students in critical thinking. These sheets can contain a variety of information, including the problem statement, probing questions, URLs, tips for using the technology, and self-reflection questions. For some lessons, it may be beneficial to have more than one Think Sheet to guide student thinking through various stages. For example, two Think Sheets could be used if you want students to make predictions before starting the problem solving process. Therefore Think Sheet 1 would ask stimulating and thought-provoking questions, and then Think Sheet 2 would contain further questions and suggestions for manipulating the data and interpreting the information. Another time you may want to use more than one Think Sheet is when a lesson includes several activities, for example, conducting an Internet search, creating and using a database to answer specific questions, entering data into a spreadsheet and charting results, and then creating a PowerPoint presentation of the findings. A lengthy Think Sheet with the guidelines and student questions for multiple activities is not only cumbersome but may overwhelm some of your students. A sample Think Sheet can be seen in Chapter 13 (see Figure 13-5).

Technical Step-by-Step Guides

If students are doing a computer task that is new or fairly new, it will be worth your time to create or use previously developed step-by-step job aids to assist students. These job aids will better enable your students to work through the lesson independently rather than needing extra assistance from you or others. There are three ways to present the guidelines: on the Think Sheet, on a separate handout, or on a sheet that stays with each computer. The job aids may be generic or lesson specific, in that they will refer to the actual formulas to be used or to the layout of a newslet-

CHECK IT OUT 11-1

Title: Where Does It Come From?

Grade: High School

Problem: *Rumors indicate that the United States has become dependent on oil from the Middle East. Is this true?*

Activity: This lesson requires students to do Internet research, create a spreadsheet chart, and create a presentation that provides evidence to answer the question in the problem statement shown above. The teacher has three Think Sheets planned for this activity; however, they are only partially developed. Your task is to download the Think Sheets and add the remaining questions.

Link to these resources and activities in the Check It Out module for this chapter of the Companion Website.

ter to be developed. For information on creating job aids, please refer to Chapter 13, Managing the Classroom.

Resource Guides

When a lesson requires students to use multiple resources, it may be useful to create a resource guide to assist students in using their time wisely. The amount of information needed on the guides will decrease as students become more familiar with using resources. A sample resource guide is seen in Table 11-1.

Rubrics

Even though it is highly recommended to involve students in the development of rubrics, it is advisable to create a sample rubric to help you determine critical components of the lesson that need to be reflected in the final products. Your sample rubric more than likely will be altered as students provide input, but this rubric will enable you to guide student thinking and ensure the critical aspects are incorporated into the instrument. You may want to develop a template for the lesson that includes a place for the lesson title, the objectives or performance, and a blank grid for the levels of performance and rating scale. Students would then complete the rubrics during the brainstorming session and use as it a guide when proceeding through the lesson (Figure 11-1). A detailed discussion of rubrics is located in Chapter 14, The Role of Assessment.

TABLE 11-1 Resource Guide

Coast-to-Coast Excursion

Problem: You want to plan the trip of a lifetime that will allow you to visit the biggest and best that America has to offer (tallest mountain, one of the seven wonders of the world, tallest building, most populated city, most visited park, etc.). You live in New York city, so want to travel from the Atlantic to the Pacific coast, but only have 2 weeks' vacation. (*Note*: You can fly home, so the 2 weeks can be spent traveling from coast to coast.) Create a travel brochure that would convince people that this would be the trip of a lifetime.

RESOURCES AVAILABLE

RESOURCE	TYPE	WHERE LOCATED	INFORMATION PROVIDED
Worldbook	Encyclopedia	Resource Bookshelf	Basic information on U.S.
Our Exciting Country	Book	Resource Table	Basic information on U.S.
Fun Vacations in the U.S.	AAA Magazine	Resource Table	Basic information on U.S.
Compton's	CD-ROM Encyclopedia	Computer #2	Basic information on U.S.
*e*Go Travel Guide	Website	Computer #1 *http://www.ego.net/us/textnav.htm*	Site-seeing guides
TripSpot	Website	Computer #1 *http://www.tripspot.com/*	Site-seeing guides
World Atlas	Book	Resource Table	Distances between cities
World Atlas	CD-ROM	Computer #3	Distances between cities
Traveling the Northwest	Travel Brochure	Resource Table	Ideas for designing a brochure
Summertime in the Rocky Mountains	Travel Brochure	Resource Table	Ideas for designing a brochure

Tech Prep

We have found that it is not appropriate to include technology in every lesson. So, remember to follow the guidelines presented in the earlier chapters to determine if student learning would be enhanced with the use of computers. If the answer is yes, please note that technology, as wonderful as it is, does take some careful planning

FIGURE 11-1 Rubric Template

Lesson Title: ______________________________

Overall Objective: ______________________________

____

Objective or Performance	Beginning 1	Developing 2	Accomplished 3	Exemplary 5	Score

and extra time to ensure smoother integration into a lesson. The following section describes how you can create computer-based folders for student work, generate digital templates, load software, add bookmarks, and get the computers up and running before class to increase the amount of learning time available to students.

Create Computer-Based Folders

When students work on the computer, it is critical that they save their work frequently. If they are using floppy disks or lab computers, it is often wise to save the file to a hard drive, network drive, or some other drive to have a backup. If ample hard drive space is available, you or your computer support person can create specific folders for a class or individual students to use for saving files. Make the folder titles meaningful and easy to locate; that is, have some logic to the path. Using main folder names such as Ms Smith, with subfolders 5th Grade and 6th Grade, is much more meaningful than SMClsrm and Sec003 and Sec004 as the folders. If more than one group of students use the same computer, make sure the folder names distinguish the difference, for example, Group2_flowers. More information about creating folders can be found in Chapter 13, Managing the Classroom.

Create Templates

If students are working with a database, spreadsheet, presentation, word processing, or other type of document that may require detailed setup and initial formatting, a

Student time can be better utilized when needed Internet sites are bookmarked before the lesson starts.

template created by you can save time and help avoid frustration. This process might involve creating the fields and pull down menus in a database or entering in the row and column names and formulas in a spreadsheet. Another example might be setting up a word processing template for a student report (Figure 11-2). The use of templates not only saves time but also shows students how to properly format different documents. Make sure to review the format, pointing out the specific features, for example, "Remember to bold your headings and make the size of the font 14."

Load Specialized Software

Another task that can be completed before implementing the lesson is to load any specialized software on the student computers. For example, if students are going to use a world atlas, writing, tessellation, or clipart software, it again saves time and frustration to have the software installed or CD loaded. If you only have a single copy of the software or CD, load it on one computer then indicate with a sign what is loaded—for example, World Atlas—to direct student traffic to correct computer.

Bookmark Internet Sites

It is very helpful to provide guidance to students as they search for information on the Web. One way to accomplish this is to create bookmarks (within the browser) for Websites that contain information relevant to your lesson. These can be sites with

FIGURE 11-2 Report Template

REPORT TITLE

Written by:

Student 1

Student 2

Student 3

Introduction

Write your introduction here. The paragraph is set up to automatically indent on the first line. If your introduction has more than one paragraph, the second paragraph will automatically indent the first line.

Methods

Write your methods here. Use the table for your timeline of activities.

Date	Person Responsible	Activity

Results

Write your results in this section. After you describe what happened, include a chart showing the results.

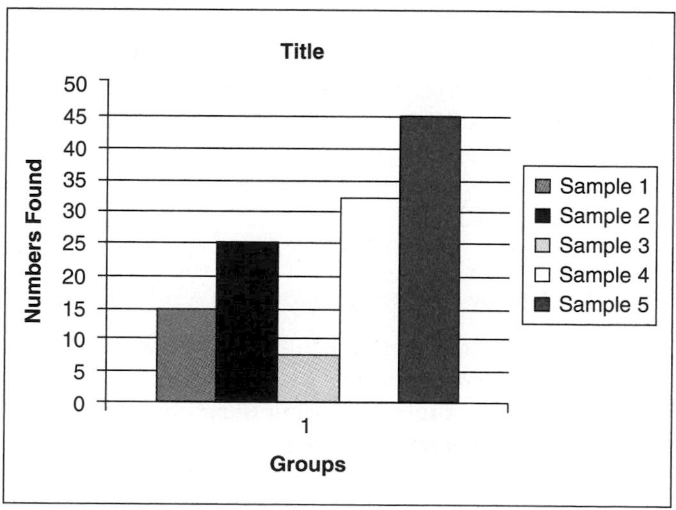

Conclusions

Write the conclusions of your study.

CHECK IT OUT 11-2

Title: Creating Templates

Grade: Any Grade

Problem: *How do you make templates for different software applications?*

Activity: The Check It Out for this problem has a partially complete template for word processing, spreadsheets, databases, and presentation. Your task involves three steps: (1) Download each template and the corresponding instructions; (2) select a lesson for which the template would be appropriate; (3) complete the template to fit the selected lesson plan.

Link to these resources and activities in the Check It Out module for this chapter of the Companion Website.

very specific information or more general sites that may have multiple links to related sites. For example, if you are doing a unit on weather, you can bookmark *http://www.nws.noaa.gov/* and have your students stay within that site by using the "Back" function. Or if you want your students to use a broader yet controlled search, you can bookmark a site designed for student research, such as "Ask Jeeves for Kids," *http://www.ajkids.com*, which provides links to pages that are "G-rated" and specifically written for children. If the automatically assigned bookmark names will not be meaningful to your students, most browsers offer the capability to change the name. More information about the Internet can be found in Chapter 9, The Internet in the Classroom.

Turn on Computers and Open Applications

One last thing that can help prepare for class implementation is to turn on the computers and open software applications before the lesson is to begin. This step is especially helpful when using older computers that have a longer "boot-up" time than newer computers. The same can be true for the time it takes to open a software application. Some of the Internet browsers or large word-processing applications can take several minutes to open and be ready for student use. It is also helpful to have students leave applications open when finished with their work to avoid start-up time for the next student. When student time at the computers is limited because only a few computers are available, it is important to save even a few minutes of time when possible.

Power Tip

Pages of Bookmarks

Each browser has a list of bookmarks stored on the computer that you or a student can access. But, how can you share your bookmarks with your students when there are several computers in the classroom or the lab? There are two ways. The easiest method is to cut and paste your links into a word-processing document, such as a Think Sheet, which students view on the computer rather than as a handout. Students can open the word-processing document and click on the link, which will automatically take them to the Website. The second method is to create a Web page you can post on a class, school, or district Website that has your links. The advantages to this method are that you can easily update the document and not have to provide each computer or student with a copy. Additional information on bookmarks is found in Chapter 9, The Internet in the Classroom.

CHECK IT OUT 11-3

Title: Adding Links to a Teacher Web Page

Grade: Any Grade

Problem: *How do you add links to Internet resources to a teacher Website?*

Activity: This Check It Out highlights several places on the Web that offer teachers space to create "free" Web pages. Your task is to select one of these locations and create a Website that has links to Internet resources that support a previously developed lesson plan.

Link to these resources and activities in the Check It Out module for this chapter of the Companion Website.

DURING CLASSROOM IMPLEMENTATION

Even though an NTeQ lesson involves new roles for the teacher, student, and computer, its foundation incorporates the basic components of effective teaching. Embedded within this structure is the NTeQ Problem Solving Process, which by its very nature is student-centered, multidimensional, and resource-rich. Yet, it also includes direct instruction and independent reading and writing when appropriate. This section begins with the Five Elements of Effective Instruction (Sullivan & Higgins, 1983), which are incorporated into NTeQ lessons. This list is followed by a detailed description of the NTeQ Problem Solving Process. The section ends with three approaches to implement at any time during a lesson: direct instruction, independent learning, and cooperative learning.

Five Elements of Effective Instruction

There are five basic elements necessary to achieve meaningful learning. The teacher has a lot of flexibility in how each of the elements is implemented, but each needs to be incorporated into the lesson. These five elements are seen in Figure 11-3 and discussed below.

Introduction

Every lesson has a beginning point, or a time when the activity is introduced to the students. The following activities need to happen during this opening exercise: motivating the students and informing them of what is to be learned, why it is important, and what prior knowledge and skills they will need to achieve success.

Motivation—Gaining Student Attention. A key factor in achieving student learning is gaining their interest and keeping them motivated to learn. We are by nature curious and want to discover new information. It is important to begin a lesson by sparking an interest or creating a problem to be solved. More will be provided in the following section on the NTeQ Problem Solving Process.

Purpose/Rationale. It is important for students to understand the purpose or what they are to learn during the lesson. Many teachers do this by posting the curricu-

FIGURE 11-3 Five Elements of Effective Instruction

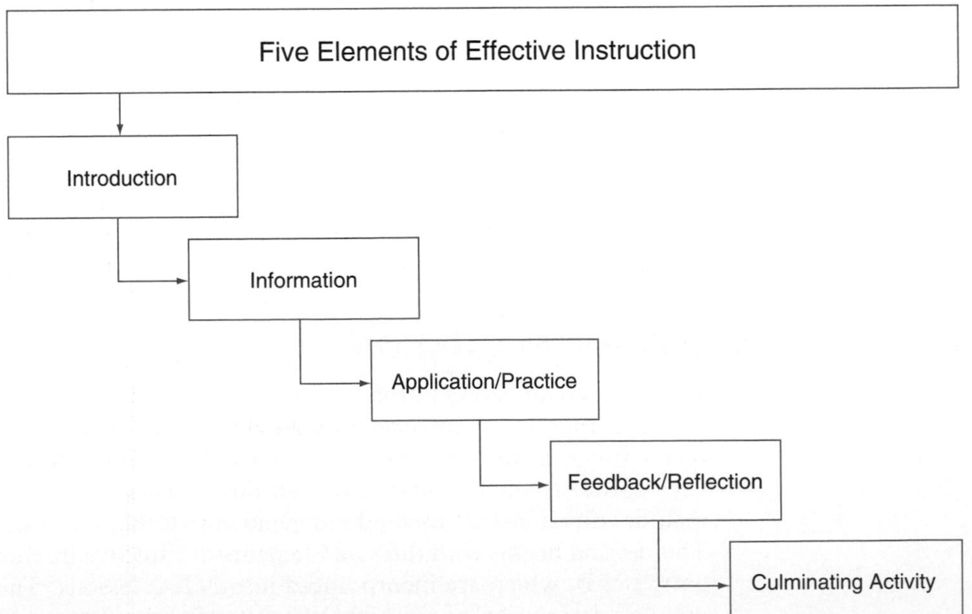

Adapted From Sullivan and Higgins (1983)

lum standards that are addressed in the lesson. This awareness lets students feel a sense of direction and accomplishment as each objective is achieved. However, just as important as listing the learning outcomes is providing students with meaningful rationales for why the information is important to learn. Whenever possible, try to make the reasoning relevant to their current world, rather than saying vague things such as, "You'll need to know this when you get to high school or college." If the new knowledge is something that will not be applied till they are adults, then relate it to a profession or career. For example, when students are learning about animal classifications and habitats, you could say that managers of zoos and wildlife parks use this information when choosing new animals to add to the park or when modifying existing zoo environments. Another approach is to create a problem or scenario that places them in the role of a zoo manager and describe the problem they must address. For example, the zoo is getting its first panda bear. What type of habitat should be provided to ensure its safety and health? Providing a rich context will help make the new information both concrete and more meaningful.

Prerequisite Knowledge. The final component to include when the lesson is introduced is to let the students know the prior knowledge and skills that will be needed to complete the activities. By sharing this information, it will help guide choices when students make decisions. For example, if students are designing a memorial flower garden to recognize American poets of the 19th century, you can remind them that they will use math formulas to find the area of a space, science knowledge of plant growth to plan the garden, and database skills to create the poet records. The new information will focus on the poets and flowers mentioned in their writings.

Information

The second element of instruction is information, or all of the facts, definitions, examples, and procedures that students must learn. This element is undergoing recent changes in that school reform measures recommend that teachers should no longer act as the primary source of information. Yet, a key factor, or perhaps the key reason for instruction, is for students to learn new information, or gain knowledge and skills; therefore, new information must be available. In traditional classrooms, the teacher provides the information in the form of lectures, textbook assignments, or handouts. In today's less traditional, more inquiry-based classrooms, both students and teachers gather the information. However, teachers still need to orchestrate the learning environment to ensure that students use the best approach for obtaining and using the needed information.

Even within a student-centered classroom, there are some areas in which well-planned direct instruction is very appropriate for demonstrating specific skills or discussing relationships among ideas or events. Guidelines for conducting effective direct instruction include presenting appropriate amounts of information in a logical sequence, demonstrating procedures, giving examples of appropriate and inappropriate choices, and providing definitions. Similar guidelines apply for students who are responsible for obtaining information. As they locate facts and figures from a variety of sources, they will need to sequence them in a meaningful manner for the task at hand. The students will need to determine if they have enough information and if the examples and definitions they located support their arguments. They will also need to learn to try out any procedures that are required to achieve the goal, for example, applying new math strategies, creating slides for the microscope, or drawing shadows in art class. This is achieved during the Application/Practice phase, which is discussed next.

Application/Practice

This phase of effective instruction is addressed very well in both the computer and supporting activities of the NTeQ model. Remember that the activities that provide practice must be relevant to achieving the lesson objective(s). It is also important for students to know what is expected of them. One way of informing the students of the expectations is through the use of a rubric or task list (see Chapter 14). To provide learners with more than one opportunity to practice and work with new information, generative learning strategies, as described in Chapter 3, can be used. These strategies ensure that students work through higher levels of learning, thus reinforcing the attainment and commitment of new information and skills to long-term memory.

Feedback/Reflection

Too often student practice is left for homework or individual seatwork that does not receive prompting and guidance to avoid the development of misconceptions or "bad" practices. When students receive appropriate and timely feedback, their learning is greatly enhanced. Students need feedback while they are engaged in the learning task or as soon as possible after completing the task. The feedback can come from peers, from the teacher, or in the form of self-reflection, guided by a task list or rubric.

For feedback to influence learning, the teacher needs to provide more than motivational comments ("good job"), instead providing feedback that is instructional and corrective. Instructional feedback provides review of previously covered or new information (e.g., "Remember that a noun is a person, place, thing, or concept."). Corrective feedback points out specific ways the student can address a problem in the work (e.g., "If you invert the fraction, your calculations will be correct."). It is often effective to combine these two types of feedback. You can also provide the feedback by asking directed questions. More information on questioning and feedback can be found in Chapter 12, Teacher as Facilitator.

Culminating Activity

The final element of effective instruction is the culminating activity. This phase is often overlooked or reduced to asking one or two questions right before the class period ends. Yet, this portion of the lesson helps to solidify and confirm that learning has occurred. This is important to not only you, as the teacher, but to the students. They need to feel a sense of accomplishment in knowing that they have attained new knowledge and skills.

During this time, you can restate the purpose of the lesson, summarize the key ideas, and ask students for their impressions. A what you Know, what you Want to know, and what you Learned (KWL) chart is an excellent tool for stimulating discussion around the lesson goals. The culminating activity involves a great deal of student input, which allows you to identify student misconceptions and reinforce key learning concepts. Your facilitation skills (see Chapter 12) will again be drawn upon during this part of the lesson. The culminating activity can include the following:

- Presentation of findings/results
- Whole-class review/summation of learning
- Discussion of implications, applications/transfer of new knowledge

The Five Elements of Instruction and NTeQ

At this point, it is clear that the NTeQ model is problem based and student centered. When first examining the Five Elements of Effective Instruction, they might seem quite traditional. However, they are actually very flexible and can be embedded within any instructional approach. When using the NTeQ approach, the lesson still begins with the introduction; however, three of the elements—information, application/practice, and feedback—occur concurrently during the computer and supporting activities. Reflection can occur during the after-computer activities, but always occurs during the assessment activity at the end of the lesson. The following section provides more detail and specific guidelines for using a problem solving process.

Implementing the NTeQ Problem Solving Process

The NTeQ problem solving process is used by students to solve a problem as part of an NTeQ lesson. These steps, as seen in Table 11-2, are heuristics that we expect you and the students to modify as you gain experience. The process is adapted to each problem rather than followed as strict rules. Students should be involved in each step of the process. As can be seen from the chart, when students apply the problem solving process, they are required to engage in a great deal of higher-order thinking. A brief description of each component of the NTeQ Problem Solving Process is presented in the following section.

Define the Problem

Let's assume that your lesson is developed and you have followed the guidelines in Chapters 2 and 3 to create a very interesting problem. Now, you have to arouse your students' interest in the problem. The key to involving them is your initial introduction of the problem. This introduction can include, for example, using props to stimulate curiosity, dropping "curiosity builders" before the lesson, asking rhetorical questions to get them thinking, or presenting data that cause puzzlement or dissonance. Curiosity props can include photos, artifacts, books, software, magazines, or newspapers with targeted headlines—the list is endless.

TABLE 11-2 NTeQ Problem Solving Process

THE NTEQ PROBLEM SOLVING PROCESS ALIGNED WITH BLOOM'S TAXONOMY*		
COMPONENT	BLOOM'S LEVEL	STUDENT ACTION
Define the problem	Comprehension Analysis	Write a statement that clearly defines the problem.
Identify what is known about the problem	Analysis	Ideas are stated as "known" information.
Identify what needs to be known to solve the problem	Analysis	List as questions.
Identify data that needs to be collected to solve the problem	Analysis	Write as action statements and indicate how to collect.
Determine how the data needs to be manipulated to solve the problem	Application Synthesis Analysis	Describe how the data will be manipulated to develop a solution.
Generate possible solutions	Synthesis	Base solutions on results of the data manipulation.
Determine how to evaluate each solution	Evaluation	Identify criteria that will be used to select the best solution.
Select the best solution	Analysis Evaluation	Consider each alternative and identify the implications of each.
Present findings	Synthesis	Publish the results.

*Bloom, Englehart, Furst, Hill, & Krathwohl (1956)

The key thing, of course, is that the props are related in some way to the problem to solve in the upcoming lesson.

You may want to use "curiosity builders" that make it easier to introduce the problem to the students on the first day of the lesson. Hints that you could drop before the lesson could include the following:

✓ I wonder if states tend to get bigger as you move west.

Teacher helps a group of students to better define their problem statement.

✓ Our family is planning to visit Nebraska next month, and I'm not sure what kind of clothes to pack.

✓ I wonder if all Native Americans use feathers in their ceremonial dress.

✓ My earlobes are attached and I can curl my tongue. I wonder if these two traits always go together.

As you introduce the problem to the students, make sure that you seem interested and curious to find the solution, even when dealing with young children and the answer is quite obvious to you. After you have verbally introduced the problem, it is critical to make sure the students have a clear understanding, or that they *define the problem*. This can be done in two ways: (1) small groups of students define the problem in their own words, then the large group reaches a common definition; or (2) the problem definition can be done as a large group by printing it on the board or displaying it with a computer. The end product should be a clearly written statement of the problem.

Identify What Is Known About the Problem

After the problem has been defined, students then need to identify what is known about the problem. Just as in the first step, defining the problem, student groups can create a list of what they know about the problem, then a common class list can be

THE TEACHER'S DIARY

I had just finished my social studies methods course in the spring of 1970 and was excited about using the inquiry method (similar to problem-based learning) while student teaching. The Cold War was still a part of our lives, as was a general fear of communism. I was teaching a high school economics unit on forms of competition. My first task was to create a dissonance in my students to arouse their interest. We started a discussion about the price of various goods and the value of having several grocery stores. I then pointed out the two gas stations by the school that offered the same services at the same price, "Why do we need two of them taking up valuable property?" Our discussion then proceeded to the phone company, electric company, and water company.

I must have succeeded in causing some dissonance in their thinking, because a few days later I had my supervising teacher, department chair, principal, and university professor visiting my class. It seems the students told their parents that evening that I was communist! I had managed to obtain their attention and to arouse their interest in economics. It soon became apparent to all that I was not a communist and there were reasons for monopolies and competition.

Gary R. Morrison
High School Social Studies

compiled. You may need to model how to identify what is known when students are first learning the problem solving process. This can be done if you identify one or two items, then ask students to identify the remaining items. For example, let's examine the following problem: Do states get larger as you move west? The "known" items include: we are looking at the size of states, we are comparing the sizes as the states go from east to west. You also can add an item that does not really fit (e.g., we are looking at the number of people per state); then show students the importance of including only "known" items.

Identify What Needs to Be Known to Solve the Problem

When a common list of what is known has been generated, students then need to determine what is needed to solve the problem. During this process, they will continually need to refer to the defined problem. This component will require students to think creatively, to make predictions and speculations, and write questions about what they want to know. For example, Do all states get bigger as you move west? Does the year of entry make a difference? Do resources matter? Or for other lessons, sample questions could include: Are presidents more likely to be Republican or Democrat? Are carnivores more likely to become extinct than herbivores? How are the works of Vincent van Gogh and Claude Monet similar? As students begin to generate a list of questions, other questions will come to mind. It is best to brainstorm and record all ideas, then to evaluate each one to determine if it is really needed to solve the problem.

Identify Data That Needs to Be Collected to Solve the Problem

The next step requires careful examination of the questions listed in the previous step and the generation of action statements indicating what data to collect and how to collect it. During this segment, you assist students with their thinking to help clarify what is needed to solve the problem, as opposed to what is "nice" to know. These discrimination skills will transfer into future workplace settings where key decisions are made. Two examples of data to collect and how it will be collected are as follows:

- Collect the following data for the 12 states in our region:
  - *What to collect:* Square miles, major cities, total population, major products, key attractions, highest point of elevation, lowest point of elevation, average yearly rainfall, average summer temperature, average winter temperature.
  - *How to collect:* The data will be collected from *http://www.50states.com* on the Internet.
- Collect genetic trait information from each group member's family:
  - *What to collect:* Hair color, hair curl, eye color, ear lobe attached, tongue curling, thumb joint.
  - *How to collect:* The data will be collected from the following, if available: parents, brothers, sisters, grandparents.

Determine How the Data Needs to Be Manipulated to Solve the Problem

After students determine the specific data to collect, they next decide how to manipulate the data to solve the problem. This will again require that students re-examine the problem statement to keep the data manipulation focused toward finding the answers or solutions. When students are just beginning to use basic computer applications, you will need to assist them in understanding the available functions. For example, students may want to use both a database and spreadsheet when examining the data from states. In the database, students could sort by elevation, population, rainfall, temperature, square miles, and products to find similarities and differences among the regional states. They could also use a spreadsheet to determine population density, state with the greatest range in average temperatures, and greatest difference between high and low elevation points.

Generate Possible Solutions

This portion of the process is often where the greatest degree of higher-order thinking occurs because students are analyzing the results of their data manipulation. For problem-based learning to be successful, the problems need to be ill-structured or ones that do not have "one" right answer but have multiple solutions. Therefore, as students come to this portion of the problem solving process, they generate several ways that the problem can be solved. For example, if students were investigating whether or not genetic traits were grouped by the type of trait (e.g., if people who rolled their tongues tended to also have attached earlobes), the students more than likely could generate data to support more than one argument.

Determine How to Evaluate Each Solution

When students have a list of multiple solutions, they then need to determine a consistent way to examine each one. To do this, a list of evaluation criteria is generated. These criteria could involve meeting specific numeric ratings (must have five or more), containing specific content (must address setting and characters), or other guidelines needed to solve the problem.

Select the Best Solution

At this point, use the criteria to have students examine each solution and choose the "best" solution. In doing this, they should keep track of the reasons why it is the best and implications for choosing the other solutions. There may be times when more than one solution could be considered as the "best" solution. In this case, students can use both or choose one based on other criteria; for instance, one more fun, more current, or more relevant to the school's context.

Present Findings

The findings can be published in a variety of ways, as can be seen in Chapter 8. The most appropriate method is determined when designing the lesson. The key consideration for this portion of the problem solving process is not *how* to present the findings, but rather *what* to present. Students need to determine what information is critical to understanding the problem and the resulting solution. If, in their data set, students found that people who could roll their tongues had attached earlobes, what supporting information needs to be included to ensure understanding? Does their PowerPoint presentation need to include descriptions of different genetic traits, how they collected the data, what other findings were recorded, and the final results? When the lesson involves different groups of students reaching solutions to a common problem, as each group shares their findings, students expand what they have learned by realizing that the problem had many possible solutions.

As-Needed Activities

There are three basic approaches that can occur at any time during implementation of an NTeQ lesson or, for that matter, any lesson: direct instruction, independent learning, and cooperative learning. These strategies are discussed below.

Direct Instruction

As mentioned earlier, although a strong emphasis is being placed on creating a more student-centered learning environment in today's classrooms, there are times that it is best for students to receive information directly. For example, direct instruction can be used to provide new or background information (telling the students about the Underground Railroad), demonstrate processes and procedures (how to measure an object to determine volume), or review basic skills (use of end punctuation). A common misconception is that this type of instruction has to be dry and uninteresting and that students have to be passive. Quite the contrary can occur. We're sure you can think back to a time when you had a teacher or college professor who kept your attention and engaged the class in dynamic discussions. Or you probably have seen an instructor demonstrate procedures so clearly that you were better able to complete a specific calculation, triturate the correct amount of reagent into your formula, or write a persuasive argument on the basis of what was demonstrated.

The key to "good" instruction, whether it is direct, independent, or cooperative, is to engage students in multiple levels of learning. Let's reexamine Bloom's Taxonomy (Bloom, Englehart, Furst, Hill, & Krathwohl, 1956):

Knowledge
Comprehension
Application
Analysis
Synthesis
Evaluation

Even though students cannot have hands-on involvement with application, analysis, synthesis, or evaluation during direct instruction, you can have them think about or virtually engage in these higher-order processes. This can be achieved through asking questions and creating "What-if" scenarios, remembering to allow enough wait time for all students to formulate possible solutions. Guidelines for asking questions are included in Chapter 12, Teacher as Facilitator. Sample question stems that can be integrated into your direct instruction are seen in Figure 11-4. As mentioned earlier, we no longer are striving for students to just "know the facts," so when you implement direct instruction, strive to include strategies that engage your students in multiple levels of thinking.

Independent Learning

The careful use of independent learning will better prepare students to be more actively engaged during direct instruction and cooperative learning situations. When students have the opportunity to read or complete various assignments on an individual basis, completion of the assignment can be adapted to meet specific needs. In other words, a student can reread until the information is understood, use reference materials to look up definitions of unfamiliar words, check and recheck answers, or refine a paragraph. However, as stated in the first sentence, independent learning needs to be carefully planned and implemented for its use to be successful.

When implementing the use of independent learning, you will need to address three main things: the *timeframe, expectations* of what is to happen during that time, and *audience,* or with whom the student's work will be shared. The following section discusses and provides examples of these three areas.

Timeframe. When setting the timeframe, it can be specific ("Papers are due in 30 minutes.") or left somewhat open, but have checkpoints ("You have 45 minutes

FIGURE 11-4 Sample Question Stems

Knowledge
Who is the person who . . .
When did this happen . . .

Comprehension
Write a statement that summarizes what we have covered so far . . .
Tell me your perception . . .

Application
How would you approach the following . . .
If you had to solve this, where would you start . . .

Analysis
Why do you think it happened that way . . .
What would it take to change . . .

Synthesis
What would happen if you combined . . .
How does this fit together . . .

Evaluation
Explain why this is the most appropriate way to . . .
If you were in charge, what would you have done to . . .

to investigate and record the differences between the two Internet articles. After 45 minutes, we'll check to see if more time is needed."). You can write the "finish" time on the board to help keep students on track ("Questions are due at 10:30 a.m.").

Expectations. There are several things to consider when determining what is expected during and at the conclusion of the independent work time. You not only need to determine the content to be included (definitions of this week's spelling words or a list of questions to ask during group time) but also the format (e.g., hand-written notes, word-processed paper, oral communication of ideas), the amount (2 pages, 10 questions, models of 4 triangles) and interaction guidelines (is this truly independent, or can students ask questions of you and/or a peer?).

Another consideration is the quality of work. This is when a task list or rubric is invaluable because it provides clear guidelines for what the ideal final product will contain. We all know that just because a student "completes" an assignment, it does not mean that the learning objectives are fulfilled. For example, a task list that students might use to review an assignment before it is due might include items similar to the following:

- The content of each question relates to the problem we are solving.
- Each question is clearly written.
- Each question is correctly written.
- Ten questions are written.

The highest rating of a rubric that students might use to assess and revise their work is as follows:

> Questions demonstrate a very clear understanding of the content. Each question is clearly and correctly written. The questions illustrate evidence of student analysis and evaluation of the key issues relevant to reaching a solution to the problem.

Audience. The final consideration when implementing individual work is to let students know who will be assessing or receiving the results of this independent session. The work can basically be shared with you, as the teacher; with a partner; with a small group of students; or possibly with others outside of the class such as an e-mail partner, a family or community member, or students from another class. Students will more than likely adapt the approach taken for a given assignment based on the final recipient(s). Therefore, by having this knowledge at the beginning of the assignment, there are no surprises when a student is asked to read to the group members her impressions about the use of nuclear power. You will notice that as students participate more frequently in a student-centered learning environment that openly accepts and considers all ideas, students will become better able to provide and receive constructive feedback. However, being in a more open environment does not diminish the need for sharing with the students, the intended audience for their work.

Cooperative Learning

For cooperative learning to be effective, you must create a culture of collaboration, consider group size and assignment, and use basic principles of cooperative learning.

Creating a Culture of Cooperation. Teaching students to work effectively in groups is a process of establishing group norms. By establishing and supporting group norms, in effect you are saying, "In this classroom, we work in this way for these reasons." Students are taught that collaboration is normal, expected, and valued. Following are some example group norms:

- Every team member is important.
- We work as a team and as individuals to accomplish our goals.
- Diversity in opinions is important. We respect the right to be different, but we must work toward consensus.
- Instead of blaming or criticizing, we seek solutions to our problems.
- We structure our work according to individual needs.
- We help those who request assistance.

Establishing Groups. To create effective groups, teachers need to consider the size of the groups and how students will be assigned to them. For teachers or students new to group work, it is best to begin by using pairs. Working in dyads ensures that each student participates and develops basic interpersonal communication skills. This also allows the teacher time to feel comfortable having students "talk" in the classroom. Pairing is very effective when using technology, because students teach computer skills to and learn them from one another.

Most inquiry projects function effectively with groups of three or four students. This size allows for expression of individual opinions, and yet is large enough to generate multiple perspectives and share the workload. Although groups of five or more are useful in certain situations, we do not generally recommend them for inquiry groups. Groups this size can become difficult to manage, and some students are more likely to sit back while others do the work.

In terms of assigning students to groups, teachers have one of two choices—either assign students or let students assign themselves. We have used both approaches with varying effectiveness. In terms of ownership, students are naturally more motivated when they can choose their own group members. However, this can often lead to problems in group dynamics. Two "best friends" may tend to dominate group interaction, two or more "problem" students in the same group may negatively influence group effectiveness and morale, or students may not be exposed to diverse opinions or skill levels when like minds choose to work together consistently over time. When the teacher assigns students to groups, things to consider are academic, social, and technology skills. When placing students in pairs and computer work is to be completed, it is best to pair a technologically competent student with one that is less competent in order to foster transfer of learning. However, care must be taken to routinely rotate computer tasks to ensure equality of learning opportunities. For example, every 10 minutes, have students move the keyboard from one student to the other.

Principles of Cooperative Learning. Cooperative learning has been touted as a highly effective structure for group learning. To distinguish cooperative learning from group learning in general, Johnson and Johnson (1991) describe the basic principles of cooperative learning.

1. *Positive Interdependence*—Assignments are arranged so students become responsible to and for one another. One meaningful way of accomplishing this is to have students divide tasks, keeping in mind that "dividing" does not necessarily mean among individual students, but can also include pairs of students within the group.
2. *Face-to-Face Positive Interaction*—Students support group members through "friendly" critique, praise, encouragement, and motivation. Teachers can support these interactions by directly teaching social skills (see point 4).
3. *Individual Accountability and Responsibility*—Although students may be working as a team, individuals are still required to be personally responsible for their own work. This can be achieved by assessing individual contributions, and by asking students for peer evaluation during and at the completion of the inquiry project.
4. *Social Skills Aren't Assumed*—In cooperative learning, teachers spend time teaching and reinforcing social skills. This is often the most neglected, yet most critical, aspect of cooperative learning. Many teachers are often resentful that students don't take turns listening, support one another, problem solve, or stay on task. We can't assume that our students, at any age level, have developed these skills, and therefore we must take time to reinforce them through group work.

5. *Group Processing*—Processing is the time devoted to reflection on group functioning. This can occur during group work and/or at the completion of an assignment. Processing is the means by which group norms and social skills are reinforced. Group processing is the key to creating a culture of collaboration in the classroom.

SUMMARY

As seen in this chapter, it takes careful thought and planning to effectively implement an inquiry-based lesson that has students use technology. This is done in two phases, one before classroom implementation and one during classroom implementation. Before the lesson is to begin, teachers make support documents that will help guide student learning. These include the Think Sheet, technical step-by-step guides, resource guides, task lists, and rubrics. This is also the time to prepare the computers for the lesson. Preparation activities can include creating desktop student folders for student computer work, creating templates for students to use when producing their computer projects, loading any specialized software, and bookmarking key Internet sites.

During lesson implementation, teachers are reminded to follow the Five Elements of Effective Instruction. Basically this means that they will begin with an introduction that gets the students interested in learning, tells them what they are going to learn and why it is important, and covers prior knowledge they will need to complete the lesson. This is followed by presentation of the actual information, which can be done by the teacher or students collecting the information. After this, students apply or practice with the new information while receiving feedback or reflecting on the learning process. The lesson ends with a culminating activity that summarizes the learning and identifies any misconceptions.

To further expand on implementing an NTeQ lesson, this chapter discussed how to guide students through the problem solving process. The steps include defining the problem, identifying what is known about the problem, what needs to be known, data that needs to be collected, and how the data needs to be manipulated to solve the problem. It also involves generating possible solutions, then determining how to evaluate each solution to select the best one. It ends with presenting the findings.

The chapter ends with a summary of three basic approaches that can occur at any time during implementation of an NTeQ lesson: direct instruction, independent learning, and cooperative learning.

AT THE CLASSROOM'S DOORSTEP

Questions Teachers Ask

The NTeQ approach seems great, and I think kids will learn more if it is used. But, this is a totally new way of teaching for me and I feel very overwhelmed. What do I do?

It can be overwhelming to think about changing the way you teach—especially when you have not seen this method implemented or modeled. You do, though, already have one of the greatest obstacles overcome, that of believing that the NTeQ approach will benefit student learning. This is the first and most critical step. After that, you begin slowly, and adopt what you can handle. Please note that we did not say what you are comfortable with, because change is typically a little uncomfortable at first. Begin with one lesson that is fairly simple or even a portion of a lesson. If your students are not used to working together in groups, this too needs to be done slowly and with very careful planning and execution. Also, make sure the first attempts involve tasks that will result in positive outcomes, such as a very simple database or spreadsheet with just a few entries. A problem that has several solutions will spark conversation among your students. Choose a topic that you feel is one of your best, so you feel comfortable assuming the role of facilitator. Once you see the lights of learning in your students' eyes and hear them actually discussing a historical event, asking thoughtful questions, and bringing in additional resources, you will begin to increase the implementation of NTeQ because you are reminded of why you became a teacher.

TECHNOLOGY INTEGRATION ACTIVITIES

To access the activities that connect the content of the text with the Companion Website and other technology, please go to the Activities module in Chapter 11 of the Companion Website at *http://www.prenhall.com/morrison*.

NTEQ PORTFOLIO ACTIVITIES

Please complete the following activities as part of your NTeQ Portfolio on classroom implementation.

Reflections

The "Getting Started" portion of this chapter asked three questions that teachers might commonly ask. In this portion of your journal, a reflection question has been added to address how you would answer each question. Please use information from this chapter to answer the questions.

1. What can I do to "get ready" for a lesson that has my students using computers?
   - *Reflection Question:* Create a step-by-step sheet that you and other teachers could use when planning the implementation portion of an NTeQ lesson.
2. Where does the "computer part" come when I am teaching a lesson?
   - *Reflection Question:* Use the guidelines presented in the During Classroom Implementation section to develop a detailed description of how you would implement the computer activities described in an NTeQ lesson you have developed.
3. I've never used a problem-based approach, much less computers—so how is a teacher supposed to do both of these at one time?
   - *Reflection Question:* Write a description that shows how technology supports a problem-based learning approach.

NTeQ Problem Solving Process

Select an NTeQ lesson that you have developed and generate a sample table similar to Table 11–2 that represents how each component of the NTeQ Problem Solving Process would be addressed by filling in the Student Action cells.

Direct Instruction Questions

Begin with one of your favorite topics for which direct instruction would be an appropriate part of an NTeQ lesson. Generate a list of questions for this lesson by using the stems or similar stems provided in Figure 11–4. Make sure to generate questions for each level of Bloom's Taxonomy.

Cooperative Learning

Again, select a previously developed lesson that engages students in cooperative learning. Write a reflection paper that demonstrates how this activity will meet the guidelines presented above: create a culture of collaboration, consider group size and assignment, and use basic principles of cooperative learning.

REFERENCES

Bloom, B. S., Englehart, M. D., Furst, E. J., Hill, W. H., & Krathwohl, D. R. (Eds.) (1956). *Taxonomy of educational objectives: The classification of education goals. Handbook I: Cognitive domain*. New York: David McKay.

Johnson, D. W., & Johnson, R. T. (1991). *Learning together and alone*. Upper Saddle River, NJ: Prentice Hall.

Sullivan, H., & Higgins, N. (1983). *Teaching for competence*. New York: Teachers College Press, Columbia University.

KEY TOPICS

Teacher Versus Facilitator

What Does It Take to Be a Facilitator?

Foster Meaningful Learning

- Use Appropriate Learning Strategies
- Ask Appropriate Questions
- Provide Appropriate Feedback

Create an Open and Supportive Culture

- Promote Development of Cooperative/Social Skills

Meet the Diverse Needs of Learners

- Meeting the Needs of Multicultural Learners
- Meeting the Needs of Students Living in Poverty
- Meeting the Needs of Students with Disabilities

Chapter 12

Teacher as Facilitator

Constructivist perspectives are causing us to re-examine the role of a teacher (Murphy, 1995). Traditionally, a teacher's job was to "fill" the minds of students with deposits of "true" knowledge (Freire, 1971). Students were expected to recite or "regurgitate" specific information back at appropriate intervals. This approach to education may have served its purpose during the Industrial Revolution, when many people were hired to work passively in factories or to return to the farm. However, the complex nature of today's society requires citizens who can conceptualize ideas, work as part of a collaborative team, problem solve, and take action. In today's world, the teacher must go beyond knowledge transmission. A teacher must engage and empower students and educate for insight.

In this chapter, we take an in-depth look at what it means to be a facilitator in an NTeQ environment and how this is different from the role of a traditional teacher. We then examine some of the key components involved in assuming the role of a facilitator, including fostering meaningful learning, creating an open and supportive classroom culture, and meeting the special needs of learners.

GETTING STARTED

What Do I Know?

1. I thought all teachers were facilitators—what is the difference?
2. How can I be sure students learn information covered on the state tests when I am just a "guide on the side"?
3. Isn't it very difficult to meet the varying needs of all my students in a classroom that doesn't appear to be well structured?

Classroom Snapshot

Mr. Bernstein has been teaching the introductory chemistry class at Craigmont High for 27 years and has always been disappointed in the low performance of students in his classes. This summer, he attended a professional development seminar on how to be a facilitator, which at first sounded like a crazy idea. The session began by the leader placing teachers into groups and assigning them to a computer. The lesson was inquiry-based and used computers as tools. The leader did not lecture, but rather introduced a problem the teachers were to solve and then provided guidance and support to each group. Mr. Bernstein was amazed because during this experience he gained deeper understanding of information he had been teaching for years. So, he decided he would use this method to teach the first lesson of the year: the Periodic Table of the Elements—a topic that is difficult for students to grasp. He downloaded a table with information for each element and created paper copies with the elements listed in alphabetical order. He then removed the Periodic Table of the Elements from his wall before students came to his class.

Mr. Bernstein began the lesson by handing out the list of elements and telling students that this is the ingredient list of our world. In other words, everything in our world is made from different combinations of these elements. He had the students take 2 minutes to examine the list of elements and come up with two questions and two comments regarding the elements. After 2 minutes, he called on five students and asked them to share one comment each. Mr. Bernstein remained quiet. He asked two students to summarize the comments, then asked another student to add any other details. He used a similar approach to review the questions. In the midst of the questions he was able to solicit the idea that the information was somewhat difficult to use because of its list format and asked for possible solutions. The students suggested creating a database of element information, sorting the information to find common groupings, then create a table or chart of information that is easier to understand (which followed Mr. Bernstein's lesson plan).

During the lesson, Mr. Bernstein walked among the groups and was elated as he heard his students actually discussing properties of the elements rather than memorizing them—a first in 27 years!

TEACHER VERSUS FACILITATOR

Some might assume that classroom teachers are automatically facilitators of learning. However, when exploring synonyms for the words "teach" and "facilitate," the *Microsoft Word Thesaurus* (2003) generated the terms listed in Table 12-1.

Notice that words listed under "Teach" represent more of a one-way transmission of information from the "one who knows" to the "one who does not know." However, the terms used for "Facilitate" portray a different type of relationship between the teacher and the student. Thus, to better understand what it means for a teacher to be a facilitator, insert the word "learning" with the "Facilitate" synonyms. For example, when a teacher assumes the role of being a facilitator, she does the following:

Makes learning easy

Promotes learning

TABLE 12-1 Synonyms for Teach and Facilitate

TEACH	FACILITATE
Educate	Make easy
Instruct	Promote
Inform	Expedite
Tutor	Simplify
Train	Assist
Direct	Ease
Enlighten	Help
School	Advance

Expedites learning
Simplifies learning
Assists learning
Eases learning
Helps learning
Advances learning

To achieve these types of activities, the teacher, as a facilitator, must create a classroom environment that is open and supportive of all learners. In this environment, students engage in active listening, reflection, explanations, and questioning as the teacher guides them through the learning process in both a directive and nondirective manner.

The positive aspects of facilitation become clear from the above description, and most teachers would probably indicate a desire to provide this type of classroom environment for their students. However, if a teacher wants to assume the role of a facilitator, he or she will not only need to change from using a traditional role when interacting with students in the classroom, but also change other teacher roles to reflect this different approach. These changes would include the way a teacher designs lessons, implements classroom instruction, facilitates learning, manages classroom activities, and assesses student outcomes (Table 12-2).

WHAT DOES IT TAKE TO BE A FACILITATOR?

Most of us attended school in educational settings that were fairly traditional, that is, where the teacher lectured rather than facilitated learning. As shown in Table 12-2, all of the processes involved in the role of a facilitator require the teacher to perhaps go beyond personal experiences and think creatively. For example, if a teacher wants to assume the role of a facilitator, he or she will need to develop meaningful, yet fun, problems for the students to solve and to visualize student-teacher interactions, and

TABLE 12-2 Traditional Versus Facilitator Role*

Teacher Role	Traditional Role	Facilitator Role
Design (*Chapters 2 and 3*)	Begin with learning objectives Obtain all resources Create lectures, and/or demonstrations to "present" information to students Create/locate activities for students to practice and "learn" the content/skills	Begin with learning objectives Identify multiple resources Create problem for students to solve Create activities that require student groups to solve the problem and "discover" the content, while using basic and research skills
Implementation (*Chapter 10*)	Direct all learning activities	Guide learning activities
Facilitation (*Chapter 12*)	Oversee student work Answer student questions Tell students how to complete work	Facilitate student learning Ask students directed questions Model procedures and thinking processes
Management (*Chapter 12*)	Provide all needed resources Direct all rotation, if multiple activities occur	Provide access to multiple resources Help students determine activities and movement between them, if multiple activities occur
Assessment (*Chapter 13*)	Create test or measure to determine degree to which the right answers were "learned"	Create assessment tools, with student help, to both guide students as they complete learning activities and assess attainment of the learning objectives

*Chapters which provide further explanation are noted in the Teacher Role column.

create generative learning activities that actively motivate and engage the students. As these activities are implemented, the teacher will need to ask questions that require higher-level thinking, listen carefully to student responses, and provide the most appropriate type of feedback. The teacher must also create a classroom environment that is open and supportive—one in which students feel comfortable to express their opinions and in which they feel their individual needs are understood, are being met, and are important.

You may feel a bit overwhelmed with all that is required to facilitate a class. However, if the knowledge and skills are examined, three prominent areas of focus emerge: fostering meaningful learning, creating an open and supportive culture, and meeting the special needs of your students. As you gain understanding and practice within each area, your confidence and ability to successfully facilitate a learning environment will increase. The three areas are discussed in the following section.

TEACHER'S DIARY

What I liked most about using the NTeQ model in my classroom was that I became a facilitator of learning. As a facilitator, I was able to let my students help me determine how and some of what they would learn in my classroom.

At the beginning of a thematic unit on trains, I asked my students to fold a piece of paper into fourths. I then asked them to write the following headings on their papers: (1) "What I Know About Trains," (2) "What I Want to Know About Trains," (3) "Where Can I Find Information About Trains," and (4) "Who Would I Like to Work With." My students' responses to "What I Know About Trains" reflected a diversity of knowledge about trains. They wrote about freight trains, passenger trains, subways, monorails, model trains, and famous trains. I noticed a pattern in their responses to "What I Want to Know About Trains." Many of them were interested in learning about passenger trains, particularly eating and sleeping on trains. Because of their interest in passenger trains, I arranged a field trip to the Historic Train Display. Here my students were able to go into different types of passenger train cars and experience first hand what it was like to be a passenger on a train. I also used these responses to develop a series of class projects. These projects encompassed everything from train history timelines to student-created train safety cartoons.

My students' responses to "Where Can I Find Information About Trains" were very interesting. Their responses went beyond the usual library books, CD-ROM encyclopedias, and Internet resources. One student wrote that she had a grandmother who lived near the Casey Jones Village in Jackson, Tennessee, and that her grandmother could send the class some things from there. Another student wrote that he had an aunt who worked for Norfolk and Southern Railroad and that she could send the class some information about the railroad. Another student wrote that his dad had a model train and that his dad could set it up in our classroom. Some students wrote that they could get information about trains from the mayor. They knew that he had a model train that went around his office. They even mentioned watching a current TV program about a train station. Many suggested taking a field trip to a train station.

As for their responses to "Who Would I Like to Work With," they all picked a friend to be their partner. I asked them to write a paragraph to tell me why I should let them work with that person. Most students wrote that they should work together because they liked each other, got along well together, and could help each other.

At the end of the train unit I asked my students to fold another piece of paper into fourths and put the following headings on it: (1) "What I Learned About Trains," (2) "What I Learned About the Computer," (3) "What I Learned About Getting Along with Others," and (4) "Project Review." They wrote about what they had learned about trains. Their new knowledge came from taking a field

Continued

trip to the Historic Train Display, listening to guest speakers invited into the classroom, watching train videos, reading library books, and using CD-ROM encyclopedias and the Internet to search for information.

They wrote about some of the things that they had learned to do on the computer. They wrote about how to use the Internet to find information and graphics, how to use word processing to write a business letter, how to use the draw and paint applications to make labels and illustrations for displays, and how to use the HyperStudio program to create multimedia presentations. They wrote about what they had learned about getting along with each other. They wrote about sharing ideas and supplies, doing their best, staying on task, being a responsible partner, and compromising to solve differences.

One student summed up the feelings of her classmates when she wrote, "I liked this project. It was really fun. The project helped me too. It taught me about trains." For a class review, they all gave this project a "Thumbs Up."

Fran Clark
Third-Grade Teacher

FOSTER MEANINGFUL LEARNING

In the introduction we described the type of learning required for today's students as vastly different from what was required in the past. It is no longer essential that students memorize large amounts of information such as the 50 states and their capitals or the presidents and their terms in office. In contrast, today's workforce needs personnel who can competently work with resources, other people, information, a variety of systems, and, of course, technology (SCANS, 1991). Specific knowledge and skills related to these five areas are as follows:

Resources:	Identifies, organizes, plans, and allocates resources
Interpersonal:	Works with others
Information:	Acquires and evaluates information
Systems:	Understands complex interrelationships
Technology:	Works with a variety of technologies

By incorporating the NTeQ Model, which involves the teacher assuming the role of a facilitator, students engage in the five activities listed in the SCANS report. However, just because students engage in "activities" does not ensure that meaningful learning will be fostered or that students will acquire the knowledge and skills needed to be successful in today's world of work. To facilitate the process of meaningful learning, the teacher must carefully plan and implement appropriate learning strategies, ask appropriate questions, and provide the appropriate feedback.

Use Appropriate Learning Strategies

Before a teacher as facilitator can foster meaningful learning in the classroom, he or she must make sure that the learning is *meaningful.* There are two important characteristics of meaningful learning (Ormrod, 2000). First, students must make connections between the new information and what they already know. These associations result in easier retrieval of the information for later application. Second, meaningful learning is more likely to be transferred to a new situation.

One tool we can use to help us determine if our instruction will lead to meaningful learning is Bloom's Taxonomy for cognitive objectives (Bloom, Englehart, Furst, Hill, & Krathwohl, 1956). Instruction that leads to meaningful learning has more objectives and activities grouped at the higher levels as opposed to the lower or rote levels in the taxonomy. Objectives and activities that concentrate only on the knowledge and comprehension levels are less likely to facilitate meaningful learning because of their emphasis on rote memorization. The higher levels of the taxonomy encourage the student to actively engage with the content and to apply, analyze, interpret, and judge the information. Of course, having all your objectives and activities focusing on higher-level skills does not guarantee that your instruction will produce meaningful learning. You will not only need to ensure that lessons address appropriate levels of learning, but also ensure that learning occurs. This is where generative learning strategies are applicable (see Chapter 3, Teacher as Designer 1: Teacher's Toolbox). Thus a teacher can use Bloom's Taxonomy and generative learning strategies to foster meaningful learning.

As you plan lessons in which you will assume the role of a facilitator, review the content and skills students are to learn and determine at which level on Bloom's Taxonomy they fall: *knowledge, comprehension, application, analysis, synthesis,* or *evaluation.* If the majority of the learning objectives fall within the "knowledge" or "comprehension" level, rethink your goals, modify existing ones, or add new ones that require higher levels of learning.

The next step is to plan your activities. This step is where you use the list of generative learning strategies as your assessment criteria: *recall, integration, organization,* and *elaboration.* If you carefully plan learning strategies that require integration, organization, and/or elaboration, your students are more likely to engage in all six levels of learning. The following examples show how the use of generative strategies can assist a teacher in the role of being a facilitator.

Recall. Strategies for recall include rehearsal and practice as well as mnemonics. As a facilitator, you can help students structure their rehearsal and practice for efficient learning, possibly creating a challenge to enhance motivation. You can also provide students with a mnemonic or help them create one to facilitate recall.

Integration. As a facilitator, the teacher assists students with integrating new information with what they already know. As an example, he could help students use a thesaurus as they rewrite the Preamble into their own words.

Organization. The teacher guides student thinking as students create organizational charts, for example, (1) students enter basic information from the periodic chart into a database, then (2) create their own representation of the groupings by generating their own chart.

Elaboration. The teacher also, through activities or questioning, provides multiple opportunities for students to expand upon or elaborate beyond the new information. For example, the teacher can ask, "What impact do you think global warming will have on the polar ice caps? . . . the Sahara Desert? . . . our city?" Elaboration also can be used to remember facts. For example, having students explain why a fact is true can enhance the recall of the fact (Woloshyn, Paivio, & Pressley, 1994).

Ask Appropriate Questions

Research has shown that the use of questioning increases student involvement and achievement (Pratton & Hales, 1986). All questions, however, are not alike. A teacher can ask one type of question that leaves the student in a passive role by simply expecting the student to give a rote-level response. A different type of question, though, can more readily engage a student and cause the student to conceptualize ideas in new ways by articulating thought processes and opinions. It has been demonstrated that this second type of questioning can actually create "neural branching," or, literally, strengthening of the brain (Cardellichio & Field, 1997). Even though higher-level questioning has proven beneficial, most teachers lack the understanding or experience to use this strategy, and, as a result, 80% to 90% of teachers typically ask closed-response questions aimed at factual recall or at getting the "right" answer (Dillon, 1988; Gall, 1984; Wragg, 1993).

Another critical skill needed to become a successful facilitator is that of asking appropriate questions. Because most of us were not taught this way, the process doesn't come naturally, but with constant reflection and awareness of the questioning process being used, the skill is one that we can develop (Kerman, 1979; Rowe, 1986). To develop this skill, it is important to know or be aware of the internal processes required to actively engage students in a questioning session. Eggen and Kauchak (1994) have examined the process of asking questions and have identified the following four things that a teacher must simultaneously consider:

- Remembering the goals of the lesson
- Monitoring verbal and nonverbal behaviors
- Maintaining the flow of the lesson
- Thinking about the next question

Meaningful learning can be fostered by asking appropriate questions.

In addition to knowing the thought process required to engage students in questioning activities, you will also need to know which higher-level questioning strategies and which questioning techniques are most productive.

There are two different styles of questioning that can be used to promote higher-level thinking. These include higher-level (analytical) versus lower-level (factual) questioning and convergent (one answer) versus divergent (several possible answers) questioning.

Higher-Level Versus Lower-Level Questions

Recalling the six levels of Bloom's Taxonomy, we saw how they can serve as a guide for ensuring meaningful learning and for developing generative learning strategies. The six levels can also be used as a model for developing sequential questions (Bloom et al., 1956). To develop sequential questions, establish an information base at the beginning of a lesson by asking knowledge and comprehension questions. Once a common foundation is laid, it is easier to proceed to the higher levels of analysis, synthesis, and evaluation. Sample questions by level of learning are presented in Table 12-3.

Convergent Versus Divergent Questions

Labeling questions as convergent and divergent is another way to think about levels of questioning. Convergent questions are closed-ended; the teacher is seeking one right response. Examples of convergent questions include "When was Dr. Martin Luther King, Jr., assassinated?" and "Who authored *Sula?*" Divergent questions are open-ended and have a range of answers that are considered acceptable. However, not every answer to a divergent question is correct. Divergent questions are often those at the upper levels of Bloom's Taxonomy. Table 12-4 contrasts convergent and divergent questions.

Techniques of Questioning

In addition to the types of questions a teacher can ask, the following six effective techniques can be used when questioning students:

- Redirecting
- Wait time
- Active listening
- Reinforcement
- Prompting
- Modeling

The first technique is *redirecting*. When redirecting, the teacher asks several students to respond to a question without answering the responses or acknowledging the responses as right or wrong. The question is simply redirected to another student.

TABLE 12-3 Example Questions Using Bloom's Taxonomy

Category	Example Questions
Knowledge	Who were the major leaders in the Civil Rights Movement? Who wrote *Uncle Tom's Cabin*?
Comprehension	Given the present rate of growth of the number of Internet Web pages, how many sites will be available in the year 2007? Where is an example of a simile in the poem?
Application	How has the ruling in Brown vs. the Board of Education affected schooling in this country? Let's measure the square footage of this room. How should we proceed?
Analysis	What are the facts and opinions in today's assigned reading? Why is this quote such a powerful way to begin this article?
Synthesis	How could we communicate the findings of our project to the greater community? How can we work with our city to promote recycling in the schools?
Evaluation	What were the successes and failures of the women's movement in the 1960s? What are the weaknesses inherent in the Big Bang theory?

TABLE 12-4 Comparing Convergent and Divergent Questions

Convergent Question	Divergent Question
Who were the disciples of Christ?	What roles did Christ's disciples play?
When was the first airplane built?	How did mass production of the airplane change transportation in America?
What is the area of a square 4'6" × 2'?	What procedures would you use to figure the area of a square 4'6" × 2'?
Who wrote *Little House on the Prairie*?	What aspects of *Little House on the Prairie* appear fictional? What's your rationale?

This technique is often used to build broader perspective in possible responses and to engage more students in the discussion.

A second and valuable questioning technique is *wait time*. Past research has shown that teachers usually wait only 1 second for students to answer. By waiting 3 to 5 seconds before calling on an individual, all students formulate a mental response, plus confidence, speculative thinking, and questions from students increase (Rowe, 1978).

A third technique used in the successful questioning process is *active listening*. A good active listener doesn't interrupt the speaker to provide correct information. Active listening involves waiting until the speaker is finished and restating the main ideas heard. At this point, a teacher can then intervene with more information, ask a rephrased question, or redirect the question to another student.

A fourth technique used in questioning is *reinforcement,* which is praise or a positive comment following an acceptable response. Responses such as "Intriguing idea!" "Great," or "Now you're thinking!" can be a powerful technique for encouraging students to participate. However, overuse of praise could have negative results. Students who don't get praised may begin wondering if their answers are inadequate and become hesitant to participate further. Or, if praise is offered too early in the answer, the students may not be motivated to elaborate on their thinking.

A fifth questioning technique is the use of *prompting*. A prompt is any question or directive the teacher makes after receiving an incorrect or incomplete answer. Some commonly used prompts include "Can you explain your thinking?" "Ann, do you agree or disagree with Bob? Why?" or "Are you saying (restate the answer)? So how do you account for (whatever was left out of the answer)?" The point in using prompts is to avoid making a student's answer "wrong." Instead, think of prompts as a way to help students understand the fallacy or misconception of their thinking without damaging their willingness to participate further in class discussions.

A final questioning technique involves *modeling*. With this technique, a teacher models his or her thought processes with students by "thinking aloud" (Collins, Brown, & Newman, 1990) while working through a given problem. For instance, when using the NTeQ Problem Solving Process, a teacher might assist students by asking them questions that will move them from one stage (What do we want to know?) to the next (How will we find out?). The following dialogue demonstrates teacher modeling during a questioning session:

Ms. Chen: I see that you are interested in knowing more about space exploration, especially forms of space travel as they exist now and as they exist in fiction. I'm wondering what might be some effective ways to get answers to your questions?

Brenda: We could look on the CD-ROM.

Enrique: I have science fiction books at home that I could bring to class.

Glorius: We could look up NASA on the Internet.

Ms. Chen: Those are some interesting ideas. It sounds like you have some good investigative work to accomplish. How could each group delegate tasks for finding out information so everyone can be involved without being overwhelmed?

This sharing of mental processes in the form of questions helps the students to focus on the content as well as the processes used as part of the inquiry. Students begin to learn how to generate questions for themselves, which is a critical component of higher-level cognitive ability (Scardamalia & Bereiter, 1985).

As you can see, it will take practice and experience to obtain a level of questioning that carefully monitors the required processes and uses the appropriate type of question and techniques. After a while, though, the practice becomes second nature—even to the students, who begin to start asking *you* higher-level questions. It becomes very exciting to see the growth and expansion of their minds—and yours!

Provide Appropriate Feedback

Most teachers are quite good at providing motivational feedback to students. For example it is common to hear: "Great Job!" "Very good!" "That's wonderful." or "I'm very proud of you!" Even though these types of responses are important and necessary to build student confidence and self-esteem, they are limited when it comes to promoting actual learning. Feedback needs to specifically address the knowledge or skills to be learned. These types of responses or feedback to student answers can be classified into five levels (Draper, 1999):

1. *Correctness of response:* Letting the students know if the answer was correct or incorrect
2. *The correct answer:* Providing the right answer if the response was incorrect
3. *Procedural or surface explanation of the right answer:* Letting the student know the correct answer if his or hers was incorrect and explaining why the answer is correct
4. *Explanation of what makes the right answer correct:* This feedback goes into more explanation and rationale than the previous one
5. *Explanation of what's wrong about the learner's answer:* This level of feedback helps students to identify misconceptions while reinforcing the intended learning

Examples of the levels of feedback are provided in Table 12-5.

Obviously, as a facilitator, it is important to strive for the level 5 type of feedback, which will reinforce learning. Yet, instructional feedback can be given even when students do not ask questions by providing elaborative comments when monitoring student work. For example, after listening to a group explain an article they are writing for a newsletter, the teacher could add, "Please remember that the mail system was not yet established at that time, and it often took weeks for colonists to receive news from other settlements." This type of feedback builds on their existing knowledge by introducing new content and helps diminish misconceptions by providing correct information.

TABLE 12-5 Levels of Feedback

LEVELS OF FEEDBACK	EXAMPLE
Level 1 Correctness of response	Yes, your answer is correct.
Level 2 The correct answer	The correct answer is carbon.
Level 3 Procedural or surface explanation of the right answer	The answer is carbon. Remember that carbon has four possible bonds.
Level 4 Explanation of what makes the right answer correct	Remember that carbon has four possible bonds and therefore can combine with four elements, for example, four hydrogens.
Level 5 Explanation of what's wrong about the learner's answer	Remember that carbon has four possible bonds and therefore can combine with four elements, for example, four hydrogens. However, your response of oxygen is not correct because it can only accept two elements, for example, like water (H_2O).

CREATE AN OPEN AND SUPPORTIVE CULTURE

If students are to engage in a higher level of learning and if they are to respond to meaningful questions, they will need to feel confident that they are respected and valued as individuals. When this occurs, students are better able to believe that their expression of thoughts and ideas also will be respected and considered in the overall scheme of learning. For a teacher to create this type of atmosphere, it is critical that students be taught appropriate social skills to be used when interacting with fellow class members.

Promote Development of Cooperative/Social Skills

Based both on research (Cohen, 1994) and our own personal experience, the time used to develop social skills through direct instruction ensures that group work is productive. To highlight what social skills need to be taught, Johnson, Johnson, and Holubec (1994) outline the following four levels of cooperative skills:

1. *Forming skills.* These include skills such as transitioning into groups quickly and quietly, using soft voices, taking turns, using group members' names, making eye contact, and respecting all opinions.

2. *Functioning skills.* These include group management skills such as restating the purpose of the assignment, keeping track of time limits, expressing support and praise for other members, clarifying, paraphrasing, and sharing feelings and humor.
3. *Formulating skills.* These include skills necessary for critical thinking and processing of the material being learned such as summarizing, seeking accuracy, elaborating to other material and ideas, seeking alternative means of processing information (drawing flow charts, visuals, etc.), and explaining the reasoning process.
4. *Fermenting skills.* These include reconceptualization skills such as criticizing ideas, not people, integrating various ideas into a new perspective, asking probing questions that lead to a deeper understanding, problem solving several alternative explanations or solutions, and justifying a solution.

When you are ready for your students to use these skills, you may want to begin by introducing one skill at a time. Let students know that along with academic objectives, you also have a social objective for the lesson. Another way to think about it is that every group lesson should include academic tasks as well as social skills. Introduce the tasks and the social skill at the beginning of the lesson. Let students know why the skill is important in the real world—this step is critical. Start with forming skills when new groups are initiated. Add additional skills each time groups work together.

At the completion of the group work (usually at the end of the period or the end of the week), allow 10 to 15 minutes for the group to process its effectiveness with the targeted social skills. As groups become more efficient at processing, less time will be required. Encourage honesty and risk-taking during processing. Have students share in their group, one by one, how they felt the group performed on a given skill. Following is a scenario of what skill instruction and group processing might look like in a sixth-grade classroom.

> Mr. Rosen is forming new groups for a social studies inquiry project. Students are already sitting in groups of four. Mr. Rosen begins by saying, "As you work in your groups today, I want you to focus on taking turns speaking. Be sure that everyone has a chance to share his or her opinion. If one person is speaking too much, the group should feel free to encourage others to participate. It's important in team efforts that the discussion includes everybody's opinions. This is how we become aware of the world around us and how we get new ideas and learn."
>
> After the groups start working on their task, Mr. Rosen monitors each group. He drops by and listens to the conversations. In one group he asks, "Has everyone had a chance to share their ideas?" In another, he notices that one student is overly quiet and withdrawn. At an appropriate interval in the conversation he draws this student in by asking, "Michael, what do you think about what's just been said?"
>
> After the groups have had a chance to work together, and then discuss their results in a whole-class discussion, Mr. Rosen asks each group to spend 10 minutes responding to the following: "Processing is a time for each group member to reflect on how their group functioned today. Today, I asked you to focus on taking turns. One by one, go around the group and share how well you think your group achieved this task. In addition, share what you would like to see the next time your group works together. I en-

courage you to be honest with one another because that is how you will learn to work together and trust one another. Remember, no put downs."

Notice that Mr. Rosen is facilitating the groups—he directs and guides them to achieve both the academic task and the social skill he has assigned for the day. He keeps the dual objectives in mind and supports students so they can effectively achieve in both domains.

MEET THE DIVERSE NEEDS OF LEARNERS*

Many of the classrooms of today are very diversified in that they have a greater percentage of students from a variety of cultural backgrounds, students from low-income families, and students with disabilities. To effectively facilitate and foster meaningful learning with such a variety of specialized needs, a teacher must understand how to implement the most appropriate approach for the different circumstances.

Meeting the Needs of Multicultural Learners

The necessity to be sensitive to the needs of multicultural learners is greater than at any time in our country's history. Minority populations now account for 30% of the population, and a greater percentage of our students come from non–English speaking families and families living in poverty (U.S. Bureau of the Census, 2001). How can teachers address the acquisition of English using technology? As a teacher, you can use language buddies and build on the students' native language and culture. Let's examine these two approaches.

Language Buddies

First, teachers can assign "language buddies" to new students (Campbell, 1996). These buddies are viewed as assisting the teacher by working alongside the new non–English speaking student in the first few weeks of school. This pairing is particularly helpful when working with technology. The buddy is able to demonstrate and then support the various uses of technology tools. Non–English speaking students can experience almost immediate success with a spreadsheet or other math-related computer tools that don't require an extensive knowledge of English. Using language buddies, non–English speaking students are empowered through the successful completion of assignments and begin creating new friendships.

As a facilitator in a classroom that is using a language buddy system, it is important to carefully watch the interactions to ensure that the English-speaking buddy is open and supportive to working with the student and that the experience does not detract from learning. It is often helpful to present the option of serving as a language buddy as an *opportunity* to learn about a new country and make a new friend. This

---

* Dr. Tom Buggey of the University of Memphis contributed the section discussing assistive technology.

opportunity should be rotated among several student volunteers to eliminate the possibility of overworking one student and to increase the circle of new friends for the non–English speaking student.

Celebrate the Culture

Second, teachers might consider how to build on and use the new language(s) that his students bring to the classroom as a way of celebrating all cultures. Classes can engage in inquiry projects via the Internet, share stories or weather information over e-mail, participate in foreign language newsgroups, or create multimedia reports about life in the student's home country. Through your facilitation skills, the non–English speakers will be seen as a true asset to the multidimensional classroom.

Meeting the Needs of Students Living in Poverty

Haberman (1994) makes the case that any schooling that begins with an assumption that children are deficient in some way because they aren't reflective of the established norm is "miseducative and leads to more negative than positive achievements" (p. 3). Rather, he suggests that teachers learn to recognize signs of four prevalent issues he has identified among poor children. These issues include lacking trust, suffering violence and abuse, living under bureaucracies, and "being done to."

Many children in poverty grow up with adults they cannot trust. These children include latchkey children, abused children, children without an extended family immediately available, or children whose parents suffer from substance abuse. This lack of trust often carries over into the school environment, where students can be fearful and suspicious of teachers. Students learn strategies of self-protection and survival by avoiding adults. To survive and overcome feelings of manipulation, those who live in poverty learn to manipulate the system to their advantage. Satisfaction is derived from having control over others or learning to comply with others to fill needs. Haberman (1994) asks, "Does the school seek to change what these children bring to school or does the school deepen and enhance these themes?" (p. 7).

Thus a role for the teacher of children who live in poverty is to assist them in developing trust of others, including school personnel, as well as offer alternative forms of interaction and communication strategies. This development of trust can be promoted with the use of technology. For example, students can use word processing or e-mail as a means to developing an ongoing communication with an author they might be studying or with students from another school. A high school social studies teacher might encourage her students to meet with the local chamber of commerce to develop a Website for the city. As a part of math instruction, a teacher could bring in a small business owner who needs assistance developing a spreadsheet. In each of these examples, students are connected in positive ways with adult members of the community. This strategy enables students to see themselves as part of a larger community and reconceptualize and formulate a more positive belief system concerning adults.

Meeting the Needs of Students with Disabilities

As a result of the Individuals with Disabilities Act (1997), an increasing number of students with disabilities are included in today's regular classrooms. This Act states that a regular educator must be part of a multidisciplinary team that determines placement and services for all students who qualify for special education. When addressing the needs of learners with disabilities, the multidisciplinary team is to work with an assistive device center or a technician employed by the school district to determine the most appropriate type of assistive technology for identified students.

Assistive Technology

The term *assistive computing/technology* refers to any method or device that makes the computer more accessible for a user with a disability. Students with disabilities typically need access to a personal computer for the same reasons as students without disabilities. However, adaptations and even alternatives to standard computer hardware and software are often necessary to make the computer accessible to the user with a disability (Wilson, Kotlas, & Martin, 1994). Some common access problems include difficulty using the keyboard and mouse, inserting disks or CDs, viewing the monitor, and hearing software directions or instruction.

Access to the computer for persons with visual impairments may require either speech output, screen magnification, or Braille input with text-to-speech translation. Adapting the computer for persons with *motoric* impairments can be accomplished if they have only the slightest voluntary muscle control. Switches can be designed for

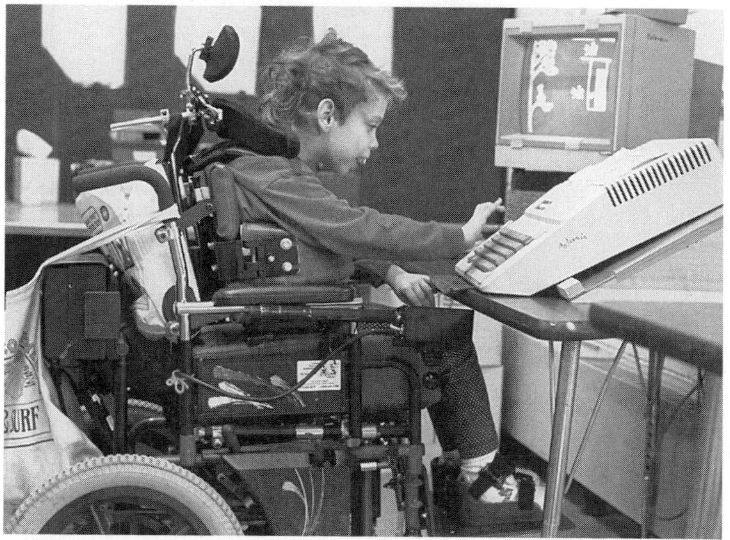

Classroom resources can be adapted to meet the special needs of students with disabilities.

use with a toe or even eyebrow movements, and keyboards can be modified for persons with gross motor control over arm and finger movement, but limited fine motor skills. For example, a key guard, which helps direct fingers to the keys, can be used in conjunction with a program that inhibits the repetitive production of a letter when it is held down too long (e.g., Easy Access, or AccessDOS). If the person's physical disability is such that use of the conventional keyboard with modifications is not an option, alternative keyboards, ability switches, headpointers, and joysticks can be used. Whatever the method, the computer treats the input from these devices as if it had been received through the standard keyboard.

As a facilitator of learning, you not only need to ensure all students have accessibility to learning resources, but you also must ensure that your classroom environment includes adaptations necessary to ensure successful goal attainment by students with disabilities. This adaptation may require changes in the communication methods or the physical arrangement.

Communication Adaptations

Adaptations to the communication environment may include a range of materials and methods such as signing, communication boards, picture-symbol cards, and high-tech devices. It may be necessary to modify classroom materials to accommodate these alternative forms of communication. The use of Braille, signs, or symbols with the related printed word on materials may facilitate learning of these techniques by all class members, thus improving accessibility of children who are nonverbal by providing a universal method of classroom communication (Buggey, 1998).

The advent and subsequent development of assistive devices in the area of mobility, computer access, and communication have eradicated barriers that have existed for centuries for persons with disabilities. The ability to speak and to access knowledge is now possible for almost all individuals with cognitive, physical, and sensory impairments. It is imperative that teachers learn how to use these technologies to ensure that persons with disabilities have equal opportunities for participation in our classrooms and communities.

Physical Disability Adaptations

As a rule, adaptations to an environment to accommodate a student should be kept to a minimum. In other words, adaptations should be as unobtrusive as possible to minimize pointing out the "differences" in the student with the disability (Buggey, 1998). The needed adaptations will depend on the type and severity of the disability. Students with severe physical disabilities will need additional space for maneuvering and therapy and may require a range of adaptive equipment to facilitate therapy and to aid in accessing aspects of the school program. Equipment often used in this context includes wedges, wheelchairs, prone standers, sidelyers, posture chairs, and support bars. Teachers must work closely with physical and occupational therapists and parents to ensure that individual needs for successful participation are met. For example, the purpose of a wedge is to give the lower trunk and torso support so that head, arms, and hands are free to manipulate objects. A child using a wedge may freely participate in activities such as reading, art, science labs, and computer activities.

SUMMARY

This chapter examined the role of teacher as facilitator in an NTeQ environment. The key components involved in assuming the role of a facilitator include fostering meaningful learning, creating an open and supportive classroom culture, and meeting the diversified needs of learners. When a teacher changes from a traditional teaching role to the role of a facilitator, he or she will change the design of lessons to ensure that he or she implements appropriate learning strategies, asks appropriate questions, and provides the appropriate feedback. The teacher will need to ensure that the students engage in active listening, reflection, explanations, and questioning as the teacher guides them through the learning process. In the midst of these activities, the teacher as facilitator will need to provide opportunities for all students to work cooperatively in well-structured activities that emphasize the growth and development of social skills, while meeting the diverse needs of students.

AT THE CLASSROOM'S DOORSTEP

Questions Teachers Ask

At my school, a noisy classroom indicates a teacher who has lost control. How do I explain the group noise to my principal and co-workers?

You must first reframe your own thinking. Examine the nature of the "noise." Is it due to children being off task and goofing around, or is it the result of students truly engaged in a social learning process? Help your colleagues understand the value of social learning—children need opportunities to express their opinions, verbally explore their thinking with others, and brainstorm various ways of problem solving. This type of learning cannot take place when students sit quietly in rows completing worksheets. Once you believe in the value of social learning, and can articulate that value to others, you'll be on your way to converting other teachers to join the bandwagon. Good luck!

I want to ask higher-level questions, but when I get involved in a discussion, they often slip from my mind. What can I do?

Take a few minutes before each lesson to develop some higher-level questions based on the objectives for the lesson. Record your questions on note cards or something that you can comfortably carry with you during class. When you begin the discussion, you can easily refer to your questions to prompt your thinking. You also may want to keep a pencil handy to make notes of ideas or questions raised during the discussion. File these questions and notes with the lesson to help you prepare for the next time you implement it. The extra time you take to prepare can mean a world of difference in the understandings your students develop during the lesson.

TECHNOLOGY INTEGRATION ACTIVITIES

To access the activities that connect the content of the text with the Companion Website and other technology, please go to the Activities module in Chapter 12 of the Companion Website at *http://www.prenhall.com/morrison*.

NTEQ PORTFOLIO ACTIVITIES: TEACHER AS FACILITATOR

Please complete the following activities as part of your NTeQ Portfolio on Teacher as Facilitator.

Reflections

The "Getting Started" portion of this chapter asked three questions that teachers might commonly ask. In this portion of your journal, a reflection question has been added to address how you would answer each question. Please use information from this chapter to answer the questions.

1. I thought all teachers were facilitators. What is the difference?
   - *Reflection Question:* Create a concept map that illustrates the differences between a traditional teacher and a teacher as a facilitator.
2. How can I be sure students learn information covered on the state tests when I am just a "guide on the side"?
   - *Reflection Question:* Review the chapter and write a response to the question that explains how students can actually learn more when teachers are facilitators.
3. Isn't it very difficult to meet the varying needs of all my students in a classroom that doesn't appear to be well structured?
   - *Reflection Question:* Review the section on meeting the diverse needs of students and generate a list of ideas that you can use to address the needs of all students in a classroom.

BLOOM'S TAXONOMY QUESTIONS

Select an NTeQ lesson that you have developed and generate a sample discussion question for each level: Knowledge, Comprehension, Application, Analysis, Synthesis, and Evaluation.

CONVERGENT VS. DIVERGENT QUESTIONS

Use the same lesson as above and create several questions that are written as a convergent and a divergent question. See Table 12-4 for examples.

LEVELS OF FEEDBACK

Select the lesson from above, or a new lesson, and write sample student questions and an incorrect and correct student response. Then write five levels of feedback for sample student responses. See Table 12-5 for examples.

REFERENCES

Bloom, B. S., Englehart, M. D., Furst, E. J., Hill, W. H., & Krathwohl, D. R. (Eds.) (1956). *Taxonomy of educational objectives: The classification of education goals. Handbook I: Cognitive domain.* New York: David McKay.

Buggey, T. (1998). Arranging preschool environments. In S. Graves & R. Gargle (Eds.). *Early childhood special education.* St. Paul, MN: West.

Campbell, D. E. (1996). *Choosing democracy: A practical guide to multicultural education.* Upper Saddle River, NJ: Merrill/Prentice Hall.

Cardellichio, T., & Field, W. (1997). Seven strategies that encourage neural branching. *Educational Leadership, 54*(6), 33–37.

Cohen, E. G. (1994). Restructuring the classroom: Conditions for productive small groups. *Review of Educational Research, 64*(1), 1–35.

Collins, A., Brown, J. S., & Newman, S. E. (1990). Cognitive apprenticeship: Teaching the crafts of reading, writing, and mathematics. In L. Resnick (Ed.), *Knowing, learning, and instruction: Essays in honor of Robert Glaser* (pp. 453–494). Hillsdale, NJ: Erlbaum.

Dillon, J. T. (1988). *Questioning and teaching.* New York: Teachers College Press.

Draper, S. W. (1999). Feedback. [Online] Available http://www.psy.gla.ac.uk/~steve/feedback.html.

Eggen, P., & Kauchak, D. (1994). *Educational psychology: Classroom connections* (2nd ed.). Upper Saddle River, NJ: Merrill/Prentice Hall.

Freire, P. (1971). *Pedagogy of the oppressed.* New York: Seaview.

Gall, M. (1984). Synthesis of research on teacher's questioning. *Educational Leadership, 42,* 40–47.

Haberman, M. (1994). Contexts: Overview and framework. In O'Hair and Odell (Eds.). *Diversity and teaching: Teacher education yearbook one* (pp. 1–8). New York: Harcourt Brace Jovanovich.

Individuals With Disabilities Education Act Amendment of 1997 (1997). Amendments to the Individuals With Disabilities Education Act [Online]. Available: http://thomas.loc.gov/cgi-bin/query/D?c107:3:./temp/~c107h55i7n.

Johnson, D. W., Johnson, R. T., & Holubec E. J. (1994). *The new circles of learning.* Alexandria, VA: ASCD.

Kerman, S. (1979). Teacher expectations and student achievement. *Phi Delta Kappan, 60*(10), 70–72.

Microsoft Word Thesaurus (2003). Microsoft Corporation.

Murphy, J. (1995). Changing role of the teacher. In O'Hair & Odell (Eds.), *Educating teachers for leadership and change* (pp. 311–333). Thousand Oaks, CA: Corwin Press, Inc.

Ormrod, J. E. (2000). *Educational psychology: Developing learners* (3rd ed.). Upper Saddle River, NJ: Merrill/Prentice Hall.

Pratton, J., & Hales, L. W. (1986). The effects of active participation on student learning. *Journal of Educational Research, 74*(4), 210–215.

Rowe, M. B. (1978). *Teaching science as continuous inquiry.* New York: McGraw-Hill.

Rowe, M. B. (1986). Wait time: Slowing down may be a way of speeding up. *Journal of Teacher Education,* Jan/Feb, 43–50.

SCANS (June 1991). *What work requires of schools: A SCANS report for America 2000.* Washington, D.C.: U.S. Department of Labor, pp. xvii–xviii.

Scardamalia, M., & Bereiter, C. (1985). Fostering the development of self-regulation in children's knowledge processing. In S. F. Chipman, J. W. Segal, & R. Glaser (Eds.), *Thinking and learning skills: Vol. 2. Research and open questions* (pp. 563–577). Hillsdale, NJ: Erlbaum.

U.S. Bureau of the Census (May, 2001). *Profiles of general demographic characteristics* [Online]. Available: http://www2.census.gov/census_2000/datasets/demographic_profile/0_United_States/2kh00.pdf.

Wilson, L., Kotlas, C., & Martin, M. (1994). *Assistive technology for the disabled.* Institute for Academic Technology (Information Resource Guides Series #IRG-20). Chapel Hill: University of North Carolina.

Woloshyn, V. E., Paivio, A., & Pressley, M. (1994). Use of elaborative interrogation to help students acquire information consistent with prior knowledge and information inconsistent with prior knowledge. *Journal of Educational Psychology, 86,* 79–89.

Wragg, E. C. (1993). *Primary teaching skills.* London: Routledge.

KEY TOPICS

Chapter 13

Managing the Classroom

At first view, a student-centered classroom can appear as anarchy to an administrator, mass hysteria to a fellow teacher, or a total loss of faith in our educational system to a parent who is used to traditional seat work. What the outside observer often fails to notice is the underlying planning, management, and organization that are guiding each student's endeavor. Granted, our first view of a student-centered classroom did not exactly match our expectations. The teacher, however, was the calmest teacher we have ever seen, even though her students were talking, moving about the room freely and even in the hallway. After a few minutes of explanation, we began to see the implementation of her planning. Her room was probably managed better than the "quiet" rooms down the hall. Changing to a student-centered learning environment requires careful management of a variety of resources and activities, but the benefits and rewards are well worth the effort.

In this chapter, we will discuss how to create and manage a classroom environment for using the computer as a tool for learning. We will also introduce the three stages that teachers go through while learning how to manage the integration of computers into the curriculum. Next we give some practical guidance for managing the multidimensional environment, such as rotation of students to the computers, managing the students while they are working on the computers, and managing the resources that accompany the use of technology.

GETTING STARTED

What Do I Know?

1. Do you know that teachers typically go through three distinct stages as they learn to manage the integration of computers into their classroom—with "survival" being the first stage?
2. How do you ensure equal access when you have 26 students and only three computers?
3. How do students keep track of their work when 26 students are using three computers?

Classroom Snapshot

Mrs. Jones arrives to school early because she wants to set up her room for today's science lesson on soil. She chose "The Creatures Below" as the title to build interest in the topic. The students are going to collect a 6-inch cube of soil from different locations around the school ground: the edge of the playground next to the woods, next to the parking lot, in between the outdoor classrooms, and in the middle of the playground. They will collect the organic material found in the soil and count the number of worms, insects, and plants on their piece of earth. Next they will use a spreadsheet to determine if the number of organisms changes based on where the soil was collected. Mrs. Jones only has one computer in her classroom; therefore she planned multiple activities for her students and a rotation schedule for using the computer. She has five activities: (1) a soil collection center, (2) an examination center to collect the "creatures" from the soil and record the number on the spreadsheet handout (NTeQ before computer activity), (3) a videotape that shows how soil is developed, (4) a set of books with diagrams of the earth's topsoil, and (5) an investigation station with soil in a clear glass container to observe the ants and worms and completing Think Sheet Questions (NTeQ after computer activity).

Her early morning preparation for this lesson includes loading the spreadsheet template on the computer, creating desktop computer folders for each group to save their spreadsheets, placing spreadsheet job aids next to the computer, hanging a "How to Save Your Work" poster on the wall behind the computer, labeling one floppy disk for each of the four groups, and loading the printer with paper. When the students arrive, Mrs. Jones introduces the lesson problem, "Did you know that when you go out to the playground there are lots of creatures living right below your feet! Today you are going to investigate the impact of humans on these creatures. In other words, do places that are real busy, like the center of the playground or next to the parking lot, have fewer creatures than less busy spots?" She then passes out the lesson handout that has a schedule for each group, specifics for entering the "creature" data into the spreadsheet, and the Think Sheet Questions. The schedule has Groups 1 and 2 start by collecting their sample of soil (with a teacher aide), Group 3 watching the video, and Group 4 reading the books. When Group 1 and 2 return, the next two groups collect their samples. The handouts were clear and easy to follow, and the job aids and poster helped with basic computer questions. With these tasks managed, students could focus their time and energy on solving the "Creatures Below" lesson problem.

CLASSROOM MANAGEMENT

The addition of computers to a classroom brings another dimension to the role of teacher as manager. When a teacher uses the NTeQ model, he is responsible for managing a multidimensional environment that integrates technology. If you examine this multidimensional environment during a lesson, it is almost impossible to separate the instructional aspects from the managerial aspects of the classroom (Weade & Evertson, 1991). Computers can be introduced without dramatically changing the instruction, but they cannot be introduced without making immediate shifts in classroom management processes (Sandholtz, Ringstaff, & Dwyer, 1990). In addition, Sandholtz et al. (1990) indicate that "instructional innovation is not likely to occur until teachers have achieved a significant level of mastery over management issues" (p. 2). They also suggest the following points:

- Classroom management is not a skill that is mastered once and for all. As classroom contexts change, so do the classroom management issues.
- Educational change takes time. Teachers tend to focus on the increased workload and drawbacks associated with the innovation before the benefits of change emerge and the innovation takes hold.

Managing a classroom that uses an innovative approach (such as the NTeQ model) involves much more than just keeping the students quiet, in their seats, and working. To effectively manage a classroom that is integrating computers in a *meaningful* way, the teacher must create an environment that is conducive to learning. In this environment, she must manage the movement of students to and from various activities, manage them while they are engaged in the activities, and oversee the management of extra resources that are used in these activities. If Internet access is available, the teacher must also manage student use of these Web-based resources. All of these managerial responsibilities may seem overwhelming at first, but with careful planning and practice they will, over time, become part of everyday routines.

THE TEACHER'S DIARY

I had been in the public school classroom for 20 years when I received my computers. I had seen a lot of innovations come and go. I felt like technology was going to be around for a long time and that it was time for me to become more technically competent. When I got the computers, I felt excited, but also overwhelmed. How was I ever going to learn how to use the equipment and remember how to create a spreadsheet or a database? There was so much to learn! I spent many hours just learning how to operate the equipment and how to use the basic computer applications. By the end of that first year, I had become comfortable with the computer and had discovered that it was going to be a useful tool for me. I could see how it was making my job easier.

When school started the next year, I was ready for a change. I had mastered the computer, so to speak, and I wanted my students to master it too. I began to look at education from a more constructivist point of view and wanted my classroom to become child centered. One of the first things I learned was my role as a teacher had to change. I had to become a facilitator of learning, not a director. Once I accepted that role, I began to look at how I had been teaching and realized that I was going to have to make some significant changes in how I approached learning and classroom management. I had many frustrations that year as I began to make those changes! It took me more time to plan my lessons. I had peers question what I was doing. I had to develop alternative assessments.

Continued

I had to learn that a noisy classroom was OK. I had to let go and allow my students to have some input into what and how they were going to learn. There were days when I questioned what I had gotten myself into. Sometimes, I wondered if my students were really learning.

When working on thematic unit projects about trains, I grouped the students into pairs to work on different topics related to trains. Some were working at desks, some were working at the computers, and some were working on the floor. The room was noisy because the students were talking as they worked together on their projects. There was a lot of movement to and from the computers. I was on the floor helping some students work on a model of a freight train. I was so engrossed in what they were doing, that I did not realize a supervisor from Central Office had come into the room until she was standing over me. She had come to visit. She said she'd only be able to stay for a few minutes, and that she would just walk around the room to see what was going on. She told me to continue what I was doing. So, I got back on the floor and continued helping. I wondered what she was thinking as the room was noisy and no one was at their own seat working!

I continued to watch her as I worked with other groups, and I noticed that she was moving from group to group talking to the students about their projects and what they had learned. Her "few minutes" visit turned into the rest of the afternoon. I apologized for the noise level and what appeared to be "organized" chaos. I thought that she might be disappointed because I was not "teaching" a lesson. She wasn't disappointed. Instead, she thanked me for letting her spend the afternoon with my students. She told me that I needed to remember that learning is not always going to be neat and tidy! She said that noise and "organized" chaos were sometimes part of an effective learning environment. She said she could tell that my students were learning and that was what was really important.

Fran Clark
Third-Grade Teacher

Classroom Environment

The NTeQ model emphasizes an environment that is student-centered. The students are actively engaged in the learning process and assume the roles of researchers. To engage students in this manner, the teacher must work with the students to create an atmosphere or culture that fosters and supports a high level of student involvement, not only with the information they are learning, but also with each other. Ryba and Anderson (1993, p. 5) provide the following six guidelines that students can follow to help create what they call a "computer learning culture":

- Helping one another solve problems
- Openly sharing information and ideas
- Reinforcing each other for making progress
- [Effectively] working in physically close proximity to one another

- Collectively supporting anyone who has a personal "crisis"
- Extending the effective working relationships beyond the computer environment

Another important aspect of managing a classroom environment that promotes student learning is to establish classroom rules and routines early in the school year. Mayeski (1997, p. 2) suggests three general guidelines to consider when establishing classroom rules.

- Make only a few rules—neither you nor the students will remember a long list.
- Select rules because they establish an orderly environment and contribute to successful learning—gum chewing probably does not impede learning.
- Make the rules as unambiguous as possible. They should be stated behaviorally. For example, "keep your hands and feet to yourself" is clearer than "no fighting."

The NTeQ model is based on a student-centered classroom; thus it is important to involve students in the formation of classroom rules and routines to give them a sense of ownership and responsibility for their learning environment (Mayeski, 1997).

Changes Over Time

When teachers are faced with adopting a new innovation, such as integrating computers into their classroom instruction, as seen in Figure 13-1, they evolve through three stages: survival, mastery, and impact (Hall & Loucks, 1979). In the *survival* stage, teachers' concerns are directed toward their personal knowledge and skills. They often do not know enough about the computers to anticipate problems; therefore they have to react to problems. After time and experience, the teachers move into the *mastery* stage, where they are able to plan for possible problems in advance. When teachers

FIGURE 13-1 Managing the Use of Classroom Computers: Three Stages of Adoption

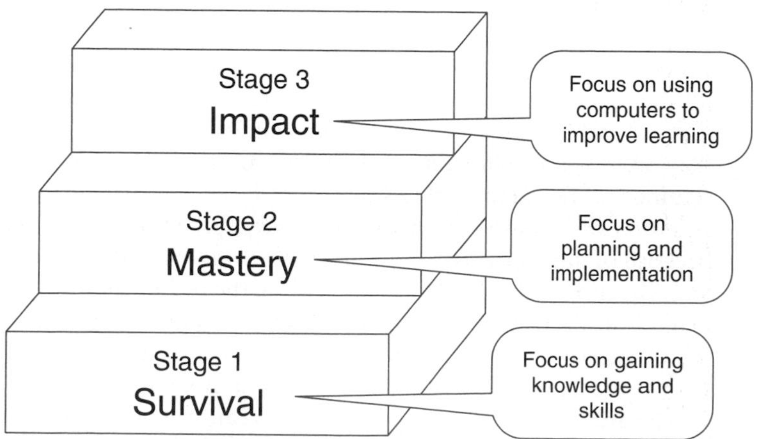

Adapted from Halls & Loucks, 1979. Teacher concerns as a basis for facilitating and personalizing staff development. In A. Lieberman and L. Miller (Eds.), *Staff development: New demands, new realities, new perspectives*. New York: Teachers Press.

In a well-managed classroom, students learn in whole-group activities as well as small-group activities.

have established a comfortable routine, they move into the *impact* stage, where they focus more on the impact the computers have on student learning. In this stage, the teachers begin to modify and improve the integration strategies used with computers.

These stages were seen in a study of how teachers in Apple Classrooms of Tomorrow (ACOT) managed their classrooms (Sandholtz et al., 1990). The study revealed four areas related to managing a classroom with computers: student misbehavior and attitudes, physical environment, technical problems, and classroom dynamics. During the survival stage, teachers struggled with students copying work from other students' disks (because the teacher could no longer tell who did the work by examining the handwriting) or with students experimenting to see if magnets really do erase disks. Teachers also found that some students enjoyed the computers so much that they were quite reluctant to leave the computer area or complete handwritten assignments. Teachers at this stage were faced with classrooms that were now overcrowded with computer hardware and equipment that was sometimes difficult to use because of improper lighting, glare from windows, or bad weather conditions. Along with the introduction of computers came the technical problems: software and equipment failures, bad disks, trouble logging onto the Internet, and printing problems. A final concern of some teachers at the survival stage was that they were often faced with students who knew more about technology than they did.

The study found that by the second year, teachers moved into the mastery stage. In this stage, the teachers' knowledge and skills had increased so they could better plan for and anticipate technology-related problems. They handled student misbehavior by restricting computer access, and they found ways to reorganize their classrooms to provide more open space and utilize the best lighting. Contingency plans were developed to handle bad weather and equipment failures. Procedures were developed to handle printing problems, and the teachers became more comfortable using their students' expertise.

After teachers mastered the management challenges presented in a technology-rich classroom, they moved to the impact stage. In this stage, they used computers to assist them with their instructional and maintenance tasks, as well as to modify and improve their management techniques.

Teachers from over 200 schools in 18 states participated in the ACOT study. These teachers were like pioneers when it came to integrating computers into their curricula. They indicated that local and peer-to-peer resources were the most valuable for technology-related issues (Casson, Bauman, Fisher, Sumpter, & Tornatzky, 1997). Today, teachers can learn from the ACOT experiences but also from the experiences of teachers who are successfully integrating technology into their current classrooms. Therefore, as you begin to integrate technology into your curriculum, it is important that you find other teachers in your school or district or through an online teacher discussion group that have experience and are willing to assist you. Perhaps these resources will make your survival stage shorter and easier.

MANAGING THE MULTIDIMENSIONAL ENVIRONMENT

The following sections provide practical guidelines and advice on how to manage a multidimensional environment. This environment has students engaged in computer use and other activities such as researching for information from books and magazines, collecting data from observations, sketching storyboards for a multimedia presentation (Chapter 8, Publishing and Presentation), gathering information from a videotape, or conducting an experiment. As you can see, this type of environment is student centered, very active, and requires careful planning and cooperation from and among the students. Plans are needed for moving students to and from the various activities, for managing the students while they are at the computers, and also for managing the extra resources required by the technology.

Managing the Rotation

There are several factors to consider when planning student rotation through multiple activities. Your plan will vary according to computer access. For example, will your students use computers in the classroom, in the lab, or in both places? If you have computers in your classroom, then you need to consider the room layout and how the students will rotate through the available computers. Both of these considerations are discussed in this section.

Working with What You Have

As you develop your NTeQ lessons, it is important to build them around the resources that you have available. The types of computer access can be categorized into four typical groups:

Single Use: One to two computers per classroom

Small Group: Three to six computers per class

Computer Lab: Room of computers with one to two students per computer
Laptop Classroom: Each student has access to a laptop during class time

Single Use. If you only have one computer in your classroom, lessons should require only minimal computer access for students. Activities are typically focused toward creating a "class" product that is produced from group or individual student work. Examples are as follows:

Small Group Work

- Groups collect and enter data for designated sections of a *class* database; for example, each *group* could collect and enter the following:
  - One state from each region
  - Five presidents
  - Endangered species from one country
  - Examples of a particular shape (squares or rectangles)
- Student groups enter their specific data into a class spreadsheet, for example, the following:
  - Each group collects and enters different weather data
  - Each group conducts the same experiment, then enters their data for comparison (e.g., how high do ping pong balls bounce when dropped from different heights, or the number of people wearing seat belts at different times of day)

Individual Students

- Each student creates one page of a classroom HyperStudio stack, for example, the following:
  - An original poem in a class book of spring poems
  - A definition and example in a "Correct Grammar" stack
  - A brief biographical sketch of a famous scientist
- Each student or pair of students adds a paragraph to an original class story.

McClelland (1996) and Wiebe (1993) suggest that cooperative learning is very successful when you are limited to one or two computers. McClelland emphasizes the importance of establishing student roles for computer use and ensuring that the roles are rotated to provide equal access to all students (see Chapter 11, Implementation: From Plan to Action, for more on cooperative learning).

Small Group. When a teacher has access to three to six computers in the classroom, student use of technology can be routinely included in the lessons. Students can be involved in the same types of activities listed for the one-computer classroom; however, the projects would be *group* projects rather than *class* projects. Even in a setting with more computers, though, cooperative learning is still effective for student learning at the computer (Willing & Girard, 1990).

Computer Labs. Computer use also can be routinely included in lessons if teachers regularly have access to a lab. The number of computers in the lab may require that students work together, or each student may work at an individual computer. It is important to encourage students to share ideas and provide assistance to one another in a lab setting to ensure that the "computer-learning culture" is maintained.

Laptop Classroom. Some schools provide laptop carts that teachers can reserve for the class, whereas other districts may have a laptop program in which students have their own laptop computers. The laptop classroom offers both challenges and opportunities. You can easily plan integrated lessons that make extensive use of the computers. Students can work individually or in small groups. Managing the classroom, however, often becomes a challenge because you must now keep an eye on 20+ computers rather than four or five. Even when students have laptop computers, we encourage teachers to design their lessons for small groups to encourage collaborative learning.

Managing the Move

Once you know where your students will use the computers, you can determine the best layout for your computers and plan for student movement to and from the computers. Moving to a computer lab involves taking the whole class; thus we will focus on rotation schedules for classroom computers. You can plan lessons around two primary types of schedules: group rotation or independent rotation.

Group Rotation

With group rotation, small groups of students stay together as they move from one lesson activity center to another (Figure 13-2). To manage this type of rotation, the teacher needs to determine approximately how long the activity at each station or center will take. If possible, each center should take about the same amount of time for completion. This scheduling helps students rotate through the centers at regular intervals.

Another consideration is to have more than one center for activities that take longer. For example, if students are collecting information about several different categories from a variety of travel brochures, the research activity may take longer than setting up the database and entering the collected information. In this case, you may want to set up two research centers so students can spend twice as long on this activity. One center could be for researching historical sites, and the other could be for researching weather patterns. The rotation can be managed by having students move through the stations in a clockwise or other predetermined pattern. You can use a kitchen timer to alert students when it is time to move. If the timer is set for 2 minutes before they need to move, the students will have time to finish the task at hand and straighten the area. When group rotations are used, the

FIGURE 13-2 Classroom Layout for Group Rotation

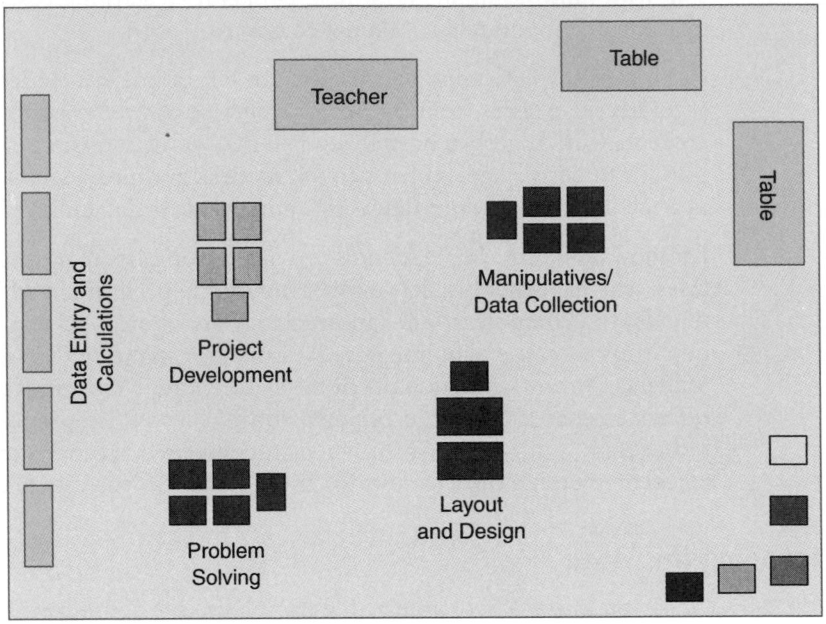

Table
Teacher
Table
Data Entry and Calculations
Project Development
Manipulatives/ Data Collection
Layout and Design
Problem Solving

student-to-computer ratio is often one to one, which ensures equal computer access. But again, just as was mentioned for the lab, you need to encourage students to work as a team.

Independent Rotation

The second type of rotation, independent rotation (see Figure 13-3), still has students in small cooperative groups, but the groups do not rotate to each activity in an established pattern. Rather, in this setup, students can access all the resources needed to solve the problem designated in the lesson, thus allowing the students to use the resources on an as-needed basis. With independent rotation, each group is assigned a computer. (Sometimes, though, more than one group has to be assigned to a computer, as was seen in Mr. Carter's class in Chapter 1.) If more than one group is assigned to a computer, you will need to establish a schedule for computer use. The teacher can create a schedule, or the student groups who are sharing the computer can establish their own schedule. It is probably wise to have the teacher create the first schedules so students can experience well-planned routines. After students have been involved with several integration lessons, they will become more adept at planning their own rotation schedules. In either situation, however, computer tasks must be divided equally among the group members.

As you plan your classroom layout, it is important to keep in mind that the setup of your classroom environment will affect the nature of your learning groups (Freiberg & Driscoll, 1996). For groups to work effectively over time, there must be

FIGURE 13-3 Classroom Layout for Independent Rotation

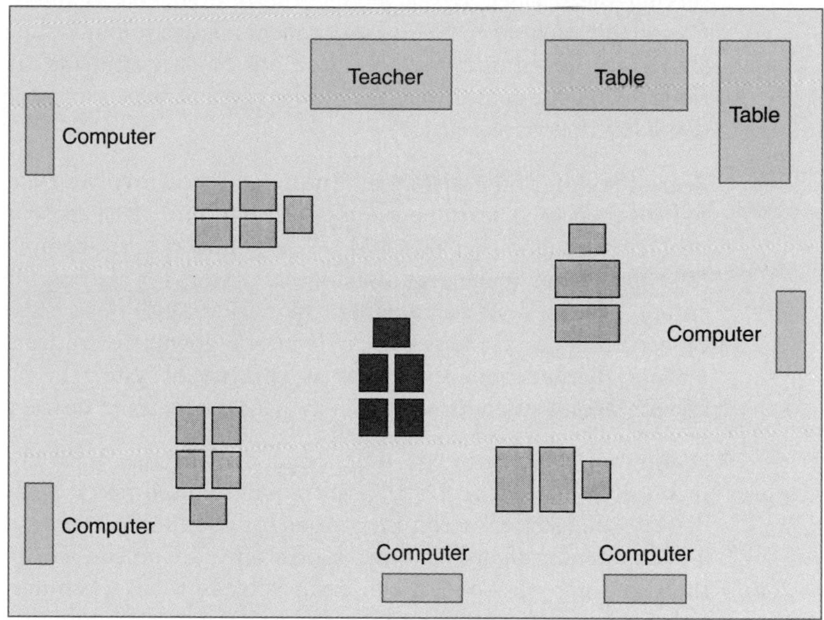

space and time to meet. Some teachers solve this dilemma by grouping desks into teams of three or four students. When planning for the layout of computers in the classroom, if at all possible, arrange the computers with enough room to accommodate from two to three chairs to better facilitate group work.

Managing Student Activities

Once students are using the computers, the teacher must facilitate student learning and manage three primary types of student activities: assisting students who need help with computer skills, dealing with any technical problems, and keeping students on task. Management suggestions for these activities are described in the following paragraphs.

Assisting Students with Computer Skills

When computers are added to a classroom, many teachers are faced with not only teaching subject-matter content, but also with teaching computer skills. There are several ways to help students acquire and use new computer skills. We will discuss four of those methods.

- Teacher modeling/demonstration
- Peer-modeling and assistance
- Technology posters or job aids
- Student handouts

Teacher Modeling/Demonstration. Students can learn new computer skills by observing the teacher as she models the desired task (Churchward, 1997). Monica Campbell teaches her fifth-grade students new computer skills by first modeling the skill with the aid of a large monitor. She has her students take notes and ask questions during the demonstration. Student groups then rotate to the computers to practice what they have learned.

Peer-modeling and Assistance. Another method involves training a corps of students to help their peers learn new computer skills and assist students that are experiencing problems (Sandholtz et al., 1990). When students at the computers need help, they can raise their hand or they can use another system for alerting the teacher or student assistant. One method uses a paper cup marker. With this system, a paper cup is placed on each monitor. If the paper cup is upside down, the students are OK; if it is turned upright, the student needs assistance. This type of system, or another type of "marker" system, avoids students waving their arms and causing distractions to get attention.

Technology Posters or Job Aids. Students can also learn computer skills by using technology posters or job aids of frequently used tasks. Technology posters consist of very brief step-by-step instructions for common computer tasks such as saving to a disk, opening an application, or printing a document. The posters are displayed by the computers so students can easily refer to them when needed (Figure 13-4). Job aids also provide easy, step-by-step instructions for commonly used computer functions and applications. They typically include more information than a poster can display, however, and are often kept in folders, in notebooks, or on note cards. The job aids are not put on display because they are created for tasks that are not completed every day. For example, job aids might be made for creating a simple database, a simple spreadsheet, or mail merge documents.

FIGURE 13-4 Technology Poster

Student Handouts. You can also assist with computer skills by including step-by-step instructions with the handouts used for a lesson. This method automatically integrates the content with the technology guidelines. Many times the teacher can create one handout that serves several purposes. The handout can include the problem statement, general instructions for the lesson, step-by-step guidelines for using the computer as a tool to solve the problem, and the Think Sheet questions (Chapter 3). Mary Kemp, a middle-school teacher, uses the following student handout shown in Figure 13-5 for a lesson she created on vertebrates.

Assisting with Technical Problems

The most frequent complaints of teachers in the ACOT classrooms were those related to technical problems (Sandholtz et al., 1990). The teachers indicated that their curriculum "got bogged down and students fell behind in their work" when the computers malfunctioned (p. 4). Teachers who participated in the Southern Technology Council study reported similar concerns (Casson et al., 1997). These concerns may have stemmed from school districts employing only one to three computer technicians for all the schools within their districts. When computer technicians are not available for teachers, they must then rely on some of the following methods for support (Casson et al., 1997; Sandholtz et al., 1990):

- Advice from other "expert" teachers in the same building, on an email list, or a Website
- Advice from "expert" students
- Troubleshooting handbooks or hotlines
- Adult volunteers (parents, college staff, business or government employees) willing to assist teachers and students with technological concerns
- Attendance at seminars and workshops to learn technical troubleshooting

Keeping Students on Task

Keeping students on task is often more challenging when students are working at computers. Computers are equipped with many fascinating features that beckon to inquisitive student minds. There are intriguing screen savers that can be modified, games to be played, and, of course, little mischievous pranks to be pulled. Students quickly learn that they can easily change the names of folders, (e.g., "Susie" to "Skinny Susie") or hide a student's file in an obscure folder somewhere on the hard drive. However, many of these student diversions occur because the required computer tasks are not relevant, interesting, or challenging. The following guidelines will help to keep students on task:

- Implement the NTeQ model:
    - Present students with interesting problems that use real-world information and data that they collect.
    - Use collaborative learning groups.
    - Involve students in decision making.

FIGURE 13-5 Lesson Handout with Technology Guidelines

Vertebrate Unit

Problem Statement:

Do all vertebrates lay eggs? If not, which groups do not? Are there any exceptions?

Directions:

To answer these questions, you will go to the computer assigned to your group and use the vertebrate database compiled by the class. Follow the directions below and work cooperatively with your group to sort the data by different fields, analyze the data to answer some questions, and complete a word processing document (using the format previously taught in class) that answers the questions. You will have the entire class period to complete the assignment. Turn the word processing document and the printouts of your database sorts by the end of the class.

Step-by-Step:

- Open the vertebrate database and select **Layout 2** under **Layout** on the menu bar.
- Select **Sort** under **Organize** on the menu bar.
- Select **Vertebrate Group** under the **Field List,** and click the **Move** button to move it to the **Sort Order** box. Click the **Ascending Order** button and then click **OK.** Print your sorted list.
- Following the directions above, select the fields listed below from the **Field** list, one at a time, and **Move** them to the **Sort Order** box. Be sure to **Move** the previous field from the **Sort Order** box before clicking **OK.** Print each sorted list before choosing the next field.

Sort by the following fields and print your sorted lists:

- Body Temperature
- Body Covering
- Method of Fertilization
- Method of Birth

- Review your sorted lists and work together to answer the questions listed below.
- Use word processing to answer the questions. Be sure to type the questions and then a short paragraph answering it.

Think Sheet Questions:

I. Do all vertebrates lay eggs? If not, which groups do not? Are there any exceptions?
II. What is the main body covering for each vertebrate group? Compare body temperature to body covering. How would you explain the major differences in body covering for cold-blooded versus warm-blooded vertebrates?
III. Compare body temperature to method of fertilization. Which groups are alike? Which group is different from the others?
IV. Compare method of fertilization to method of birth. What is the main difference between vertebrates with external fertilization versus those with internal fertilization? How do you explain this?
V. What are the major subgroups for each vertebrate group?

- Monitor student activities (Churchward, 1997):
  - Pass through an area about two minutes after students have started a new assignment. This delay allows the teacher to determine if the students understand what is required.
  - Provide individual assistance to students as it is needed.
  - Make general announcements only if several students are experiencing the same problem.
- Make it a habit to check the Internet sites the students have visited while conducting a search (e.g., use the **Go** option on Netscape's menu).
- Involve students in establishing class rules for using the computer. These rules could include the following:
  - Only use the computer for the assigned lesson unless special permission is obtained. Special permission might be given for students who have completed their assignments and want to create a customized screen saver, conduct an Internet search for an upcoming vacation, check on their favorite football team, or find the admission requirements for a college.
  - Never open or alter another student's computer files or any computer files other than your own.

The amount and type of materials that teachers manage changes when computers are added to the classroom.

MANAGING THE RESOURCES

Computers require more "stuff" to make them work than other learning tools, such as calculators or VCRs. Computers often need floppy or zip disks, software, CD-ROMs, a printer, and ink cartridges. Besides the computer needing more resources, the desktop of the computer also needs to be managed, and the computer itself needs to be maintained. This section provides some practical guidelines for managing these components.

Student Storage Devices

Each student should have at least one USB storage device, high-density floppy disk, zip disk, and/or CD-RW, based on the type of computers available. If students are going to create multimedia projects, such as PowerPoint presentations or HyperStudio stacks, they will need more than one disk if the computers do not have zip or CD-RW drives. Encourage students to purchase disks from a well-known company to avoid disk failures that result in the loss of student work. It is often best to keep the student disks in a centralized location rather than have the students keep track of their own disks. In a self-contained class, the teacher can have one disk storage box that holds the labeled student disks in alphabetical order by the student's last name. In a departmentalized setting, the teacher can have one disk storage box for each period. The disk storage boxes should be kept in a dry location without temperature extremes or direct sunlight. It is also important to keep the disks away from magnetic fields such as TVs, computer monitors, or speakers.

THE TEACHER'S DIARY

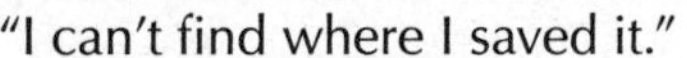

"I can't find where I saved it."

"I deleted it."
"I can't open the file."
"I have a virus!"
"I copied my friend's work."
"I copied my work and gave it to my friend."
"I deleted the printer driver."
"I can't connect to the Internet."
"I dropped my computer."
"I was playing a game when I should have been doing my work."
"I didn't back up my files and my computer crashed."
"My sister changed the settings on my computer."
"I know I wasn't supposed to be at that Internet site."
"Somebody took my power cord."
"I can't hear you because the printer is running."
"I left my computer on the bus."
"My computer keeps shorting out."
"I don't have my computer today. It's getting fixed."

Continued

Welcome to my world. Managing a computer classroom involves many unique problem solving situations, and new problems appear all the time. I've learned a lot over the course of the year and know that I have more to learn.

My students think that having a computer is really cool. One thing that students learn very quickly is how fun and easy it is to change their computer settings. Some enjoy doing this so much that they spend their class time looking at screen savers when they should be doing their work. Students learned how to have their work open while fiddling with the computer settings. They do this so that when I come by, all they need to do is exit out with a simple click of the mouse, and I'll never know what they were doing. Something that I have found that helps me monitor the computer use is to turn the students around so that their backs face my desk. This makes their computer screens visible to me from my desk (or other places in the room), and they don't know when they are being monitored.

Using a filtered e-mail service to transmit files has been a tremendous time saver. Because of the use of e-mail, I no longer copy files onto floppy disks and pass the disks around the room. Students can no longer say, "I didn't get the file." My response to them now is "You must have deleted it. Look in your recycle bin." Having a filter is helpful to prevent inappropriate picture files or messages from being passed around the classroom.

Something that I did not do this year, but intend to do next year, is to have a labeled floppy disk for each student to be kept in the classroom that is only for backing up files from "My Documents." Once per week I will give students 5 minutes to back up documents.

I think that setting up guidelines and expectations regarding computer use at the beginning of the year is very important. The majority of students will be responsible and trustworthy. However, inappropriate use of the computer by even one student can affect the integrity of the entire program. It is wise to prevent problems before they occur whenever possible.

Pam Shoemaker
Sixth-Grade Teacher

Software and CD-ROMs

Computers need software applications to be useful. Many computers come equipped with applications already loaded on the hard drive; however, most people want to enhance their computers by adding new applications. This new software normally comes with a CD-ROM containing the actual application and sometimes the user's guide. The CD is used to load the application on the hard drive. After the installation, the teacher needs to find a safe location to store the CD-ROM and the user's manual, if supplied. Some software includes a "key" or code to activate the software. We have found it useful to record the code on the CD storage case and on the inside cover of the manual. You will need this code if you ever reinstall or upgrade the software. If you are using software that is licensed by your school or district, you can probably obtain the key from your support group. The manuals need to be kept in a place that is easily accessible for quick reference. The CDs can be stored in a box

Power Tip

Managing CD-ROMs

There are several applications such as encyclopedias that require the CD-ROM to be in the drive to run the application. You should review the software documentation and/or contact the CD-ROM company, because some allow teachers to install the software on more than one computer. The software (i.e., a search engine) is useless without the CD-ROM. If you are *allowed* to install the software on more than one computer, your students will have more flexibility in using the application, but only one student can use the CD-ROM at a time.

marked as "Master Software Disks." There are strict copyright laws regarding software applications; therefore, it is very important to always have the original software for all applications on each computer.

Printing Supplies

When students complete their assignments on a computer or do an Internet or CD-ROM search for information, they have to use a printer to see a paper copy of their work. For printers to function, they need paper and some form of cartridge, both of which can become costly if a monitoring system is not used. The cost of printer cartridges can be reduced by purchasing recycled ones or refilling them with ink when using an ink jet printer.

The amount of printing can be minimized by having students complete the majority of their editing on the computer. When students are conducting searches from the Internet or a CD-ROM, have them use the Preview function of the Print dialog box to determine how many pages the document contains. They can then print only the pages they actually need. If students are mainly interested in the text information from a Web page, the text can be highlighted, copied, and pasted into a word processing document that will typically use less ink and paper than printing original Web pages.

File Management

There are multiple ways to manage the files stored on a computer. Following are some guidelines for managing the desktop of a classroom computer.

It is helpful to designate one folder for student work. This folder can be titled "Student Folder." Folders within the "Student Folder" can be arranged by either student's last name (Figure 13-6) or subject area, with student work by last name within each subject area folder (Figure 13-7).

Establish a specific file name for the students to use for each assignment to make it easier to locate their work. For example, the file name can include the initial for the subject area, date, and student initials. The file name for a math paper completed on February 11 by Tina Grimes would be: M2_11TG.doc; a science assignment, completed on November 7 by Kenneth Thompson would be labeled: S11_7KT.doc.

FIGURE 13-6 Student Folder by Student Last Name

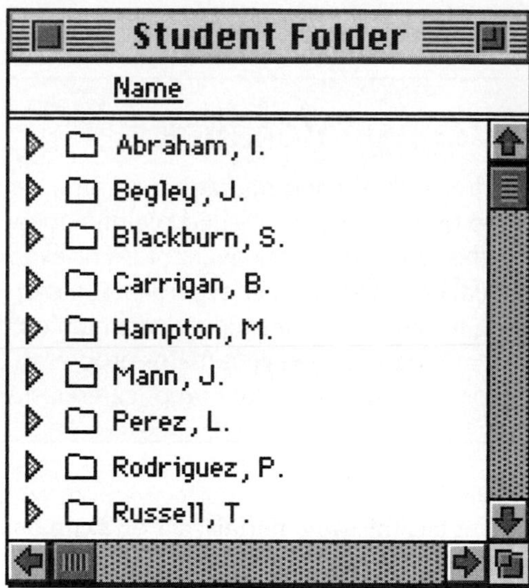

FIGURE 13-7 Student Folder by Subject Area

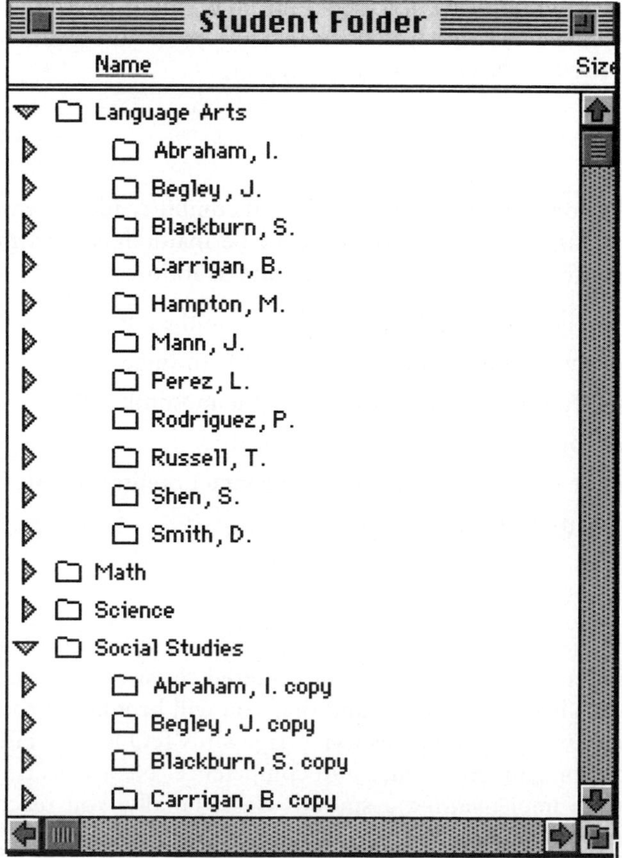

Power Tip

Computer Maintenance

Computers are kind of like cars and children—they need maintenance on a regular basis. Unfortunately, most teachers do not have the time to perform this needed maintenance, and they may even lack the expertise. Have you considered the other resources available? For example, you might find that many parents in your school have a great deal of computer expertise. You can form a parents group that might meet at the school one evening a month to do computer maintenance. Often, this simple routine maintenance that takes only a few minutes can prevent major problems. Similarly, some parents might be willing to donate time to more serious repairs or complicated tasks.

If more than one student has the same initials, a 1 or 2 can be added after the initials. To help students remember how to label their files, a poster with labeling keys could be displayed in the computer area. Also, require each student to include his or her name in the document in case there is confusion about the file name.

Computers also need frequent maintenance. You may want to establish a time once a week for students to copy files from a hard drive to a floppy or removable disk and then delete them from the hard drive. Additional maintenance suggestions are discussed in the next section.

Computer Care

Not only do the computer resources and computer file systems need to be managed, but the computers themselves need to be maintained and managed. Some simple guidelines for computer management are as follows:

- Do not allow any food, drinks, or gum in the computer area.
- Avoid touching the computer monitor with fingers.
- Use screen saver software to protect the monitor.
- Secure cords and cables away from traffic.
- Clean the mouse tracking balls and contact points with alcohol on a regular basis.
- Use a virus protection software.

SUMMARY

A key theme that runs through this chapter is that it takes time and careful planning to achieve a well-managed student-centered classroom that has students using computers. It is helpful to understand that you will be going through three stages as you gain the knowledge and skills to manage an NTeQ lesson. First is the survival stage, in which you gain confidence and competence. Next is Mastery, in which you concentrate on implementing a smooth class. Finally, you reach the impact stage, in which student learning is the center focus because technology use has become routine. When establishing your management plan it is important to assist your students in achieving a computer learning culture and to follow the basic guidelines for setting classroom rules. Your assignments will vary based on the number of computers available to the students and the rotation plan chosen: group or independent rotation. You will need to assist students with learning computer skills, keep students who are using the computer on task, and solve technical problems. A final aspect of managing classroom use of computers is taking care of the extra resources, managing the computer desktops, and maintaining the equipment.

AT THE CLASSROOM'S DOORSTEP

Questions Teachers Ask

It sounds good to have a corps of students who are trained as computer assistants, but how do we get these students trained?

Students can become knowledgeable about computers in several different ways. One approach is to include a group of students when the teachers receive technology training. Another way is to have technology-savvy teachers offer mini-lessons before or after school or at lunch. If a school has a computer lab that is staffed with a computer teacher, this teacher may offer specialized training to future student technology assistants. Business or university personnel or parents can also volunteer to train students in basic computer troubleshooting or operations.

Managing computers in my classroom sounds expensive. Are there some ways to save money?

Teachers can save money on disk storage boxes by creatively using inexpensive plastic bins. Note cards can be used to create alphabetical dividers for the disks. Money can be saved on paper by printing on both sides of paper that has not been wrinkled or damaged. Businesses often will give classroom teachers paper from discarded reports, letterhead that has changed, or other documents that are no longer used. The recycled paper can be used for draft copies of student work. Similarly, some businesses will donate older computers for classroom use.

How do I find "good" floppy disks?

We wish we had a good answer for this question, because we have many stacks of bad disks. One class project is to track the number of bad disks and the reliability of others. Once you find a reliable brand, stick with it as long as it works. Floppy disks seem to have a limited lifetime based on use. Some users state that you should never use a floppy disk for more than 100 save operations. A good defense is to have a good disk utility software that you can use to recover files on a damaged disk. Once a student has a problem with a floppy disk, copy the files to another floppy and discard the bad disk. We have found it is better to be safe than sorry when dealing with disks.

TECHNOLOGY INTEGRATION ACTIVITIES

To access the activities that connect the content of the text with the Companion Website and other technology, please go to the Activities module in Chapter 13 of the Companion Website at *http://www.prenhall.com/morrison.*

NTEQ PORTFOLIO ACTIVITIES: MANAGING THE CLASSROOM

Please complete the following activities as part of your NTeQ Portfolio on managing the classroom.

Reflections

1. Do you know that teachers typically go through three distinct stages as they learn to manage the integration of computers into their classroom—with "survival" being the first stage?
   - *Reflection Question:* Create a table that lists the key traits of a teacher at each of the three stages: survival, mastery, and impact.
2. How do you ensure equal access when you have 26 students and only three computers?
   - *Reflection Question:* Choose an NTeQ lesson you developed for an earlier chapter and create a computer rotation schedule that provides the 26 students equal access to the three computers.
3. OK, I have 26 students using three computers—how do we keep track of their work?
   - *Reflection Question:* Use a draw program or a table to create a desktop filing system for the 26 students to use on the three computers. Write a brief scenario of how you would explain the system to fifth-grade students.

Classroom Computer Rules

Create a poster that displays the rules your students will follow when using computers in your classroom.

Job Aids

Choose a previously developed lesson that includes student use of computer tasks that may be unfamiliar to them. Create a step-by-step job aid for this lesson.

REFERENCES

Casson, L., Bauman, J., Fisher, E., Sumpter, J., & Tornatzky, L. G. (1997). *Making technology happen: Best practices and policies from exemplary K–12 schools.* Report. Southern Technology Council, Research Triangle Park, N.C., Southern Growth Publications.

Churchward, B. (1997, September 11). *The honor level system: Discipline by design—11 techniques for better classroom discipline* [On-line]. Available: http://members.aol.com/churchward/hls/techniques.html.

Freiberg, H. J., & Driscoll, A. (1996). *Universal teaching strategies.* Needham Heights, MA: Allyn & Bacon.

Hall, G. E., & Loucks, S. (1979). Teacher concerns as a basis for facilitating and personalizing staff development. In A. Lieberman and L. Miller (Eds.), *Staff development: New demands, new realities, new perspectives.* New York: Teachers Press.

Mayeski, F. (1997, May 6). The metamorphosis of classroom management [On-line]. Available: http://www.mcrel.org/products/noteworthy/noteworthy/franm.asp.

McClelland, S. (1996, March 20). The one computer classroom [On-line]. Available: http://www.indep.k12.mo.us/THS/lesley/mcclelland/one%20computer.html.

Ryba, K., & Anderson, B. (1993). *Learning with computers: Effective teaching strategies.* Eugene, OR: International Society for Technology in Education.

Sandholtz, J. H., Ringstaff, C., & Dwyer, D. (1990). *Teaching in high tech environments: Classroom management revisited, first–fourth year findings.* Apple Classrooms of Tomorrow Research Report Number 10. [On-line]. Available: http://www.apple.com/education/k12/leadership/acot/library.html.

Weade, R., & Evertson, C. M. (1991). The construction of lessons in effective and less effective classrooms. In U. Casanova, D. C. Berliner, P. Placier, & L. Weiner (Eds.), *Classroom management: Readings in educational research* (pp. 136–159). Washington, DC: National Education Association.

Wiebe, J. (1993). *Computer tools and problem solving in mathematics.* Wilsonville, OR: Franklin, Beedle & Associates Inc.

Willing, K. R., & Girard, S. (1990). *Learning together: Computer-integrated classrooms.* Markham, Ontario: Pembroke Publishers Limited.

KEY TOPICS

The Role of Assessment
- What Is Assessment?
- Assessment and the NTeQ Model

Assessment Tools

Task List
- When to Develop Task Lists
- What Is Included
- Types of Task Lists
- Creating the Task List
- Using the Task List

The Rubric
- When to Develop Rubrics
- What Is Included
- Types of Rubrics
- Creating a Rubric
- Using a Rubric

Chapter 14

The Role of Assessment

To achieve a level of successful performance in our society, it is no longer enough to know factual information and how to perform specific tasks; rather it is critical to also know when to use the information and tasks and how to adapt them to new situations. Therefore, to better prepare students for this environment, we must shift our thinking to realize that "what is important is how and whether students organize, structure, and use that information in context to solve complex problems" (Dietel, Herman, & Knuth, 1991, p. 2). In looking at this type of learning, it becomes apparent that traditional testing methods are inadequate measures of student achievement. Therefore new or alternative forms of assessment are necessary. This chapter discusses both traditional and alternative forms of assessment, with particular emphasis on the use of task lists and rubrics.

GETTING STARTED

What Do I Know?

1. At what level should students be involved with creating assessments for their schoolwork?
2. How well do tests really demonstrate what students know and are able to do?
3. How can assessments help students to improve their thinking and level of achievement?

Classroom Snapshot

BACK IN TIME IN BROWNSVILLE

Every year Mrs. Burbage teaches a unit about Brownsville, the town in which the school where she teaches is located. This year she chose the history of Brownsville. Her principal is emphasizing the use of lessons that are more authentic, so she decided to go beyond her typical history lesson from the Chamber of Commerce publication "The History of Brownsville" and have students create "Brownsville: Back in Time" booklets. She told the class that each student was to create a Brownsville history booklet on a topic of their choice. The booklet was to have a cover sheet with a student-drawn color picture, along with five pages of historical information about the selected topic. She reminded the students that they must do their "best work" because the booklets are going to be displayed in the hall for parent night.

At the end of the unit, Mrs. Burbage was very pleased with the student booklets. Although there were varying levels of performance, it was obvious that most students had done careful research, analyzed their collected information, and selected appropriate areas of focus for the final product. The results were far beyond her expectations. As she graded each one, she felt limited in being able to express the key areas of success to the students. She did add comments like "very good paragraph," "nice organization," "great description of the photo," but the words didn't really tell the students *why* it was good. On the other side, when student work did not reflect a "best effort," she was again limited to comments such as "paragraph needs more research support" and "rewrite so it is easier to understand." Mrs. Burbage found it difficult to provide consistent feedback, plus it became very time-consuming to add detailed comments. She wished she had some way of communicating expectations about the work before students completed the assignment and a way to let them know the specific areas of success and needed growth. She decided to do an Internet search to determine if there was an alternative way to assess her students. Her search led her to the discovery of rubrics and task lists.

THE ROLE OF ASSESSMENT

What Is Assessment?

We all have a general idea of what it means to assess "something," but let's examine two definitions of the term to align our thinking. The *American Heritage Online Dictionary* (2000) provided the following definition of *assess*: "to determine the value, significance, or extent of [what is to be assessed]." To place this in the context of education, Black and Wiliam (1998) define assessment as ". . . all those activities undertaken by teachers—and by their students in assessing themselves—that provide information to be used as feedback to modify teaching and learning activities (p. 1)." In today's classrooms, assessment of student learning has been expanded to include not only traditional types of assessments, but also some forms of alternative assessment measures. The following section discusses both methods.

Traditional Assessment

When describing traditional assessments, we are referring to tests, quizzes, or exams. As we know, these types of instruments typically comprise multiple-choice, true/false, fill in the blank, matching, and, of course, the dreaded essay questions. The primary purpose of traditional assessments is to measure the degree to which students have learned content knowledge and simple process skills, such as long division or punctuation rules, rather than to measure more complex skills and processes (Marzano, Pickering, & McTighe, 1993). However, multiple-choice questions can be written to assess all levels of Bloom's Taxonomy (Morrison, Ross, & Kemp, 2004). For specific instruction on writing these types of items, see the Resources list at the end of this chapter.

Black and Wiliam (1998) issue three areas of caution when using traditional assessments: effective learning, negative impact, and managerial role. The first concern deals with the influence that traditional testing can have on effective learning. They conclude that the "tests used by teachers [normally] encourage rote and superficial learning even when teachers say they want to develop understanding" (p. 1). The second issue concerns the often negative impact of "overemphasizing" the process of scoring and assigning marks while the "giving of useful advice and the learning function are underemphasized" (p. 2). The last area deals with using the process of assigning grades as a way to serve "social and managerial functions, often at the expense of the learning function" (p. 2). Or, "the collection of marks to fill in records is given higher priority than the analysis of pupil's work to discern learning needs" (p. 2).

The above concerns, though, are more a result of practice than of the limitations of the assessments. All assessments can be used to monitor progress and diagnose student strengths and weaknesses (Herman, Aschbacher, & Winters, 1992). The traditional types of assessment are very useful for monitoring whether or not students have acquired specific knowledge and skills; however, they are limited in measuring the *application* of more complex skills and processes such as problem solving or setting up and conducting an experiment. Therefore a need for an alternative type of assessment has been established.

Alternative Assessment

Alternative assessment, also referred to as authentic, direct, and performance based, is defined as "a process of gathering evidence and documenting a student's learning and growth in an alternative context" (Ryan, 1994, p. 1). These measures serve to not only "monitor" or keep the teacher informed of student acquisition of knowledge and skills, but also to diagnose specific learning needs in order to modify learning and instructional approaches (Herman, et al., 1992). In other words, the assessments can be used in a formative manner, to guide student learning during the lesson, as well as in a summative way to assess learning at the end of a lesson (Black & Wiliam, 1998). The key thing to remember is that alternative assessments are intended to measure the *application* as well as the acquisition of knowledge and skills.

So what does it take to use alternative assessments? Unfortunately, it is not as easy as copying one out of a book and using it in your "regular, quite traditional" classroom.

To effectively use alternative assessments, the classroom environment needs to reflect new approaches to learning and instruction. Below are some common components that are necessary for successfully implementing the use of alternative assessments:

- Students are involved in setting goals and criteria for assessment.
- Students are actively involved in the learning process.
- Students use higher-order thinking and/or problem solving.
- Tasks are meaningful and often contextualized in real-world applications.
- Metacognitive, collaborative, and interpersonal skills are often assessed.
- Student responses are scored according to specified criteria, known *in advance,* which define standards for good performance (Dietel et al., 1991).

When examining these components, it becomes clear that they reflect the NTeQ approach to learning and integrating computers into the curriculum. The next section describes the role of assessment within this model.

Assessment and the NTeQ Model

The NTeQ approach to integrating computers into the classroom is problem based, real world, student centered, hands on, collaborative, and dependent on using the computer as a tool. Within this environment, a combination of traditional and alternative assessments can be used; however, because of the nature of the engaged learning environment and the NTeQ final products, it is apparent that alternative assessments are an imperative component and that traditional types of assessments will be used less frequently.

Traditional or Alternative?

To determine which type of assessment to use, begin by reviewing the learning objectives for the lesson (Figure 14-1). Identify what the student needs to recall and what the student needs to apply (Morrison et al., 2004). An example that involves recalling information might be to list the presidents in sequential order from first to current. If this same objective was presented in a manner in which students applied the information rather than recalled it, they could group the presidents by four common traits found among all presidents. The next step is to decide if students need to *specifically* demonstrate acquisition of the information (e.g., identify parts of a sentence). If the answer is yes, create a traditional form of assessment, such as students circling the nouns and underlining the verbs in sentences. It also may be necessary to use traditional tests when students are required to take standardized tests that contain information covered in your lesson to provide practice within this type of assessment.

If students are not required to specifically demonstrate *acquisition* of knowledge, its attainment can be ascertained through the completion of the *application* portion of the learning objectives. If you look at the example above, when students group presidents by common traits, the task demands a higher level of processing and requires students to apply knowledge and skills. With this type of a task, there is no "right" answer because students can choose any number of categories for grouping the presidents—gender, party, previous employment, college, birth order, to name a

FIGURE 14-1 Traditional Versus Alternative Assessment Flow Chart

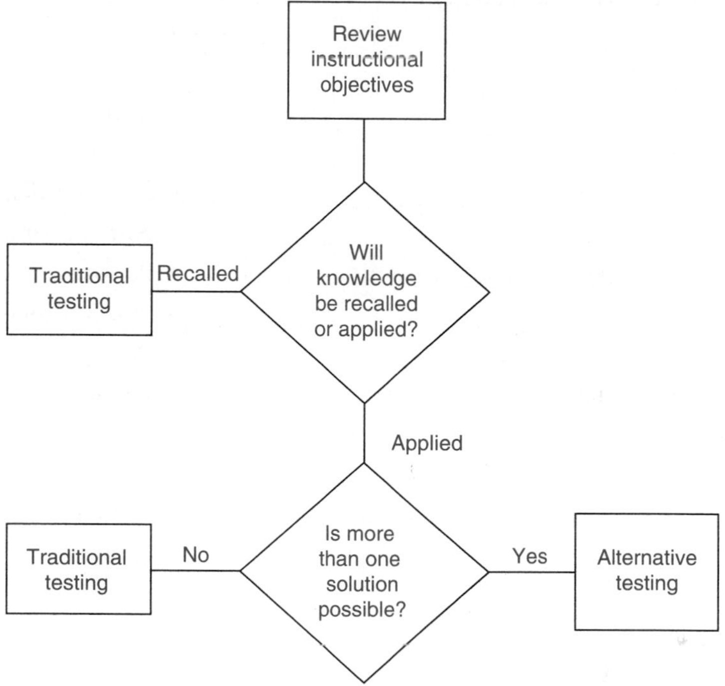

few. It would be very difficult to derive a traditional form of assessment for this type of task. Therefore an alternative form of assessment will need to be used. The types of alternative assessments will be discussed in a later section of this chapter.

While using the NTeQ model, you also may want to assess other types of learning that go beyond the content domain. These could include the application of technology skills, as listed in the National Education Technology Standards for Students (NETS, 2000), collaborative skills, or metacognitive skills. The section on rubrics will go into detail on identifying the types of learning to assess. Next we will discuss the types of products that can be used with these new forms of assessment.

What to Assess

As presented in Chapter 4, it is obvious that with the NTeQ model students produce a wide variety of products that require alternative assessments. A partial list of items that can be used for alternative assessments is seen in Figure 14-2.

As you examine these items, you may be thinking that some of these aren't "new"—you created a salt map *exhibit* of your home state in fifth grade, *demonstrated* an erupting volcano for seventh grade science, and wrote a *report* about democracy when in high school. Your grade for each product was more than likely determined by whether or not the student included "all the pieces," if it looked good, and if it was "right." Did the salt map have everything labeled, were the labels neatly written, and was it "right?" The volcano needed to explode, the drawings needed to show how volcanoes erupt,

FIGURE 14-2 Appropriate Student Products for Use with Alternative Assessments

- Billboard
- Book
- Brochure
- Collage
- Collection
- Comic strip
- Computer-based instruction
- Database
- Demonstration
- Diorama
- Editorial
- Exhibit
- Experiment
- Game
- Graph
- Illustration
- Interview
- Limerick
- Magazine advertisement
- Map
- Mobile
- Multimedia simulation
- Mural
- Museum display
- Newspaper article
- Performance
- Photo display
- Play
- Poetry
- Puppet show
- Report
- Riddle
- Slide show
- Song
- Timeline
- TV news report
- TV weather report
- Website

and again everything needed to be "right." The "rightness" is determined by the teacher's knowledge and skills, but most of the time you and your classmates do not know until it is too late, and sometimes not even after the grade is assigned, what it takes to be "right." Here is an example to show the difference between a traditional type of scoring and a more alternative measure:

> *Traditional:* [Students] will demonstrate an understanding of the scientific method.
>
> *Alternative:* [Students] will build into his or her investigation a definition of the problem, a review of literature about the topic, a listing of hypotheses that could be tested, an experimental design that controls for all variables except those in the hypothesis that are being tested, and an explanation of how findings were used to find the solution for the original problem (Herman, et al., 1992, p. 3).

As you can see, the traditional assessment described above is vague and assumes that there is only one "true" scientific method. With this type of assessment, each student has to assume that he or she can also ascertain what the true scientific method

Students soon learn to use task lists and rubrics to help improve performance.

is and that the final product will demonstrate the needed "understanding." On the other hand, the alternative assessment clearly delineates the specific components deemed necessary to "demonstrate an understanding of the scientific method." Therefore the students not only know what is expected to demonstrate this understanding, but the assessment, which the students have at the start of the lesson, also serves as an instructional tool to teach the scientific method as students complete the work. Two primary tools used to share the assessment criteria with students are the task list and the rubric.

ASSESSMENT TOOLS

One of the greatest differences between alternative assessments and traditional assessments is the degree of student involvement with the assessment process and student knowledge of what is expected to achieve success. In this section, the task list and rubric are presented as a means of guiding student learning during the instructional process and ascertaining the degree to which students applied the specified knowledge and skills. The task list is basically a check sheet that students use to guide them while working on a project. The list goes beyond being a tally, though, in that students not only mark off each step, but also assess the quality of what is produced. In Figure 14-3, you can see that students circle the face that shows how they feel about each item they complete.

The task list, in and of itself, is a great tool and would improve the completion and quality of student work if it were used consistently. But as you and I know, a student product can have all of the components and still not represent a high level

FIGURE 14-3 Sample Task List

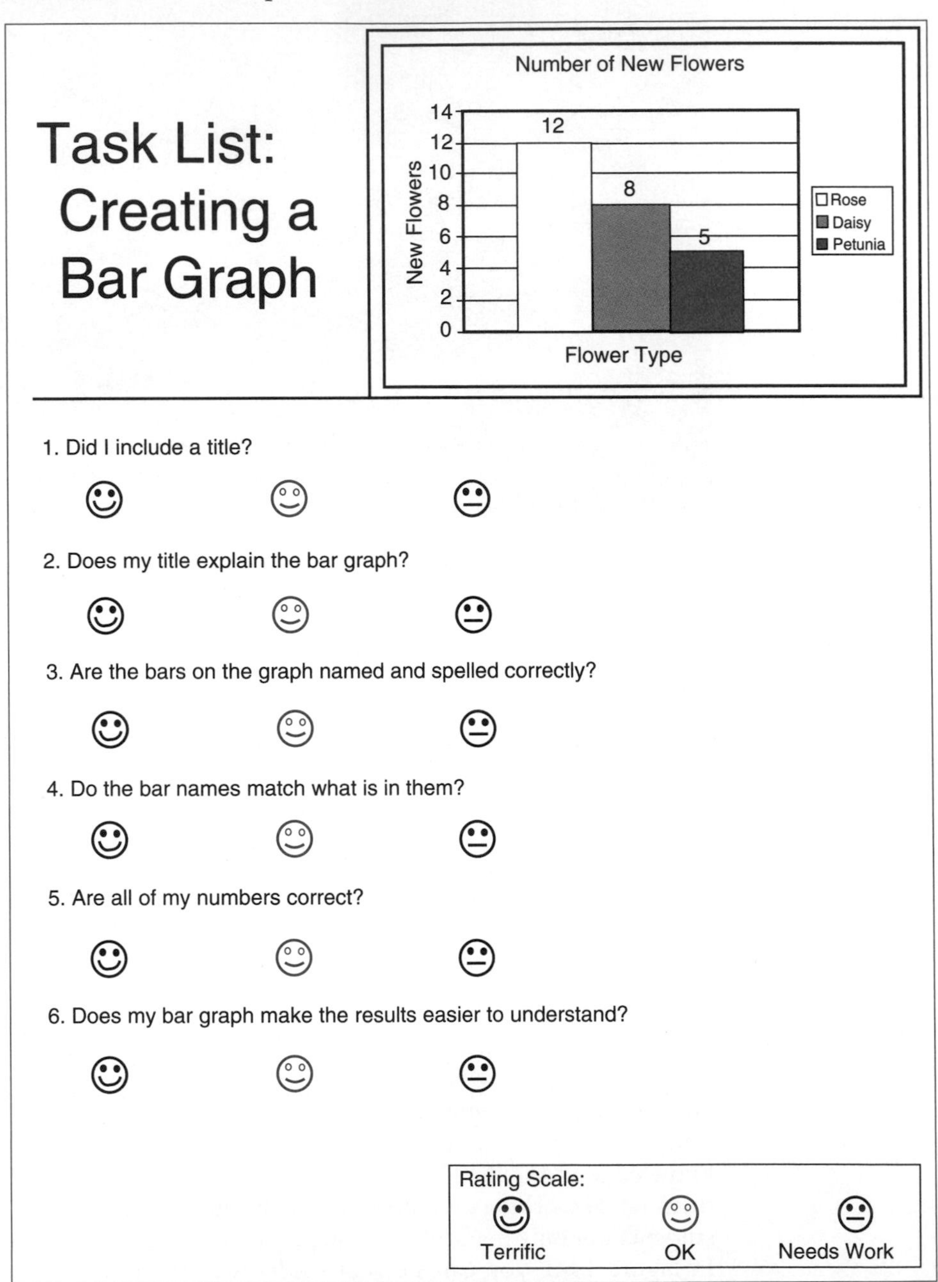

of understanding and achievement. The overall product may lack cohesiveness. The overall findings may lack sufficient support for the conclusions reported. The presentation of ideas may be concise and complete, but the overall flow of the material may not create a relevant or interesting depiction of the content. These aspects of

TABLE 14-1 Sample Rubric

Newspaper Article on Seatbelt Safety

Objective or Performance	Beginning 1	Developing 2	Accomplished 3	Exemplary 4	Score
1. Students will write a persuasive article on why drivers should wear seat belts.	Persuasive arguments are not clear or concise and had very poor references made to supporting graphics.	Persuasive arguments are fairly clear and concise. References made to graphics provide limited support.	Persuasive arguments are clear, concise, and articulate. References made to supporting graphics are useful.	Persuasive arguments are very clear, concise, and articulate. Excellent references made to supporting graphics.	
2. Students will generate spreadsheet charts that demonstrate a trend.	The charts show very little about seat belt use. The title, labels, and legend are missing or incomplete.	The charts show limited aspects of seat belt use. The title, labels, legend, and type of chart provide incomplete support.	The charts demonstrate trends in seat belt use. The title, labels, legend, and type of chart support understanding.	The charts clearly demonstrate trends in seat belt use. Excellent choice of title, labels, legend, and type of chart.	

student work comprise what was described earlier as being "right"—or that vague knowledge possessed only by the teacher. Not anymore!

The rubric defines what is meant by being "right" in a clear and understandable manner. It takes all the pieces and places them into descriptions of final student products—ranging from ideal to did not fully "meet the lesson requirements" (Table 14-1). It is the assessment tool that ties it all together and shows both the teacher and student where specific support is needed and where praise should be given. Both forms of assessment tools are discussed in the following sections.

TASK LIST

Task lists, in general, are not anything new. For some time, teachers have provided students with assignment sheets, or a list of what a particular student product should include. The difference, as mentioned, is that in the past it was generated solely by the teacher; its purpose was limited to what should be included, and it typically did not address quality of the work, although at times the list would contain things like "use correct grammar" and "check your spelling." Following are some guidelines for developing task lists.

When to Develop Task Lists

A task list obviously is developed after the lesson is planned and the student products have been defined. With the NTeQ model, this would refer to the assessment portion of the 10-step planning model. If you want to involve your students in developing a task list, it is best for you to initially develop a draft of critical items that need to be included. This draft will help you to guide student input to ensure that all critical components become part of the final task list.

What Is Included

A task list can include anything that needs to be emphasized with a particular lesson. Typical items that can be included are seen in the following list:

- *Lesson content* (endangered species, Civil War, fractions, folk dances)
- *Process skills* required to complete the task (outlining, multiplication, concept mapping)
- *Work habits* (writing neatly, organizing materials, staying focused)
- *Social/group skills* (completing assigned tasks, taking turns, listening)
- *Technology skills* (saving on disk, formatting margins, labeling a graph, inserting graphics)
- *Metacognitive or thinking skills* (logging activities, think-alouds, self-reflection)

Educators in Connecticut's Pomperaug Regional School District 15 (1996) suggest that the following *key* question be asked to determine which items should be included on the task list: "What are the elements of quality for this project?" (p. 86). The answers to this question will serve as an outline for items to include on the task list. Of course, as you can see, the list could easily become very long when assessing a variety of areas. To help alleviate this concern, a set of task lists that concentrate on a different subset of skills, such as work habits or social skills can be developed. Then these "generic" assessments can be added to lessons on a rotating basis.

Types of Task Lists

There are two basic types of task lists: *generic* and *content specific* (Educators, 1996). It is often helpful to create several generic task lists for commonly performed tasks, such as creating a poster, generating a graph, developing a PowerPoint presentation, writing a persuasive paper, or writing a book summary. Once a set of generic task lists is created, the content-specific task lists can refer to fulfilling all of the criteria on a specified generic task list, as well as the content-specific items. For example, if students were creating a poster on bridges, the content-specific task list could include the following:

- Sample drawings of the three types of bridges
- Written descriptions of each bridge type

- Translation of bridge types into basic geometric shapes
- Fulfillment of all criteria on poster task list

The sample task list seen in Figure 14-2 is an example of a generic list for creating a bar graph that could be used with students in early elementary grades.

Creating the Task List

The three main things to consider when creating the task list are as follows:

1. *Write* with easy-to-understand concise wording
2. *Group* items by type of learning
3. Choose appropriate *rating scales*

Write

When writing the items, make sure they clearly define what the student is to accomplish. For example, rather than using "Did I correctly apply the rules of grammar?" use more explicit descriptions, such as "Did I capitalize the beginning word?," and "Did I use correct ending punctuation?"

Group

The next considerations for writing a task list are to group items by categories of learning tasks and clearly label each set of items in the classification. The group titles will be determined by each assignment, but some sample group headings might include the following:

- Content
- Use of language
- Organization
- Mechanics
- Graphic layout
- Technology skills
- Cooperation skills
- Thinking skills

Scale

The remaining consideration is the rating scale. The rating scale needs to clearly denote different levels of performance, yet not demean the students. Notice in Figure 14-4, the "faces" go from a very big smile, to a partial smile, to a neutral look rather than to a sad face. If a student's performance is less than ideal, it is important to use the assessment feedback to show students that they can *always* improve. Smiley faces tend to work well with young students, but as students progress to upper grades, you

FIGURE 14-4 Task List by Grade Level

Task List Rating Scales by Grade Level

Grade 2—Persuasive Communication

I drew a picture of my favorite part of the story.

I drew details.

Grade 3—Persuasive Writing

Opening Statement

T: I stated my opinion very clearly.
O: I stated my opinion.
W: I did not state my opinion.

Reasons for My Opinion

T: Reasons for my opinion are well supported.
O: Reasons for my opinion are somewhat supported.
W: I did not include reasons for my opinion.

T = Terrific **O = OK** **W = Needs Work**

Grade 5—Persuasive Writing

	Assessment Points		
		Earned Assessment	
Element	Points Possible	Self	Teacher
My position is stated clearly.	______	______	______
I have at least two reasons to support my position.	______	______	______

Grade 9—Persuasive Writing

	Assessment Points		
		Earned Assessment	
Element	Points Possible	Self	Teacher
Writer introduces and clearly states a position.	______	______	______
Position is supported by at least four main points.	______	______	______

Adapted from *A teacher's guide to performance-based learning and assessment,* Educators in Connecticut's Pomperaug Regional School District 15. 1996, pp. 95–98

can replace the faces with an actual rating scale that uses terms or terms and numbers. For example, Figure 14-4 depicts how a rating scale might change across grade levels (Educators, 1996, pp. 95–98).

CHECK IT OUT 14-1

Title: Famous Bridges

Grade: High School

Problem: *Students are to create a task list to assess a "Famous Bridges" poster they are to create. The poster is to compare and contrast the geometric aspects of the support structure of the three famous bridges.*

Activity: Download the task list template and the "Famous Bridges" assignment sheet. Open the template in a word processing application and use information from the assignment sheet to create a task list for the poster.

Link to these resources and activities in the Check It Out module for this chapter of the Companion Website.

Using the Task List

As mentioned, students should be involved in the creation of a task list, if at all possible. By participating in the creation of the task list, the students gain some ownership in determining what is to be assessed. You may find that students often set goals higher than you might. Once the final task list is determined, review each item with the class to ensure that students understand the specific requirements. It is important that this session is very open and all students feel comfortable to seek clarification. Students must understand what is required of them if they are to achieve the expected outcomes.

Encourage students to frequently refer to the task list as they proceed through the various steps of assignment completion. If, during the lesson, students ask you questions regarding specific requirements, you can refer them to the task list, indicating that they can then ask additional questions if they still need clarification. An additional benefit of using a task list is that it saves you from repeating lesson requirements to individual students who may not have been paying attention.

With the use of a task list, students learn to self-reflect on their work to determine progress and quality of individual components. If the task list includes a section for peer review, students can not only improve their individual quality of work, but also reinforce the content and skills being learned by examining how other students approach the same learning tasks. When the products are complete, students can submit the completed task list with the final product, and teacher rating and comments can be added, if appropriate.

Students may need teacher guidance when first using self-assessments such as rubrics.

THE RUBRIC

We described the rubric as an assessment tool that examines the final product in its totality. Stix (1996) provides the following description of a rubric:

> A rubric is a carefully designed ratings chart that is drawn up jointly by the teacher and students. Along one side of the rubric are listed the criteria that the teacher and students decide are the most important ideas to be mastered in the lesson. Across the top of the rubric are listed the ratings that will be used to assess how well students master each of those criterion. . . . Within each ranking, there may also be numerical gradations, depending on whether a student performs at the higher or lower level of that category. (p. 1)

In the following sections, we will discuss when to develop rubrics, what to include, types of rubrics, how to create a rubric, and how to use rubrics to enhance and assess student learning.

When to Develop Rubrics

Just as with task lists, rubrics are developed during your lesson planning process after you have defined the final student products. This, again, may be a draft of the final rubric, because students need to be involved in the process of determining the final components to be included. By having a draft of the critical items for which students need to be assessed, you can guide student thinking during the time that the students are developing the rubric, to ensure that they "add" these critical items to the final measure.

THE TEACHER'S DIARY

Believe it or not, I had never been exposed to using a rubric in college. The first I had heard of them was when our staff was sent to a conference on authentic assessment. Our school district was working on incorporating more writing across the curriculum and we needed help on assessing this work. I teach ninth-grade science, so I was very familiar with grading lab reports, but not grading larger projects. I had incorporated several projects into my instruction, but was still not satisfied with the grading procedure I used.

After the conference, I was still unsure about the usefulness of the standard rubric that uses a ranking of 1 to 5. I thought my procedure needed work, but the rubric appeared to be just more work, not a cure for my problem. We agreed, as a staff, to go ahead with incorporating a 1 to 5 rubric across the curriculum. I worked out what I felt would be a 5 project—all requirements met and surpassed, and felt I might have a good plan for the project *Minerals Used in Industry.* I took my rubric and presented it to the class. I was in for a surprise. They wanted to add requirements! Their ideas were a stroke of luck. I always encourage the students to have input into the requirements for a project. I passed out the new and improved rubric with the instruction sheet and discussed it with the class. There were questions, but it seemed as if they understood the requirements.

Presentation day was a big surprise. It was so easy to grade the projects! Everything was so clear. If they did not meet the requirements for a 5, then they dropped to a 4, and so on. Students had few questions or complaints on their evaluations because the rubric was reviewed beforehand. The parents were aware of the grading rubric and used it to help prepare their student. It was a success all around.

The rubric has allowed our staff to compare data across the curriculum. We compared students' scores on reading skills and math skills. The staff was able to design strategies to improve reading and comprehension skills for all of our students based on this information. The data was that easy to apply.

Rubrics for assessment did not just give us an easier and more reliable method of grading in our own classrooms, but also provided important data used in school improvement.

Tracy Lamerato
Ninth-Grade Science Teacher

What Is Included

Most rubrics comprise three primary components: (1) assessment criteria, (2) rating scales, and (3) levels of performance, although other components, such as a comment section, can be added. A great deal of flexibility exists within each component to assist the teacher in creating rubrics that meet the individualized assessment needs of a wide variety of student products.

Assessment Criteria

This component of the rubric defines the specific areas of assessment for the student product. The terms used are typically very precise and descriptive. The rubric can be designed to have one overarching criterion, such as scientific drawing, or it can be broken down into more specific criteria under a more generalized topic. For example, a math rubric may have computation and logical reasoning as its criteria, and a writing rubric may have consistency of thought, completeness, grammar, and spelling. Assessment criteria may also address different areas of learning, for example, technology skills, social skills, or work habits. If you use a task list for a lesson, the areas of emphasis on the task list could become the assessment criteria on the rubric.

Rating Scales

The rating scale of a rubric depicts how many levels of performance will be included. The scale ranges from little or no performance to the best possible performance. Typically the fewest levels on a rubric would be three and the most would be six. A three-point rating scale might include: (1) Needs Work, (2) Good, and (3) Excellent. A six-point scale might include: (0) Minimal/No Evidence, (2) Limited Evidence, (3) Some Evidence, (4) Satisfactory Evidence, (5) Commendable Evidence, and (6) Superior Evidence. When designating the levels, you can use descriptive terms, as seen in our three-point scale, or a combination of numbers and terms, as seen in our six-point rating scale. The range of levels is determined by student ability and the complexity of the final student product being assessed. Some products would not exhibit enough diversity to justify the use of a six-point scale.

Levels of Performance

This is the most significant component of the rubric because it is the part that clearly defines what it means for the work to be "right"—that mystery component discussed earlier in this chapter. A very clear and concise description is written for each level of the rating scale. Please refer to Figure 14-3 to examine how the descriptions change across levels of performance.

Types of Rubrics

Rubrics can be divided into two types: holistic and performance specific. A holistic rubric addresses multiple aspects of achievement, for example, writing, grammar, technology skills, and presentation within each level of performance (Table 14-2). A performance-specific rubric has assessment criteria divided into subcategories, similar to those found in a task list, and a description would be written at each level of the scale for each individual area (Table 14-3).

Creating a Rubric

Our next discussion focuses on some of the considerations for creating a rubric. You start with identifying the assessment criteria, then determine the rating scale and write descriptions for each level of performance.

TABLE 14-2 Holistic Rubric for Recycling Presentation

Objective or Performance
Students will use PowerPoint to create a presentation that provides a convincing, research-supported argument to recycle.

Level 4: Exemplary
The flow of the presentation is very logical and extremely easy to follow. The content is accurate, complete, and written in a very interesting manner. The spreadsheet chart is very appropriate and provides distinct details that correctly support the conclusions. The graphics clearly add meaning to the overall presentation. The choice of background design, fonts, and animations blend together to create a very esthetically pleasing presentation. The overall product presents a very persuasive argument on the need to recycle.

Level 3: Accomplished
The flow of the presentation is logical and easy to follow. The majority of the content is accurate, complete, and written in an interesting manner. The spreadsheet chart is appropriate and provides details that support the conclusions. The graphics add meaning to the overall presentation. The choice of background design, fonts, and animations create a pleasing presentation. The overall product presents a persuasive argument on the need to recycle.

Level 2: Developing
The flow of the presentation is somewhat logical and fairly easy to follow. The content contains a few errors and is missing some information. It is written in a moderately interesting manner. The spreadsheet chart is not the most appropriate possible, and therefore the details do not fully support the conclusions. The graphics add little meaning to the overall presentation. The choice of background design, fonts, and animations create a somewhat disconnected presentation. The overall product offers limited support for the persuasive argument on the need to recycle.

Level 1: Beginning
The flow of the presentation lacks a logical sequence and is somewhat difficult to follow. The content contains multiple errors and is missing key information. It is written in a manner that promotes little interest. The spreadsheet chart is not appropriate and therefore provides very limited if any support for the conclusions. The few graphics that are used add very little meaning to the overall presentation. The choice of background design, fonts, and animations create a disconnected presentation. The overall product offers very limited if any support for the persuasive argument on the need to recycle.

Assessment Criteria

When identifying the assessment criteria, you need to determine the type of focus or emphasis that is critical for this assignment. If your students are at a beginning level of development, you may want to use the performance-specific type of rubric to

TABLE 14-3 Performance-Specific Rubric for Recycling Presentation

Objective or Performance Students will use PowerPoint to create a presentation that provides a convincing, research-supported argument to recycle.					
OBJECTIVE OR PERFORMANCE	**BEGINNING 1**	**DEVELOPING 2**	**ACCOMPLISHED 3**	**EXEMPLARY 4**	**SCORE**
Presentation Flow	The flow of the presentation lacks a logical sequence and is somewhat difficult to follow.	The flow of the presentation is somewhat logical and fairly easy to follow.	The flow of the presentation is logical and easy to follow.	The flow of the presentation is very logical and extremely easy to follow.	
Content	The content contains multiple errors and is missing key information. It is written in a manner that promotes little interest.	The content contains a few errors and is missing some information. It is written in a fairly interesting manner.	The majority of the content is accurate, complete, and written in an interesting manner.	The content is accurate, complete, and written in a very interesting manner.	
Spreadsheet	The spreadsheet chart is not appropriate and therefore provides very limited if any support for the conclusions.	The spreadsheet chart is not the most appropriate and therefore the details do not fully support the conclusions.	The spreadsheet chart is appropriate and provides details that support the conclusions.	The spreadsheet chart is very appropriate and provides distinct details that correctly support the conclusions.	
Esthetics	The choice of background design, fonts, and animations create a disconnected presentation.	The choice of background design, fonts, and animations create a somewhat disconnected presentation.	The choice of background design, fonts, and animations create a pleasing presentation.	The choice of background design, fonts, and animations blend together to create a very esthetically pleasing presentation.	
Overall argument	The overall product offers very limited if any support for the persuasive argument on the need to recycle.	The overall product offers limited support for the persuasive argument on the need to recycle.	The overall product presents a persuasive argument on the need to recycle.	The overall product presents a very persuasive argument on the need to recycle.	

FIGURE 14-5 Sample Terminology for Rating Scales

Attempted	Acceptable	Admirable	Awesome
Byte	Kilobyte	Megabyte	Gigabyte
First Base	Second Base	Third Base	Home Run
Novice	Apprentice	Proficient	Distinguished
Freshman	Sophomore	Junior	Senior
Glass	Garnet	Ruby	Diamond

guide student learning in each area. If students are more experienced with what is expected, you can use a holistic approach. When using a holistic method, your students will need to be able to discern the subtle differences among the listed performances. In other words, they will need to be able to detect that the description addresses the fonts, the background design, and the animations, plus all the other related criteria (refer back to Tables 14–2 and 14–3).

Rating Scale

The first step in creating a rubric rating scale is to determine how many levels are needed and how the levels will be designated. When deciding the number of levels to include, you need to consider the ability level of your students and the complexity of the student product to be assessed. When beginning to use rubrics with younger students, it may be difficult for them to distinguish the subtle differences among multiple levels; therefore you may want to begin with a three-level rubric. As students progress to higher grade levels and become more experienced with the use of rubrics, a rating scale with additional levels can be used.

Even though students in upper elementary, middle, and high school may better be able to distinguish requirements at more than three levels, you will need to determine if the student product is complex enough to have five or six distinct levels of performance. For example, will you be able to clearly define differences between a product that has *limited* evidence of achievement and one that has *some* evidence of achievement? If the distinctions are not clearly evident, you may want to reduce the number of levels on your rating score.

When determining how to designate each level, a variety of terms can be used as descriptors. The important thing to remember is that you want to use terms that do not indicate failure or that the student is incapable of learning. Stix (1996) has compiled a list of terms that can be used for rating scales. A sample of these terms is seen in Figure 14-5.

Levels of Performance

To write the levels of performance for your rubric, begin by describing the ideal performance. Write at a level that is developmentally appropriate for your students, and write in a clear and concise manner. Another consideration is that the terms must represent *measurable* aspects of the student work. For example, if you examine the

"Exemplary" description from the holistic rubric in Table 14-2, you will see that each item is measurable.

> *Level 4:—Exemplary.* The flow of the presentation is *very logical and extremely easy to follow.* The content is *accurate, complete,* and written in a *very interesting manner.* The spreadsheet chart is *very appropriate* and *provides distinct details* that *correctly support* the conclusions. The graphics *clearly add meaning* to the overall presentation. The choice of background design, fonts, and animation *blends together* to create a *very esthetically pleasing presentation.* The overall product presents a *very persuasive* argument on the need to recycle.

After you have written a clear description of an ideal student product, identify the terms within the performance indicator that can vary, for example, "clearly," "distinct," "correctly," and "very." The italicized portions of the description just presented are the terms that can be modified to reflect different levels of student achievement.

As you review the holistic rubric (Table 14-2), note how the key terms are changed at each level of the rating scale to demonstrate differences in student performance. When starting to write your own rubrics, sometimes finding just the right descriptor for your performance levels can be challenging. To assist with this, you may want to reference the following list, which contains terms that are useful for describing performances at different levels of achievement (Pickett, 1999, p. 1):

- Presence to Absence
- Complete to Incomplete
- Many to Some to None

CHECK IT OUT 14-2

Title: Writing Performance

Grade: Middle School

Problem: *Students are to create a presentation for the City Council that describes the results of their study on hazardous waste at the city landfill. They have a description of the "ideal" presentation, but need to develop the remaining levels of performance.*

Activity: Download the description of the "ideal" Hazardous Waste presentation. Use this to devlop from two to five levels of performance for the assignment. Label the performance levels with an appropriate rating scale.

Link to these resources and activities in the Check It Out module for this chapter of the Companion Website.

- Major to Minor
- Consistent to Inconsistent
- Always to Usually to Sometimes to Rarely

Using a Rubric

The concept of using a rubric may be new to both you and your students. You may want to begin by using a "ready-made" rubric that you get from the Internet or from your curriculum materials. The rubric should not be complex, the descriptions should be short and easy to understand, and the levels of performance should be easily distinguishable. Or, you may decide to begin with one that you have planned and designed.

The key thing to remember is to engage students in the assessment process. If you begin with a ready-made rubric, review each component with your students to ensure understanding. Share with them that they will help design and create the rubrics to be used for future lessons. Once your students are familiar with a rubric and its purpose, always involve them in describing what the ideal product should look like. You may want to create a large laminated blank rubric that can be filled in as your students offer suggestions. Students can have copies of the blank rubric that they can fill in after the large one is completed. Make sure they use a pencil, because developing a rubric is an iterative process that will involve changes. Or, if you have a digital projector available, you can create the rubric and immediately print copies for each group.

The rubric describes the final product, not individual steps to be completed: thus students may not need to reference it as frequently as the task list. They do need to be reminded though, to review the description of an "Exemplary" final product and use it to conduct periodic self-assessments to ensure that the "pieces" fit together to create a meaningful and cohesive representation of their knowledge and skills. You will use the rubric to determine the degree to which students fulfilled the specified criteria of the lesson assignment.

SUMMARY

As seen in this chapter, there are many benefits of using alternative assessments when implementing an NTeQ or problem solving approach. Of key importance is the increased level of student involvement with the assessment process. By engaging students in the development of assessment criteria, they begin processing the new information and understanding in what ways they can demonstrate newly gained knowledge and skills. Therefore the use of alternative assessment tools actually helps guide and support the learning process by providing detailed direction during the learning task and feedback after completion of the task. Black and Wiliams (1998) indicate that performance will improve when students have access to feedback that indicates specific areas of *weakness* as well as identifies known areas of *strength*. As you continue to use this process, it is very helpful to collect samples of student work that reflect the various levels of performance. These student products can serve as useful guides for students in future classes.

AT THE CLASSROOM'S DOORSTEP

Questions Teachers Ask

Using alternative assessments seems like the right thing to do, but how can I not feel quite so overwhelmed with all the changes it will take to use this process?

As with any change, it is always best to start small. You may want to begin by creating a task list for a lesson that is one of your favorites. If you feel comfortable, you can create a simple three-level rubric to go along with the task list. Or, as mentioned, you can use a rubric that another teacher at your school has created or one from the Internet.

Please keep in mind that it can take some time to get rubrics that work "just right." Both you and the students may think that the rubric you jointly developed will accurately assess a product, but during its use you may discover that an important aspect is missing. At this point, students can just pencil in that aspect and it can be added next time. It is helpful to keep notes of these refinement ideas.

You may also want to begin a collection of task lists and rubrics to use "as is" or for examples of wording or layout. Anything that you can do to save time is a worthy endeavor. You can also check out some of the online teacher lists or chat rooms to see how other teachers use alternative assessments.

It seems like cheating to let the students know exactly what they will be "tested" on. If I use a task list or rubric, how can I be sure they "know" the information?

The majority of student products that are appropriate for use with authentic assessments require such a depth of information processing and the application of knowledge and skills that it would be almost impossible for students to complete them without "knowing" the required content. Please remember that alternative assessments play a dual role: the obvious role is to assess student achievement and attainment of stated objectives, but the additional role is that of guiding student learning during the lesson.

Aren't the "user-friendly" rubric ratings a waste of time to use when they have to be translated into grades anyway?

Unfortunately, many teachers are still required to use a standardized method, such as letter or numerical grades, of recording student progress. So, as you mentioned, the rubric scores do need to be changed into the traditional format. But, because one of the main purposes of alternative assessments is to promote learning and guide students to better achievement, the rating scales provide a more supportive approach than assignment of a grade. A letter grade of "D" seems to reflect failure more than terms such as "developing" or "apprentice." Therefore, with a rubric, students not only feel more encouraged to improve, but the task list and rubric let them know exactly where they need to improve.

TECHNOLOGY INTEGRATION ACTIVITIES

To access the activities that connect the content of the text with the Companion Website and other technology, please go to the Activities module in Chapter 14 of the Companion Website at *http://www.prenhall.com/morrison.*

RESOURCES

Writing Traditional Test Items

Morrison, G. R., Ross, S. M., & Kemp, J. E. (2003). *Designing effective instruction* (4th ed.). New York: John Wiley.

Student Technology Standards

National Education Technology Standards for Students (NETS): Connecting curriculum and technology. (2000). Eugene, OR: International Society for Technology in Education in cooperation with the U.S. Department of Education.

Sample Assessment Measures

Educators in Connecticut's Pomperaug Regional School District 15. (1996). *A teacher's guide to performance-based learning and assessment.* Alexandria, VA: Association for Supervision and Curriculum Development.

Performance Assessment

Marzano, R., Pickering, D., & McTighe, J. (1993). *Assessing student outcomes: Performance assessment using the dimensions of learning model.* Alexandria, VA: Association for Supervision and Curriculum Development.

NTEQ PORTFOLIO ACTIVITIES: ASSESSMENT

Please complete the following activities as part of the Assessment section of your NTeQ Portfolio.

Reflections

The "Getting Started" portion of this chapter asked three questions that teachers might commonly ask with regard to the assessment of student learning. In this portion of your journal, please use information from this chapter to answer the opening questions.

1. At what level should students be involved with creating assessments for their schoolwork?
2. How well do tests really demonstrate what students know and are able to do?
3. How can assessments help students to improve their thinking and level of achievement?

Task Lists

When using the NTeQ model, students create products with the use of computer tools. As noted, these tools include word processing, spreadsheets, databases, presentations, and the Internet. Products from these tools would each have a basic set of criteria that could be used to assess the degree that it was appropriately applied for the age of the students. For this section of your portfolio, create a Task List for each computer tool that would be developmentally appropriate for students in your class. Use the Spreadsheet Task List as a model.

Rubrics

Student learning can be enhanced when rubrics are used to guide and assess problem-based learning activities. It is critical for today's teachers to utilize alternative assessments, such as rubrics, to assess learning. To demonstrate your understanding of rubrics, create a holistic and performance-specific rubric for an instructional unit of your choice. To demonstrate your understanding of how to effectively use alternative assessment, write a brief description of how you will engage your students in the development of a rubric (holistic or performance specific).

Alternative Assessment Resources

Create an annotated list of alternative resources that are appropriate for the subject areas and grade levels of your students. Use a format similar to the following example.

- Name of assessment resource
- Location (e.g., URL, book page number)
- Specific description of how you will use the resource

REFERENCES

The American heritage dictionary of the English language, 4th ed. Boston: Houghton Mifflin, 2000. Available: www.bartleby.com/61/.

Black, P., & Wiliam, D. (1998). *Inside the black box: Raising standards through classroom assessment* [Online]. Available: http://www.pdkintl.org/kappan/kbla9810.htm.

Dietel, R. J., Herman, J. L., & Knuth, R. A. (1991). *What does research say about assessment?* Oak Brook, IL: NCREL. Available: http://www.ncrel.org/sdrs/areas/stw_esys/4assess.htm.

Educators in Connecticut's Pomperaug Regional School District 15. (1996). *A Teacher's guide to performance-based learning and assessment.* Alexandria, VA: Association for Supervision and Curriculum Development.

Herman, J. L., Aschbacher, P. R., & Winters, L. (1992). *A practical guide to alternative assessment.* Alexandria, VA: Association for Supervision and Curriculum Development.

Marzano, R., Pickering, D., & McTighe, J. (1993). *Assessing student outcomes: Performance assessment using the dimensions of learning model.* Alexandria, VA: Association for Supervision and Curriculum Development.

Morrison, G. R., Ross, S. M., & Kemp, J. E. (2004). *Designing effective instruction* (4th ed.). New York: John Wiley.

National Education Technology Standards (NETS) for Students: Connecting curriculum and technology. (2000). Eugene, OR: International Society for Technology in Education in cooperation with the U.S. Department of Education.

Pickett, N. (1999). *Guidelines for rubric development.* [online]. Available: http://edweb.sdsu.edu/triton/july/rubrics/Rubric_Guidelines.html.

Ryan, C. D. (1994). *Professional's guide: Authentic assessment.* Westminster, CA: Teacher Created Materials.

Stix, A. (1996). *Empowering students through negotiable contracting to draft rubrics for authentic assessment.* U. S. Department of Education [Online]. Available: http://www.interactiveclassroom.com/articles_006.htm.

Appendix

LEARNING TASKS AND COMPUTER FUNCTIONS

Learning Task	Computer Function Examples
Alter, Change, Convert, Modify, Vary	Use a spreadsheet to alter the data to produce a different graph. Convert a picture to create a different perspective, meaning, etc. Modify a sentence to create an opposite meaning.
Analyze	Use a spreadsheet to determine the smallest, largest, middle, etc. Use a database to find the most or least common characteristics. Use a spreadsheet to make a graph or chart.
Appraise	Use a graph to determine the solution to problem. Use a spreadsheet to evaluate.
Arrange	Use a database to arrange the states by their order of entry into the Union. Use a spreadsheet to arrange the cells from smallest to largest. Use the draw program to arrange pictures in correct sequence.
Assemble, Produce	Produce a drawing of how you would assemble the equipment for this experiment.
Assess	Use a digital camera to compare and contrast. Use word processing to write an evaluation. Use word processing to create a survey or record data on a spreadsheet or database.
Calculate	Create a formula to calculate the area of rectangles. Determine the average weight of five pumpkins.
Choose, Select, Categorize	Use a database to sort or match records according to common characteristics. Use the database of the presidents and select all who served two terms. Categorize the states by their electoral vote in the last three elections.
Classify, Identify, Isolate, List, Recognize	Identify the plants in the database that have particular characteristics. Use a word processing program to keep a list of your new words.
Collaborate, Cooperate, Contribute	Use e-mail to collaborate with other students at a distant location. Use a word processing program to share ideas and conclusions with others.

Continued

LEARNING TASK	COMPUTER FUNCTION EXAMPLES
Collect, Observe, Gather	Enter your data from the observation into the database. Observe how the line changes as you change the first variable. Use the Internet to gather information and data.
Combine, Match, Tabulate, Sequence	Use a spreadsheet to determine the most preferred drink and snack from your taste test. Determine how many perennials and annuals you have observed. Sequence the states according to their joining the Union.
Compare, Contrast, Differentiate, Discriminate, Relate	Compare last year's cookie sales to this year's cookie sales. Draw two pictures to help you differentiate between rotation and revolution. Use a spreadsheet with charts to show similarities and differences. Use a database to find common/uncommon characteristics. Use word processing to communicate similarities and differences. Use draw and copy functions to compare geometric shapes.
Deduce, Infer, Generalize	Use a database to analyze information to support generalizations. Based on the graph of the cookie sales for the last 2 years, how many will this class sell this year? Based on plants with similar characteristics in the database, how would you classify this example?
Describe, Outline, Paraphrase, Reconstruct, Rephrase	Use a word processor to outline the chapter. Paraphrase the information you found in the CD-ROM encyclopedia. Based on your research, write a story to reconstruct the events leading to the railroad strike.
Design, Plan	Create a drawing showing your plan for the house of tomorrow. Use the draw program to create a safe playground. Make a map of your neighborhood.
Diagram, Draw, Graph, Illustrate, Plot	Use a spreadsheet to make a chart. Use the digital camera to illustrate safety in the classroom. Use clip art/draw program to illustrate your newsletter.
Edit, Punctuate, Write, Report	Allow students to print their first drafts and then exchange with other students to proofread. Create a worksheet. Use spell check to correct spelling errors. Type a story and have members of the group proofread, make suggestions to clarify ideas, and edit the final copy. Gather information on a given topic and write a report.
Estimate, Predict, Formulate	Use a spreadsheet to manipulate data for estimations and predictions with graphs. Use a database to sort, categorize, and support predictions. Use a database to predict the basketball scores for the teams in the NBA. On a spreadsheet, write formulas for students to multiply, subtract, add, and divide the NBA scores. Use the Internet to have the students estimate how much they would spend at three different stores.

Interpret, Interpolate, Extend	Analyze data collected on the spreadsheet and determine which planet will show your lowest and highest weight. Determine how many years it will take to arrive at a planet going a designated speed and record that on a database and spreadsheet. Then calculate your age upon arrival. Use the digital camera to take pictures of an experiment in various stages. Use the pictures and presentations in class.
Judge	Use the Grolier CD-ROM encyclopedia to review periods of history such as the World Wars and decide or judge which had the greater impact on modern life.
Judge, Evaluate	Make a judgment based on data collected from CD-ROM encyclopedias, the Internet, books, and *National Geographic* animal software as to which animal should be adopted as a pet. Use word processing to prepare a written report justifying your position. Use charts to make comparisons for evaluations.
Plan	Write a letter about opening your own business. Draw a floor plan in the draw program. Use a spreadsheet to plan your daily expenditures.
Solve, Determine	Use a spreadsheet to determine the classroom with the most square feet. Use a spreadsheet and database to solve word problems. Use the spell check to check spelling. Determine the mean, mode, and median scores from a basketball game. Determine which graph will best show the results.
Synthesize	Write a report using word processing, a spreadsheet, and a database.
Verify	Use a spell checker to check your spelling words. Estimate math problems and then use a spreadsheet to verify the exact answers. Use databases to verify predictions.

This chart was prepared as part of a class exercise by teachers who participated in the 1996 Project SMART summer training at the University of Memphis.

Index